INQUIRIES
INTO THE ORIGIN
OF LANGUAGE

STUDIES IN LANGUAGE

Noam Chomsky and Morris Halle, Editors

INQUIRIES INTO THE ORIGIN OF LANGUAGE

THE FATE OF A QUESTION

JAMES H. STAM

Upsala College

HARPER & ROW, PUBLISHERS

NEW YORK   HAGERSTOWN   SAN FRANCISCO   LONDON

Sponsoring Editor: George A. Middendorf
Project Editor: Holly Detgen
Designer: Andrea C. Goodman
Production Supervisor: Francis X. Giordano
Compositor: Bi-Comp, Incorporated
Printer and Binder: Halliday Lithograph Corporation

INQUIRIES INTO THE ORIGIN OF LANGUAGE: THE FATE OF A QUESTION

Library of Congress Cataloging in Publication Data
Stam, James H 1937–
    Inquiries into the origin of language.

    (Studies in language)
    Includes bibliographical references and index.
    1. Language and languages—Origin. I. Title.
P116.S68   409   76-232
ISBN 0-06-046403-8

T O

WOLFGANG MAX ZUCKER

ἀνδρὶ   πολυτρόπῳ

CONTENTS

THE RISE AND FALL OF A FINAL SOLUTION

PREFACE

This book treats the classic theories concerning the origin of language which were proposed during the eighteenth and nineteenth centuries, together with their background in ancient and early modern philosophy. It does not advance any solution to the puzzle of language origin but is rather a work of interpretation and analysis. It is not only a presentation of the sequence and pattern of different answers to the question, but an attempt to look at the nature and status of the question itself, to see what questions the various thinkers were actually asking through the vehicle of this common theme.

When I first concerned myself with the general topic of this book, as an undergraduate and graduate student in the late 1950s and early 1960s, there was relatively little professional interest in the question of language origin. Linguists were, for the most part, reluctant to put forward speculative hypotheses on incomplete or inaccessible evidence, and philosophers either reinterpreted the question as one to be approached on some basis other than the testimony of historical linguistics or they dismissed the issue itself as a pseudoproblem. This general skepticism toward the very attempt to inquire into the matter of language origin was a final by-product of both a satiation and frustration with the topic, which had developed in the latter nineteenth century when audacious attempts to solve the riddle collided with positivist strictures against metaphysical and nonempirical investigations. That clash itself, however, came in the aftermath of a century of the most active and productive pursuit of this elusive theme.

I was intrigued by the circumstances which would have led not only philosophers of positivist leaning, but linguists themselves, to abandon and even proscribe a whole area of investigation which had been of such central importance to their predecessors. I undertook to investigate the various contexts in which the question of language origin had been raised. I wanted neither to give a merely doxographic account of the different hypotheses nor to analyze the validity of these alternatives as such, but to interpret the different meanings which the question had for those who asked it. I tried to place the discussions of the problem in the context of intellectual history, to see whether those who placed restrictions on the question late in the nineteenth century were even addressing the same issue as those who had speculated about it in earlier years. Thus I have used the history of ideas as a way of clarifying the question asked, at the same time that I have taken the question as one focus for a history of ideas.

In the years since I commenced work on this project there has been a marked renewal of interest in the matter. New trends in psycholinguistics during the 1960s and intensified research into primate communication suggested new possibilities. Above all, the "revolution in linguistics" of the late 1950s showed the instability of established certainties and stimulated a fresh and open curiosity about the history of the philosophy of language: A mood arose which would ill receive the pronouncement, "The door is closed on that issue." The Conference on Origins and Evolution of Language and Speech, sponsored by The New York Academy of Sciences in September, 1975, is one sign of this revival and would have been almost unimaginable twenty years earlier. Thus the positivist obituaries to the topic were in fact the lullabies of a temporary dormancy.

During the years that I worked on this topic, the project itself expanded considerably. The present book has been cut down from a manuscript nearly twice the length, and readers should be informed what material has been excluded from the present version. First of all, I have omitted most of the draft material dealing with the philosophy of language in German romanticism and idealism—the metacritiques of Hamann and Herder; most of the themes in Schiller, the Schlegel brothers, Hegel, Schleiermacher, and so on—and I have included only a truncated version of Humboldt, largely without interpretation. For these thinkers the problem of origin was secondary to other considerations about language, and I have only used such material as directly related to the present topic. Secondly, I have dropped one major theme which ran through the earlier draft: the curious attribution of truth or falsity, nobility or baseness, beauty or ugliness to individual (natural or artificial) languages themselves. When nationalists asserted that German was an organically continuous original language, they were in effect making a truth claim for the German language itself. That differed only slightly from the claims sometimes made for proposed universal characteristics, for the *clarté universelle* of French, and for disambiguated *langue bien faite*—the scientific language of the future in which, some alleged, untruth would be virtually impossible. It is my hope to deal with both of these themes at some future date.

Another area of omission may prove more disappointing to some readers: I have not discussed contemporary parallels to the material under consideration and have avoided twentieth-century names and references except in footnotes. Readers familiar with recent philosophy of language and linguistics will immediately recognize that themes abounded in the eighteenth and nineteenth centuries which are better known to most of us from the works of Heidegger, Wittgenstein, Cassirer, Skinner, Chomsky, and others; and these readers may wonder why I have not devoted more direct discussion to these correspondences. There are several reasons. The book was already lengthy and somewhat cumbersome: precision about contemporary analogies would have overburdened its structure to the breaking point. I conscientiously desired to avoid anachronism and the sorts of misunderstanding bred when we see in past thought a series of "anticipations." My deepest concern in this matter has been the status of studies in the history of philosophy. It is my conviction that present-day philosophy stands deeply in need of the history of philosophy as relevant discipline, of studies which are both scholarly and philosophical, which involve both exegesis and argument. Two pitfalls must be avoided: doxography, first of all, which treats the history of philosophy as a succession of opinions. By treating philosophical statements as opinionated utterances and philosophers as opinion-givers or opinion-makers, doxography either ignores or denies the original claim of philosophy that it could (or at least sought to) rise above opinion. A second danger is "seculocentricity," a time-boundedness to the current generation and its concerns, which can distort perspective as much as the place-boundedness of ethnocentricity. Surely the greatness of the great philosophers consists in more than the fact that they said things which would be elaborated by other thinkers who happen to be our contemporaries. Not all the theorists dealt with in this book are great philosophers, and some are not philosophers in any sense. Nonetheless, they deserve to be considered in their own right and on their own terms and through the avenues of their own questions: We can no more force our questions upon them than we need feel compelled to accept their answers.

The translations of both classical and modern texts are, for the most part, my own. Therefore I have usually cited classical sources according to the pagination, lineation, and subdivisions of the accepted standard editions. Thus, for example, I have cited Plato according to the "Stephanus numbers," usually included in the margin of modern editions; Aristotle according to the "Becker numbers"; and so on.

Where available translations were particularly good, however, I have employed them. I would like to thank Cornell University Press for permission to use quotations from *The New Science of Giambattista Vico,* translated from the third edition (1744) by Thomas Goddard Bergin and Max Harold Fisch (Ithaca, New York, 1948). I am also indebted to Michael Hamburger for giving permission to excerpt from his translation of Hölderlin's "Brod und Wein," *Hölderlin: His Poems,* translated by Michael Hamburger, second edition (London, Harvill Press, 1952).

During the years of preparation of this book I received indispensable financial support from several sources: a semester sabbatical from Upsala College; a Fellowship for Younger Scholars from the National Endowment for the Humanities; and a grant-in-aid from The Newberry Library, Chicago, Illinois, where I was able to use the Prince Louis–Lucien Bonaparte Collection, a goldmine of sources in nineteenth–century linguistics. I am much obliged to these institutions and to their staffs for the personal encouragement given to me.

I also wish to thank those who read some or all of this book in manuscript: Jeffrey Cain, Alan Kusinitz, C. Alfred Perkins, Robert W. Rieber, David H. Stam, and John Wallhausser. Their criticisms were well taken and their suggestions invariably an improvement. My wife, Līga Ziemelis Stam, was proofreader at the several stages and assisted in countless ways and I am grateful for her patience with me and with this project. The staff at Harper & Row, and particularly Holly Detgen, have been competent, exacting, and cooperative. The editors of this series, Noam Chomsky and Morris Halle, were ever generous with their time, knowledge, and insight, providing suggestions which led me to give the book its present shape.

I first worked on the material covered in Part II of this book in a seminar with Professor Frank E. Manuel at Brandeis and expanded that work in my dissertation, "The Question of the Origin of Language in German Thought, 1756–1785," under Professor Manuel's direction. I am most appreciative of the way he has shared his comprehensive knowledge of eighteenth- and nineteenth-century texts and the sensitivity of his readings of them. In a more general way, my interest in this area of thought was first aroused in an undergraduate course in the philosophy of language at Upsala, which is only one of the very many reasons why this book is dedicated to Professor Wolfgang M. Zucker.

J.H.S.

PROLEGOMENA

I

Our questions fix the limits of our answers. Our answers, even the best of them, may only lead us on to new or renewed questions. Refusal to question is the mark of a closed mind and the opposite of philosophy, if not of wisdom as such. These principles are as rarely weighed as they are regularly conceded.

This book is primarily about questions, secondarily about the diverse answers given to a particular question, that concerning the origin of language. Different questions come to the fore at different times: Many current questions were hardly asked a decade ago, and one can only guess what will be the focal ones a decade hence. The question of language origin gained immense popularity around the 1740s; it waxed, then waned for a few decades; it was heartily revived in romantic literary criticism and comparative linguistics, but, as if by a dialectic all its own, interest died and the question was virtually abandoned in the last decades of the nineteenth century—only to be raised again in our own times. On the other hand, the same question may be asked differently by different thinkers: Approaches to political or philosophical problems, for example, may diverge so radically that one might think the antagonists were asking different question altogether. The deeper concerns of eighteenth- and nineteenth-century writers with linguistic origins were in some cases so thoroughly alien that it could only be misleading to categorize the theories on the basis of the answers alone.

Questions themselves can be of different sorts, just as they can be asked at different levels. A request to the corner policeman for directions to the nearest filling station must be distinguished from inquiries into the true, the good, and the beautiful. But why? If the policeman can answer my question, he has disposed of it, and I no longer have a question; whereas if the philosopher offers an answer to my queries, I still have (or should have) a question. The philosopher's answers may lead to dead-ends, perplexities, further complications, wonder, or perhaps even bedazzlement—that is, new questions.

The importance of questions does not mean that all answers are equally valid or satisfactory. Answers can be foolish, irrelevant, mendacious, misleading, erroneous. How, then, can an answer to any philosophical question be satisfactory? *Satisfaction* denotes a pleasurable state distinguished from satiation. When we are satisfied we have "had enough" in moderation—we are content for the moment, but we shall return to the pleasure again. A satisfactory philosophical answer sheds light, perhaps brilliant light, but we may have to return to the question again. The question is preserved at the same time that it is canceled. Were the question not disposed of at all, the answer would hardly be satisfactory; were the question disposed of entirely, the answer might well be unphilosophical.

There are also questions about questions. Socrates often turned the questions of his interlocutors; and analysis of the meaningfulness of questions is a prevalent mode of twentieth-century philosophy. Despite superficial similarities in techniques of definition and dialectic, however, there are profound differences between the two. Generally, linguistic analysis operates under the postulate of Hume, related to earlier strictures of Locke and later ones of Kant, that philosophy should be purified of all improper questions. To paraphrase (and admittedly misrepresent) the seventh proposition of Wittgenstein's *Tractatus:* Whereto one cannot give an answer, thereof one must not ask. In many modern philosophical exercises, the intent to dismiss case from court has been the predisposition of both the judge and a majority of jurors. Socrates' questioning of questions was undertaken in a different spirit. The man who said that a life without questions would not be worth living could not have had as his purpose the purgation of questions, but rather of unexamined answers. When Meno, slinking away from defeat in argument, asked Socrates how he could go around asking questions that he could not answer, Socrates replied that the whole argument was "eristical" (80e). When Socrates, in the sixth book of *The Republic,* ridiculed other explanations of the Good and implied that philosophy would be useless if it could not address itself to this question, he went on to admit that he himself had no direct explanation, but could at best speak by analogy about the sun (505–509). Socrates regularly coupled his admissions of ignorance with expressions of willingness, eagerness to pursue the question.

The question about the origin of language was disposed of toward the end of the nineteenth century. The question was, in effect, abolished. Among many signs of this, the clearest was the second article of the bylaws of the Parisian *Société de linguistique,* founded in 1865, which prohibited all communications on the subject. The question was banned because it was deemed unanswerable in any verifiable way. The reader may be judge whether the proscription was justified under the circumstances. Questions, however, are of different kinds. Before answering, therefore, the reader should ask: Is this question on the order of a query to the corner policeman or of inquiries concerning the true, the good, and the beautiful?

II

Questions can suffer their own fates and undergo their own histories. We have already indicated that the question of language origin came, so to speak, to a bad end. But it also had its days of glory. We shall witness its rise and fall over a period lasting somewhat longer than a century.

The theme had been raised before the epoch of our specific investigations: Some classical authors gave it extensive treatment; some medieval theologians and Biblical scholars commented on the problem; polyhistors, missionaries, and travelers in the early modern centuries offered random hints. It is not our purpose, however, to present a survey of opinions about the origin of language, nor even exhaustive coverage of authors during the eighteenth and nineteenth centuries. This task has already been performed.[1]* It is our greater interest to look at the dynamics of the ways in which the question was raised and then resolved, asked again, and brought to its final disposition.

Although concern with language origin was on the rise earlier in the eighteenth century, it is convenient to begin with the 1740s; and although decreasing interest and increasing disapproval of the question was also a gradual phenomenon, the 1860s can serve as an approximate terminus. During these years there was an unfolding pattern of refinements and changed understandings of the question, enrichments and transformations of the answers. There were perceptible waves of interest in discussion and alterations of its terms. It was during this span that investigations of the problem were most prolific, but also most productive; the whole inquiry took on some qualities of classic stature. In the 1740s appeared the poetical explanation of Vico, the mechanical one of La Mettrie, and the empiricist one of Condillac. Rousseau's remarks on the matter came a few years

* Numbered notes begin on page 263.

later and were partially responsible for the rapid spread of concern in England and Germany—a wave which reached its peak in Herder's famous prize essay and Hamann's rebuttal of it. German and English romanticists took up the problem once again, and from there it disseminated to inspire the confidence of nationalists, the effusions of mystics, and profound analysis by some idealist philosophers. Two nineteenth-century developments seemed to promise well for the possibility of an adequate solution to the dilemma of the beginnings of speech: The rise of comparative linguistics and of evolutionary theory. In the end, however, the methods of both sciences were used to substantiate the growing suspicion that the question was unanswerable in any scientific sense. And so arose the open attacks on the question and its fall into disrepute.

Preliminary comments may help clarify why this particular question should have come into such prominence in the 1740s. What was involved was not only increased concern with language, but with the specific question of origins. We can simplify the causes somewhat by analyzing them in terms of reactions to Descartes and his immediate followers, who were generally interested in other aspects of language than its origin—its volitional character, its rational structure, and so on. Vico rejected Descartes's natural science in favor of historical science, and was thus led back to the beginnings. La Mettrie extended Cartesian mechanism from beast to man and thus put exclusive emphasis on material and efficient causes; but it has been clear since Aristotle that such explanations are limited unless they push back to initial efficient causes. From Locke on, empiricists rejected innate ideas; but this obliged them to supply some other interpretation of the origination of ideas and consequently of language. The cults of sensibility and pietism saw language as an expressive outpouring of inwardness, feeling, the heart; but this focus also implied that language should be viewed in terms of its sources. Finally, there was the phenomenon which Lovejoy has referred to as the "temporalizing of the chain of being."[2] The breakdown of metaphysics invited its subtle, almost unconscious translation into an evolutionary schema. Structural principles, under the aspect of time, become origins. This very transformation can be taken as a consequence of the breaks in the "chain of being" as such. When the nature of reality itself is in question, the structure of language can hardly be taken for granted. There is a pressing need to return *ad fontes*.

The question of language origin, at least at first, was no one's exclusive preserve. It was asked by philosophers, psychologists, anthropologists, biologists, aestheticians, theologians, historians, and poets themselves, as well as philologists and linguists. Indeed, many of these disciplinary distinctions had not yet been made. The very word *origin* is as equivocal as the Greek *arché,* Latin *principium,* and German *Ursprung.*[3] Depending on emphasis and perspective, concern with origins could center on problems of temporal beginnings, of psychological genesis, behavioral stimuli, creative sources, cultural forces, rational foundations, transcendent grounds, or divine inspiration. Could it be that the very ambiguity of the word enriched some of the discussion about it?

I

PATHWAYS
TOWARD THE
BEGINNINGS

[1]

LANGUAGE POETICAL OR LANGUAGE MECHANICAL?

Prospects of a New Science

It is fitting that these inquiries should begin with Giambattista Vico. Vico was the herald of a "new science"; he also viewed himself as a rediscoverer of "ancient wisdom." The new science of which he spoke was history, the ancient wisdom was poetry, and philology was key to both. These phrases, however, had been used before and during Vico's times in contexts and with meanings different from those which he impressed upon them.

More familiar usage, then as well as now, has associated the "new science" with a conscious rejection of "ancient wisdom." Bacon delighted in attacks on Aristotelity; Descartes' method of universal doubt required that philosophy start out with a clean slate. The tradition of philosophy, it was implied, had distorted or destroyed the original purpose of philosophy: Philosophy had come to encourage opinion and dogmatism instead of counteracting them. The new science was to be philosophy reconceived, in combat with inherited philosophical dogmas as well as common opinion. The revolutionary scientific movement, fully launched by the seventeenth century, promoted a new understanding of nature and a new attitude toward her. Especially novel was the supposition that the study of nature could not and should not be separated from man's desire for mastery over natural forces. In general, ancient and medieval philosophy had affirmed that the proper goal of such study was harmony with nature, contemplation, or even stoic acceptance of fate. The new outlook saw man in contrast with nature, in conflict with her, ultimately in a life-and-death struggle.

The changed view of man's place and role in the world required abandonment of the traditionally sanctioned understanding of *sophía* and *scientia,* wisdom and knowledge. First, the new science implied that the student of nature should approach her in a different spirit. Second, the quest for certainty became a preeminent concern: The ancient notion that the working out of knowledge may lead to the knowledge of ignorance and the medieval belief that science may lead without contradiction to the "uncertainties" of faith were either de-emphasized or ignored. It has often been remarked that the term *natural science* has no appropriate employment for premodern times, because the knowledge of nature was never before so fundamentally distinguished from other kinds of human knowing. Some of the successes of modernity, however, have been so startling that the very word *science* has become the popular synonym for *natural science.* All other inquirers and researchers who make some claim to knowledge must qualify their title. Chemists and physicists may, without blush, refer to themselves simply as scientists; but the self-respecting sociologist or psychologist remains a "social scientist," the philologist a *Geisteswissenschaftler,* still others, "humane scientists."

Vico's "new science" stands midway between the revolutionary new science of the seventeenth century and the science of "the establishment" in the twentieth. Early in his life Vico had concerned himself with the "dispute of the faculties" or "hierarchy of the sciences." His first work of lasting significance, *On the Study Methods of Our Time* (1708), treated the different methods and objectives of the various disciplines.[1] Although the subject of history is never mentioned, this work is considered an outstanding defense of humanistic studies, because in it Vico questioned the universal applicability of what was then called the "geometrical method"—the attempt to employ in nonquantitative questions a mathematical model of deductive reasoning—and because he called for more serious study of ethics and jurisprudence, poetry and philology. Evidently, Vico intended a mediation between the warring factions in the Quarrel of the Ancients and the Moderns, the extensive debate on the relative merits of antiquity and modernity which dominated literary criticism in the last decades of the seventeenth century and colored viewpoints on many a dispute concerning theology and science, history and taste. Vico used the phrase *Scienza nuova* in his own new sense in 1725 as title for the first edition of his now famous work. Vico must have been aware, when he entitled a work *Principles of a New Science,* that few of his readers would suspect that the science involved was history.

Opposition to ancient philosophy by the founders of modern thought was not a contempt born of ignorance. Both Bacon and Descartes betrayed a deep respect for the genius of Plato and Aristotle and others, but protested that their original intentions had been undone by those schools and movements which adopted the founders' names. Bacon even wrote a work, which Vico knew and often cited, *On the Wisdom of the Ancients.* Here, however, Bacon did not deal with the recognized philosophers, but with the earliest Greek poets. *De sapientia veterum* is a detailed allegorizing exegesis of the wisdom concealed in ancient myths and fables, wherein Bacon found a kind of original wisdom. Vico concurred that the deeper wisdom lay in the earliest poets of antiquity—"Poetic Wisdom" and "Discovery of the True Homer" are section titles of Vico's magnum opus—but he did not believe that Bacon had understood the true significance of that poetry: Bacon could only detect wisdom in ancient myth and fable by reinterpreting it into a kind of cryptophilosophy.

The discovery of the origins of poetry does away with the opinion of the matchless wisdom of the ancients, so ardently sought after from Plato to Bacon's *De sapientia veterum.* For the wisdom of the ancients was the vulgar wisdom of the lawgivers who founded the human race, not the esoteric wisdom of great and rare philosophers.[2]

According to Vico, ancient wisdom is not to be found in myth allegorized and philosophized, but in myth historicized. Poetry must be understood in the light of all the social forces which created it and as an historical force itself. Vico's peculiar version of "new science" would be needed for the recovery of Vico's version of "ancient wisdom."

Vico's embrace of history forced his break with Cartesianism, though he only worked out the principles of his opposition gradually. Philology, for Vico, was principal handmaiden to history, the critical tool for the new science. In the first part of the *Discourse on Method,* Descartes had dismissed the studies of language, history, and fables as incompetent for attainment of any true or certain knowledge. Vico's distance from Cartesianism, however, by no means constituted a total breach with the underlying principles of modern science and philosophy. The epistemological key which Vico found and which emboldened him to open the gates of historical science was the maxim *Verum ipsum factum,* "The true is the same as the made"; that is, man can only know that which he himself helps to make. Man can have no knowledge of nature, since it is made for men by divine or other forces. Comprehensive history, in contrast, encompasses all those things which man makes: language, institutions, poetry, monuments, gods, myths, indeed philosophy and all the sciences themselves. This fundamental of Vichian epistemology was taken from Thomas Hobbes, who wrote: "And to know truth is the same thing as to remember that it was made by ourselves by the common use of words."[3] Hobbes's famous encounter with Euclid's geometry—when his skepticism about the Pythagorean theorem forced him to go back to the initial axioms and definitions—led him to the conviction that the truth is a human construction. Order can be established, in science and in society, if and only if there is agreement about terms and first principles, which, though they must be consistent with one another, may be more or less arbitrary in themselves. Hobbes's interest, surely, was not the rejection of the new scientific wave, but rather the application of its methods to civil philosophy.[4] In the same way, Vico was not merely a defender of the "humanities" against the "sciences." Vico's quarrel was not with mathematicians but with physicists, for the former could easily admit, whereas the latter denied, that they were dealing in manmade truths. Vico did not totally break away from the *esprit géométrique:* After all, he refers to the first book of *The New Science* as a set of axioms and continuously enumerates corollaries to his propositions. Rather, the turn to history is a shift from one to another version of the geometrical approach. Vico still argued hard for the unity of the sciences, and it was far from his intentions that history, or any other discipline, should be pursued from a standpoint of moral neutrality.

Obviously, Vico was not the inventor of history, nor even the first modern thinker to be its special champion. What was new in Vico was the defense of history *as a science*—a science understood, to a considerable extent, in the modern sense of that term. Vico's concern, less persistently carried out, is loosely analogous to the problems posed later by Kant and Hegel. Kant's basic question in the *Critique of Pure Reason* was, How is metaphysics *as a science* possible? Kant was well aware that people had and did engage in metaphysical speculations, but he considered many of them dreamers and ghost-seers. The difficulty was whether metaphysics, and ethics and aesthetics, were possible as sciences. For Hegel, the desperate need was to reestablish philosophy in general *as a science*. Likewise, the achievement which Vico would have claimed for himself was the establishment of the study of history on a scientific basis. His effort might appropriately be called an attempt to found the "new" new science.

The specific and connoted meanings of the terms *history* and *historical science* have changed considerably between Vico's time and our own. But it is not surprising that there have been many contending voices raised against Vico and his heirs, insisting that the claim of a scientific basis for history was exaggerated, unfounded, and pretentious. It was in the latter half of the nineteenth century that German scholars made the distinction between *Geisteswissenschaften* ("sciences of the spirit or mind") and *Naturwissenschaften* ("sciences of nature")—and the common translation of these terms as "the humanities" and "the sciences" is not only a distortion, but a capitulation by the translators. What underlay this distinction was the question, Can there be "sciences of the spirit" at all? The question itself is ambiguous. For the more skeptical it meant, Can spirit properly be captured in scientific systems? For others it meant, How can the techniques of modern science be applied to human things?

It is fitting that this study begin with the man who awakened a deeper interest in history and introduced the problem of history as a science. There is something fundamentally, inescapably historical about man's language. The simplest definition of history is that it is, or is the study of, the past as it flows into and affects the present. When we speak, we speak a language which, to an overwhelming extent, has already been created for us. We always employ a tongue which comes to us out of the past; yet the act of speaking takes place in the present, and we participate in creating the language of the future. In language perhaps more than in any other human activity, we make the past no longer past. And if we speak well, we put the future in our debt.

One of the simplest, and still one of the best, definitions of language comes from Aristotle: Language is "sound with meaning" or "sound with a soul."[5] Sound, by itself, is studied by acousticians. But how study sound with meaning and soul? One way to classify theories of language is to distinguish those which exaggerate sound, as if language had no meaning, from those which exaggerate soul, as if language required no physical medium. The fact that language is embodied thought put linguistics in a place of special contention in the dispute between the *Naturwissenschaften* and *Geisteswissenschaften*. Indeed, the uncertainty as to the status of linguistics was partial reason for the undoing of interest in language origins. Should the study of language belong with the new sciences of Galileo, Bacon,

Newton, and Darwin? Or with the new science of Vico, Herder, and Hegel? Or with something newer or something still older?

Man the Language-Maker

The Greek word *poíēsis* means "poetry," but also "making" or "creation" in a general sense. Vico's contention that the true and knowable must be made by man is closely related to his belief that the wisdom of antiquity is best revealed in its poets. Primitive myth and poetry were not simply an igniting spark toward civilization, not the mere monuments of its early dawn; they stand as the prototype of man's making of language. For Vico, man is *homo faber* poetically conceived, the fabricator of speech, tales, poems. In his schema of historical recurrences, or *ricorsi,* it is during the "age of heroes," rather than the preceding "age of the gods" or the succeeding "age of men," that Vico places the heyday of poetic imagination and creativity— the time when man lived at his fullest, best, and most human.

The stages in the recurrent order of world history relate to the varieties of human language.[6] Up to the grand deluge, Vico allows no division between sacred and profane history, nor does he deviate from Holy Writ. Except for a brief reference to "what must have been the sacred language invented by Adam, to whom God granted divine onomathesia,"[7] Vico does not presume to inform us as to the nature of antediluvian speech, nor whether it had any postdiluvian remnant. After the flood, the Hebrews alone maintained the traditions of revealed truth and lived by its law, in isolation from every other people, a special exemption from the laws governing ordinary history. All other descendants of Shem, Ham, and Japheth scattered over the earth and reverted to a state of bestiality. Forsaking religion, they abandoned the humanizing customs of marriage and burial. They suffered not merely a confusion of tongues, but aphasia, the loss of human speech altogether.[8] Vico gave man after the great flood some two hundred years to become a beast, to dehumanize himself and lose all memory of language. Enormous physical growth accompanied this mental and spiritual shrinkage, as these beast-men grew into giants. During the same centuries occurred a physical process momentous in its impact on the human future. Evaporation from the deluged world was slow enough and the earth itself moist enough, so that it was a long time before a natural balance was restored and rain, thunder, and lightning recurred. The thunderbolts of Jove inspired terror in the beast-men, their first inspiration. The "age of the gods" was issued in.

In fear of natural force and reprisal for shamelessness, men returned to belief in the gods. Thus their bestiality was brought under control and authority reinstituted, marriage and the family reestablished, burial rites resumed. Festivals and ceremonies brought order back to human life.

The "age of the gods" was a stage in the development toward civil society: It included the oncoming of agriculture, then of property, then of a nobility in control of that property. The age of the gods was the womb of human civilization and history, a place and period of formation. (Vico repeatedly asserts that the main national languages first grew in protected isolation and he refers to a language which remains free of foreign influence—he mentions German—as a *lingua madre*.) In that age were shaped the institutions required for the birth of law, something which could be embodied in tradition, and for the emergence of poetic wisdom. The language of this age was not yet poetry. Vico speaks of it vaguely and variously, using these formulations almost in succession: "a divine mental language by mute religious acts or divine ceremonies"; "imaginative characters of animate and mute substances"; expression "by means of gestures or physical objects which had natural relations with the ideas"; "a language with natural significations"; "language . . . hieroglyphic, sacred, or divine"; and, with an allusion to Homer, "the language of the gods" themselves.[9] Vico seems to be groping for some way to characterize language precedent to articulate speech, yet suddenly transformed from animal mutism, the language which would be mother to poetic imagination.

Recognizable poetic language flourished during the next, "the age of heroes." It was a language of "symbols . . . , metaphors, images, similitudes or comparisons, which, having passed into articulate speech, supplied all the resources of poetic expression."[10] In Greece, Orpheus lived near the beginning of heroic times, the first of the "theological poets," and Homer near the end. Among the Chaldeans, Zoroaster, and among the Egyptians, Hermes Trismegistus are considered "poetic characters."[11] The whole of ancient Roman law and jurisprudence is viewed as a solemn, severe kind of poetry. Vico stressed the association between poetic myth and lawful authority by identifying poetic with civil theology.[12] The oldest poets were at once theologians and legislators. Their work was both *onomathesía* and *nomothesía*, both name-giving and law-giving.

The tradition of the heroic age found in civil-theological poetry was the culture of nobility, the most mythic and traditional of the commonly recognized forms of social organization. Despite his sympathetic fascination with aristocracy, Vico perceived in it one fatal defect: It was based on profound inequality. Since noblemen owned the land and serfs tilled it, conflict between patricians and plebeians was inevitable. If the aristocrats were accommodating, they could easily lose their privilege; if they were unyielding, they might very well lose their lives. Out of the dynamics of this struggle emerged the "age of men," and with it the political institutions of republic and monarchy, democracy and dictatorship. Gradually philosophy replaced religion, but licentiousness also replaced law, and plebiscite or edict replaced tradition—until a new barbarism set in and the age of men degenerated to inhumanity. Finally the *ricorso* would begin anew and the cycle be repeated.

The order of ideas must follow the order of things.

This was the order of human things: first the forests, after that the huts, thence the villages, next the cities and finally the academies. . . .

Men first feel necessity, then look for utility, next attend to comfort, still later amuse themselves with pleasure, thence grow dissolute in luxury, and finally go mad and waste their substance.

The nature of peoples is first crude, then severe, then benign, then delicate, finally dissolute.[13]

And prose replaced poetry.

Language ran in course with men. *The New Science* is full of correspondences. Those between the varieties of men and the modes of speech are specially treated in a chapter of the second book, "Corollaries concerning the Origins of Languages and Letters." Vico actually advances two contradictory theses concerning the origin of language. Near the end of the chapter Vico says, "as gods, heroes and men began at the same time . . . , so these three languages began at the same time, each having its letters, which developed along with it."[14] Of these, divine language is almost entirely mute, heroic language a mixture, and human language "almost entirely articulate and only very slightly mute, there being no vulgar language so copious that there are not more things than it has words for."[15] This view is in harmony with one aspect of Vico's treatment of history as a whole: In some passages the emphasis seems to imply that history is not so much a succession or cycle of three distinct ages as a continuous struggle between patricians and plebeians, in which the earliest formative period was favorable to *nobilitas* but the subsequent course of events increasingly advantageous to the *vulgus*. Each class or party might be said to speak its own language, and linguistic history is essentially a question of dominance. Earlier in the chapter, however, and much more frequently throughout the book, Vico speaks of three ages and successive types of language: Each epoch develops its own appropriate form of speech. This, the prevailing view, leads Vico to contrast the metaphorical, sensuous, spontaneous poetry of the age of heroes with the utilitarian prose of the age of men. Here the history of man, his mind, and his language is seen as a conquest of imagination by abstraction. The tension between these contradictory theses yields discrepancies even in particulars—for example, the simultaneous interpretation of Aesop as a "vulgar moral philosopher" who wrote in prose and as the "poetic character" of the serfs who probably wrote in verse.[16]

Vico's apparent inconsistency can best be explained by his dual intentions of having the new science serve both as "a history of human ideas" and as "an ideal eternal history traversed in time by the histories of all nations."[17] Vico intended both a descriptive history and an historical paradigm providing a model for human virtue or excellence. In the "Conclusion of the Work: On an Eternal Natural Commonwealth, in Each Kind Best, Ordained by Divine Providence," Vico followed on the track of Plato's *Republic,* wherein Socrates constructed an "ideal state" or "city according to the *lógos*" (369a5), but also described the course of its probable or inevitable destruction, were it ever to be achieved. Despite the unlikelihood that philosopher-kingship would ever be realized, the logical city could serve as a standard whereby actual and not-so-logical cities could be judged. Evidently Vico's "ideal eternal history" was meant to have somewhat the same purpose: The universal pattern of recurrence would serve both to illuminate the individual histories of nations and as a guide and model. It was Vico's hope that a recovery of the beginnings would bring with it a return to principles (*principi*). Although Vico viewed man as a language-maker, by his own account men are capable of being myth destroyers as well as myth creators. Individual men and individual ages do not measure up to the standard of human nature. This is necessarily so, because it is the nature of men and of ages that they should change. Vico, who never tired of etymology, regularly referred *natura* to *nascor* ("to be born") and *phýsis* to *phýō* ("to generate or grow"). Vico could not identify with those classical thinkers who saw the changeability of things as essential deviation from their true forms; but he cannot yet be identified with those who temporalized the chain of being entirely. The dual purpose of the new science reflects an unresolved dual interpretation of "nature."

Man the language- and myth-maker is not always at his best, though Vico recognizes something clearly best in the poetic wisdom of the heroic age. Mythic poetry is the prototype of human language because it encompasses tradition (the basis of society and law), religion (something which points to a realm beyond man and makes him aware of his limits), and self-expression. This poetry and language best manifest that faculty of the human mind which Vico considered the most unique and powerful—not reason, but *ingenium,* inventiveness or creativity.[18] Vico's emphasis on *ingenium* over man's other mental powers was corollary to his initial and axiomatic principle, that man knows that which he makes. Reason might re-present a picture of the world, but it could not make it. The priority of reason led Descartes to a doctrine of innate ideas, ideas which men did not participate in making but which were simply given. Spontaneity and imagination ruled in the earlier periods, because reason had not yet become the great usurper. Consummate originality, especially in language and poetry, is found at or near the beginnings.[19] At the same time that Vico emphasizes the creativity of language, he sees poetry as the source of traditional authority. Ironically, the tradition which develops out of original poetry may tend to discourage the inventiveness which was its initial inspiration. Once again Vico is caught between his commitment to the transistory and historical nature of all things and his search for ideals and models. The prototype of poetic wisdom does not mean that all men in the earlier age spoke with equal poetry, heroism, or wisdom. So too, the departure from this standard in the later age need not mean that all language becomes uncreative, unpoetical, and unwise: "The poetic speech . . . continued for a long time into the historic period, much as great and rapid rivers continue far into the sea, keeping sweet the waters borne by the force of their flow."[20]

A bewildering aspect of Vico's treatment of linguistic origins is his vague reference to a language of the gods themselves. He cites the Homeric passages where the gods are said to call things by special names, speaks of nature as "the language of Jove," and describes Greek theology as the "science of the language of the gods."[21] He further refers to the Platonic tradition that there was once a completely natural and adequate language, spoken perhaps on Atlantis, and to Plato's injunction that men should not presume to name the gods or use their names or speak their language.[22] Vico's numerous allusions of these themes with no further explanation seem to have as their purpose an indication of the limits of our own clarity. In at least three places Vico states these intentions quite explicitly:

In reasoning of the origins of things divine and human in the gentile world, we reach those beginnings beyond which it is vain curiosity to demand others earlier. . . .

Later men were unable to enter into the imaginations of the first men who founded the gentile world, which made them think they saw the gods.[23]

Vico also indicates the limitations on man's understanding of absolutely original things in the frontispiece which he explicates in such detail. In that iconographic allegory Homer is separated by dark thundering clouds from the brightness surrounding the eye of God and representing divine providence and wisdom. Homer's illumination comes indirectly by reflection from a jewel on the breast of world-transcending poetic metaphysics. The discovery of the "true Homer" represents the final limit of the philological-historical reconstruction allowed by the new science. For Vico himself, however, this may have been one of its most fruitful successes—so much so that he renders a line from the *Odyssey,* in obvious mistranslation, as saying that the Muse gave to Homer "a knowledge of good and evil."[24] Although consummate divine wisdom may be unattainable, and though we may be removed from the language of the gods by a veil thick as the thunderclouds of Jove, remnants can be found memorialized in poetry and myth. The poets, Vico vaguely suggests, may have expressed superior wisdom precisely because there lingered in them some hazy recollection of the earlier language of divinity. Language itself can preserve: In his work *On the Most Ancient Wisdom of the Italians* Vico attempts to locate that wisdom in the very storehouse of language. But surely such wisdom as there may be in ancient poetry and myth is manifest to us only if we are looking for it and only if we are ready and able to listen to the language in which it is spoken. This is the probable reason why Vico concludes the main body of his book with words from Seneca: "This world is a paltry thing unless all the world may find therein what it seeks."[25]

Vico's new science leaves us with many perplexities and paradoxes. He proposed to recover wisdom by returning to origins, yet he cautiously avoided the pretense that this was a return to absolute beginnings. There is a tension between the function of the new science as a "history of human ideas" and as "ideal eternal history." Vico was evidently disturbed and discontent with the present. He protests his faith in divine and historical providence; but when he speaks near the end of the book about "the most recent barbaric history," although his factual detail is taken from the fourth century, his message seems to be addressed to the eighteenth. Would the "age of men" live up to its name?

Man the Language Machine

The explanation of linguistic phenomena generally, and of origins particularly, within the framework of mechanistic physics, derived from the extension of the Cartesian notion of the beast-machine to include the man-machine.[26] Descartes had argued that animals are machines and that their organization and behavior are susceptible of mechanical analysis. At the same time he averred that there are aspects of human activity which cannot properly be interpreted in mechanistic terms. After much experimentation with automata, Descartes concluded that there are two commonplace features of human behavior which no robot could imitate: first, the use of speech; and second, the wide range and diversity of actions which men perform.

It is essential to understand what precisely is involved in these two tests. According to the second, Descartes asserted that man has a nature superior to machines and brutes, not because of the precision or expertise with which he can perform a single given task, but rather because of the generality and wide range of which he is capable. Machines might well be devised to perform calculations more quickly and more accurately than human beings, but "it is morally impossible that there should be sufficient diversity in any machine to allow it to act in all the events of life in the same way as our reason causes us to act."[27] Descartes implies that ethical decisions entail a kind of complexity which cannot be reduced to a mechanical weighing of pros and cons, which may indeed be computable, but rather a complexity which involves the capacity for judgment and which best grows on a wide field of activity, the sort of field where it is the unexpected that crops up. Genuinely ethical decisions are of the kind that we cannot be "programmed" to make: It is only in the face of the unexpected and unknown that decisions have a truly ethical character.

Descartes's first criterion for distinguishing man from beast, human language, is our more immediate concern.

We can easily understand a machine's being constituted so that it can utter words, and even emit some responses to action on it of a corporeal kind, which brings about a change in its organs. . . . But it never happens that it arranges its speech in various ways, in order to reply appropriately to everything that may be said in its presence, as even the lowest type of man can do.[28]

Man's possession and the beasts' lack of language does not result from physiological differences. On the contrary, combinations of physical sounds can indeed be imitated by some animals, whereas some human beings do not have the physiological apparatus necessary for articulate speech. Nonetheless, it is the latter who exhibit the form of behavior closer to human speech. Deaf-mutes, despite their handicap, find means of communication which give them a broad range of response and expression. The phonomimetic animals, in contrast, show no evidence that there is thought behind their sounds: There is no reason to believe that their utterances are responses to particular situations or words or that they are expressions of any state of mind, but only that they are imitations of sounds.

For it is a very remarkable fact that there are [no men] so depraved and stupid . . . that they cannot arrange different words together, forming of them a statement by which they make known their thoughts; while . . . there is no other animal, however perfect and fortunately circumstanced it may be, which can do the same.[29]

Outside the realm of phonomimetics, there are many domesticated animals that respond to utterances or commands for which they have been trained. These stimulated reactions also fall short of the basic elements of human language: A situation in which obedience within the boundaries of physical limitation is the only possibility—a situation in which it is impossible to say no or to ask questions in return—is less than human because it makes ethical decision either impossible or negligible.

Descartes's two tests of human distinctiveness can now be seen as related to one another. Animal communication, complex though it may be, does not show the range and the freedom found in even the simplest uses of language by man as a thinking being. A thinking being, by Descartes' definition, is "a thing which doubts, understands, conceives, affirms, denies, wills, refuses, which also imagines and feels."[30] In modern parlance this is referred to as "the creative aspect of language use."[31] With the instrument of already established languages, men can say new things, they can lie, they can give expression to the powers of their imagination, they can disagree. There is no evidence of any of these capacities in the sign systems of animals or in so-called computer languages.

Although Descartes dilated on some of these points in his copious correspondence, nowhere does he offer an extensive analysis of man's language. The member of the Cartesian movement who did give it more special treatment was Géraud de Cordemoy, whose *Physical Discourse Concerning Speech* (1666) gained status as the Cartesian orthodoxy in matters linguistic. The then prominent discussion of the relation between body and soul led Cordemoy to questions of language and to a distinction: "In *Speech* there are alwayes [sic] two things, viz. the Formation of the *Voyce,* which cannot proceed but from the *Body;* and the *Signification* or the *Idea,* which is joyn'd therewith, which cannot come but from the *Soul.*"[32] Parrots, musical instruments, even echoing rocks make sounds; but since there is no reason to believe that thought lies behind these sounds, we cannot conclude that there is a soul either. The surest sign of the presence of thought would be innovation. "For it seems to me, that to *speak*, is not to repeat the same words, which have struck the ear, but to utter others to their purpose and sutable [*sic*] to them."[33] "I conceive . . . that *Art* may go so far as to frame an Engin, that shall articulate words like those, which I pronounce; but then I conceive at the same time, that it would only pronounce those, that were design'd it should pronounce. . . ."[34] Genuinely human, "soul-filled" language must include "signs of Institution," conventional rather than necessary signs. This provides the possibility of novelty for the speaker, even though it also means that "I can render those signs very deceitful."[35]

Descartes's remarks about language were meant to show the distinctness of man as a thinking being and the exemption of *res cogitans* from the mechanical laws which regulate the extended world. It was a small step—albeit one which ignored or contradicted many Cartesian arguments—to take one side of Descartes's explanation and use it to defeat the other. Pierre Gassendi, most influential of the revivers of Epicurean atomism, was among the first to take Descartes's own principles of mechanics and apply them to thinking beings. The fifth set of objections to the *Meditations on First Philosophy*, which Descartes published together with his own replies, were criticisms by Gassendi. In one passage Gassendi made passing reference to Descartes's use of langauge as a test of humanity:

You say that the dog barks by mere impulsion and not owing to resolve, as in the case of men speaking. *But in the case of man there are causes at work too, and hence we might deem that his speaking was due to impulsion; for that also which we attribute to choice is due to the stronger impulse, and the brute also exercises his own choice when one impulse is greater than the others. . . . You say that they do not reason to conclusions. But though they do not reason so perfectly and about so many things as man, they still do reason; and the difference seems to be merely one of more or less.*[36]

Man's language, that is to say, is merely better developed and more complex than a dog's; it involves a question of degree, not of kind. Descartes does not isolate these comments in his reply, although he does say of the general section that Gassendi is "carping," and that he has not addressed himself to the substance of the arguments he tries to criticize.

We must agree that Gassendi's comments do not rebut anything that Descartes says about man's employment of speech. There is one clause, however, which, if conceded, would indeed undermine the whole of Descartes' argument: "for that also which we attribute to choice is due to the stronger impulse." But should one concede this premise? There is first of all the classical distinction between cause and *conditio sine qua non:* The cause explains why something happens, whereas the condition merely identifies something without which an event could not have happened. Even though we may admit that secretion by the adrenal glands always accompanies anger, it would be transparent nonsense to answer the question, "Why are you angry?" with the reply, "Because my adrenal glands are secreting." It takes no assembly of philosophers to demonstrate the circularity—"I exhibit the effects associated with anger because there are operating in me the causes associated with anger." Surely the most common reasons for anger are that we or someone else have done or said something stupid or vicious. The distinction between cause and condition is equally clear in the case of language. If a child were asked, "Why did you say such an embarrassing thing in front of our guests?" we would have to consider him either idiot or premature sophist if he answered, "Because my lips and tongue moved in such and such a way, thus forming articulate sounds out of the air emitted from the lungs past the larynx." Such a child does not know the meaning of the word *why.*

It is hard to understand what exactly Gassendi meant by stronger and weaker impulses with regard to language. Certainly not that the decibel level would be proportionate to the pleasure or pain of the stimulus? Nor that the intensity of words corresponds to the extent of feeling or depth of thought behind them? The strongest point can often be made with understatement, and overstatement is sometimes necessary to make a minute or obvious one. And what of those who remain silent in the face of circumstances that elicit a response from others? Their silence may result from thoughtfulness or ignorance, from courage or cowardice, or from many other things we do not know. Did Gassendi have in mind psychological conditioning or compulsion? When someone is compulsively angry we say that he is angry "without reason" or that he has "lost his head." In the case of language we should have to explain by psychomechanical impulsion not only the phenomenon of speaking, but the content of a speaker's statements as well. Should compulsive talking serve as the model for all human speech? It may yet prove possible, by physical or political or psychological techniques, to bring men to a state where everything they say or do not say is determined by controlled conditioning. Should one then conclude that language is by nature mechanical? Or that such men and such language have lost their nature and been reduced to the level of machines?

Gassendi was an exponent of Epicureanism, one of the schools of ancient philosophy which had a full-blown theory of language origin. Epicurus's own preliminary comments were embellished by his poetic systematizer, Lucretius; and the arguments of Lucretius were reiterated by Diodorus Siculus and Vitruvius, all of whom became standard references in eighteenth-century footnotes.[37] The relevant passage from Epicurus is brief and somewhat confusing:

Hence even the names of things were not originally due to convention, but in the several tribes under the impulse of special feelings and individual sense impressions primitive man uttered special cries. The air thus emitted was moulded by their individual feelings or sense-impressions, and differently according to the difference of the regions which the tribes inhabited. Subsequently the whole tribes adopted their own special names, in order that their communications might be less ambiguous to each other and more briefly expressed. And as for things not visible, so far as those who were conscious of them tried to introduce any such notion, they put in circulation certain names for them, either sounds which they were instinctively compelled to utter or which they selected by reason of analogy according to the most general cause there can be for expressing oneself in such a way.[38]

Epicurus's remarks should be considered in the context of two disputes. There was, first of all, a debate going back to the fifth century whether names are according to nature (*phýsis*) or convention (*thésis, synthéke, nómos*). On this, Epicurus's position is that words were first natural, but that the growth of language brought an increase in the use of conventional terms. More important was the general argument between Epicureans and Stoics. Each school claimed that language was "natural," but they used that term in very different senses. The Stoics considered language "natural" in two regards.[39] First, it was natural for man as a rational creature to employ a rational instrumentality for expression and communication, and the Stoics viewed language as one manifestation of divine rationality. Second, insofar as Stoics tended to identify nature with reason, they took the rational structure which they saw in language to be an aspect of its naturalness. The Epicureans, when they referred to language as "natural," did not mean that verbal elements are correct or imitative of nature, nor that the structure of language is rational; on the contrary, they believed that the world is ruled by chance. Rather, they meant that the phenomena of language proceed from sensation and instinct and can therefore be explained in physical terms.

A more elaborate account of language origin is found in the fifth book of *On the Nature of Things*. Like Epicurus, Lucretius combined the idea that there is a native physiobiological impulse which drives men to speak, with the concession that most individual words are agreed upon by arbitrary compact. Lucretius compared verbal differentiations to variations of tone and mood in the lowing of cattle, the barking of dogs, neighing of horses, and singing of birds. "If various feelings compel animals, even though they are mute, to emit varied sounds, then how much more likely is it that mortal men should be able to denote dissimilar things with one and another sound."[40] Elsewhere Lucretius compared man's power of speech to the calf's growing of horns, the whelp's development of claws, and the bird's use of wings: Man has a tongue, so he will gradually learn to use it. Beyond this, Lucretius maintained that mankind was at first a mute herd, and that the origin of language preceded the formation of political societies. He objected to the idea that there could have been any single person at that time who would stand out among men and be accepted as an authority in the designation of things. Why, he asked, should any one man have had the capacity to do what others could not do? and how would he have imposed his will? But if a dictating sovereign is eliminated by this argument and if consensual agreement is eliminated by the prepolitical condition, how did differences of linguistic usage emerge? Lucretius' physicalistic explanation leaves the origin of language as mysterious as it does the formation of political society.

Julien Offray de la Mettrie was the eighteenth-century Epicurean who gave the most systematic exposition of man as a machine and language as a mechanical invention. According to La Mettrie's best-known work, *Man a Machine* (1748), there is some physical impulse behind every physical response. Man's "superiority" over other animals is not to be denied, but rather to be explained by superior organization of the brain and nervous system. Differences between men and beasts are of degree rather than of kind and have come about by a gradual evolutionary process. In explaining man's evolution into a speaking animal, La Mettrie is more sophisticated than his masters, Epicurus and Lucretius. He adds the importance of neurological mechanisms to the mere presence of a biological apparatus enabling man to articulate sound. "Nothing, as any one can see, is so simple as the mechanism of our education. Everything may be reduced to sounds or words that pass from the mouth of one through the ears of another into his brain. At the same moment, he perceives through his eyes the shape of the bodies of which these words are the arbitrary signs."[41] Man possesses an organism well suited to make associations through verbal signs. "As a violin string or a harpsichord key vibrates and gives forth sound, so the cerebral fibres, struck by waves of sound, are stimulated to render or repeat the words that strike them."[42] The inappropriateness of this simile is glaring: Violins and harpsichords do not play themselves; and they do not choose to remain silent when played, nor to play something totally capricious and quite unexpected by their performers.

La Mettrie was fascinated by the possibility of constructing a talking robot, "a mechanism no longer to be regarded as impossible, especially in the hands of another Prometheus."[43] There was at least one such attempt later in the century, by Wolfgang von Kempelen, but we are ill informed of its results.[44] Almost unanimously, the biologists of the day were skeptical about the possibilities of language among simians. Buffon and Cuvier denied that apes had the necessary mental powers; and Pieter Camper conducted anatomical researches which convinced him that orangutans lacked even the physical apparatus for articulate speech.[45] Nonetheless, some, such as Gottfried Wenzel, tried to reconstruct and translate the rudiments of animal communication.[46] The details of Wenzel's conversations with his dog, however, and his dictionary of the elementary animal sounds are so primitively ludicrous that they seem like caricatures. Long since, the Abbé Bougeant and Cyrano de Bergerac had made much sport with the possibilities of animal language—when Cyrano voyages to the moon, the four-legged lunar inhabitants determine that he must be a featherless parrot, since as a biped he clearly lacked reason, and yet he could imitate the sounds they spoke.[47]

From the perspective of a neurologist, La Mettrie recognized one difficulty: Although men may be anatomically of a kind, there are considerable variations in native intelligence, and these seem to be related to verbal ability. For this reason, La Mettrie accepted that which Lucretius rejected—that it was only one or relatively few members of the human species who instructed the others in the customary usage of words. "But who was the first to speak? . . . The names of these first splendid geniuses have been lost in the night of time. . . . We must think that the men who were the most highly organized, those on whom nature had lavished her richest gifts, taught the others."[48] These geniuses, physiologically or neurologically superior individuals, must have been especially sensitive and would therefore "express their new feelings . . . by spontaneous sounds, distinctive of each animal, as the natural expression of their surprise, their joy, their ecstasies and their needs. For doubtless those whom nature endowed with finer feeling had also greater facility in expression."[49] Even if we admit that there are physiologically determined differences of intelligence and that such differences translate into degrees of verbal ability, we are left with an enormous question. Is there any guarantee or even probability that such "geniuses" will speak reasonably, let alone wisely? There may be some likely correlation, but it is vague indeed, hard to define and harder to measure. The wise, after all, are often laconic. And wise things can be said by fools, children, and drunkards. Wisdom is often simple; and its opposite is often complex, sophisticated, intelligent, ingenious. La Mettrie specifically refers to a "greater facility in expression." But what, ultimately, does it mean to "speak well"?

Elementa Verbalia

If the foregoing interpretations of language were explicitly mechanical, the next are implicitly chemical. These were attempts to break language down into its primordial elements, the original syllables or single sounds of human speech. By methods of reduction these authors sought to arrive at basic verbal atoms from which were composed all the molecules, and then the more complex and synthetic structures, of later languages. These were not always the terms of analogy used by the authors themselves. Some had in mind a more biological model: The original roots were the seeds out of which grew all subsequent blossoms and branches. For these writers about language origin, the main task was a reconstruction of the first spoken sounds. They wanted their researches to have a "tangible" result, substantiated with maximum etymological certainty. Unfortunately, many of the same authors employed that sort of etymology in which, as Voltaire said, "vowels do not count for anything, and consonants for very little."[50]

Charles de Brosses and Antoine Court de Gébelin were explicit about their principles of derivation: All vowels are interchangeable, all dentals with other dentals, labials with other labials, etc., and the order of syllables was subject to frequent alteration.[51] De Brosses filled 12 volumes and Court de Gébelin 9 with countless etymologies, all with some seemingly ponderous but seldom very clear significance, and which all pieced together in a grand scheme of magnificent eternal verity. Somehow, this great manifold of vestiges led back to one original and very sparing language. "Since the germs of speech are of a very small number, intelligence can do nothing other than rehearse them, assemble them, and combine them in all manners possible in order to manufacture words both primitive and derived."[52] De Brosses, president of the *Académie des inscriptions et belles-lettres,* was vitally interested in primitive antiquities and it was he who first theorized that *fétichisme,* a term of his own coinage, was an important phase of pagan religion. Ungenerously, one might regard the primitive roots as the fetishes of President de Brosses himself. The vocabularic primitives had to be as they were, according to de Brosses, just so by natural ordination, under the combined influence of climate and the very structure of the speech organs. The one *langue primordiale* diversified only as mankind moved out from its first single dwelling place, and language, as well as the vocal organs themselves, came under the influence of different climes. De Brosses exerted considerable influence in France even before publication, and, despite the lampooning of the *Traité* by Voltaire, there and abroad after it. In England, John Horne Tooke made ample use of de Brosses' materials. In Germany, Thomas Abbt and Winckelmann lifted the climatological theme.[53] In France, Bergier and Abbé Copineau invoked the etymological authority of de Brosses, but turned his evidence into confirmation that the original language was Hebrew and was inspired by God.[54] For his part, Court de Gébelin constructed an architectonic system half sacred and half secular, with alternating appeals to God and to Nature, and founded on the integrating principles of *ordre* and *besoin* ("need, function"). Somehow this beladen creation all balanced out to its author's satisfaction. The second and third volumes of his *Primitive World* were specifically devoted to the "natural history of speech." Court de Gébelin pleased himself that he had lifted the question of origin out of the "vagueness of hypothesis" and rescued etymology from its state as a "vain and frivolous science, fastidious and without principles." "In effect, if we succeed in demonstrating the analogy of all languages and in reducing them to a single primitive language given by Nature, from which men always have and shall be obligated to borrow their words, there will be no doubt left about the other portions of our enterprise. . . ."[55]

John Horne Tooke published a compilation, nearly as prolix, which had an even greater, and more deadening, influence on English philology.[56] His ΕΠΕΑ ΠΤΕΡΟΕΝΤΑ, or *The Diversions of Purley* consists mainly of lengthy and seemingly erudite disquisitions on the importance of etymology and countless derivations of individual words. Horne Tooke made no claim that he had arrived at the beginnings of all language, but he did believe that present-day words could be decomposed into their original elements through etymology, which is "like a microscope . . . useful to discover the minuter parts of language which would otherwise escape our sight."[57] Two main principles informed *The Diversions.* First, Horne Tooke maintained that all linguistic progress has consisted in increasing efficiency, that is, greater and greater abbreviation through the atrophy of unnecessary parts. Second, he believed that all the later parts of speech could be derived from original nouns and verbs—indeed, he would have preferred it had he been able to reduce all to nouns alone. Hazlitt made note of the reductive aspect of the method: "Mr. Tooke . . . treated words as the chemists do substances; he separated those things which are compounded from those which are not decompoundable."[58]

Occasional theories of a reductionist sort continued through the nineteenth into the twentieth century. Franz Wüllner inferred the "make-up of the *Ursprache*" and the "derivation of the *Urstämme*."[59] Alexander Murray was a Scotch autodidact, but quite confident that his method was reliable: "The account, exhibited in these pages of the rudiments of speech, depends not on hypothetical but inductive reasonings."[60] All tribes and nations, according to Murray, speak dialects of a single original language, which consisted exclusively of monosyllables used either as nouns, verbs, or adjectives. This original language itself derived from nine primordial syllables: *AG, BAG, DWAG, GWAG, LAG, MAG, NAG, RAG,* and *SWAG,* all of which meant some variety of "striking" or "pressing."[61] Despite the monotony of sound and meaning, the remainder of Murray's two-volume work shows with elaborate and inventive detail how each of these syllables was composed and decomposed, extended and contracted, into all the words of all the languages of the human race.[62]

The extreme conclusion of attempts to reduce language to primordial verbal elements is assignment of fundamental signification to each of the alphabetic sounds. This notion also had its tenacious adherents during the eighteenth and nineteenth centuries. For some this was a matter mystical or dogmatical; for others it was the clear result of empirical science.

Rowland Jones believed that language, in all probability Celtic, was instituted by God and that divine wisdom ordained correspondences between the shape of written letters, the shape of the mouth in forming their sounds, and the transcendent mysteries of their individual significance.[63] James Gilchrist also held that words are resolvable into a few primitives and these into the letters of the alphabet. In fact, written letters preceded sounds, which were produced when the form of the lips was made to imitate the character of script. Of all letters— Gilchrist emphasized the "curiologic (or circle-graphic) method of significancy"—the first was *O,* a written circle, whose sound is produced by rounded lips, and whose original meaning was infinite circularity.[64] W. Hornay considered himself a Hegelian. In 1858 he philosophically generated all the original letters: Diphthongs and umlauts represented the unity of opposites, but in consonants the subject becomes actual; the subject becomes active in *D*, energetic in *T*, it recognizes a second subject in *N*, recognizes itself in *L*, "posits itself in self-certainty" in *R*, and so on. To this is added the bonus that the physical motions and positions of the vocal organs in producing each sound correspond to the appropriate stage of spirit. With the aspirates the breath is rolled in the mouth and only reluctantly exhaled—the subject desires to remain in its subjectivity; with the sibilants the breath is freely and noisily ejected—subjectivity expresses itself in objectivity.[65]

Considering such lucubrations, one cannot withhold sympathy from those who came to view all theories of language origin as fools' fantasies, distrusted schemes and speculations, and insisted that philology stay with known or knowable facts. An abundance of nonsense paraded as sublime wisdom and grand discovery. In 1842 the error was well stated by F.-G. Bergmann, who unfortunately subscribed to it and developed a hypothesis similar to Hornay's: "Articulate sound, by the nature of its vibrations, indicates the state of the soul, in the same way that acoustical sounds reveal the molecular composition of more or less sonorous bodies. Thus it is that articulate sounds are significant in and of themselves. . . ."[66] All reductionists held in common the assumption that individual sounds have significance in and of themselves and that the key to these elemental meanings would unlock a kingdom of mysteries.

The more far-fetched of these theories seem like parodies. Plato himself had given a humorous version of such reconstructions in the *Cratylus*. In that dialogue about the "correctness of names" Socrates is approached by two men of contrary disposition and mind. The title character is dogmatic in his conviction that individual words have a natural meaning and that all deviations therefrom are misnomers; Hermogenes takes the view that words are conventionally agreed upon through some vaguely defined social process and that any term can be exchanged for any other, if only there is common consent. In the first part of the dialogue Socrates argues with Hermogenes and against Protagorean relativism, that there is a better and a worse in our use of language and that the better use is that which comes closest to that of those best able to ask and answer questions, dialecticians. In a second section of the dialogue Socrates offers a series of etymologies, revealing the "true meaning" of the names of heroes, gods, parts of the soul, planets and elements, the virtues, philosophical terms, and so on. It has been remarked that this is one of the most playful sections in all of Plato's writings.[67] Socrates repeatedly makes comments like "This will strike you as absurd"; "I think I am going to get caught up in some nonsense"; "I have to laugh when I say this." When he derives the names of Dionysos and Aphrodite, Socrates says he prefers a facetious explanation, "for the gods love to play around too" (406c). It has also been pointed out that Socrates and Plato were often the most serious when they seemed the least so: The similarity of *paideía* ("education") with *paidiá* ("child's play") afforded Plato one of his favorite puns. Some of the etymologies are indeed revealing of the nature of the things named, even though they may be wildly incorrect derivations in the modern sense. For example, Hermogenes inquires about "the greatest and most beautiful," namely truth (*alḗtheia*) and falsehood (*pseûdos*) and being (*ón*) and name (*ónoma*) itself. According to Socrates all of these derive from roots meaning "to search." *Ónoma* was combined from *ón oû zḗtēma* ("being which is sought out"), and *onomastón* ("famous, of great name") is said to imply very clearly that "that is real for which there is a search" (421a).[68]

After performing these etymological exercises, Socrates suggests that further reduction must be possible and that each letter must have some naturally correct meaning: rho expresses motion, delta and tau, rest; alpha, size, eta, length, omicron, roundness. With that Socrates concludes the etymological section and turns to conversation with Cratylus. The scheme, however, is bait for the over-willing Cratylus, and Socrates quickly introduces contrary examples. At the outset of the whole section of derivations, Socrates stated the principle which could stand as the refutation of overweening literal reduction: "Be on your guard, lest I mislead you with deceptive motions hard to parry. . . . It is no matter whether it is these syllables or those, so long as the meaning is the same; nor does it make any difference if some letter or other is added or dropped, so long as the essence of the thing is steadfast and manifest in the name" (393c–d). And just before analyzing the individual letters, Socrates remarked: "That which I think about the first names is, it seems to me, extremely arrogant (*hybristiká*) and laughable. Nonetheless, I will share it with you if you wish . . . " (426b). This is a typical commencement of Socratic dialogue, but Cratylus, who lacked a sense of humor, did not detect Socrates' foils. We can loosely paraphrase that problem of the *Cratylus* which goes beyond the literal question as follows: If the real issue of correctness does not lie in syllables and letters, then wherein consists the better and the worse in man's use of language?

[2]

THE LINGUISTIC
PROGRESS OF THE
HUMAN MIND

The Naming of Things

The most eminent British empiricists, although they had important things to say about other problems of language, concerned themselves little with the specific question of its origin. Francis Bacon
iconoclastically exposed the "idols of the marketplace," misunderstandings due to defective communication, but showed no interest in origins.
In his *Leviathan,* Hobbes disposed of the inventions of printing, letters,
and speech in two brief paragraphs, then moved on to questions of
more pressing concern: "For words are wise men's counters, they do
but reckon by them; but they are the money of fools, that value them
by the authority of an Aristotle, a Cicero, or a Thomas. . . ."[1] Aside
from his treatment of "visual language" and "natural signs," Berkeley's
principal concern was to avoid misleading language and "to get clear
of all controversies purely verbal" and "confine my thoughts to my
own ideas divested of words."[2] Although Hume is often cited as a
founder of analytic philosophy, he engaged in no extended discussion
of the nature of language; nor did he raise the problem of origin,
which he probably would have consigned to the limbo of those questions better left unasked.[3] Thomas Reid introduced language at the
appropriate place in his psychological hierarchy—at the level of abstraction, posterior to sensation, memory, and conception; but it is
little more than a neglected detail on the fuzzy edges of a picture
sharply focused on the theme of "common sense."[4]

The case of Locke is instructive as much for what is omitted from the theory of origin as for what is actually asserted. The second book of the *Essay Concerning Human Understanding* is entitled "Of Ideas" and the third book "Of Words." They follow roughly the same sequence of analysis, since, according to Locke, words are the signs of ideas in our mind—that is, they are the signs of subjective ideas rather than objective things, with *idea* defined simply (albeit untraditionally) as any content of the mind or anything which is an object of the understanding.[5] Since the mind at birth is a blank tablet, according to the thorough-going critique of innate ideas in the first book of the *Essay,* all ideas can be traced to their origins either in sensation or reflection. All the eventual thinking of the mind has a traceable genesis going back to the discrete data which sensation and reflection first supply, "simple ideas," the original atoms of consciousness. By associating and disassociating simple ideas the mind forms "complex ideas" of substance, mode, and relation. For example, a complex idea of substance is formed when the mind notices that "a certain number of . . . simple ideas go constantly together [and are] presumed to belong to one thing."[6] It is complex ideas of individuals or things that we designate when we employ proper names, though the vast majority go nameless. The greater importance of language arises when the mind generalizes from complex ideas to form "general ideas." "Words become general by being made the signs of general ideas: and ideas become general by separating from them the circumstances of time and place and any other ideas that may determine them to this or that particular existence."[7] Abstraction, the ability to separate out from a like group of complex ideas those essential properties which make for a class of things having the same name, is the specific faculty of humans which differentiates them from mute beasts.[8] For Locke, then, the linguistic function is partly social, allowing the significant communication of general ideas to others, and partly cognitive. Language has a classificatory purpose, because Locke considered the formation of general ideas equivalent to the division into genera and species.[9] Ordinary language is a kind of taxonomic protoscience, but one which is often indistinct or inconsistent. At the same time, words are the medium of exchange in the marketplace of ideas, but a coinage dangerously subject to devaluation.

Language has its allotted place and functions in the Lockean scheme; yet there is something incomplete and unsatisfactory in his treatment. In somewhat the same way that he evasively solved the dilemma of substance by asserting its existence as an "I know not what," Locke was irresolute about the real status of genera and species.

He endowed the mind with the active power to classify and assign names accordingly; yet he stipulated that the classification should be correct and that the names should have a "clear and steady meaning." In what sense could names be correct, however, unless there were some natural order of classes but passively reproduced in thought and speech? The same incertitude can be detected in the passage where Locke came closest to stating an overt theory of language origin:

I doubt not, but if we could trace them to their sources, we should find, in all languages, the names which stand for things that fall not under our senses, to have had their first rise from sensible ideas. By which we may give some kind of guess, what kind of notions they were, and whence derived, which filled their minds, who were the first beginners of languages; and how nature, even in the naming of things, unawares suggested to men the originals and principles of all their knowledge.[10]

Nature is vaguely introduced, but with the same vagueness individual men are left as inventors of language. Nature is called to the rescue whenever Locke comes upon dilemmas that he cannot resolve—and nature is always conformable to whatever Locke deems reasonable. Locke occasionally conjectures how children, or Adam, or tropical savages might come to designate things. In such passages, he speaks as though these children or savages would by their own free decision necessarily arrive in a world much like that of late seventeenth-century England, and as though they would perceive things quite in the manner of any Englishman of sound sense. When Locke speaks of children as denominators of things, he conveniently forgets that children *learn* an already spoken tongue. There is in Locke's epistemology a concealed *petitio principii:* It is asserted that the mind at birth is a blank slate, but for unexplained reasons the mind is then seen as developing according to a fixed pattern; hence the mental structure of which Locke purports to show the genesis is in fact assumed from the beginning. A like begging of the question can be found in the Lockean analysis of language: At that point in the mind's development when language is called for, language is, without explanation, already there.

David Hartley extended and specified the application of Lockean psychology to the problem of language. It was Locke who coined the phrase "association of ideas," but it was Hartley and Hume who gave to associationist principles a central place in epistemology. The first and more influential volume of Hartley's *Observations on Man, His Frame, His Duty, and His Expectations* (1749) was a thorough exposition of associationism; the second an apology for the Christian religion on the basis of that theory. Hartley held that sensation, the sole "primary source" of human ideas, is a process whereby external objects cause vibrations of varying intensity, which affect the sensory apparatus and are transmitted to the brain; there they become *vibratiuncles,* lesser and lingering vibrations preserved in the memory storehouse of the nervous system. Violent vibrations are painful, mild ones pleasurable. This physiopsychological process provides the stuff of ideas, which are formed when association operates on these stimuli. Ultimately, this leads to six classes of "intellectual pleasures and pains": those of imagination, ambition, self-interest, sympathy, theopathy, and of the moral sense. Even the belief in God and consent to ethical principles, Hartley derived from associations pleasurable or painful.

Hartley devoted lengthy sections of the *Observations* to problems involving language and its development. Whereas Locke had treated the mind as though it underwent a process of self-development—autogenesis, as it were—unaffected by language up to the formation of general ideas, at which point language is suddenly available, Hartley saw speech as one of the effective factors in mental development. He enumerated ways in which words themselves, spoken or written, can act as the auditory or visual stimuli which are associated into a specific idea. Words also help to fix associations and to pass on already associated ideas among the generations of a society.[11] Moving beyond Locke, Hartley admitted that the learning of language is a factor in the formation of man's mental frame at an early stage in its genesis. This very point propelled Hartley into excursuses on child psychology and some vague suggestions of a progressive mental development of mankind related to changes in language.[12] The projection of individual psychic development as an historical progression was, however, a task which Hartley could perform only with the greatest difficulties. He was committed to the literal truth of Scripture—although his own account deviated from its few details about language—and was obliged to tell his story in terms of the generations of Adam, Noah, and Abraham. Also, since his associationism led him to think of visual and auditory images as conjoined, he maintained that the evolvement of writing and speech must have been simultaneous, and thus suggested that God gave letters to Adam in Eden.

Hartley's floundering in these matters still went beyond Locke to the extent that interpersonal or social aspects of language were considered a factor even in the very origin of ideas. If mental and linguistic development both involved social relations, and not merely the psyche's relation to the external world, how then would man treat his fellow human beings in and through his language?

The Money of Fools or the Wealth of Notions?

Bernard de Mandeville denied man's inherent sociability in his *Fable of the Bees; or, Private Vices, Publick Benefits*.[13] This satire was aimed at the third earl of Shaftesbury, who had criticized Hobbes's depiction of man's natural estate as the presocial condition of warring individuals, and had insisted that sociability is one of man's "natural affections," that sympathy and compassion are native human characteristics, and that man is endowed with a "moral sense." Infected by the skepticism of Bayle and La Rochefoucauld toward all rational truth and human virtue, Mandeville emigrated to England from Holland as an open partisan of Hobbes. He held that man is by nature neither sociable nor compassionate, that human character is distinguished more by corruptibility than perfectibility, and that men are motivated by pride, competition, and self-interest. Such private vices, however, work toward the public good, since the spirit of competition creates a productive society and the spirit of domination a well-ordered society. This is the point of the versified fable with which the work begins. The allegory describes a hive in which many bees are successful, many exploited, but all ambitious and active. When grumbling members of the apiary's "lower classes" demand justice and equality, it is Jove's inclination to ignore them, but he risks his divine reputation in such tolerance of moral laxity. At long last he makes public display of indignation and institutes that honesty, altruism, and compassion should henceforth prevail. The poem then describes the progressive deterioration of the hive as all its members become good but lazy, humble but unindustrious, equal but disorderly. Mandeville sums up the moral of his tale:

> Then leave Complaints: Fools only strive
> To make a Great an Honest Hive.

> T'enjoy the World's Conveniences,
> Be fam'd in War, yet live in Ease,
> Without great Vices, is a vain
> Eutopia seated in the Brain.

> Fraud, Luxury and Pride must live,
> While we the Benefits receive:
> . . . .
> So Vice is beneficial found,
> When it's by Justice lopt and bound;
> Nay, where the People would be great,
> As necessary to the State,
> As Hunger is to make 'em eat.

Bare Virtue can't make Nations live
In Splendor; they, that would revive
A Golden Age, must be as free,
For Acorns, as for Honesty.[14]

The importance of Mandeville's *Fable* lies in more than its defense of the Tory order—inclusive of imperialism, mercantilism, and preindustrial capitalism—or its precursory position in a line of socio-economic thought leading up to social Darwinism and the ideology of the "robber barons." Mandeville's radical denial of human sociability led him to a vital concern with the genesis of language. In the dialogues which comprise the second part of the *Fable*—between Horatio, a follower of Shaftesbury, and Cleomenes, speaking for the author—Cleomenes insists that speech is no more natural to man than the social state, and hence it must have undergone some gradual process of development. Mandeville used a device later employed by Condillac: He affirmed his belief in Scripture, but went on to speculate how two savage children might have developed their native capacities. Savages (who, as distinguished from barbarians and primitives, have neither language nor civilized society) and children alike, Mandeville proposed, have a thickness of tongue relative to total mouth formation, which makes them ill adapted for articulate speech. If grown savages were suddenly introduced into the civilized world, hearing language, they could hardly recognize its usefulness; and should they be made sensible of its purpose, they could not master the art of speech, for suppleness of tongue is a matter of civilized practice.

Men are neither sociable nor compassionate, according to Mandeville, but they are more intelligent than other animals, and some men more than others. Intelligent men realized that they might better preserve themselves by communal efforts. As societies were formed—either through the common self-interest of contracting parties or the individual self-interest of persons powerful enough to compel others—language developed apace. Like the brutes, earlier men may have given vent to their passions in cries, but such emotive ejaculations or warning howls have little to do with articulate speech. Once socialized, men first used visible gestures to convey their wants and meanings; but soon enough articulate speech came to dominate, because men could invent a greater variety of expressions by employment of the vocal organs, and the use of these organs in turn widened the range of possible articulation. Mandeville's account of the original motivation for developing language is nearly unique:[15]

Horatio. The Design of Speech is to make our Thoughts known to others.
Cleomenes. I don't think so.
Hor. What! Don't Men speak to be understood?
Cle. In one Sense they do; but there is a double Meaning in those
    Words . . . ; If by Man's *speaking to be understood* you mean, that
    when Men speak, they desire that the Purport of the Sounds they
    utter should be known and apprehended by others, I answer in the
    Affirmative: But if you mean by it, that Men speak, in order that
    their Thoughts may be known and their Sentiments laid open and
    seen through by others . . . , I answer in the Negative. The first
    Sign or Sound that ever Man made, born of a Woman, was made
    in Behalf, and intended for the use of him who made it; and I am
    of Opinion, that the first Design of Speech was to persuade others,
    either to give Credit to what the speaking Person should have them
    believe; or else to act or suffer such Things, as he would compel
    them to act or suffer, if they were entirely in his Power.
Hor. Speech is likewise made use of to teach, advise, and inform others
    for their Benefit, as well as to persuade them in our own Behalf.
Cle. And so by the help of it Men may accuse themselves and own their
    Crimes; but no Body would have invented Speech for those pur-
    poses; I speak of the Design, the first Motive and Intention that
    put Men upon speaking. We see in Children that the first things
    they endeavour to express with Words are their Wants and their
    Will. . . .[16]

In this intriguing passage Mandeville does not bluntly assert that the
purpose of language is lying, exploitation, and enslavement; but he
does affirm that the reason for the creation of language lies in man's
pursuit of self-interest, self-interest bridled at best by the forces of
competition.

Adam Smith combined the principle of self-interest from Mandeville with the emphasis on naming from the Lockean tradition. Smith
appended a dissertation, "Considerations Concerning the First Formation of Languages, and the Different Genius of Original and Compounded Languages" (1761), to the second edition of his *Theory of
Moral Sentiments.* Smith subscribed to the idea—which Locke had
suggested, but then rejected—that language began with the giving
of proper names to particular familiar objects. Subsequent linguistic
development was an extension of individual names, first into nouns
substantive, signifying classes of things, and then into nouns adjective,
designating qualities. Prepositions were invented to express the relations among these terms. Verb development followed a similar pattern.
The first verbs were impersonal, such as "It is raining," referring to
particular events; others were originally nominal in their signification. *Venit,* for example, may at first have meant something particular,

such as "The lion came," actually serving as the name for the lion, and only later designating the action associated with the lion. Pronouns were formed only after nouns and verbs had been clearly distinguished. Adverbs were extensions from nouns adjective, and conjunctions were invented when there was a need to express the relationship between sentences. In sharp contrast with later romantic theorists—who, to the contrary, emphasized the priority of verbs over nouns—Smith omitted any explanation of original interjections.

In support of his hypothesis Smith introduced evidence, most of which was conjectural, and some of which was dubious. One of his key arguments concerns the way children refer to adults other than their parents as "mama" and "papa." It is doubtful that these words should be considered proper names at all—and no matter if a child calls its parents "John" and "Mary." Indeed, such extension may prove the opposite of Smith's point. When a child, seeing a strange dog, uses the name of his family dog, this probably means that the verbal expression which adults use as a proper name, the child is using as a generic term. A proper name emphasizes the individuality of a member of the species, whereas the child's extension indicates his recognition of similarities among members of a species. Smith's explanation is also vitiated by his reificiation of relations. He speaks of relations as though they were themselves things, just as he speaks of qualities as particulars which can be experienced and denominated separately from the things *of* which they are attributes and *to* which they belong. Smith failed to grasp the fundamental that things themselves exist in and as relations, just as humans exist as human in relation to other humans. The nominalization of all actions and reification of all relations is the sure giveaway of Smith's capitalist ideology. (As Hegel analyzed the former, so Marx exposed the latter.) Human and other relations are "handled" as though they were things—money in the bank, so to speak. The "wealth of notions" consists in the transformation of ideas into exchangeable and marketable commodities.

Smith's confusion comes out on the subject which, by his own admission, gave him the greatest difficulty: the genesis of the personal pronouns. He explains the third-person pronoun as a simple process of nominal substitution and abbreviation, but it was the first and second persons which caused problems. The passage, though lengthy, is revealing.

The first formers of language . . . might have said *ego venit, tu venit,* as well as *ille* or *illud venit.* And I make no doubt but they would have done so, if at the time when they had first occasion to express these relations of the verb there had been any such words as either *ego* or *tu* in

their language. But in this early period of the language . . . it is extremely
improbable that any such words would be known . . . : they, both of
them, express ideas extremely metaphysical and abstract. The word *I*,
for example, is a word of a very particular species. Whatever speaks may
denote itself by this personal pronoun. The word *I*, therefore, is a general
word, capable of being predicated . . . of an infinite variety of objects.
. . . The word *I* . . . is far from being the name of a species, but, on
the contrary, whenever it is made use of, it always denotes a precise
individual, the particular person who then speaks. It may be said to
be, at once, both what the logicians call, a singular, and what they call,
a common term; and to join in its signification the seemingly opposite
qualities of the most precise individuality, and the most extensive general-
ization. This word, therefore, expressing so very abstract and metaphysical
an idea, would not easily or readily occur to the first formers of language.
What are called the personal pronouns . . . are among the last words of
which children learn to make use. A child, speaking of itself, says, *Billy
walks, Billys sits,* instead of *I walk, I sit.* As in the beginnings of language, therefore, mankind seem to have evaded the invention of at least
the more abstract prepositions, and to have expressed the same relations
which these *now* stand for, by varying the termination of the co-relative
term, so they likewise would naturally attempt to evade the necessity of
inventing those more abstract pronouns by varying the termination of
the verb. . . .[17]

Although this is not on a par with Hegel's analysis of the "here and
now"—perhaps not even our common awareness of the "I and Thou"
—the passage deserves commentary on several counts.

In the opening sentences there is the same circularity regarding
the origin of words and of ideas which we noted in the epistemology
of Locke. Surely words are not just "there," ready to be used at the
appropriate point of mental awareness, like preserves standing on a
shelf, a supply waiting for a demand. How should they have been
invented unless their prospective employers had some awareness of
their use and meaning, in this case one's own and another's personal
identity? Secondly, one is struck by Smith's use of the phrase "whatever speaks" and his remark that the word *I* is predicable of an infinite number of objects. Surely its applicability is not universal—
unless one identifies all substance with subjectivity. (This last Smith
clearly does not do, for in his economic thought and elsewhere he
is clearly committed to the Baconian project of expanding the "bounds
of human empire," i.e., the conquest of substance by subjects.) Broadly,
I could denote all creatures showing some semblance of an ego in
actions which display rationality, will, or passion; narrowly, it is restricted to those creatures who say "I," speaking beings. And then, by

sudden transformation, the self becomes not one out of an infinity of particular objects, but the most abstract and metaphysical of all ideas. Surely the reader must exclaim: "Who, me?"

Next, there is Billy. It is true that the correct use of personal pronouns comes late in a child's language development, but once again that may prove the opposite of Smith's point. There is no reason to suppose that Billy's problem of expression stems from a lack of self-awareness per se. It more likely comes from an inability to recognize why he and others together should have rights to the first-person pronoun. And at the point when Billy could understand that, he would not only have discovered the meaning of the word *you*, but simultaneously of *I*, which Smith correctly identifies as one of the most logically mysterious expressions in all human language.

Finally, by a literal reading Smith suggests that the early framers of language deliberately avoided some things; therefore we should notice the specifics which Smith evades, or in any case omits. First, he makes no differentiation between *he* and *she* as opposed to *it*. Second, although he admits the peculiar difficulties of both the first- and second-person pronouns, he never speaks about the latter.

There is no statement in the dissertation which specifically connects it with the ethical philosophy expounded in the *Theory of Moral Sentiments*. Dugald Stewart even suggests that Smith had a self-interested motive in using it as an appendix, to assure it a wider circulation. There are, however, curious parallels between the main work and these addenda. As the title suggests, it was Smith's burden to prove that ethics can be derived from man's instinctive feelings. Although man is natively a creature of self-interest, he is also possessed of natural sympathy, which Smith specifically associated with the powers of imagination. If one child sees another suffer, he can imagine himself in a like situation, and thus suffer together with the other. The sight of pain elicits "instinctive benevolence," but a strange sort, because it is one where self-interest and sympathy are supposed to be fully in harmony—that is, I sympathize because it would be against my self-interest to be in your situation. (Smith's reasoning was rather more far-fetched, it should be added, when he implied that men are inspired with similar sympathetic reactions at the sight of someone else's prosperity.) He tried to derive approbation and disapprobation, ultimately all the moral sentiments and social affections, from such responses.

Smith made qualified criticisms of Mandeville in a chapter entitled, "Of Licentious Systems," but similarities between *The Fable of the Bees* and Smith's *The Wealth of Nations* are obvious. The harmony of self-love and sympathy in *The Theory of Moral Sentiments* turns up in the later work as the identification of a more or less unrestrained pursuit of self-interest with the production of the public good. Is it too much to ask whether Smith's moral philosophy might have been more adequate had he given deeper and more serious consideration to the genesis of the personal pronouns?

Jeremy Bentham, in several unfinished manuscripts found with his literary remains,[18] also put forward a language theory tailored to the *homo economicus,* one which emphasized instrumentality and efficiency, which implied a supply-and-demand theory of words, and which made the origin of speech into something like a primitive business proposition. Evidently unacquainted with all those who had protested the inadequacy of the metaphor, Bentham presupposed that language was a tool, invented much like other human implements. The uses of language are either "extra-regarding" or "self-regarding." By the former we communicate with others either to convey information, excite emotions, or prompt certain courses of action. In its self-regarding aspect language is a tool which can be applied to itself: We can use it for the improvement of our thinking, which will in turn improve our language. Language owes its origin, however, strictly to its extra-regarding functions, which remained its sole purpose for a long time, since meditation was impossible in the early stages of society. Material wants required the formation of language, and material things were the first designated.

In the case of each tribe the objects of which the use and thence the possession is most necessary . . . to subsistence, to enjoyment, to exemption from pain—the necessity must have been earliest and most urgently felt. Hence these must have been the objects to which the denominations must have been earliest attached. Without an entire sentence of no necessity, of no want, can any intimation be conveyed.[19]

Like more romantic thinkers, Bentham believed that single primitive utterances were equivalent to whole sentences, and saw modern interjections as remnants of these antiquities. He did not attribute this, however, to a primitive capacity for emotive or poetic expression— in the above quotation the use and possession of objects even precedes pleasure and pain; rather it was the aboriginal means for making commands and transactions, for the expression and satisfaction of wants. Linguistic progress, in contrast, came with analysis, the breaking down of primitive one-word sentences into their component parts.[20] Underlying Bentham's theory of language is the substructure of an economics of scarcity, even perhaps a certain poverty of spirit—a striking contrast with those thinkers who taught that speech originated in the luxurious outpouring of irrepressible emotions, in fact the desire to share such fullness of heart with fellow human beings.

Elsewhere Bentham had a different explanation of man's evolution from the bestial state, attributing it to the formation of "fictions."

Names of real, names of fictitious entities, in the division thus expressed, may be seen [as] one exhaustive division of the whole stock of *nouns substantive*. Strict, to the highest pitch of strictness, as is the propriety with which the *entities* here called *fictitious* are thus denominated, in no instance can the idea of *fiction* be freer from all tincture of blame: in no other instance can it ever be equally beneficial; since, but for such fiction, the language of *man* could not have risen above the language of *brutes*.[21]

Some nouns designate real entities, perceptible and concrete individual things, whereas others stand for fictions. Such fictions—names of classes, of quality and quantity, psychological terms, etc.—have a useful purpose despite their lack of material reality. "To language then—to language alone—it is, that fictitious entities owe their existence; their impossible, yet indispensable existence."[22] These same "blameless falsehoods" and "profitable fictions," however, can be the source of incalculable human error, if men cease to be mindful of their real status. Then the "counters of wise men" become "the money of fools," as men fall prey to the "tyranny of words." Then the fictions are indistinguishable from the fabulous entities of poets, priests, and lawyers.[23]

To avoid confusion, we must employ these fictions with clarity about ther status. To that end a new organon was needed, one even newer than Bacon's, whch was unclear on the very point of the natural status of classes. Bentham's new organon was the critical analysis of linguistic usage, "disambiguation" and "exposition."

A proposition is *clear*, in proportion as it is *clear*—that is, *free*—at the same time from *ambiguity* and *obscurity*. . . .

In so far as the seat of the unclearness is in the words taken singly, *clearness* has for its *instrument, exposition*. Exposition is a name which may, with propriety, be applied to the designation of every operation which has for its object, or end in view, the exclusion or expulsion of unclearness in any shape; to the operation, and thereby, (for such on the present occasion is the poverty, and thence the ambiguity, of language) to the portion of discourse by which the end is endeavoured to be accomplished, and by which the operation of accomplishing it is considered as performed.[24]

Bentham busied himself with the compilation of philosophical dictionaries, critical glossaries, and handbooks of deceptive fallacies.[25] Rather than the usual definition *per genus et differentiam,* Bentham proposed a method of "paraphrasis," the resolution of abstract and composite figments into simple sensory ideas, and analysis of complex propositions into their material components. As the ultimate instrument of disambiguation, Bentham projected, but did not live to complete, some means for the systematic analysis of propositions similar to his own "felicific calculus," which quantitatively measured pleasure and pain.[26] With all these novel tools the bewitching powers of the fictions could be dispelled.

Bentham, like John Horne Took and Noah Webster, thought that linguistic progress consisted in increasing abbreviation,[27] and speculated that the original linguistic shorthand must have consisted exclusively of nouns. In fact, Bentham harbored a passionate hatred of verbs. "Where a substantive is employed, the idea is stationed as it were upon a rock:—where no substantive is employed, but only a verb, the idea is . . . a twig or a leaf floating on a stream, and hurried down out of view along with it. . . ."[28] "I use a verbal substantive where others use a verb. A verb slips through your fingers like an eel—it is evanescent: it cannot be made the subject of predication—for example, I say *to give motion* instead of *to move.* The word *motion* can thus be the subject of consideration and prediction. . . ."[29] On the basis of his "substantive-preferring principle," Bentham favored the use of nouns with primitive auxiliaries, invented a host of neologisms, and in the notoriously obscure style of his last writings he attempted to avoid verbs altogether. Bentham warned against the insidious personification of fictions—references to kings as "the crown," to lawyers as "the law," and to rich men as "property." He did not object to the nominalization of all actions: For Bentham language began with things, and it ends with "thingification."

Bentham's substantive-preferring principle was closely related to his deep distrust of all rhetoric and poetry, just as the priority of the verb in romanticist thought was a corollary of their exaltation of poesy.

Between poetry and truth there is a natural opposition: false morals, fictitious nature. The poet always stands in need of something false. When he pretends to lay his foundations in truth, the ornaments of his superstructure are fictions. . . . Truth, exactitude of every kind, is fatal to poetry. . . . [The] exceptions do not counteract the mischiefs which have resulted from this magic art. If poetry and music deserve to be preferred before a game of push-pin, it must be because they are calculated to gratify those individuals who are most difficult to be pleased.[30]

The disenchantment of poetic magic would come with the critical employment and analysis of "impossible, yet indispensable" fictions. Quite unexplainably, language was made into the simultaneous cause-all and cure-all for man's mental and social maladies. Bentham displayed more skepticism toward the tyranny of language than he had for the potential tyranny of actual governors. The very purpose of the felicific calculus was to provide legislators with a mechanism to compute the pleasure and pain which different policies would stimulate in the populace at large.[31] It does not seem to have occurred to Bentham that the technique might be used as an additional means of manipulation, that this tool too might be a weapon. Are sophists any the less dangerous when they use a disarming, disambiguated language? And what might Yahoos do with such a language?

Well-Formed Formulae of Linguistic History

Locke was, to a great degree, as much "The Philosopher" for the French *philosophes* as he was for the English. Voltaire popularized the master in the *Philosophical Letters* (1733); Condillac further systematized empiricism in his *Essay on the Origin of Human Knowledge* (1746). Diderot, Turgot, Holbach, Helvétius, and others all made contributions toward establishing the authority of Locke and of sensationalist epistemology. Influence brought with it transformations. Condillac "radicalized" Locke into a more consistent form of genetic sensationalism, so that the existence of human language, ready and waiting at a certain point of human development, could no longer be taken for granted the way it was by Locke. Condillac's revisions compelled him to consider linguistic development. Another aspect of Locke's transformation in France was the extent to which Condillac, Turgot, and Condorcet projected empiricist epistemology onto an historical screen. Locke's explanation of psychological development became a model for the historical progression of the race. This historicizing of the sequence of intellectual faculties was parallel to the "temporalizing of the chain of being," the change from a metaphysical explanation of natural hierarchy to the first evolutionary schemes of natural history.[32] In the French appropriation of British empiricism, the sensation of simple ideas became the perceptual mode of primitive men; maturation became progress; clarity about abstract ideas became the keystone for the age of scientific revolution.

The subtitle of the *Essay on the Origin of Human Knowledge* modestly advertised it as a "Supplement to Mr. Locke's *Essay on the*

Human Understanding," but in fact Condillac revised Locke as well. The initial point of emendation concerned Locke's doctrine of autonomous reflection. Locke considered sensation a *sine qua non* for reflection and prior to it, since the mind cannot be aware of its faculties until they are operative; but Locke stoutly maintained that reflection is nonetheless independent, because its contents cannot be reduced to more primitive sensory data. Thus Locke was a consistent empiricist— all contents of the mind are derivable from experience of some sort; but he was not a strict sensationalist—not all experience is of a sensuous kind. Condillac objected that Locke's explanation of reflection was an unnecessary concession, an inconsistency which weakened the entire edifice. It implied that there was something innate in the mind, incited by circumstance perhaps, but not explicable as a response to the stimulative phenomena of the world perceived by sense. Condillac tried to show that all supposedly independent reflections are derivable as compositions from the data of sense. Ideas are formed by a prereflective process of association requiring the use of signs. "The ideas are connected with the signs, and it is only by this means . . . they are connected with each other."[33] For Condillac, the seeds of language, if not its full flower, were present and well rooted prior to reflection. Locke sometimes spoke as though little babies not only sensed, for example, a cube of sugar, but as though they recognized it *as* cubical, white, and sweet. The fact is, however, that we do not interpret sense data by native instinct; rather we must learn how to "use" our senses, which requires the employment of signs.

In Condillac's revision of empiricist doctrine, the connection or association of ideas (*la liaison des idées*) must come into play before the emergence of reflection.[34] The mechanism of liaison, the "real cause of the progress of the imagination, contemplation, and memory," is the use of signs which reinforce and preserve associations. These signs may be internal or private and are not yet equivalent to human language in the full sense; but they are the necessary precedent to it and to the operation of reflection, because it is only at this point that the mind can become aware of the complexity of its own operations. Reflection and language reciprocally influence one another, leading to the further progression of each and the emergence of more advanced mental faculties: abstraction, judgment, understanding, and reason.

The importance of signs for Condillac led him to criticize Locke on still another point. Locke did not recognize the deeper epistemological relevance of signs, or of language generally, because he saw the main purpose of language in the communication of already formed ideas and overlooked its role in the very process whereby such ideas are formed.[35] According to Condillac, the function of signs is so basic that deaf-mutes or isolated children would, in order to reason, have to contrive some system of internal signs. He distinguished three types of signs: accidental (when the circumstances or part of an experience evokes association with the whole), natural (cries or gestures expressive of passionate response), and instituted (conventional words or other arbitrary means of signification). In imagination and contemplation all three kinds may be operative, and for memory all three are necessary. Thus the brutes, who have no instituted signs, cannot advance beyond reminiscence, or at most imagination. The use of signs puts the mind in command of itelf and raises it to a human level. On the other hand, the necessity for signs stems in part from the limitations of human understanding: Signs assist the finite mind when ideas involve such a manifold of qualities that it is impossible to grasp them all at once. Condillac even remarked that an infinite being would have no need of any language or sign system. Through the use of signs, mere consciousness passes over into meaningful reflection and the mind becomes aware of its strengths as well as its limits.

Condillac's amended version of empiricism, with its emphasis on signs and its different account of reflection, forced the question of language and its origins. The entire second half of the *Essay* treated language and method, beginning with a lengthy section, "Of the Origin and Progress of Language." Condillac began by affirming (perhaps sincerely, but in any case conveniently) that all mental operations and the gifts of speech were bestowed upon "our first parents . . . by the extra-ordinary assistance of the Deity. . . ."[36] But he immediately went on to suppose how two children, alone and astray after the deluge, might have gone about the invention of signs. Such a supposition would allow investigation of the way in which language *might have been* invented by man. The remainder of the second part, of course, was an elaboration of the supposition, with no regard to the initial affirmation of miraculous origin.[37] As further protection against attacks from the quarters of theology, Condillac evoked the authority of Bishop William Warburton, who had said that "judging only from the nature of things and without the surer aid of revelation," the secular explanations of linguistic origins in Diodorus and Vitruvius would almost convince, as they did indeed persuade such a saintly man as Gregory of Nyssa and such a learned one as Richard Simon.[38] In implying basic agreement with the eminent English divine, however, Condillac was distorting his source; for Warburton found the natural explanation a temptation to unregenerate reason. Warburton himself held that God, by instructing Adam in speech, also awakened man's reasoning powers and religious capacity. In the ambiguous passage from Genesis, Warburton interpreted the apparently passive role of God, looking on as the animals paraded before Adam to be named, as the fitting image for a tutor giving his pupil an unannounced examination. Condillac regularly bowed to Warburton's authority, only to use it to undermine the authority of Scripture.

Condillac's epistemology already explained the necessity of "inward language," the use of signs for the advancement of thought; but the device of an isolated boy and girl allowed him to sketch a conjectural account of the way in which external language, language for interaction and communication, might come about. Like other living creatures, the children would have expressed their states of pleasure or pain, fear or satisfaction, with natural cries, facial expressions, or emotive gestures. Because human beings are innately compassionate, such gesticulations would gradually become the basis for mutual understanding. The first of the hypothetical children might have moved his arms and hands in a certain way in pressing need or danger. The second child would have responded with automatic sympathy and would assist the other.

Thus by instinct alone they asked and gave each other assistance. I say *by instinct alone;* for as yet there was no room for reflexion. One of them did not say to himself, *I must make such particular motions to render him sensible to my want, and to induce him to relieve me:* nor the other, *I see by his motions that he wants such a thing, and I will let him have it;* but they both acted in consequence of the want which pressed them most.[39]

The origin of language, although human, was not viewed by Condillac as an invention in the way that one imagines civilized man inventing a mechanical tool. Machines require already rational creators, whereas man cannot become rational without the aid of language. The roots of language, therefore, must reach into the deeper, earlier, and more primitive recesses of the psyche.

It took some time before fully articulate language developed. First, some of the manual gestures and bodily movements must have come to be associated with particular causes of concern, sources of contentment, or objects of the world. Condillac lingered long on the theme of chironomic and pantomimic media of expression—a theme which became important for aesthetic theories of the day, was taken up by Diderot in his *Letter on the Deaf and Dumb for the Use of Those Who Hear and Speak* (1751), and was given practical application in the sign language devised for the instruction of deaf-mutes.[40] Once reflection was activated by the use of signs, the hypothetical children (or the actual children of the human race) would have become aware that vocal sounds can serve as easily as conventional gestures to convey meaning. Language then became a mixture of articulated voice with the "language of action." Gradually, articulate speech came to predominate and nearly replace gesture and mimicry, because it was economical and convenient, and because it allowed a greater range of variety and subtlety—all of which the mind would not have recognized in its prereflective state. In primitive understanding and communication, linguistic signs were already created, and without them the mind would never have progressed.

For Condillac, psychogenesis was a near-perfect recapitulation of phylogenesis. The progression of mental powers could be temporally projected as a tableau of the historical advancement of the human mind. The progression from the sensate to the rational in individual development had its correlative in the passage from a primitive poetry of vague but concrete images to a modern science of abstract but precise formulas. Linguistic history is a miniature of the forward movement of humanity. Primitive language was metaphorical and sensuous, like the primal operations of the psyche. Early speech featured the visual and active along with the articulate; highly figurative and rhythmic, it was a medium well suited to poetry. Verbs, the most active element, probably came first, then nouns representing undifferentiated wholes, and so on. The evolution of writing followed similar course: first picture-writing, then hieroglyphics in which a partial image represented a whole idea, and finally the more abstract and entirely conventional use of alphabets. With the increasing domination of abstract rationality, language became characteristically prosaic. Poetry was lost, but knowledge gained. As the art of reasoning is inseparable from that of speaking, so every language is itself a kind of method. Improvements in language and the advancement of science move in parallel progression, "for it is the method that does the inventing, just as telescopes do the discovering."[41]

Condillac's documentation for this historicolinguistic sketch was, to be sure, rather meager. He lifted a few examples from Hebrew out of his reading of Warburton; otherwise all his evidence for "primitive language" was taken from classical Latin, the only foreign language Condillac knew. But he was modest and acknowledged the speculative nature of his work. He took the motto for the entire *Essay* from Cicero: "As far as I am able, I will explain; not, however, like Pythian Apollo, as though the things which I will say are certain and fixed; but, simply as a limited man, following probable conjectures."[42] Condillac did not claim to deal with necessary truths, but with reasonable possibilities. And although a stiff dogmatism would eventually develop out of sensationalist epistemology, Condillac himself was cautious.

Anne Robert Jacques Turgot, baron de l'Aulne, systematized the doctrine of progress, much as Condillac had systematized Lockean epistemology. He too made the sensationalist explanation of linguistic progress a prominent feature of the grand historical scheme. Turgot formulated the law of progress in two lectures delivered at the Sorbonne in 1750. The first, "Discourse on the Advantages Which the Establishment of Christianity Has Procured for the Human Race," was backhanded praise of the Christian religion. Christianity had a civilizing influence and was a powerful agent of human advancement. It was an institution which, if it did not always promote learning, had at least passed it on. And Christianity had tamed the passions of men, so that even war was no longer such a fearsome thing:

Because of it the atrocious consequences of victory have ceased—the cities reduced to ashes, the nations put to the edge of the sword, the prisoners and wounded massacred in cold blood. . . . All these barbarities of the public law of the ancients are unknown among us: victors and vanquished receive the same aid in the same hospitals.[43]

For its historic role, Christianity is worthy of admiration—if not necessarily of preservation. The second *Sorbonnique,* "Discourse on the Successive Progress of the Human Mind," further elaborated the law of progress.

For Turgot, progress was a law. Newton discovered the law of gravity governing natural phenomena, Turgot the law of progress regulating human and social events. It has been well remarked that Turgot raised "the spirit of novelty to the level of a major passion of human nature."[44] Innovation and change are not only inevitable but intrinsically desirable. Even when its consequences are disastrous, error is preferable to constancy, because men learn from their mistakes, but stagnation teaches nothing. Turgot's progress theory was clearly sensationalist; but, like Diderot, he was wary of a pitfall: The empiricism of either Locke or Condillac can all too easily be turned into solipsism or Berkeleian idealism.[45] To avoid this, Turgot gave sensationalism an opposite emphasis. Because all knowledge derives from sense, man is completely open to the outside world, rather than being shut up within himself, and is sensitive to a constant barrage of new impressions and associations, which keep the mind open and progressive. The physical and the moral universe operate according to fundamentally different laws. Gravity is a law of constancy and regularity; progress a rule of perpetual change. Some centuries earlier, in his *Oration on the Dignity of Man,* Pico della Mirandola had pictured man as a movable being who can either rise to the level of angels or fall to the level of beasts. And, in his *Fable About Man,* Juan Luis Vives had man, the Protean actor, taken up into the very circle of the gods. There was a veritable chorus ready to sing the powers of human ascension, writers who lived and wrote under the happy assumption that in this one case the forces of gravity would be nonoperational—not only could man rise, he must inevitably do so. Just so, for Turgot, gravity and progress differ in their direction; much as earth and water move downward, fire and air upward, in the ancient scheme of elements. Turgot did not say whether progress would be more ethereal or more fiery.

Turgot distinguished four separate arenas in which progress may occur: theoretical knowledge, technology, morality, and the arts. Progress of language is not a special subdivision, because advancement in each of these areas would depend on linguistic developments. In fact, Turgot remained neutral, even skeptical, on the question whether there really is significant advancement in poetry and the other beaux arts on specifically linguistic grounds. Poetry, he felt, thrives on figurative language, on the imprecision which is the death of science. Increasing clarity of terms, however, has promoted progress in all other domains—science, technology, and morality—even if it has occurred at an uneven pace, and with apparent setbacks ultimately vindicated. The history of language most vividly embodies the record of progress. "A well-made study of languages could well be the best logic. . . . This type of experimental metaphysics would at the same time be a history of the human mind and of the progress of its thoughts, always in relation to the needs which brought them to birth. Thus languages are simultaneously the evidence [*l'expression*] and the standard. The history of peoples would then take nothing less than the knowledge of languages."[46]

Turgot proposed various projects to trace the development of the human spirit through linguistic remains, but he himself never carried them out, although he did contribute the article on etymology to Diderot's *Encyclopedia.* He did, however, make some intriguing comments, in the *Sorbonniques* and elsewhere, on the parallelisms of linguistic and intellectual progress. Turgot made much of the relatively novel notion of original genius, the individual especially gifted because of his intense receptivity to new ideas. Genius is an important component in the machinery of progress, but its influence is in proportion to the times. The grand genius can only remake history when language has advanced to the point where it can adequately express his novel intuitions. As already implied in Condillac, it is not only the man but also the medium which is discoverer. Another observation concerned the dialectics of progression. Turgot was careful to maintain that progress takes place in subtle and sometimes devious ways. Individual nations may fall and be corrupted even while humanity as such and the general historical movement go forward. Here too language can be the unrecognized agent of advancement. Turgot used the example of the Romans: The decadent late Roman imperialists were defeated by the barbarians, but in linguistic history they were victorious. The barbarians inevitably adopted the language of their conquered victims, because the Latin language expressed a superior state of mind and contained a greater store of accumulated knowledge: Even in adversity progress was on the march. The history of language proves that that apparent setback was ultimate victory. Individual societies become decadent and may come and go; but in language, high civilization retains its dominance regardless of ephemeral conqueror and vanquished.

This sort of linguistic history does not only temporalize empiricist epistemology; it historicizes the older optimism, such as that expressed in Pope's famous lines:

> All nature is but art unknown to thee,
> All chance, direction which thou canst not see;
> All discord, harmony not understood;
> All partial evil, universal good;
> And, spite of pride, in erring reason's spite,
> One truth is clear, WHATEVER IS, IS RIGHT.[47]

The historical rendering of metaphysical optimism into the doctrine of human progress constituted a special form of secularized universal theodicy.[48] Progressive theories of history became grand-scale rescue operations, recovering beauty from ruins, reason from error, authors from oblivion, fortune from disaster, and real victory from apparent defeat. In the spirit of his age, Turgot was tolerant—generous with error, which would ultimately be righted, tolerant of ignorance, which would finally be illuminated. Right and reason would triumph in the end, even if it required the forceful leadership of genius, or an elite of geniuses, or a virtual army. History would vindicate them; indeed, history would apparently give everyone a clean slate. Yet there is something frightfully ironic in this grandiose rationalization of past catastrophes. One is forced to wonder, for instance, how much comfort imperial Roman generals would take in their linguistic conquests and how much sympathy they could have for the aloofness of the later historian's perspective. It is all somehow reminiscent of Gulliver. Gulliver was at a loss to understand the ingratitude of the Lilliputian queen, whose life and palace he had saved, even if he had used an unorthodox method to extinguish the flames which entrapped her—just as the overprivileged cannot fathom the ingratitude of the underprivileged toward their charities, or overdeveloped experts belittle underadvanced peasants who are unthankful for their aid. These anomalies entail fundamental problems of perspective. Were Turgot a poet writing his own *Essay on Man,* one can imagine emendations in Pope's famous line: "Whatever is, is right for the time being" or "Whatever is, is right in proper historical perspective." But even if one could make it scan and rhyme, it could hardly be rendered in authoritative boldface with the confidence of a Pope.

The marquis de Condorcet wrote his *Sketch for a Historical Picture of the Progress of the Human Mind* shortly before his imprisonment and death in 1794, while hiding from Jacobin terrorists. Condorcet also took novelties in language—the first formation of articulate speech, the invention of printing, and the devising of a language for the future—as steps in human improvement. Sanguine despite present adversities, confident despite his insistence on the need to contrive the proper instrumentalities of progress, Condorcet prophesied a glorious future in "The Tenth Epoch" of the *Sketch:* "Our hopes for the future condition of the human race can be subsumed under three important heads: the abolition of inequality between nations, the progress of equality within each nation, and the true perfection of mankind."[49] These happy results would be brought on by the abolition of inequalities of wealth, status, and education. Natural inequalities of intelligence and potential would not be eliminated, but the conditions for the flowering of genius would be equalized. Universal popular education would promote human perfection in two ways: It would facilitate the detection of genius and remove artificial barriers against the natural development of talent; also, it would make knowledge more accessible, so that many persons below the level of genius could participate in the scientific enterprise.

Equality and universality of language were important ingredients in Condorcet's prescription for future well-being. Condorcet, like Condillac, inclined to the notion that all science is really *"langue bien faite"* and that the impurity of natural language is the greatest single impediment to the advancement of learning. Like Jeremy Bentham, who devised a "felicific calculus," Condorcet worked on a *mathéma-*

tique sociale.[50] Unlike other inventors of universal characteristics, however, Condorcet hoped to achieve more than a well-formed language for the technical expert; indeed, he suspected that such pure systematizations were inimical to the egalitarian spirit. The split between vernacular and scientific language had been one of the instruments of deception and social injustice used by priests and despots in previous epochs. By using a language unintelligble to the populace, hieratic philosophers had preserved their own and their masters' power by the illusion that knowledge was available only to themselves. Differences of speech and manner endanger democracy whether they are the distinctions between aristocrat and bourgeois or between scientist and layman. The universal language which Condorcet planned, one which would dissipate human ignorance and bring perpetual peace, should have all the clear consistency of science and all the easy comprehensibility of vernacular tongues.

Death in a prison cell at Bourg-la-Reine prevented him from completing his plans for such a language.[51] Condorcet was unbounded in his enthusiastic hopes for the influence such a language could exercise. He spoke of it in one vein with his confident prediction that medicine would prolong human life and that education would lead to man's moral perfection. "We shall show that this language, ever improving and broadening its scope all the while, would be the means of giving to every subject embraced by the human intelligence, a precision and a rigour that would make knowledge of the truth easy and error almost impossible."[52]

[3]

THE INSPIRATION
OF ANTIQUITY

Introduction: Gulliver's Language Lessons

Jonathan Swift, the literary giant, did not compose a theory of the origin of language in the usual sense; yet *Gulliver's Travels* can be used as a popular source to gain insight into the technical philosophy of the period in somewhat the same way that *Through the Looking Glass,* Lewis Carroll's nonprofessional work, has become a source for professional philosophy of language in more recent years. Swift's remarks about language are not lengthy, but they are weighty.

The first two voyages of Lemuel Gulliver, to Lilliput and Brobdingnag, the lands of the miniscule and the gigantic, contrast the extremes of human stature, both physical and moral. Since Lilliput is obviously a satire on the pettiness of modern politics, particularly British and French, and since Brobdingnag represents the grandeur of the ancient polis, the work is clearly intended as a further statement concerning the Battle of the Books and the Quarrel of the Ancients and the Moderns.[1] Specific contrasts regarding language are brought out primarily in the third and fourth parts of Swift's masterpiece.

During the varied wanderings of the third voyage, Gulliver is first taken up to the flying island of Laputa, whose residents are of a strange form, with two eyes, befitting Cartesian dualism, one "turned inward, and the other directly up to the Zenith."[2] By disposition and location the Laputans show themselves to be given to "higher things," the theoretical sciences of mathematics and music. "It seems, the Minds of these People are so taken up with intense Speculations, that they neither can speak, nor attend to the Discourses of others, without being rouzed by some external Taction upon the Organs of Speech and Hearing. . . ."[3] They therefore require a special sort of servant called "flappers," who alleviate the harsh sensations of their speech by flapping mouth and ear with bladders full of pebbles.

Ill at ease and unadmired in Laputa, Gulliver next goes to Lagoda, which is peopled by creatures who are strange in dress and aspect, but at least human in form. Their society is undergoing revolutionary transformation because of events some 40 years earlier.

Certain Persons went up to *Laputa,* either upon Business or Diversion; and after five Months Continuance, came back with a very little Smattering in Mathematicks, but full of Volatile Spirits acquired in that Airy Region. . . . These Persons upon their Return, began to dislike the Management of every Thing below; and fell into Schemes of putting all Arts, Sciences, Languages, and Mechanicks upon a New Foot.[4]

Earthbound, the Lagodans were given to the applied sciences, and for their pursuit they obtained royal permit to establish an extensive Academy of Projectors. Swift's detailed description of this technological institute is clearly a spoof both of Bacon's *New Atlantis*—instead of a College of Six Days Work, in the Lagoda Academy there is a six-hour work day—and of the well-established Royal Society.[5] Among the many useful projects undertaken—everything from the invention of gunpowder to attempts to capture sunbeams in cucumbers as a heating device—experiments were also conducted in the School of Languages.

The first Project was to shorten Discourse by cutting Polysyllables into one, and leaving out Verbs and Participles; because in Reality all things imaginable are but Nouns. The other, was a Scheme for entirely abolishing all Words whatsoever: And this was urged as a great Advantage in Point of Health as well as Brevity. For, it is plain, that every Word we speak is in some Degree a Diminution of our Lungs by Corrosion; and consequently contributes to the shortening of our Lives.[6]

Instead of speaking, the projectors advised that people carry with them the objects they wished to signify, which would both be good exercise and have superior clarity over verbal ambiguities. The scheme would have caused some considerable inconveniences, to be sure, but its ultimate undoing was a rebellion by women and the vulgar and illiterate, who insisted on their rights of free speech.

The Laputans and Lagodans represent the contrast between theoretical and experimental science. Both exhibit hostility toward language which is seen either as unpleasant or deceptive. The Laputans, capable of introspection through one eye and cosmic speculation through the other, could grasp the abstract directly through the mind alone, so that language, which entails the actual physical production and reception of sounds, seemed an unfortunate nuisance. This is carried over into the Lagodan fear that speaking may wear out the lungs. The main issue for these experimental scientists, however, was that they were dealing with things rather than ideas (in either the ancient or modern sense), that words are inferior to things, and hence that language is something the practical man would best be rid of. The Laputans are annoyed by the physical side of language, whereas the Lagodans are fearful of its mental or spiritual side and desire to replace it with something entirely concrete, the parade of things.

Gulliver's final voyage is to the land of the Houyhnhnms. Here the contrast is not so much between the physical and spiritual sides of language as between the two aspects of human nature. The Yahoos have human bodies, but are dominated entirely by their passions and appetites: They have no capacity for reason or language and are unable to produce anything but howls with their vocal cords. The Houyhnhnms, in contrast, have the body of a horse, but are governed totally and absolutely by reason—their name means "perfection of nature"—and have the ability to speak through their nose.

The language of the Houyhnhnms is in several regards an imperfect model of human speech. First of all, their language is the only one of all those reported by Gulliver which is unpronounceable by any standards of orthography or phonetics. Only two of the words mentioned by Gulliver are clear exceptions: the word *Yahoo* itself and *Luhimuh,* a sort of wild rat. Other words can only be pronounced in part. For example, the last syllable of "Yahoo" and the first of "Houyhnhnm" sound alike and suggest various wordplays: a *who?* and a *why?* linked by affixes suggesting an affirmative and a negative as well as the second and third personal pronouns, *you* and *him*—and the whole combination evocative of a distorted *human.* No doubt Swift was playing the absurd with the unspeakability of this language, as contrasted with the unspeakable deeds of the Yahoos, but one wonders how many flappers the Laputans would have required had their ears been accosted by such neighings.

Secondly, the Houyhnhnms had very few words, because they had very few wants. This despite the fact that poetry of a very traditional, epic sort was held in great honor among them. Just as the Laputans had no words in their language for imagination, fancy, or invention, so the Houyhnhnms lacked terms for anything evil. Even for the inconveniences or displeasures in their lives they only added

Yahoo as a suffix to one of their usual terms: *Ynholmhnmrohlnw Yahoo,* for example, meant "an ill-contrived house."

Thirdly, the Houyhnhnms were unable to lie. It was only with great difficulty that Gulliver could even convey to his masters the conception of lying:

For [Gulliver's master] argued thus; that the Use of Speech was to make us understand one another, and to receive Information of Facts; now if any one *said the Thing which was not,* these Ends were defeated; because . . . I am so far from receiving Information, that he leaves me worse than in Ignorance; for I am led to believe a Thing *Black* when it is *White,* and *Short* when it is *Long.* And these were all the Notions he had concerning that Faculty of *Lying,* so perfectly well understood, and so universally practiced among human Creatures.[7]

The subject of lying comes up again in the very important fifth chapter, where Gulliver begins to tell his master about the human way of life in England and generally in the "civilized world." Gulliver concentrates on two aspects of European manners which are found particularly obnoxious: warfare and constitutional law. Gulliver relates specific details about the conduct of military campaigns and the invention of destructive weapons, until the Houyhnhnm commands him to be silent and observes in disgust that civilized Yahoos must be even more vile than those of his own land.

He thought his Ears being used to such abominable Words, might by Degrees admit them with less Detestation. That, although he hated the Yahoos of this Country, yet he no more blamed them for their Odious Qualities, than he did a Gnnayh (a Bird of Prey) for its Cruelty, or a sharp Stone for cutting his Hoof. But, *when a Creature pretending to Reason, could be capable of such Enormities, he dreaded lest the Corruption of that Faculty might be worse than Brutality itself.*[8]

From discussion of the means of violence, Gulliver proceeds to describe law, which should control violence, but does not do so, because the experts in the law are professional liars: "I said there was a Society of Men among us, bred up from their Youth in the Art of proving by Words multiplied for the Purpose, that *White* is *Black* and *Black* is *White,* according as they are paid."[9] Not only do lawyers deceive, but they have developed "a peculiar Cant and Jargon of their own, that no other Mortal can understand, and wherein all their Laws are written, which they take special Care to multiply; whereby they have wholly confounded the very Essence of Truth and Falsehood, of Right and Wrong. . . ."[10]

It is not only the mendacity of lawyers which shocks Gulliver's master, but the very possibility of such disputatiousness. In their total reasonableness the horses had neither inclination nor necessity for argument or dialectical discussion of any kind. In a most significant passage, Swift wrote:

As these noble *Houyhnhnms* are endowed by Nature with a general Disposition to all Virtues, and have no Conceptions or Ideas of what is evil in a rational Creature; so their grand Maxim is, to cultivate *Reason,* and to be wholly governed by it. Neither is *Reason* among them a Point problematical as with us, where Men can argue with Plausibility on both Sides of a Question; but strikes you with immediate Conviction; as it must needs do where it is not mingled, obscured, or discoloured by Passion and Interest. I remember it was with extreme Difficulty that I could bring my Master to understand the Meaning of the Word *Opinion,* or how a Point could be disputable; because *Reason* taught us to affirm or deny only where we are certain; and beyond our Knowledge we cannot do either. So that Controversies, Wranglings, Disputes, and Positiveness in false or dubious Propositions, are Evils unknown among the Houyhnhnms. In the like Manner when I used to explain to him our several Systems of *Natural Philosophy,* he would laugh that a Creature pretending to *Reason,* should value itself upon the Knowledge of other Peoples Conjectures, and in Things, where that Knowledge, if it were certain, could be of no Use. . . .[11]

If all of this is true, however, one wonders: Why did the Houyhnhnms ever speak at all?

For all these reasons, the unpronounceable equine neighings cannot serve as a model of human language. In the strange inverted mirror images that Swift uses, the beasts become men and men beasts, but in partial aspects. The Yahoos, human in body, represent all that is worst in human nature; the Houyhnhnms, human in rational capacity, represent all that is best. In each case even the representation of partial aspect is distorted, because it is cut off from the totality. Lemuel Gulliver, as gullible as his name suggests and certainly neither saint nor philosophical genius, is the only real man on the scene. As such, he is caught in between, just as his size is a median between the Lilliputian pygmies and the Brobdingnagian giants. Gulliver was most apprehensive about telling his master, who reacted with particular resentment, about the castration of horses in the civilized world. But the Houyhnhnms themselves are like castrated men, humans with neither spirit nor passion. Even their nasal language suggests a falsetto. To the extent that virtue comes easy to the impotent, one must say that the vaunted superiority of these horses is as priggish and prideful as anything to be found in England. Is it instinctive benevolence, the social character of the Houyhnhnms, or tamed passion and the control of violence which is the more admirable and virtuous among human beings?

The same deficiency pertains to their language. One wonders what the Houyhnhnms used or wanted language for. People who instinctively understood would not need it to teach or communicate. People who had no disagreements would not need it to learn or to dispute. People who had no desires would not need it to gain or to control. People who were instinctively benevolent and never showed grief would not need it to comfort or console. Even if some schemers of universal characteristics imagined a language in which error was nearly impossible and deception improbable, the Houyhnhnms' could not have been a philosophical language either. The usual pedagogical problem for the philosopher is to indicate that knowledge is even possible—which sophomores doubt too early and sophists doubt too late. But the Houyhnhnms could hardly conceive that opinion is possible. Language could have been important to the Houyhnhnms only at the point where they were confronted with something totally strange, such as Gulliver himself.

There is another motif in Swift's symbolism. It is intimated in several ways that the Houyhnhnms represent the gods, just as the Yahoos represent the beasts and Gulliver is in between. For one thing, the Houyhnhnms have no gods. The most explicit reference comes when Gulliver reluctantly admits that he is a Yahoo and undresses in front of his master: "I let my Shirt down to my Waste, and drew up the Bottom, fastening it like a Girdle about my Middle to hide my Nakedness."[12] This wandering, confounded Adam does not want to be recognized as a beast in the eyes of a god, although the master cannot understand why any gift of nature should be concealed. Gulliver is ashamed, whereas the Yahoos are before shame and the Houyhnhnms are beyond it. Aristotle said that life outside of all society was only possible either among beasts or among gods; and, related to this, that beasts have no capacity for rational language, whereas gods have no need of it.[13] The only reason gods would need language would be to communicate with men. And so, the Houyhnhnms would only require speech to communicate with Gulliver. If these creatures are gods, however, they are intolerant and even misanthropic ones, who refuse to meet Gulliver's problems of communication at anything like his own level. To whatever extent the metaphor holds that language is the cloth of thought, it is not only ornamentation but concealment. Despite all the lessons he was given by the Houyhnhnms,[14] could Gulliver ever truly learn the language of these rational beasts?

Mute Beast or Eloquent Savage?

At the same time that the theory of progress was achieving such dominance, especially in France, there was a different mood and movement afoot, especially in Scotland. Despite its anachronism, the term *preromanticism* fits this movement to the extent that it involved a rejection of neoclassicist aesthetics and did ultimately influence the outbreak of full-blown romanticism in England and Germany late in the 1790s. The term *primitivism* is misleading, since it was rare that anyone blindly eulogized mindless acorn-eaters. Nor were the "primitivists" necessarily committed to a notion of historical regression. More commonly they perceived in the past certain periods of maximum human creativity, "axial periods" of human development. Thomas Blackwell, James Beattie, Adam Ferguson, and Richard Hurd, for instance, all suggested that Homer's grandeur derived from the reservoir of creative energies supplied by his age. Numerous variations on the theme were possible. History could be seen, as by Monboddo, as a progression toward a pinnacle and subsequent descent from it. Or history could be interpreted as a series of relatively sudden breakthroughs followed by longer, less exciting, derivative leveling-off periods—something like the "normal science" which follows scientific revolutions.[15] Such a series could itself be pictured as a cycle or as a progression over the whole, with epicycles of regression during any given epoch.

A "balance of history" was made to replace the more traditional "balance of nature." It was sometimes argued that the draining away of artistic genius coincided with the accumulation of scientific data and techniques, so that there was an overall compensation. On the other hand, a standard argument of the orthodox against modern science and, in the Quarrel of the Ancients and the Moderns, of partisans of antiquity against modernism in general was the notion that there is an inevitable and irreversible "decay of nature."[16] Something like a law of historical entropy was incorporated into the schemes of those who believed in a sudden coalescence of creativity at particular times which provided the energy for years to come. The prevalent version of the idea, however, was flexible enough to allow hope for the future, hope for resurgence, for a renaissance in the full sense—not merely an imitative revival of an old culture, but a rebirth of its creative resources. This theme led to remarkable differences between the primitivists of the middle and later eighteenth century and the earlier defenders of the ancients, even though primitivism was an extension of their side of the quarrel. The "Ancients" could at least agree on a common poetical and philosophical standard, but the primitivists were not interested in standards so much as "energies" or creative powers, and their renewal. Increasingly, as the century wore on, this hopeful search for reawakening meant that the primitivists tended to have one eye toward the past and one toward the future. Like Swift's Laputans, they represent a mediation or compromise between antiquity and modernism.

James Burnet, Lord Monboddo, was a Scotch judge and a prolific dilettante in philosophy and literature. He published only two major works—*Of the Origin and Progress of Language* (1773–1792) and *Antient* [sic] *Metaphysics, or the Science of Universals* (1779–1792)—but both were so full of lengthy digressions that they ran to six volumes apiece. Monboddo imagined himself the reviver of ancient philosophy, who would restore Aristotelian metaphysics to its original dignity, whereupon its superiority would be so clear to all men of sound reason, that they would forthwith abandon the prevailing empiricist epistemology and its insidious skeptical consequences. Monboddo's popular reputation derived from a thesis widely viewed as a philosophical eccentricity, the idea that orangutans are human beings *in statu naturali*. In the tenth footnote to the *Discourse on Inequality*, Rousseau had discussed travel reports about the orangutan and suggested that it might be a species somewhere between the baboons and human beings. Beyond this, Rousseau thought it possible that these caudates might even be humans in a presocial state, that they might possess an as yet undeveloped capacity of *perfectibilité*, which he considered the specific difference of the human species. Rousseau's cautious conjecture was adopted by Monboddo as an unqualified assertion. He thus transformed the orangutan into a true primitive, giving body to Rousseau's phantom, *l'homme naturel*.

It took some juggling of Aristotle to support the contention. Monboddo made a fourfold distinction which, he claimed, was based on Aristotle: "energy," the operation and exercise of faculties; "faculty," the immediate cause of energies; "habit," the disposition productive of the faculty; and "mere power," the capacity to acquire such a *habitus*. It is not entirely clear which Aristotelian distinctions Monboddo was using here,[17] but he clearly went beyond Aristotle when he subdivided the last category between "that power which immediately produces the act, and that which is remoter, and may be said to be only the *power of power,"* and designated this last "capacity."[18] The importance of this hair-splitting becomes clear when Monboddo, using the Peripatetic definition of man as "a rational animal, mortal, capable of intellect and science," puts special emphasis on the word *capable.*[19] Man, accordingly, is a creature distinguished not by his express or actualized powers, but by his potential powers. In respect of pure capacities, Monboddo claimed, the orangutan is one with both the civilized and barbarous varieties of the human species. Orangutans possess all the anatomical features necessary for speech, but happen never to have employed their physical apparatus for the actual development of their latent capacity.

The interpretation of the orangutans as creatures possessed of the "power of power" of language derived from more fundamental principles in Monboddo's theory of language. He stated his points of departure in the descriptive titles to Books I and II, *Of the Origin and Progress of Language:* (I) "That Language is not natural to man, proved, first, from the origin and nature of the *Ideas* expressed by Language; and, secondly, from the nature of *Articulation*"; (II) "That the Political State was necessary for the Invention of Language. That such state is not natural to man, any more than Language, to which it gave birth." Language is an accident contingent upon and posterior to man's political organization, which is itself accidental. Language, then, is one among the many arts developed subsequent to man's socialization.[20] The orangutans' "aphasia" is explained by their coincidental failure to have taken the step into social life, for which reason they never actualized their capacities. In all this Monboddo invoked the authority of Aristotle, who had himself affirmed the opposite. Aristotle felt that social life was man's necessary condition; that life outside of society is only possible either among beasts or among gods; and that man's possession of language is the supreme demonstration of this. When we speak either of "animal language" or of a "language of the gods," we are engaging in paradox, perhaps meaningful or illuminating, but paradox nonetheless.

Today Monboddo is best known as the butt of Dr. Johnson's jokes and conversational polemics. Boswell had a weakness for primitivist theories and was a personal friend of Lord Monboddo—and Johnson liked to tease, especially when a Scotsman was involved. Johnson quipped: " 'Other people,' said he, 'have strange notions, but they conceal them. . . .' He said Monboddo was as jealous of his tail as a squirrel."[21] Boswell relates a reference to Monboddo as "a Judge *a posteriori.*"[22] Johnson ridiculed attempts to defend the superior happiness of beasts, and added: "Rousseau *knows* he is talking nonsense, and laughs at the world for staring at him. . . . Monboddo does *not* know that he is talking nonsense."[23]

He attacked Lord Monboddo's strange speculation on the primitive state of human nature; observing, "Sir, it is all conjecture about a thing useless, even were it known to be true. Knowledge of all kinds is good. Conjecture, as to things useful, is good; but conjecture as to what it would be useless to know, such as whether man went upon all four, is very idle.[24]

Dr. Johnson was surely not taciturn, but a conversationalist willing to discuss virtually any subject with just about anyone. Still, he dismissed speculations about the beginnings of man and of language as useless, idle prattle. Johnson's reserved silence about language origin may be more in character than it seems. In context, it is more an example of typically Johnsonian common sense than an attempt to dampen the joys of conjecture or limit the freedom of inquiry. He knows, Johnson seems to be saying, and every straight-thinking human knows, that there are basic differences between men and animals. These differences must be recognized regardless of man's past biological evolution (which is not really at issue) and regardless of the future possibility that man might be turned into an automaton or some other sort of beast. If speculation leads to the obliteration of these distinctions, as Johnson thought it did with Monboddo, then speculation is idle and even dangerous.

Adam Ferguson, a friend and compatriot of Monboddo, also rejected the notion that man ever lived outside of society, and with it the whole idea of a prehistorical state of nature. "Where [is] the state of nature to be found? . . . It is here. . . . While this active being is in the train of employing his talents, and of operating on the subjects around him, all situations are equally natural."[25] "We speak of art as distinguished from nature; but art itself is natural to man."[26] Ferguson distinguished between associating and political animals. A political animal is not only gregarious and cooperative, but must have individual choice, real and with consequences, whether "to be a good or an ill member of the society." "To be in society . . . is the state of those who quarrel as well as those who agree. Estrangement is not always a vice, nor association a virtue. Persons may assemble for contest, as well as for concord. . . . In the choice of friendship and enmity, the task of human wisdom begins, and is there only properly exercised, where the good of society is matter of free choice. . . ."[27] Ferguson made a parallel point in a chapter which differentiated the "communication of animals" from the "language of man." Human language, like human society, must entail the possibility of free and consequential choice; it must allow for newness and invention. Man is not a "nature stationary," but rather "in the progressive nature of man, it is necessary that the stock of language should wax with the growing occasions on which it is employed."[28] Man is a mutable creature, whose language and sociability are coeval, the foundations of his artful nature.

Dr. Johnson's jibes against Monboddo helped perpetuate an error concerning him. It has been demonstrated that Monboddo, like Rousseau, was widely misinterpreted as an unqualified primitivist and that it would be more accurate to describe both as early social and anthropological evolutionists.[29] As such, they readily conceded the advantages which accrued to man from his early socialization, the emergence of rationality and art; but they felt that at a certain point this social evolution and advancement of the arts and sciences became corrupting and "dehumanizing." In the pattern of human history men rise to a peak of intense humanity and then fall from it, despite outward tokens of progress. For Rousseau this high point came with the communal life just prior to the introduction and dominance of private property; Monboddo located the singular period of greatness in ancient Greece. Monboddo's version of linguistic history fits this pattern to a detail. Man began mute; after his entry into civil society he used the natural sounds he could produce to develop articulate speech; articulate language was progressively subjected to criteria of beauty and clarity, until it attained its perfection in the dialects of Greek antiquity; since then further linguistic refinement has been at the price of vitality, increased clarity at the expense of poetry. Thus Monboddo placed Chinese and the American Indian languages in the period prior to the apex, whereas English is the prime example of later decadence. At the very acme of the rise and fall of eloquence there stood, according to Monboddo, the Olympian Homer. But just who was this Homer? And was he in fact an Olympian?

A New Homer . . . and a New Moses

The reinterpretation and reevaluation of Homer, and of primitive poetry and language generally, is one of the best foci for observing the changing canons of taste during the eighteenth century. It had its background in the Quarrel of the Ancients and the Moderns. For the *anciens* Homer was the model of literary form and fount of epic materials—indisputable proof that modern men must still take their standards from antiquity and that progress could not likely improve upon them. For the *modernes* Homer was the poet who described an uncivilized, immoral, chaotic society of petty, self-inflated "heroes," over which modern refinement had innumerable advantages; and they believed furthermore that Homer described this crude rusticity in a style disorganized and inelegant—clear demonstration of modern superiority, not only in science and society, but in taste and poetry as well. From around 1680 to 1720, progressive thinkers—Fontenelle, Perrault, John Dennis, Houdart de la Motte, and the Abbés Depont, Terrason, and d'Aubignac—attacked Homer for the infelicities of his manner and defects of his content. The defenders of antiquity met its prosecutors on essentially common ground. They—Boileau, Huet, Mme. Dacier, Boivin, Parnell—discovered eminent rationality and formal design in Homer's poetry. The following famous lines of Pope describe Virgil's use of Homer:

> Perhaps he seemed above the Critic's law,
> And but from Nature's fountains scorned to draw:
> But when t'examine every part he came,
> Nature and Homer were, he found, the same.
>
> . . . .
>
> Learn hence for ancient rules a just esteem;
> To copy nature is to copy them.[30]

Homer's very vindication against the challenge of the modernists was formulated in modern terms. No one had yet bluntly asserted that Homeric poetry was indeed rough and primitive and that this was precisely its charm and beauty. The "new Homer" would not merely entail a construction of philological method, but a shift in values whereby the primitive gained esteem for being just that.

"Discovery of the True Homer" was the title of the third book of Vico's *New Science*. Ironically, the "new Homer" was, in the first place, at least two Homers, and in the second place, no Homer at all in any individual or personal sense. Vico took up the argument of the ancient Alexandrian *chōrízontēs* that the two epics attributed to Homer could not have been composed by the same author. Instead, he suggested, the *Iliad* was composed earlier and in the northeastern area of Greece (Ionia); whereas the *Odyssey* came later from southwestern Greece (Doric territory near Ithaca). It is misleading, however, according to Vico, to refer to the "composers" of the epics in anything but a metaphorical way, as is indicated by the universal vagueness about the time, place, and circumstances of Homer's life.

That the reason why the Greek peoples so vied with each other for the honor of being his fatherland, and why almost all claimed him as a citizen, is that the Greek peoples were themselves Homer.

That the reason why opinions as to his age vary so much is that our Homer truly lived on the lips and in the memories of the peoples of Greece. . . .

Thus Homer composed the *Iliad* in his youth, that is when Greece was young and consequently seething with sublime passions, such as pride, wrath and lust for vengeance, passions which do not tolerate dissimulation but which love magnanimity; and hence this Greece admired Achilles, the hero of violence. But he wrote the *Odyssey* in his old age, that is when the spirits of Greece had been somewhat cooled by reflection, which is the mother of prudence, so that it admired Ulysses, the hero of wisdom.[31]

The poems which became the *Iliad* and the *Odyssey* were originally unwritten ballads, according to Vico, sung and danced by wandering minstrels, but even more importantly by the entire Greek people. The etymology of *Hómēros* may signify the editorial functions of the rhapsodes or refer to the common people themselves, but in no case was Homer a personal artist in the modern sense; rather he was, in a poetic sense, the "founder of a nation," a "man of the people"—the Greek people themselves.[32]

All of this accords with the axiom of *The New Science* that poetic wisdom is not recondite philosophy cryptically expressed, but something sui generis, prior and superior to philosophy. The poetic power of the Homeric epics was for Vico inseparable from the fact that their author was unphilosophical and, as it were, artless: "By the very nature of poetry it is impossible for anyone to be at the same time a sublime poet and a sublime metaphysician, for metaphysics abstracts the mind from the senses, and the poetic faculty must submerge the whole mind in the senses; metaphysics soars up to universals, and the poetic faculty must plunge deep into particulars."[33] Vico does not shy away from descriptions which would normally be censorious:

Such crude, coarse, wild, savage, volatile, unreasonable or unreasonably obstinate, frivolous and foolish customs . . . can pertain only to men who are like children in the weakness of their minds, like women in the vigor of their imaginations and like violent youths in the turbulence of their passions; whence we must deny to Homer any kind of esoteric wisdom.[34]

Vico's Homer is so new that all this is said in the poet's praise. Horace had written in the *Ars poetica* that he "became indignant whenever good Homer nods"; to which Vico retorted: "Unless he had nodded that often, he never would have been the good Homer."[35]

Thomas Blackwell was a devotee of Shaftesbury and professor of Greek at the University of Aberdeen for more than thirty years. Dissemination of the new interpretation of Homer was facilitated by Blackwell's academic position: He numbered among his students Monboddo, James Beattie, William Duff, and James Macpherson. Blackwell considered the language and poetry of a people inseparable from its geographical and social environment at a particular stage of development. Modern, no less than primitive poets are molded by their times, and it is both their duty and their fate to reflect the manners and style of the day in literary form. Blackwell saw a development, of language and of men, from a prepoetical to a postpoetical phase, from crude formlessness to superficial polish. He described the first stage: "It is certain, that the *primitive Parts* of the Languages reputed *Original,* are many of them rough, undeclined, impersonal Monosyllables; expressive commonly of the *highest Passions,* and most *striking Objects* that present themselves in *solitary savage Life.*"[36] And he commented on the last: "Does it not sound something like Treason in *Apollo's* Court, to say that a *polished Language* is not fit for a great Poet? . . . Let me only observe, that what we call *Polishing* diminishes a Language. . . ."[37] It was Homer's destiny to live at the most poetic of times, the "intermediate stage," when savagery had been tamed but civilized decadence had not yet set in, when learning was not yet so advanced as to dispel wonder, nor art to destroy the passions. The service of the Greek language spoken then was Homer's added fortune: "A flourishing, happy Nation . . . must speak the noblest Language. . . ."[38] Homeric greatness can be reduced to these ingredients: He lived in the right place at the right time and spoke the right language.

The next great monument along the road to the discovery of a new Homer was Robert Wood's *An Essay on the Original Genius and Writings of Homer* (1769). Wood's most important philological contribution on the Homeric question was his demonstration, accepted as definitive at the time, that Homer had no access to the art of writing. Consequently, Homer was in possession of no tradition of learning or wealth of erudition. Wood protested against allegorizers who saw in Homer a repository of special wisdom: "Nothing could be more contrary to our idea of the character of his writings, and to that unbiassed attention to the simple forms of Nature, which we admire as his distinguishing excellence."[39] For Wood, the language which was the source of Homer's poetic powers was a linguistic mode which preceded the invention of writing, and therein lay its very greatness. He made use of Adam Smith's notion of the division of labor. Homer, Wood asserted, lived before that "useful distribution of industry," which leads to progress in the arts and trades and sciences, but which robs life and language of its simplicity.[40] Before that great transformation of society, language too was undivided. Blackwell had already suggested that Homeric language was spoken at a higher pitch than later became customary, making it nearly indistinguishable from music. Wood asserted that the "language of Nature" combined the use of voice, countenance, and gesture, and that Homeric poetry as orally recited must have exploited all of these. The original unity of media added to the dimensions of poetic effect.

It was therefore an advantage to the Father of poetry, that he lived before the language of Compact and Art had so much prevailed over that of Nature and Truth. . . .

Homer, though the oldest, is the clearest and most intelligible of all ancient writers. The Greek vocabulary, though copious in his time, was not yet equivocal; ambiguity of expression was little known before the birth of Science; when Philosophy, adopting the language of common life, applied known terms to new meanings, and introduced that confusion and obscurity, which still continues to supply matter for polemical writings, and to be the chief support of metaphysical subtlety and refinement.[41]

Philosophy and learning actually introduced the ambiguities which they then made bold to clarify. Homer's words still had a distinct, concrete, sensuous, unmistakable meaning. Language, according to Wood, makes the man, the author, and the thinker.

In Germany, Wood's *Essay* was widely circulated and highly influential, after it was introduced to Christian Gottlob Heyne by Johann David Michaelis.[42] Michaelis's son translated Wood's *Essay* in 1773; and in 1776 Johann Heinrich Voss, an estranged student of Heyne, translated Blackwell's *Enquiry*. Hamann, Herder, and Goethe—to mention only the most notable—used Wood as the basis for a new look at the old Homer and in support of their own new literary criticism. Equally important, the Germans used philological expertise to work out the scholarly details of the "new Homer," the textual criticism which transformed brilliant intuition into thorough demonstration. Friedrich August Wolf, a casual student of Heyne at Göttingen who was named to the newly established chair in philology at Halle, published his *Prolegomena ad Homerum* in 1795. The full title discloses that it was Wolf's intention to demonstrate his hypothesis conclusively, to construct a history of the Homeric texts and thereby find the means for a probable reconstruction of the original.[43] By the argument of the *Prolegomena,* the two epics originated near the middle of the tenth century B.C., were orally transmitted and altered by rhapsodes, and were finally edited and changed again in the middle of the sixth century in the time of Pisistratus. Since the original lays came from different sources, artistic unity was imposed upon them at a later date. Homer, or two Homers, may well have existed as the first organizers of disjointed materials, but not as either the original writer or final editor of the two epics.

Simultaneous with the discovery of a "new Homer" was the philological reinterpretation of Moses and the elaboration of the "higher criticism" of both the Old and New Testaments. In 1753 Jean Astruc speculated that the two divine names used in Genesis, *Elohim* and *Yahweh,* derived from two different traditions.[44] The disentanglement of the Priestly and Deuteronomic Codes in addition to the Elohist and Yahwist would be an achievement of nineteenth-century scholarship. Also in 1753, Robert Lowth published lectures he had delivered as professor of poetry at Oxford, *Lectures on the Sacred Poetry of the Hebrews.* Influenced by Longinus on the one hand, and antagonized by the mix of literalism with paradox in Warburton's *Divine Legation of Moses* on the other, Bishop Lowth interpreted the Hebrew Scriptures as sublime primitive poetry, of which some was oracular (the Prophets), some choral (Psalms), some elegiac (Lamentations), some didactic (Proverbs), some odic (the Song of Deborah), some dramatic (Job and the Song of Solomon), some idyllic, and some epic. The same characteristic descriptions used for Homeric language were here applied to the poetry of the Hebrews. Although Lowth claimed a distinctive genius for Hebrew poetry and language, which he referred to as the *stilus parabolicus,* its main features are familiar: It is a highly figurative language, full of poetic imagery drawn from ordinary life.

Johann David Michaelis attended Lowth's lectures at Oxford in 1741 and incorporated these views in his own Bible commentaries and works on the Hebrew language. Five years after Lowth published his lectures, Michaelis translated them with an appendix of his own notes. Themes from Lowth were echoed by Hamann and Heyne; and Herder's *On the Spirit of Hebrew Poetry* (1782) became a minor classic. In 1779 Johann Gottfried Eichhorn, a student of both Michaelis and Heyne at Göttingen and subsequently professor of Oriental and Biblical literature there, interpreted Moses as a "poetic legislator." In collaboration with one of his own students, Johann Philipp Gabler, he expanded this work into a multivolume explanation of the Hebrews' mythic mentality and a painstaking analysis of the oral traditions combined in the Old Testament canon.[45] From here, the chain of research reaches over a host of scholars to Julius Wellhausen, also of Göttingen, whose *Prolegomena to the History of Israel* (1882) was as definitive as was Wolf's *Prolegomena* on the Homeric question. Parallel developments in the exegesis of the New Testament—distinguishing Judaic from Greek, and Gnostic from Pauline elements—go from Johann Salomo Semler to Ferdinand Christian Baur, and on to Rudolf Bultmann in the twentieth century.

Many of the new Biblical critics saw themselves as the first to truly appreciate, if not translate, primitive eloquence. Like Vico, Heyne thought that his labors would help restore myth to its original dignity.

Myths have regained their worth and eminence; they are to be considered as ancient sagas, as the first sources and beginnings of the history of peoples; others as the first attempts of the childish world to philosophize; in them genius strives to become poetry; through them the historical style is formulated; out of them developed writing, language, especially the poetic language from which proceeded rhetoric. . . . Art, with its ideals expressed by divine natures and pantheons, had its first complete foundation in myths and mythic images.[46]

Myth was the language of the infancy and innocence of the human race. There is, to be sure, a question whether such words do in fact describe the "original dignity" of myth. And there were many who foresaw dangerous consequences: Even Wolf, insisting that the roles of minister and philologist must be kept separate, refused admission in his seminars to theology students. The dialectics of the transition from naive mythophilia to skeptical demythologizing are curious indeed. One result of the higher criticism, one which had a more widespread immediate impact than any other, was the rewriting of the life of Jesus. Heinrich Eberhard Gottlob Paulus, also a professor of Oriental languages, wrote a *Life of Jesus* in 1828, in which he tried to explain what natural phenomena might have been confused in the recollections or fantasies of the disciples so as to be transmitted as miracles. A student of Baur, David Friedrich Strauss, when he published a life of Jesus in 1835, gained such instant notoriety that he was turned down for a university position; and the biography by Renan (1863), an expert in Semitics, was immediately condemned by Catholic authorities. In response to Strauss, Carl Ullmann, himself a learned man and no mere reactionary, wrote a book called *Historical or Mythical?*, which he said was the *Lebensfrage* of theology, its vital question but also its question of life or death.[47] The question whether history and myth are contradictory or complementary categories would dominate theology for over a century. It is ironic that Vico had predicted that history, with the tools of philological criticism, would not only lead to a new "philosophy of authority" but would restore the language of myth and poetic wisdom to its original dignity. One wonders what Vico would have thought about the results of the new science?

Originality as Novelty

Originality originally referred to that which is (or is like that which is) at or near the origins, and therefore ancient or "primitive"; *originality* has come to mean that which is creative and novel and therefore modern or avant-garde. Eighteenth-century discussion of the nature of "original language" provides the primary material on which this semantic shift is based. Given the limited historical spectrum envisioned by most eighteenth-century thinkers—since neither comparative linguistics nor evolutionary theory had yet fully developed—they considered Hebrew and Greek to be among the first languages, and Moses and Homer the original poets. As the modernists emerged victorious in the Quarrel of the Ancients and the Moderns, the Battle of the Books was transferred to a new level. The "new Homer" of Vico, Blackwell, Wood, and Wolf was not a master of clarity and design, but rather mythologue, voice of the people, the intensive reflector of his age. As the symbol of the mirror was overshadowed by that of the lamp, the powers of the poet and of genius generally came to be interpreted as active rather than passive.[48] The artist was seen as inventor rather than imitator.

The shifting meaning of *originality* was an important aspect of the eighteenth-century revolution in aesthetics and literary criticism, the transition from neoclassicism to the age of sensibility to romanticism.[49] The term *neoclassicism* itself covers a multitude of virtues inscribed in different literary canons and variously expounded. The "reign of Parnassus" was not the tyranny implied by some of those who stormed against it. There were, nonetheless, several themes related to the question of original language which served as ammunition in the rebellion against neoclassic standards of taste: the notion of the "sister arts"; the rejection or radical recasting of the Aristotelian doctrine of mimesis in favor of the idea that the arts are expressive; a novel explanation of "original genius"; and a reinterpretation of the faculty of imagination.

Ut pictura poesis, a reiterated maxim from Horace's *Ars poetica,* expressed the mimetic function of art and implied an especially close kinship between poetry and painting. Denial of this comparison and assertion of the affinity of poetry with music and dance was one point registered against neoclassical theory. Lessing's *Laocoön* (1766) may be the most famous work drawing territorial boundaries between poetry and painting, but the theme was common.[50] In England the main emphasis was on the musical properties of poetry; on the continent the principal concern was with the creation of a new operatic genre wedding music and word, as in the operas of Gluck.[51] The most comprehensive and influential work on this subject was John Brown's *Dissertation on the Rise, Union, and Power, the Progressions, Separations, and Corruptions of Poetry and Music,* first published in 1763, condensed for a wider audience, and translated into German, French, and Italian within a decade. Brown traced the emergence of the arts back to impulses of the passions, which could be expressed by action, voice, or articulate sound. Action was incorporated in gesture and dance, voice in music and song, articulate sound in speech and poetry. Since all were inspired by a single power, they were at first united, and their unity had social as well as aesthetic effects. This primitive *Gesamtkunst* was the medium of religious rite, vehicle for tradition and education, and means for announcement and propagation of the law. In time, however, the arts separated, as the dance increasingly became the domain of the martial spirit, and the functions of legislator and bard were also disjoined.[52] Separation of the arts was in part cause, in part symptom of general social dissolution. Brown enumerated some 36 stages of progressive disunity and aesthetic decadence. The empiricists had seen original sensations as essentially atomic and gave to the "higher faculties," along with language, the synthetic function of bringing together the discrete data of sense. Brown, in contrast, saw the original intuitions as being full and whole, so that the progress of abstraction had the function of analysis and the consequence of disunity. For Brown, original language was an abrupt outburst in simultaneous poetry, song, and dance.

Music had always been the most difficult art to reconcile with Aristotelian aesthetics. The thesis that poetry and music were "sister arts" was an important factor in the transition from the view of art as imitative to the view of art as expressive, and from there to Wordsworth's explanation of poetry as the "spontaneous overflow of powerful feelings."[53] In 1744 James Harris's influential essay claimed that music is not imitation at all, that poetry is imitative only in a carefully prescribed sense, and that the mimetic qualities of poetry and painting are unrelated.[54] Adam Smith suggested that the very idea of artistic imitation is paradoxical: The perfection of imitation would be in exact replicas of objects, but these we do not admire as art; rather we are aesthetically fascinated only to the extent that there is a discrepancy between the medium of representation and the thing represented.[55] James Beattie took Smith's concept of sympathy from *The Theory of Moral Sentiments* and applied it to poetics: Music and poetry arise from the emotional impulses of the artist, and it is therefore their purpose to evoke an emotional response.[56] At first music was seen as an exception from Aristotelian theory; then poetry was added to the list of non-mimetic arts; and finally it was asked whether it is not exceptional for any art to be imitative. This step was taken by Sir William Jones, the famous Orientalist, in an essay of 1772:

Thus will each artist gain his end, not by *imitating* the works of nature, but by assuming her power, and causing the same effect upon the imagination, which her charms produce to the senses: this must be the chief object of a poet, a musician, and a painter, who know that great effects are not produced by minute details, but by the general spirit of the whole piece. . . .[57]

Expression replaced mimesis as the central category of criticism. Expressive theories of language came into corresponding dominance. Daniel Webb, for example, theorized that original language must have been a simple and spontaneous outpouring of emotions in powerful verbal expressions, and first of all the interjections of emotive response.[58] Webb was so taken with the idea that language originated in passionate monosyllables that he hypothesized that Chinese was the original language and, in any case, the parent of Greek.[59]

   The expressive theory of language and art shifted the attention of criticism, so that its brightest light was shed not on the qualities of the artistic product, but on the creative process whereby art is produced.[60] The problem of the artist became one of the most prominent themes of literature itself. The psychology of "original genius" became a matter of moment around the middle of the century.[61] There is a dialectical line from Shaftesbury's *Letter Concerning Enthusiasm* (1708), through the "cult of genius," to the understanding of the poet as someone possessed, of the artist as someone suffering the morbidities of inspiration. At first genius was considered subjectively, as a psychological faculty, stronger in some, but present in all humans; then the term was applied mainly to those individuals in whom there was a special talent for originality—in Germany it was common to refer to persons, not merely artists or artistic works, as *Originale;* in the latter third of the century, especially in Germany, the term was used in an objective sense in themes like "the genius of a people" or the "genius of a language." In the earlier phase, when genius was seen as a power of the soul, *ingenium,* there was a transition from an understanding of this faculty as passive and receptive, the ability to reflect the world in its fullness and intensity, to a view of genius as inventive. Both Robert Wood and William Duff interpreted Homer as an "original genius." For Wood, Homer's ingenious originality meant that "he took his scenery and landscape from Nature, his manners and characters from life, his persons and facts . . . from tradition, and his passions and sentiments from experience. . . ."[62] Duff, in contrast, listed the following qualities of original genius: "irregular greatness of imagination," "wildness of imagination," "enthusiasm of imagination," and a "powerful bias to invention."[63] In summary, Duff wrote:

Original Genius is distinguished . . . by a more vivid and a more comprehensive Imagination. . . . It is likewise distinguished by the superior quickness, as well as justness and extent, of the associating faculty. . . . But, above all, it is distinguished by an inventive and plastic Imagination, by which it sketches out a creation of its own, discloses truths that were formerly unknown, and exhibits a succession of scenes and events which were never before contemplated or conceived. In a word, it is the peculiar character of original Genius to strike out a path for itself whatever sphere it attempts to occupy; to start new sentiments, and throw out new lights on every subject it treats. . . . It is distinguished by the most uncommon, as well as the most surprising combinations of ideas; by the novelty, and not unfrequently by the sublimity and boldness of its imagery in composition.[64]

The contrast between Wood's spontaneous and receptive original genius and Duff's spontaneous and inventive original genius could hardly be more clear.

These changes were in turn related to the redefinition of *imagination* within the empiricist tradition.[65] The older definition had it that imagination involved the mind's capacity to retain the images imprinted upon it by sense. Thus Hobbes referred to "the decaying sense" and wrote that "imagination and memory are but one thing, which for divers considerations hath divers names."[66] Though Locke and Berkeley pictured the mind as a more active agent of construction, neither emphasized the role of imagination. With Hartley and Hume, however, imagination came to occupy a central place. Using the psychology of association, both interpreted imagination as that active mental faculty which puts images together from associated ideas. Thus the conception of imagination changed from image retention to image composition. With this as his point of departure, Kant made a three-fold distinction of reproductive imagination, productive imagination, and aesthetically productive imagination. The last of these, Kant took to entail the creation of "aesthetic ideas," which, like the "ideas of reason" of the *Critique of Pure Reason,* transcend the laws of conceptual understanding—and which Kant specifically associated with the activity of genius.[67] Finally, Coleridge—under the combined influences of Hartley, Priestley, and Kant—formulated his own trichotomy of primary, secondary, and creative imagination.[68]

Originality, expressiveness, and imitation all involve intrinsic paradoxes as independent aesthetic categories. The paradox of mimesis was explained by Adam Smith—though it had been raised as a problem about language in Plato's *Cratylus* (432)— namely, that similitude is admirable only in a context of dissimilitude. The paradox of expression was formulated by Schiller and Hegel: namely, expressive theories of language and poetry emphasize the power of inward feeling, but once this is expressed it *is no longer* inward feeling. In the perceptive aphorism of Schiller: "Once the soul *speaks,* then, alas! it is no longer the *soul* that is speaking."[69] Although *originality* is made to refer to novelty or inventiveness, its etymology points in the opposite direction.[70] There is a link between the two meanings of *originality:* An unlearned primitive author who reflects his times and an inventive modern author have this in common: Whatever else they do, neither imitates those authors who have become classics. The rejection of mimesis brought questions of origins and originality to the fore in all paradoxical perspective. The discovery of a "new Homer" was not only a reinterpretation of the old but the invention of something new.

Edward Young, himself both poet and critic, grasped the dimensions of the paradox of originality.

Imitate [ancient authors] by all means; but imitate aright. He that imitates the divine Iliad, does not imitate Homer; but he who takes the same method which Homer took. . . . Imitate; but imitate not the composition but the man. For may not this paradox pass into a maxim? viz. *"The less we copy the renowned ancients, we shall resemble them the more."* . . .

Suppose you was to change place, in time, with Homer; then, if you write naturally, you might as well charge Homer with an imitation of you. Can you be said to imitate Homer for writing so, as you would have written, if Homer had never been? As far as a regard to nature, and sound sense, will permit a departure from your great predecessors; so far, ambitiously depart from them; *the farther from them in similitude, the nearer are you to them in excellence:* you rise by it into an original; become a noble collateral, not an humble descendent from them.[71]

In his *Conjectures on Original Composition* (1759), Young found originality there where genius prevails, where imitation is of nature rather than of authors, where the republic of letters is extended and a new province added to its dominion. "Born originals, how comes it to pass that we die copies?"[72] Young felt that literary tradition had become an obstacle to the vitality of literature; much as Bacon and others felt that the philosophical tradition was detrimental to philosophy itself. Young claimed Bacon as his master and his "shelter," frequently using phrases that ring of Bacon: Poetry must conquer new territories; we must not let the "blaze of even Homer's muse darken us to the discernment of our own powers"; "True poesy, like true religion, abhors idolatry."[73]

Young still addressed himself to the dispute of the ancients and the moderns. Modern authors, with the exception of Shakespeare, are inferior to ancient ones, according to him. Their shortcomings do not derive from their place in history, however, from the decline of natural or poetic powers, or from any other necessity, but rather from the folly of an enslavement to antiquity wrongly understood, imitation of ancient works instead of the spontaneous creativity and original genius which produced those works. There is hope: Originality may bring with it the dawn of a new day for poesy. Originality and genius stand like Bacon's pillars—the open gateway to a new and unknown world.

If ancients and moderns were no longer considered as masters and pupils, but as hard-matched rivals for renown; then moderns, by the longevity of their labors, might, one day, become ancients themselves. . . .

Why should it seem altogether impossible, that heaven's latest editions of the human mind may be the most correct, and fair; that the day may come, when the moderns may proudly look back on the comparative darkness of former ages, on the children of antiquity, reputing Homer and Demosthenes as the dawn of divine genius; and Athens as the cradle of infant-fame; what a glorious revolution would this make in the rolls of renown.[74]

With original genius, moderns could be not merely "on the shoulders of giants," but giants themselves. There could be not merely the slow cumulative progress of scientific knowledge, but a glorious poetic revolution. "Antiquitas juventus mundi," said Bacon. German romanticism also began with arguments about the relative merits of ancient and modern poetry. As romanticism emerged triumphant in aesthetics, but defeated and disillusioned in politics and in the sciences, the Quarrel of the Ancients and the Moderns subsided. It was transformed into the problem of the "two cultures"—the truth of poetry versus the truth of science, a theme going back to Bacon, but emphatic and clear in Coleridge—which would actually turn out to be not so much a quarrel as a failure of communication.

The discovery of a "new Homer" was proclaimed in the context of the new science of history. Ironically, for some this original interpretation of the original Homer meant the virtual irrelevance of history. If Homer's greatness was his "original genius," then the significant questions about origins are not so much historical as psychological and aesthetic. Historical research might recover traces or even reconstruct the "true Homer," but poetic genius could create new Homers. In fact, there was a new Homer, discovered or invented, in the mid-eighteenth century: Ossian, the Homer of the North. James Macpherson, a student of Blackwell, spent six months in the Scottish highlands, conversing with its humble and its poor, and listening to the age-old ballads they recited in Gaelic, a language which he never fully mastered but which he fully "appreciated" nonetheless. He published in 1760 an anthology of these poems translated into English. The next year he produced, on the basis of the alleged discovery of an ancient manuscript, *Fingal, an Ancient Epic Poem . . . , Translated from the Gaelic Language*. In 1763 Macpherson produced yet another poem by Ossian, *Temora*. Macpherson prefaced the works with dissertations on the climate and customs of the Caledonians compared with the Achaeans, and on the correspondences between the Greek and Celtic tongues. Samuel Johnson immediately suspected a hoax and demanded prompt publication of the manuscripts, which Macpherson refused on the grounds of expense, as he declined to show the manuscripts to his friends lest they plagiarize. Controversy about the authenticity—or should we say "originality"?—of the Ossian poetry raged well into the nineteenth century. It was only then that the full story was established by sound scholarship: There probably was an Ossian, at least there is someone of that name mentioned in Scottish and Irish balladry, but there were no epics *Fingal* or *Temora*, though some of the materials of both were taken from Gaelic legend.[75] A dastardly hoax to be sure, but for all one knew the real Homer of Greek antiquity may have sinned no less.

The latter half of the eighteenth century was a great age of forgeries. Thomas Chatterton, a suicide at the age of seventeen, composed poetry which he attributed to Thomas Rowley, a fifteenth-century monk. He faked an ancient manuscript well enough to deceive Horace Walpole, but not Thomas Gray, who exposed it. William Henry Ireland was a master of the arts of forgery—indeed, he raised them to the level of a science. He treated paper properly and could imitate antique script to perfection. His mistake and act of hubris was announcement of the discovery of two lost Shakespearean plays, *Vortigern* and *Henry II,* which he composed himself. One performance of *Vortigern* at Drury Lane was enough to laugh it off the stage and brand Ireland a counterfeiter. Ireland outlived the shame of exposure to write several "original" novels which have passed into literary oblivion; only the forgeries are worthy of memory.

The saddest tale of all is of a man deceived, not a deceiver. Francis Wilford was an English officer, stationed in India, interested in antiquities. He was a member of the Asiatic Society of Bengal, founded by Sir William Jones, in whose *Asiatic Researches* he published several sections of "An Essay on the Sacred Isles of the West." It was Wilford's idea that some westerly islands mentioned in Hindu myth were one with the British Isles. Unfortunately, Wilford knew no Sanskirt and had to hire pundits to confirm all this in Indian literature. Aware of Wilford's hypothesis, happy to please, not to say anxious for a source of revenue, the pundits fabricated all the evidence. Even Jones was taken in. Wilford himself discovered the erasures and mutilations in the texts whose words he could not understand. He was literally sick over the matter, but was forthright enough to notify his friends and leading periodicals, and to write a full retraction.[76]

It is all very strange indeed. When Vico and Heyne called for a restoration of myth to its original dignity, they were attacking not only allegorists, but also the proponents of the imposture thesis, those who saw myth as a history of vicious deceptions. It is as though the new interpretation called for new deceits and fresh impostors. *Antiquity, authenticity, originality*—what did the words even mean?

[4]

STRUGGLES
WITH A FLAWED
QUESTION

Jean-Jacques Rousseau represents a turning point within the modern period.[1] Sympathetic readers today generally agree that there is something more specifically "contemporary" in Rousseau than there is in most of his contemporaries. Twentieth-century themes abound in his writings, if not always by the same name: centralization versus decentralization, alienation and dehumanization, community versus mass society, the uses and dangers of science and technology, the requisites of power and its inevitable abuses. Even in those often excessive·and indulgent passages of psychological self-examination, Rousseau portrayed himself as a personal victim of an impersonal modernizing society, one of the first in a line of suffering artists.

Rousseau's attack on the grand experiment we call modernity was undertaken in a mood of bitter resignation. A simple return to the classical tradition of philosophy or imitation of classical models was, he felt, as impossible as for civilized man to attempt a return to the state of nature. In the endeavored escape man would bring his modernity, his vanity, and his civilization with him. The fight against modernity must use modern weapons, modern terrain, and modern principles of warfare. Thus, Rousseau's social philosophy was the kind of struggle which could be an enormous trap. There is ample evidence, however, that Rousseau agreed with Socrates and Plato that all political philosophy is a fight with and against a snare, because the philosopher does not have his happiest or best home in the political world, and yet he cannot remove himself from it. The philosophical critic of his society—and he will inevitably and incessantly be critical of his society, even as its forms vary—confronts a trap.[2] He risks being lured into it or ensnared by a vast supply of social blandishments and material benefits, or of falling into an ever more frenetic struggle as he is gripped in the teeth of contradiction. The struggles are not for that reason nugatory: The fly is not the born inferior of the spider. There is an obvious difference between struggling in a trap and struggling with a trap. In political philosophy, Rousseau's awareness of possible pitfalls was stronger than his confidence that he had overcome the obstacles or solved the problems.

It was Rousseau who pointed out most succinctly the difficulties standing in the way of a satisfactory solution to the question of language origin—that is, that this question too was a sort of trap. He first took up the problem in the *Discourse on the Origin of Inequality Among Men,* second of the essays submitted in the competitions of the Dijon Academy, written in 1753. In that important work, which the academicians did not see fit to honor, Rousseau traced the evolution of mankind. From an asocial existence in the state of nature, man entered the age of happy pastoral savages dominated by compassion and healthy self-love (*amour de soi*) rather than morbid vanity (*amour-propre*), an age wrecked by the development of agriculture and private property, which led men to act on impulses of acquisitiveness, domination, and competition, and consequently introduced a warfare of all against all. Such chaotic conflict being found intolerable, men formed cities and other artificial political organizations by entering into a social contract. Rousseau located the beginnings of language in the hazy and long transition between man's condition as an unsociable mute beast and his life as a "noble savage." The same era saw the invention of simple artifacts, tools, and weapons, and the evolution of natural family relations into a patriarchal social system. All of these must have taken an incalculably long period of time, but in the case of language it is hard to explain how it ever could have been instituted at all.

Rousseau specified two dilemmas or *aporiae* underlying all explanations of language origin, one involving the relation of speech to sociability, the other the relation of language to rationality. Since the state of nature is an atomistic condition of totally unsocial individuals, in Rousseau's interpretation, he could envision neither the opportunity nor the necessity for language there. On the other hand, neither could he imagine man's entrance into any form of social organization, unless men were already capable of speech, and unless communication were a factor in establishing the social union. Language appears to be necessarily prior to the formation of society, but at the same time, society seems to be necessarily prior to the invention of language. This was the inconsistency in Condillac's otherwise reasonable hypothesis: "He has assumed that which I put in question, namely, a sort of society already established among the inventors of language."³ Rousseau found no logical escape from this cul-de-sac. To say that language evolved from those primary associations among parents and children which are founded in nature alone is an evasion of the problem and "would commit the same error as those who, when reasoning about the state of nature, transport over into it ideas taken from within society."⁴ The prior existence cannot be taken for granted:

Since the child has all his wants to explain and consequently has more to say to the mother than the mother does to the child, the greater burden of invention should fall on him . . . ; for to say that a mother dictates to the child the words which he should employ in order to demand this or that thing, may well show how one teaches a language which has already been formed, but it certainly does not teach how languages were formed in the first place.⁵

The genesis of language cannot simply be assumed, and yet there is this insuperable barrier against any explanation of its genesis.

Even if there were a solution to this problem, there would remain another: "For if men had need of speech in order to learn to think, then they had a much greater need of being able to think in order to invent the art of speaking. . . . So that one is hardly able to formulate any credible conjecture about the birth of this art of communicating our thoughts and of establishing intercourse among minds."⁶ Again the *aporia:* Language seems to be necessarily prior to reason and reason necessarily prior to language. Difficulties are compounded by the expanse of time required to develop an art,

which is already so far from its origin, but which the philosopher still sees at such a prodigious remove from perfection that there is no one so bold as to assure us that it will ever arrive there, even if all the revolutions necessarily occasioned by time would be suspended in its favor, and if all prejudices would disappear from the academies or be suppressed within them, so that they would be able to devote themselves to this thorny problem for whole centuries without interruption.⁷

The past origin and future progress of language stand equally in doubt. Apparently, any human explanation of the beginnings of language will smash against one or the other of these dilemmas.

* * *

Although the explanation of these impasses was generally attributed to Rousseau, they were anticipated in Plato's *Cratylus*. Cratylus is the character in that dialogue who maintains that names are naturally correct. He takes characteristic satisfaction in Socrates' refutation of his opponent, Hermogenes, who had originally insisted that names are merely conventional and arbitrary devices used for social convenience. The tables are turned, however, when Socrates also goes on the attack against Cratylus. The inherent problems of Cratylus's position emerge when Socrates engages him in discussion about law and the lawgiver, *nomothétēs*. Socrates gets Cratylus to admit that language has the purpose of instruction and that naming is an art. The two go on to agree that legislators were the artificers of language, who invented names by imitating the natures of things. Cratylus goes beyond this to insist that these name-givers, following nature, must have been consistently correct in their designations—concluding that the knowledge of names is one with the knowledge of things (435d) and that lying, saying "that which is not," is impossible (429d). For Cratylus, the instructiveness of language depends on its consistency and inerrancy, for language is man's tutor only if it is an adequate guide to reality.

Despite all the obvious variations in known languages, Cratylus insists that the instructive function of speech is not conditioned by them. Such linguistic differences are generally associated with the different societies to which one belongs or with differences of social status, class, or consciousness. Cratylus's refusal to take these differences seriously reflects either a knowing indifference or an unknowing blindness to the power of social custom over man's ways of acting and thinking. Socrates, in contrast, was fully aware of the ambiguity of the term *nomothétēs,* which could refer both to the name-giver and the lawgiver. Socrates puns several times on the similarity between *nomothétēs,* "legislator," and *ho tà onómata thémenos,* "he who establishes names."[8] Socrates locates and exposes the Achilles' heel in Cratylus's argument, his failure to take the problem of social custom into full account. A series of questions are used as decoys in preparation for the final foil. What if the name-giver were wrong, would not all knowledge based on names be incorrect also? This Cratylus cannot accept, believing that incorrect names are no names at all, and that the consistency of language is proof of the accuracy of its originator. Suppose, Socrates asks, the legislator had given names consistently, but on false principles? Again Cratylus will not concede the point. Having distracted Cratylus, Socrates delivers his final blow: If knowledge of things comes through knowledge of names, how could the inventor of names have known anything (438a)? Here is Rousseau's *aporia* in its original form. Cratylus escapes from it with the answer used by many—Süssmilch, de Maistre, Bonald, for example—after Rousseau asked the same question: "I think, Socrates, that the truest account concerning these matters is that the first names for things were established by a power which was greater than anything human, and therefore it is necessary that the names hold correctly" (438c). Since Socrates finds imperfections in language and men's use of it, he cannot accept this notion that names were established by the gods themselves.

Aporiae had an important function in Socratic argumentation.[9] The typical structure of Socratic dialogues went as follows: A problem was introduced about which Socrates declared himself ignorant, though ever willing to discuss it; various definitions or solutions were put forward, but all found inadequate under questioning; Socrates and his interlocutor were then forced to admit the impasse at which they had arrived.[10] In the *Apology* Socrates states the principle behind his method, knowledge of ignorance. Socrates claims positively to know that, what, and why he does not know. In the aporetic dialogues he invites his interlocutors to join him through discussion in coming to a knowledge of the reasons for ignorance in important matters. Knowledge of ignorance is a fundamental for self-knowledge, but it is also related to the most important problems of political life. In the sixth book of the *Republic* Socrates ridicules all who claim to be philosophers yet cannot give an account of the good; but when Glaucon presses him to give a clear explanation of his own, he finds himself at a loss to do so. Instead, he says that he can at best speak about "the offspring of the good" (507a), the sun, which has the same relationship to the visible world that the good does to the intelligible. In choosing this analogy, however, Socrates reveals the reason why he admitted ignorance about the good: The sun cannot be looked at directly with the natural eye. As the sun can only be an indirect object of vision, so the good must be an indirect object of knowledge. We cannot directly look at the problem of the good without being blinded and dizzied. Thus, the fitting end for a "good" discussion is an acknowledged impasse.

The *Cratylus* deviates from the typical structure without deviating from the principles. The situation itself is atypical. In the *Cratylus* Socrates argues with two persons who claim diametrically opposed positions. In a way, they are not so much interested in being illuminated as they are in having Socrates crown one of them victor. Each displays an understandable tendency to take as confirmation whatever Socrates says in refutation of the other. Socrates himself does not subscribe to either of their positions. The character arrangement of Plato's work about language reflects the most common speaking situation: There is a speaker, a person addressed, and a listener.[11] This common situation can lead to special misunderstandings—misunderstandings which do not derive from the ambiguity of the terms of propositions, but from the different perspectives of the listeners. Cratylus and Hermogenes incline to take Socrates' words in different ways because of their own ambitions and opinions. There are arguments which Socrates might have used with Hermogenes had they been alone, which he did not use in the presence of Cratylus, because his purpose was to teach them both. Thus, there is something peculiar about this situation, even though it is so far from being uncommon that it is in fact the basic teaching situation.

The problem of perspective is of critical importance for an interpretation of the *Cratylus*. The two interlocutors put to Socrates a question which is deficient in perspective: Are names natural or conventional? Many questions show limited perspective. Who was right, Locke or Berkeley? Descartes or Spinoza? Who will make the best president, the Republican or Democrat? What is the best system, communism or capitalism? Who is the greatest literary character, Achilles or Odysseus? The defectiveness of these questions goes deeper than their failure to consider all the options. One would not fully expose that deficiency by answering to the above: Hume, Malebranche, democratic socialism, and Hector. In the case of the *Cratylus* it is not as though Socrates were trying to take a mediating position between the "nominalism" of Hermogenes and the "realism" of Cratylus. As the allegory of the cave suggests, limited perspective is not overcome by thinking over a broader spectrum or making more careful divisions on a line, but by turning around and looking in the other direction—and the images in that allegory suggest that this requires the shock of confronting an aporetic problem. The defect of these questions lies in the limited perspective of most people who would pose the question in that particular way. The nature of the true, the good, and the beautiful does not lend itself to easy and direct statement. The meaning and even the truth of an answer cannot be separated from the meaning and perspective of the question to which it is a response. The truth does not reside in free-floating words or propositions outside of contexts and outside of speakers' mouths. Both Cratylus and Hermogenes put themselves in a state of childish dependency on words: Cratylus thinks that he will know the truth if he knows names; Hermogenes thinks that, if names are arbitrary, then there is no truth. Cratylus questions the possibility of error, whereas Hermogenes questions the possibility of truth. Each position mirrors the other: If either is right, then all argument is puerile and irrelevant. Socrates must teach both of them to grow up.

Socrates' concluding remarks are meant to show that there are better and deeper questions to be asked:

But if this is a battle of names, in which some people say that these words resemble the truth and others say that those do, how can we come to any decision and on what basis can we choose? For there are no other words different from these existing anywhere. . . . What course would be necessary to know or find things as they really are?—that I feel is probably a bigger problem than you and I can handle, but we can easily agree that the course does not follow words; that knowledge and inquiry must rather proceed from the things themselves than from words. . . . (438d–439b)

. . . Neither would any reasonable man rely on names for himself and the training of his soul, being so confident in words and the givers of words that he consciously leans on them and condemns himself and things to a condition in which nothing is healthy, but in which everything leaks like a pot or a runny nose, as though everything existed in the state of a man afflicted with rheum and catarrh. . . . And so you should look into these matters thoroughly and courageously and like a man—for you are still young and of a fit age for such a task. . . . (440c–d)

Cratylus's (and Hermogenes') way of putting the question was "immature." That is not to say that their question is a "pseudoproblem," any more than the election of a president is a quibble based on semantic confusion. Such questions are not to be dismissed, but taken seriously at one level and not so seriously at another. That would seem to be just Socrates' attitude, not only toward the specific problem of the correctness of names, but toward the persons who raised it and toward human language in general.

From the meager historical evidence about Cratylus, it is doubtful that he heeded Socrates' hints. In Plato's dialogue Cratylus is still a young man, but Aristotle refers to him at an older age and says that Cratylus, convinced of the flux of things, gave up the use of words entirely and only pointed at things in response to his disciples' queries.[12] For all one knows, Cratylus may have thought that was the lesson Socrates taught him. Rather than changing his perspective or transcending the limitations of his original question, Cratylus merely swung from one to the other extreme, from overweening confidence in words to excessive distrust of them. But words by themselves should be the objects neither of our love nor of our hate. Interestingly,

Socrates seems more sympathetic toward Hermogenes than Cratylus. The difference of character between the two is shown by the way they answer questions. Hermogenes is cautious and uncertain in response to Socrates' points: "I suppose so"; "I am not sure what you are driving at"; "I am uncertain"; "There again I am puzzled." In contrast, Cratylus habitually answers with self-assurance: "Definitely"; "Yes, I know"; "I think your statement must be correct"; "That is absolutely true." Even their one-word answers differ: Hermogenes usually says *"Naí"*—a simple "Yes"; whereas Cratylus constantly answers *"Anángkē"*—"Necessarily so." Cratylus is certainly more sure of himself—but it is he who relies on individual words and their authority. Socrates' goal is the knowledge of ignorance, whereas Hermogenes represents a presumed ignorance and Cratylus presumed knowledge: Neither does Hermogenes know so little as he thinks nor Cratylus so much.

Socrates' own attitude is most obvious at the commencement and conclusion of the dialogue. When first asked to mediate the dispute, Socrates replies:

There is an ancient maxim that it is very hard to know the nature of the good; and even the knowledge of names happens not to be a small part thereof. If only I had heard the fifty-drachma lecture course by Prodicus, in which anyone who took the course would come to learn all about these things, as Prodicus himself said, then nothing would prevent me from knowing straightaway the truth about the correctness of names; but I did not hear those, I only heard the one-drachma course. Therefore I do not know what the truth of these matters is; but I will be happy to make a common search together with you and Cratylus. (384a–b)

Since Cratylus apparently did take Prodicus's lecture series, he should literally know fifty times as much as Socrates on the subject of language.[13] This joke involves more than the usual Socratic irony of modesty and exaggeration. The joke summarizes the point about language which must be brought home to both Hermogenes and Cratylus. Teachers know that they cannot guarantee that they will teach anybody anything, because teaching addresses students for whose varied minds the teacher cannot speak. The mere hearing of words cannot insure understanding; and therefore, if and when we would know the truth, its statement cannot be equated with its conveyance. And therefore, needless to say, attendance at Prodicus's lectures could have been fifty-drachma's worth of intellectual motion wasted. Socrates' deadpan comments are more an ambush against Cratylus than Hermogenes. Cratylus, however, falls straight into the trap, which is to say, he does not get the joke. He does not understand Socrates' words, even though they were simple ones—the kind of low-key but obvious joke which does not require an advanced course in sophistry to interpret.

Cratylus was a very serious man indeed, serious above all about himself. His failure to understand is especially evident in the last pages of the dialogue. Although Socrates had corrected him on numerous particulars and refuted him on generalities, upon further questioning, Cratylus would merely return to his dogmatic assertions, until Socrates does have to "lecture" him. Socrates finally dismisses Cratylus with gentle good humor:

Soc. And so you should look into these matters thoroughly and courageously and like a man—for you are still young and of a fit age for
such a task. And do not be satisfied too easily, but examine very
carefully; and when you have found out, share it with me.

Crat. Yes, I will do that. But be assured, Socrates, that I have not been
unreflective up to now and as far as my investigations are concerned
and bearing everything in mind, I think that it is the way Heraclitus
says it is.

Soc. Until another time, then, when you return and will teach me; for
now, as was your plan, go out into the country, and Hermogenes can
serve as your escort on the way.

Crat. So be it, Socrates. But you too should try to think about these things
directly. (440d–e)

We should be tempted to say that these comments were snide and discourteous, were we not assured that Cratylus was insensitive to both the irony of Socrates' remarks and the pompousness of his own. Cratylus was a literalist in personal character and in the doctrine which he maintained. Socrates plays with this to the end: Cratylus, who spoke so much of nature, must look at it once—literally, take a walk in the country—before Socrates can take his words very seriously. Hermogenes has apparently learned enough to be of some guidance—which proves that even the discussion of a question which was very limited in perspective from the beginning, and which came to an impasse in the end, may be instructive.

Although Rousseau stated the dilemmas concerning language origin with such clarity, he nonetheless went on to offer what he thought a probable account of its development. He did this immediately after his exposition of the *aporiae* in the Second Discourse itself, but also in an *Essay on the Origin of Languages,* which he considered using as an appendix or companion-piece to the discourse, but which was only published after his death.[14] Rousseau, then, was not deterred by his realization that the asking of a question might lead to no final solution, nor did he find such speculation inconsistent with awareness of the impasses. The hypothesis of the Second Discourse, Rousseau himself allowed, was very close to Condillac in most particulars. He emphasized the importance of cries and gestures in the early formation of language; and, consistent with his view of man, he stressed that compassion was an essential factor leading to language. Other themes are familiar: the necessity that conventional articulation dominate in fully human language; the idea that original words functioned as whole sentences; and so on. Rousseau ended the passage by admitting that he was "frightened by the difficulties which multiply and convinced of the nearly proven impossibility that language could have been born and established by purely human means," and by calling on others to attempt a solution of the dilemmas.[15]

Although the genesis of language was not the central problem of the *Discourse on Inequality,* the *aporiae* relate to the more general questions which were Rousseau's deepest concern. It was Rousseau's general purpose to find the means to distinguish the natural from the artificial in man and, by stripping man of the artificial accretions of social life, to find two things: the natural foundations on which just and well-ordered societies can reasonably be built, and a way of attaining self-knowledge.[16] The two are so inseparable that the difficulty of finding one compounds the difficulty of the other. Rousseau was scrupulously cautious in approaching both problems:

My readers should not imagine that I dare to flatter myself that I have seen that which it seems to me so difficult to see. I have begun certain lines of reasoning, I have hazarded certain conjectures, less with the hope of resolving the question than with the intention of clarifying it and reducing it to its true state. Others may easily proceed further along the same route, without it being easy for anyone to arrive at the end of it.[17]

The accumulation of knowledge does not necessarily increase the depth of knowledge and may even hinder clarity of vision:

What is even more cruel is the fact that all the progress of the human species constantly removes him further from his primitive state; and the more we accumulate new knowledge, the more we deprive ourselves of the means to acquire the most important knowledge of all; so that in a sense it is on account of our studying man that we have removed ourselves from the position of knowing man.[18]

Rousseau's description of *perfectibilité,* man's native impulse to improve and go beyond himself and make himself, gives to that quality all the dimensions of a tragic flaw.[19] It is a virtue and proof of man's freedom, but it is also what makes men constantly lose themselves and progressively become heedless of the simple truth about their nature. Perfectibility and corruptibility are inseparable, which is one reason why it is so difficult to say what man is. Borrowing another image from Plato, Rousseau wrote:

Like the statue of Glaucus, which time, sea, and storms so completely disfigured that it looked less like a god than a ferocious beast; so the human soul is altered in the bosom of society by a thousand constantly reviving causes, by the acquisition of a mass of knowledge and a multitude of errors, by changes happening to the constitution of the body, and by the continual conflict of the passions; and it has changed its appearance, so to speak, to the point where it is nearly unrecognizable. . . .[20]

Rousseau accepted the modern notion that man's nature is changeable. In a way he even adopted the modern vision of progress, though he painted that picture in dark and mixed instead of uniformly brilliant colors. If man's nature perpetually changes, then self-knowledge is impossible, since that which one might know to be true today will not be true tomorrow. Self-knowledge, in other words, is a never-ending task and obligation, which can be described either as dead-ended or as open-ended. It is the difficulty of self-knowledge that lies at the core of philosophical and political problems—one reason, no doubt, why Rousseau wrote three different autobiographical works. If man's nature is an unknown, how can men formulate natural law? All theories, ancient and modern, have shattered on this dilemma:

Thus all the definitions of these learned men, otherwise in perpetual contradiction with one another, agree only on this particular, that it is impossible to understand and hence to obey the law of nature without being a very great reasoner and a profound metaphysician: which means precisely that for the establishment of society men had to use enlightenment, but enlightenment does not develop except in the bosom of society itself and then only with great difficulty and for very few members of the race.[21]

This central impasse of political philosophy exactly parallels those regarding human language.

Because the *Essay on the Origin of Languages* was never published by Rousseau, it would be crudely disrespectful of the author's wishes to interpret it as a final statement on the problem. Rousseau announced a number of important themes, some original with him and others familiar from diverse theorists in the sensationalist and sentimentalist traditions. Language, he asserted, derives not from needs but from passions, and he vaguely suggested that love may have been parent to speech.[22] Primitive language was expressive rather than utilitarian in its purpose; and thus it was highly figurative, sensuous, and poetical. Original language played the full range of impressions on both eyes and ears: it was full of gesture and movement; it was a musical language, rhythmic and melodic.

Language, like man, is not static; it progresses. As with all human progress or perfectibility, the advancement of language was a mixed blessing. Language lost something of its original unity, charm, and power by dint of its progression. As grammar improved, the musical quality of language declined. Since history and law were originally recited and made public in musical verse, this linguistic change decreased public awareness of law and tradition, and hence public confidence and obedience were undermined. As for John Brown, so for Rousseau the separation of word and song led to the degeneration of music, a change of emphasis from melody to harmony. After writing was invented, exactitude was substituted for expression, and the range of public utterance became more restricted, rather than more free: "In writing, one is forced to use all words in their common acceptation; but someone who is speaking can vary the acceptation by his tone . . . ; less constrained by the need for clarity of expression, he can give more to its strength."[23] Rousseau thought that speaking is clearly superior to writing, both for the public welfare and for individual enlightenment. He may well have taken the principle from Plato, for whom the written word was as inferior to the spoken word as was the latter to the real being which it signified.[24] He included in the *Essay* a footnote to the *Cratylus,* which he called "one of the most interesting dialogues," because it "condemns definitively that dangerous system which would tend to substitute the study of names for the study of things."[25] He did not on these accounts abandon writing—no more than he desisted from speculation because of impasses, or thought it possible to return straightaway to nature or to antiquity: The serious treatment of defective media, imperfect questions, and inadequate answers is precisely the philosopher's task within civil society.

Language, for Rousseau, is man's "first social institution."[26] Like society itself, language is posterior to the natural state, yet it derives from man's specific native capacities, compassion and perfectibility— man's desire, for better or worse, to improve his condition and change himself. The same criterion distinguishes human language from animal

communication: Although animals do communicate signs to one another, these cannot be compared with human words, because there is
no evidence of change or progress in such signs, nor of any arbitrary
or conventional element. As Rousseau was well aware, the criterion
of perfectibility makes man's specific difference a highly wavering,
or dynamic, or metamorphic thing. Rousseau quoted with apparent
approval Montaigne's remark that, with regard to the capacities of
the soul and inward qualities, there is sometimes more difference
between one and another given man than there is between a given
man and a given beast; and Rousseau also probed the possibility that
orangutans might be men who had remained in the state of nature.[27]
Despite that, he tried to isolate something in man, expressed in language, which cannot be reduced to a physiological factor: "The
invention of the art of communicating our ideas depends less on the
organs which serve us for this communication, than it does on a
faculty peculiar to man, which leads him to employ the organs for this
purpose, and which in the absence of those would bring him to
employ others toward the same end."[28]

Some of Rousseau's most fascinating observations are contained
in the last chapter of the *Essay on the Origin of Languages,* "The
Relation of Languages to Government." In earlier chapters he had
contrasted the character of languages in the different regions of the
world, especially the divergences between equatorial, temperate, and
northern languages. As did Montesquieu before and Herder after him,
Rousseau made climate into something more than a single physical
force, but instead a whole arrangement of natural forces, an environment which molds human temperament. In the last chapter Rousseau
asked whether there is any mutuality between types of language and
types of government. Since there would arise in the near future a
host of zealous linguistic partisans—people who claimed in effect that
true virtue could only be expressed in German, or that the truth could
only be told in French, or that love could only be declared in Italian,
or that a good business deal could only be consummated in English—
it is important to avoid misunderstandings of Rousseau's comments.
He certainly attributed no magical powers to the words of language
in themselves.[29] Rather he was aiming at the distinctiveness of those
languages best suited to public speaking, eloquence, and convincing
declamation. Aesthetic and political considerations here converge. It
was not that Rousseau was confident that oratorical suasion necessarily brings on a good result: He had no more faith in rhetoricians
than he did in the wisdom of the masses or the prudence of potentates.
Although his vision was anything but sanguine, however, he was a

defender of democracy. But he believed that democracy could only function well in a relatively small community, where people know one another and come together in person—not tête-à-tête or *in camera* (not to mention in front of a television screen and behind a television camera), but in public assembly. This was not because he held to any inflexible dogmatism about free speech, but for two very practical reasons.[30] First, he felt that every community needs public expression of the principles to which it claims to adhere, even if the principles are limited and even if the community often defaults on its claims. Every political society, in other words, needs some form of public rhetoric, in which its ideals are promoted. At the same time, that rhetoric must be kept "honest": Rhetorical pleading and assertion stand in need of dialectical questioning. The need for rhetoric and patriotism in a functioning society does not mean that one should be gullible about politicians and rhetoricians. On the contrary, Rousseau's second reason for stressing the importance of public assembly was his conviction that magistrates and other public officials must always be open to questioning. It would lead us too far astray to go further into Rousseau's final statement on political philosophy, *The Social Contract.* Still, it is curious that the year in which he was working on the first draft of that masterpiece was the last year in which he did any revisions on the unfinished *Essay on the Origin of Languages.*[31]

Rousseau stated with great clarity the dilemmas confronting theorists of language origin. Rousseau thus introduced a new element into the discussion. It was no longer satisfactory for writers simply to submit hypotheses on the subject, mustering whatever support they could. It became necessary, in addition, to weigh the possibility of any answer at all and to assess the ultimate usefulness of such speculations. It went beyond the logical puzzles of the *aporiae* themselves, because it entailed not the question whether this Gordian knot *could* be disentangled, but whether it *should* be. *Aporiae,* which are originally formulated as admonitions to the philosopher to be cautious with certain problems because of their inherent difficulties, are often appropriated in an alien spirit. They then lead to that attitude of philosophical abandon which, on account of these difficulties, would cavalierly reject the problems. Statements of *aporiae* carry with them an inevitable risk: the danger that they might lead to a cessation of discussion. The immediate task for philosophers of language after Rousseau, although sometimes but dimly perceived, was to ask themselves: Is the problem of language origin a question worth asking?

II

HERDER'S PRIZE ESSAY, BEFORE AND AFTER

[5]

A QUESTION
ON THE RISE

An Academic Quarrel

Much of the German discussion concerning the origin of language had its center in the Berlin Academy of Sciences. It was there that argument first broke out in 1756, with lectures by Pierre Moreau de Maupertuis and Johann Peter Süssmilch supporting the theories of human and divine origin respectively. It was the Berlin Academy which sponsored several essay contests related to the problem, and especially the famous competition of 1770, which spawned a flurry of pertinent works. The award in that contest went to Herder, whose *Preisschrift* is probably the most famous essay on language origin ever written. It was also in the Berlin Academy that further discussion was stimulated midway in the nineteenth century. In 1850 Schelling addressed the members in recollection of Herder's prize essay and called for a reopening of the question. Jacob Grimm and Haymann Steinthal wrote works in direct response to Schelling's call.

When the academy was founded by Frederick I in 1700, it was intended to be a "German-loving and German-fostering" institution, which would promote study of the "culture of the German language."[1] When Frederick the Great assumed the throne in 1740, however, his Francophile predilections led him to reshape the academy. Its presidency went to Maupertuis, and thereafter to d'Alembert and then to Condorcet—even though d'Alembert resided in Berlin for only two months and Condorcet not at all. Maupertuis renamed the society the *Académie royale des sciences et belles-lettres*, reorganized it on the model of the Parisian *Académie des sciences*, and established French as its official language. Favoritism toward the French was displayed in the naming of officers, the awarding of prizes, and the issuing of stipends—and German members were understandably resentful.[2] When Süssmilch rose to contradict the views of Maupertuis on the origin of language, the implications were threefold: An unappreciated and unpaid member of the academy was refuting its president, who was well endowed and well revered; a Protestant pastor was protesting the secular Enlightenment; a German was raising his voice against a Frenchman.

Maupertuis's lecture, "Dissertation on the Different Means Whereby Men Are Served for Expressing Their Ideas," was delivered in May of 1756. Taken by itself, it is surprising that it should have brought on so much controversy. It is barely polemical and much like other French renditions of the subject. Maupertuis did not even attempt to prove that God was not responsible for the creation of language; he simply took human origin for granted. He saw no need to seek a supernatural explanation when a natural one was at hand. In few respects did the "Dissertation" go beyond Maupertuis's own earlier work, *Philosophical Reflections on the Origin of Language and the Signification of Words* (1748), a work widely known because of Turgot's mildly dissenting critique of it.[3]

Maupertuis described man in his prelinguistic state as expressing himself by instinctual gestures and cries, natural outbursts evoked by the most pressing needs and connected with the most elementary pleasures and pains—a child crying from hunger, a woman lifting her arm in fright, a man shouting and clapping his hands in joy. These, the unchanging expressions of basic human emotions, universally understood by men of all times and places, are natural signs. This "language," however, was inconvenient and limited: It lacked variation and flexibility and soon proved inadequate to man's expanding needs. Conventional gestures were invented to supplement it. But this expanded language of conventional gestures and natural cries also proved unsatisfactory: It was physically awkward and still lacked sufficient variety. The cries could have been further developed in a musical direction—making distinctions with nuances of tone, pitch, and timbre—but this would have been a medium understood only by the musically gifted. When men happened on the combination of sounds into words, they immediately recognized that their discovery was indeed felicitous. Articulate language could be molded into an infinity of variations, understood by all who were not deaf, and spoken by all who had a tongue. "All the rest [of the development of language] has been nothing more than particular conventions and variations of articulation."[4] From here on, the progress of language and of mind were parallel and reciprocal: Differentiation of the parts of speech bred more abstract and more precise distinctions; mental advancement led to improvements of linguistic usage.

Maupertuis emphasized an economical principle operative in the development of language. First, he understood language as evolving in response to man's specific needs, at first physical and then increasingly intellectual. With linguistic progress, man betters his mental aptitudes, develops ideas requiring an increased vocabulary, and gains a taste for accuracy which demands finer grammatical distinctions. In each case, language "does the necessary." Language is extremely practical. It does not develop out of joie de vivre, emotional outbursts, or creative impulses. The progress of language does not move in the direction of luxury (an economic situation no longer determined by needs), but of efficiency. Secondly, although language must meet these needs, it cannot become so cumbersome or intricate as to be unintelligible. Language must maintain a balance between the limitations of simplicity and those of complexity. The system of roman numerals shows the principle of economy fully at work. The method must have been inaugurated when someone made *I* stand for one, and had *II, III,* and *IIII* represent two, three, and four. This was a simple and uniform arrangement, in which one sign indicated only one thing, and only one basic sign was used. With the "multiplication of ideas," however, the very simple system would suddenly become complex and inconvenient. Twenty would have to be written as *IIIIIIIIIIIIIIIIIIII*. To make their numerical system more serviceable, the Romans substituted *V, X, L,* and so forth.[5] Spoken and written language generally strike an economical balance between the variation and complexity necessary for expression of differentiated and manifold ideas and the uniformity and simplicity necessary for convenience and general intelligibility. With this economical principle, Maupertuis intended a parallel to his *principe de la moindre action,* the scientific hypothesis that Nature always takes the most direct route to a desired result. The explanation is curiously close to the thesis of Leibniz's *Theodicy,* that God in creating the world struck the perfect balance between the greatest possible variety and the greatest possible order.

Maupertuis saw man as the inventor of language in the strict sense, the discoverer and perfecter of a useful tool. This was a basic conception of language origin, common though not universal among the French, which was to become the object of special attack by German thinkers—the idea that language is an external instrument which man uses and therefore can invent with conscious deliberation. For Maupertuis, necessity was mother of invention, but his version of linguistic history allowed for many happy accidents. Maupertuis introduced chance where and whenever it proved convenient. The looseness of his approach, the fact that no single step was demonstrated conclusively, was another point on which he was criticized. It was on this that Süssmilch felt sure of victory. Yet Maupertuis probably did not intend to prove anything rigorously with his conjectures on the origin of language. After all, what empirical evidence is there on which a conclusive argument might be based? Where are the data which the scientist could observe and interpret to come to a clear and binding solution?

The theoretical arguments against Maupertuis may have been incidental in comparison with the deep-seated resentment which his presence aroused, and there are several reminders in the "Dissertation" of the causes of that resentment. For example, after applying the principle of economy to the development of writing—with Chinese as his example—Maupertuis called for a universal language to be used among scientists and scholars.[6] French, of course, was the language most appropriate. In an earlier lecture, "On the Duties of the Academician," Maupertuis had declared:

That clarity and that precision which is characteristic of French authors is undoubtedly as much dependent on the genius of the language as the language itself has always been dependent on the spirit of those who first spoke it and formulated its rules. Indeed, it is these advantages which render it so universal that it happens that a monarch whose taste is the most decisive commendation speaks it and writes it with such elegance and desires that it should be the language of his academy.[7]

It requires little imagination to perceive how such comments, including their flattery of Frederick, would have antagonized German members of the academy.

Johann Peter Süssmilch was best known in his own day as a pioneer of statistical science. In *The Divine Order in the Variations of the Human Race Demonstrated from Birth, Death, and Reproduction* (1741), he used ecclesiastical records of baptisms, deaths, and marriages to demonstrate that the sex of newborns and the age of death are not matters of chance, but the result of divine plan. He argued that the statistics as a whole—when samples are taken for a sufficiently large number of instances over a sufficiently long period of time from sufficiently varied places—point toward a constant and reasonable pattern, even though the individual case seems to be accidental. Although he is sometimes considered the first formulator of "the law of great numbers,"[8] it was Süssmilch's purpose to show that seeming patterns of probability are in fact laws of divine providence.

In language Süssmilch saw another phenomenon which *philosophes* attributed to chance, but which he believed should be understood in the light of divine providence and revelation. Süssmilch had been working on the problem for two years before he delivered his two consecutive lectures to the academy in October of 1756, lectures which he published ten years later as *Attempt at a Proof That the First Language Did Not Have Its Origin from Man, but from God Alone*. Avoiding piety and dogma, Süssmilch informed his readers at the outset that his proof was neither Biblical nor historical, but purely philosophical and based only on the internal structure of language itself.[9] The stress in the title is negative: Süssmilch did not claim to prove formally and positively, any more than Maupertuis attempted to disprove, the divine origin of language. What he did intend to demonstrate incontrovertibly was that man could not have invented language by himself and that the orderliness and beauty of language exclude its genesis by chance processes. Süssmilch used his method carefully: He eliminated all possibilities, until divine origin was the only solution left.

The first step was to prove the orderliness, reasonableness, and economy of language. As evidence, Süssmilch used contemporary travel literature, the work of his former teacher Jakob Carpov,[10] and the arguments of Condillac and Maupertuis themselves for linguistic economy. Any given language must be simple enough for a child to learn and understand, yet complex enough for the most intricate formulations of philosophers. Süssmilch found this balance present in all known languages—and equally present in them all, *pace* Maupertuis. He noted with some enthusiasm that all languages, having alphabets of approximately twenty to twenty-six letters, are composed of a very limited number of sounds; yet these sounds in combination present endless possibilities of variation, and suffice for the expression of the entire range of human thoughts. Both the simplicity and complexity of language should inspire our wonder, but most of all their equilibrium.

On the one hand the purpose of language made it necessary that differing concepts should be connected with different signs and words, so that confusion and ambiguity could be avoided; but on the other hand it was necessary to refrain from any too extensive multiplication of the signs, which would increase the difficulties of language.[11]

Süssmilch adduced much additional evidence to show the perfect architectonics of language: the ingenious decimal system, which allows the simple burgher to reckon his grocery bill and the experienced mathematician to perform the most involved calculations; the rationality of grammar, which is essentially the same for all languages (thus proving their single origin); the beauty of the rhythms of speech and meters of poetry. There is reason in all languages, even those of peoples who have failed to make the best use of it.

This demonstration of the complete and magnificent order of language (arguable though it may be) eliminated chance, but it did not exclude the possibility of human invention. Süssmilch's next step was to prove that the orderliness of language could not have been imposed upon it by man, even gradually. He argued that man could never have possessed reason without or prior to language. If such a perfect structure as language requires a reasonable being to design it, that being could not have been man, since man first attained to reason after he had language. The similarity of this argument to Rousseau's second *aporia* is obvious, but Süssmilch came to it independently.[12]

Süssmilch used much the same evidence to which Condillac and Maupertuis had made appeal. There was the case of a ten-year-old child, purportedly reared by bears in the Lithuanian forests, who walked on all fours, showed no signs of reason, and spoke no language save the grunts and groans of animals. The life story of a French youth was reported in the journals of the Academy of Paris in 1703. Deaf and dumb from early infancy, the boy had regained his hearing. On questioning, the boy showed that he had not the slightest concept of God, the soul, immortality, or morals; and yet he had been taught by pious parents to attend church, genuflect, and cross himself at the appropriate times. For Süssmilch this was clear proof that man, no matter how adept at imitation, cannot reason without language. And in that case he could not have reasoned to invent it.

The full course of Süssmilch's argument is clear. The perfection of structure in language presupposes that it was designed by a reasonable being; man without the use of language is not a reasonable being; ergo, man was not the designer of language. The evolution of language by chance is excluded by the first premise; the invention of language by man is excluded by the above syllogism. God alone is left as sufficient cause for its development. Süssmilch found other indicators of divine origin, but was careful to use them only as corroborative evidence, not as links in the argument, which was kept negative.

Maupertuis's explanation was grounded in the empiricism of Locke and Condillac, Süssmilch's logic in the rationalism of Leibniz and Wolff. Maupertuis and Condillac readily acknowledged that their interpretations of language origin were conjectures with no more than probable validity. The philosopher, they thought, should be guided by empirical evidence wherever it is available; but, in the absence of factual data, he should realize that he is engaging in tentative speculations and hypotheses. Süssmilch, in contrast, sought all the certainty of deductive proof. He dismissed all conjectures probable or possible, limited discussion to "purely philosophical" proofs, and came to a single necessary principle. He used factual evidence only to elaborate and clarify the steps in his argument, not as the basis for it. Taking Leibniz's distinction between truths of reason (also called *eternal truths*) and truths of fact, Süssmilch saw the divine origin of language as a rational truth. *Vérités de fait* are derived from experience and observation, always tentative, but *vérités de raison* are clear, distinct, and necessary. In the words of Christian Wolff, "that thing of which the opposite is impossible, or involves a contradiction, is called a necessary thing."[13] Süssmilch thought that he had proved that the two alternatives to divine origin, chance and human invention, were self-contradictory and, hence, that he had demonstrated a necessary truth. Once his principle was established, however, Süssmilch gave no detailed description of the way in which language developed or how God had instructed man to use it. Condillac and Maupertuis spoke with no certainty, but they painted a colorful picture of the possible stages in the growth of language; Süssmilch spoke with the certitude of philosophical demonstration, but he painted no picture whatsoever.

An Ill-Formed Question

In the same year as these lectures, 1756, Moses Mendelssohn published a translation of Rousseau's Second Discourse. He appended an open letter to Lessing, proposing a solution to Rousseau's double dilemma regarding language origin. Appealing to the popular psychology of association, Mendelssohn wrote, "these transitions from one concept to another must also occur with savage peoples; for we find very clear traces of it even among animals."[14] Language could have developed gradually along associative lines. The first words may have been onomatopoeic imitations of animal sounds. But gradually the sound of the singing bird would have been associated with the bird itself, then with the tree on which the bird sat, the location of the tree, the color of the bird, the idea of flight, and so forth. There is no certain proof or testimony, but Mendelssohn saw this as a possibility and knew of no evidence disproving it. Consequently, one need not "call God down from the heavens" to escape the difficulties of natural or human explanation. Since he started out from Rousseau's *aporiae,* however, Mendelssohn had to emphasize and reemphasize the dilatory character of linguistic growth. By making the pace of development tortoiselike, Mendelssohn thought he could reach a point where the priority of either language or reason could not be distinguished. Such gradualism, however, is no real answer to Rousseau's problem: It is much like a solution to the chicken-or-the-egg question which would let both develop simultaneously, but ever so slowly.

Süssmilch's lectures brought into the open the hostilities within the Berlin Academy. The next year the membership quarrelled bitterly in determining the prize essay topic for 1759. They finally decided on a subject which related to language but did not concern its origin: the reciprocal influence between language and opinions and (where that influence is deleterious, i.e., where language leads to error or misunderstanding) proposals of means to overcome such influence. The prize-winning essay was submitted by Johann David Michaelis, the Göttingen Orientalist who was so influential in transmitting English thought to Germany. His *Dissertation,* written in German in 1758, was translated by Mérian and Prémontval so that Frederick and Maupertuis could read it, and was crowned the next year.

The first section of Michaelis's prize essay documents the influence of a people's opinions on its language. Such influence can derive from philosophy and science, but also from a people's general outlook, its religious beliefs, prejudices, and idiosyncratic assumptions. The intelligentsia among primitive races were the inventors of language, and poets transformed their contributions into universally accepted coinage by popularizing them in eloquent discourse. The elite of philosophers, scientists, and poets only initiated things, however, for language is "a democracy, in which the will of the majority decides upon usage."[15] Overzealousness in scientific regulation of language could only result in pedantry: For example, the rigid Copernican who would say that Berlin sets on the sun rather than perpetuate the error implied in the word *sunset.*

Although Michaelis's reference to the democratic constitution of speech became the most quoted figure from the treatise, there was an implicit "elitism" in his approach. In his numerous examples, he tried to show what degree of scientific awareness could be deduced from the particulars of early language: The use of both masculine and feminine gender for plants in Semitic languages indicates cognizance of the bisexuality of plants long before European scientists had discovered it; an archaic meaning of *psychē,* "butterfly," proves that early Greek thinkers chose this term to designate the soul because, observing the metamorphosis of the caterpillar, they considered it analogous to metempsychosis. Thus Michaelis gave to particular beliefs priority over the words expressing them, without explaining how such ideas originated. The second and third sections of the *Dissertation* concern respectively the beneficial and deleterious effects of language on opinions. The last section treated the ways in which ill effects might be remedied. In all, Michaelis clearly affirmed and documented the reciprocal influence of language and opinion, but he did not delve into the mechanism of that reciprocity.

Moses Mendelssohn reviewed Michaelis's prize essay in the *Literatur-Briefe,* the *Letters Concerning Current Literature,* a publishing project of Friedrich Nicolai, of which Mendelssohn was coeditor, first with Lessing and later with Thomas Abbt. Mendelssohn commenced his review lamenting the inadequacy of previous attempts to solve the language puzzle.

Why should it be so difficult to philosophize about the origin of language? I know of course that . . . we can hardly formulate anything more than conjectures. But why is it that no conjecture, no hypothesis has been successful for the philosophers? If they cannot tell us how language *really* originated, why don't they at least explain to us how it *could have* originated?[16]

He suggested that the difficulty may stem from the fact that we have all become too accustomed to language and cannot think without it. "As little as the eyes in their natural state can clearly perceive the instrument of sight, the light rays, perhaps just so little can the soul investigate language, the instrument of its thoughts, back to its origin."[17] Man is too close to language, too involved with it, to really understand it. Mendelssohn, in effect, added another impasse to the two of Rousseau, and yet he declared himself "a friend of such speculations."

Mendelssohn's review of Michaelis was critical, but it was more hostile toward the academy than toward the author himself. The formulators of the prize essay topic had built an inconsistency into the very question. The problem as posed implied that certain truths or theories are not only difficult of acquisition but actually impossible to attain or state—all according to a person's mother tongue. The framers of the question must have thought this an equal limitation on philosophers and laymen, since it is philosophers who especially concern themselves with "truths and theories." By the nature of the case, however, even the most astute philosopher could never recognize either the limitations of his own language or those truths from which his language bars him, much less could he suggest means to overcome barriers which he does not recognize in the first place. Since the question as stated implies that all languages direct human thought and therefore limit it, one would have to think in a language totally different from any human one in order to conquer these limitations. Or else, one would have to think outside the framework of language altogether, in which case the reciprocal influence of language and opinion would be nil. Ultimately, the most restrictive aspect of language is not that it channels our opinions, but that it channels them in a way which we cannot recognize. Conversely, "the limitations of language are not limitations any longer, as soon as we recognize them as such."[18] Language frees man by enabling him to think, but it thereby also enslaves man by forcing him to think in certain ways. The academicians' statement of the question did not invite contestants to probe these depths of the problem. The very question as formulated was superficial and self-contradictory.

Johann Georg Hamann—whose response to Herder's prize essay would be so influential—also reviewed Michaelis's *Dissertation* in his *Crusades of a Philologist* (1762). It is written in Hamann's usual style of obliquity (Michaelis is never mentioned by name), allusion, aphorism, and paradox. Like Mendelssohn, Hamann was more fiercely critical of the Berlin Academy than of Michaelis. He began his "Essay on an Academic Question" scornfully:

In my opinion it would be easier to survey the discussion of the question concerning the reciprocal influence of opinions and language, if the topic itself were explained before plunging into solutions to it. But since scholars do not require such tedious thoroughness in order to make themselves understandable to one another, or perhaps because they can write most affluently and yet with the least cost to themselves about vague propositions, common readers may be done a service if this deficiency, though not really corrected, is at least pointed out in the present pages.[19]

The word *opinion* in the topic, Hamann wrote, is ambiguous and the notion of language many-sided. The question as formulated presupposes an hypothesis and thus implies a particular answer. If the topic was meant to invite rigorous philosophical inquiry, it was badly worded, since rationalists and disciples of Leibniz would prefer the word *harmony* to *influence,* while empiricists and disciples of Hume would be skeptical about arguments of cause and effect.

Hamann saw three aspects under which the topic could be meaningfully examined. In the first place, there is what he referred to as a "natural mode of thinking."

If our conceptions are given direction by the point of view of the soul and if this in turn . . . is determined by the condition of the body, then something similar can be applied to the body of the entire *Volk.* The lineaments of its language will then correspond to the direction of its mode of thinking; and every *Volk* reveals the same through the nature, form, laws, and customs of its speech as well as through its external form and a whole drama of public activities.[20]

Upon this "natural mode of thinking" is based the relative wealth or poverty of a language, its peculiar characteristics, its *genius.*

Secondly, there is an "artificial or accidental mode of thinking" which includes the whole complex of truths, half-truths, and untruths, intellectual vogues and prejudices, which a people accepts as verities. The natural mode of thinking constitutes the invariable opinion of a people, whereas the conventional mode constitutes its variable opinion.

Finally, Hamann emphasized the extensiveness of the province of language, ranging from spelling to poetry, from mindless chatter to thoughtful philosophy. Even if language is simply defined as the vehicle for communicating our ideas and understanding the ideas of others, the prize essay should have investigated the relation of opinion to these. Hamann himself only offered one of his tantalizing obscurities:

We are not lacking observations through which the relationship of language to its varied usages could be defined quite exactly. The insight into this relationship and the art of applying it belong together with the spirit of laws and the secrets of ruling. Precisely this relationship makes for classical authors. The offense of confusing languages and the blind faith in certain signs and formulae are coups d'état sometimes, which have more to them in the realm of truth than the most powerful, freshly-dug-up word-root or the unending genealogy of a concept; coups d'état which would not occur to the most erudite pothouse politician or the most loquacious artisan even in their most fantastic dreams.[21]

In the footnote to this Hamann quoted in Greek an apparently innocuous passage from Aristotle's *Politics:*

Some people, trying to connect Zaleucus and Charondas, say that ONOMACRITUS first arose as an able lawgiver, and that he was trained in Crete, being a Locrian and travelling there to practice the art of sooth-saying, and Thales became his companion, and Lycurgus and Zaleucus were pupils of Thales, and Charondas of Zaleucus.[22]

The capitalization is Hamann's own and the word means "name-decider" or "name-judge." The passage, taken together with the foot-note, indicates that for Hamann the origin and formation (or re-forma-tion) of language is a problem specifically related to rulership and legal-ity. With the reference to Onomacritus, the inventor of language and the deviser of law are taken to be the same. Thales, the philosopher, is made to follow Onomacritus; while Lycurgus, Zaleucus, and Charondas—the lawgivers of Sparta, Locria, and Sicily, respectively—are placed after Thales. Implicit in Hamann's use of this quotation is an arrangement of priorities: first, the original legislator, not generally recognized as such, who was in fact the originator of language; then the first philoso-pher, known as a philosopher but not as a legislator, who contributed to the spirit of laws by molding the "formal" opinions of a people; only after these came the acknowledged legislators or popular politi-cians. Thus the "natural" and proper formation of law is based upon thought, which is in turn based upon language.

Hamann regularly used footnotes in a special way. He would quote lengthy and obscure passages in Hebrew, Greek, or Latin, with-out comment, and sometimes with intentional distortion. He left it to the reader to translate, to determine the context in the original, to decide on the meaning which Hamann himself attributed to the pas-sage, and then to puzzle out the relationship between the quotation and the words in the main text. In the *Essay on an Academic Question*, the main footnotes are taken from Plato and concern *dóxa* ("opin-ion"). When mentioning scholars—to which class he consigned Michaelis and the members of the Berlin Academy—Hamann noted Plato's use of *doxósophoi* as contrasted with *philósophoi*, the "seemers of wisdom" as opposed to the "lovers of wisdom."[23] In the next footnote Hamann quoted the Eleatic stranger: "The sophist then has been shown up as someone who has a kind of opinionated knowledge about every-thing, but not the truth."[24] Hamann used these footnotes to identify the basic weakness of Michaelis's prize essay, its unclarified and unexplained employment of the very term *opinion:* "The meaning of the word opinions (*Meynungen*) is ambiguous, since the same are sometimes equated with truths and sometimes taken as the opposite of truths."[25] In Plato, *dóxa* is generally identified with "unexamined thinking" and more specifically with the median faculty between ignorance and knowledge, which has as its object becoming, the realm between nonbeing and being.[26] Opinion is so far from being identical with knowledge that it is the task of philosophical teaching to rid people of opinion through catharsis and midwifery. This more general sense of *opinion* can be fruitfully related to language and to "the spirit of laws and the secrets of legislation."[27] The failure to take account of this broader meaning and the two-sidedness of the term itself explains the triviality of both the academy's question and Michaelis's answer. Did Michaelis even know what question he was answering?

In 1762 Jean Henri Samuel Formey, permanent secretary of the Berlin Academy, delivered a "Review of the Principal Means Employed to Discover the Origin of Language, of Ideas, and of Human Knowledge," which he included in his *Anti-Émile* the next year.[28] Formey was a critic of Rousseau, and the "Review" attacked the "genuine chimera," the "gross absurdity" of the state of nature. Rousseau was correct in saying that the state of nature would have to be devoid of all vestiges of social or political life, but such a condition never has and never will exist. How can one arrive at it or at the origin of language? Formey proposed an experiment, though he did not seem entirely serious about it. There would have to be at least two generations of children brought up in isolation and without exposure to human language. The first would have all their needs provided for, would presumably copulate and reproduce, and then should be left on their own with their young. With this second generation one could find out how and if men could invent language by themselves. Tales and proposals of like experiments went back to antiquity—Herodotus reported that Psammetichos of Sais conducted one, and that the two children first said the Phrygian word for bread[29]—and through the Middle Ages—the Hohenstauffen emperor Frederick II apparently did have some children raised in isolation by mute nurses, but they all died. Formey himself considered it most likely that language was a gift of the Supreme Being. But, in the absence of a scientific experiment with verifiable results, he wondered, is the origin of language an answerable question?

Refining the Question

Contributions to language theory during the first half of the 1760s criticized the accepted ways of asking the question; in the last half of the decade there was the more constructive consideration of what the question really implied, how it might be answered, and what the term *origin* should mean. Thomas Abbt, coeditor of the *Literatur-Briefe* after Lessing's withdrawal, devoted one fragment to man's original estate and its implications for the beginnings of speech. Most of this unfinished essay concerns method: How can one reliably get to the origins? The philosopher can accept the Biblical explanation or, if he rejects it, rely on speculation and "bright ideas"; in the latter case his speculations can be based either on logical arguments or empirical evidence. One must keep these approaches separate and not "thoughtlessly melt together these antithetical and nonmixing elements."[30] If the philosopher of language accepts the Mosaic account, he works with a picture already begun for him, but only as a sketched outline; onto this sketch he can superimpose the omitted details. If he rejects the Pentateuch stories, he begins with a blank canvas, a clean slate; but he is then confronted with countless difficulties. He does not know whether to place man in the world as a child or grown-up, alone or in a group. Hoping for the best and assuming a favorable environment, the *philosophe* may decide upon a pair of children; but he then comes upon the most problematic puzzles: the relationship of the origin of language to the origins of society and rationality. "With fear and trembling he begins to draw a few lines and then, anxious and discontent with his work, immediately erases them. In the end he lets a few things stand, not because they were the things which pleased him most in his drafts, but simply because he has become tired.[31] The tabula rasa becomes a tablet of erased errors. If the thinker ignores the difficulties and holds to the "likely explanations" provided by onomatopoeia, the association of ideas, and so on, then he must "leave everything else to the accidents of genius or stupidity" and "grope about in darkness and uncertainty."[32]

Against rationalist and empiricist speculation, Abbt defended the Mosaic description of human beginnings, but on heuristic rather than authoritative grounds.[33] The account in Genesis is acceptable precisely because it is so incomplete, because it leaves open more questions than it answers. In Genesis we first see man already grown-up, in need of woman (i.e., companionship and society), with full use of his faculties, engaged in adult conversation. Despite Adam's naming of the animals, Abbt judged that this portrait presupposed man's possession of language. Thus there is as much room for conjecture about the origin of language within the Mosaic account as there is without it. Did God endow man with language piecemeal or all at once? Did he merely assist man in the invention of language, did he lead man, or did he actually instruct? If God taught man language directly, how could he have done so unless man were already in possession of language? Was this language Hebrew? If so, the Hebrew we know or something different? an idiom sensuous, metaphorical, or abstract? It is useful to accept the Mosaic account because then, should speculation falter, it would not have to retreat into embarrassed silence: "Such conjectures certainly serve to make that picture more complete; however, if they should be erased again, it would still leave an impressive and clear picture from which we could recognize the beginnings of mankind."[34] The argument is unusual: the stories of Genesis should be credited, not because of Biblical authority, but because acceptance facilitates discussion.

Abbt died in 1766 at the age of twenty-eight. One of Herder's earliest projects was a memorial tribute to him,[35] and Herder's first important work, *Concerning Recent German Literature,* generally known as the *Fragments,* was explicitly a continuation of the defunct *Literatur-Briefe.* Together with the *Critical Forests* (1769), the *Fragments* became the programmatic and nearly canonical statement of aesthetics and literary criticism for the younger generation of German writers. The first section of the *Fragments* concerned language and included a sketch, "Concerning the Life Stages of Language."

Language, Herder began, is a necessary instrument of the arts and sciences and simultaneously a part of them. "The people which has great poets without a poetic language, great prose writers without a flexible language, great philosophers without an exact language does not exist."[36] However, Herder added quickly, language is more than an instrument. With tools men produce artifacts which, though made with an instrument, are ultimately external to it and independent of it. The brush of the painter is an important tool, but the finished painting can be understood separately from the brush. The arts and sciences, in contrast, cannot be understood as though language were only the exterior tool used to make and design them. Man is not master of language in the same way that he is master when he uses a tool. Language controls man as much as man controls language. Herder preferred the metaphor of skin and body to describe the relationship between language and thought. Language is not a neutral medium, but a treasure house of ideas, sentiments, and intuitions. Each succeeding generation, each great poet, and each thoughtful person makes new contributions to the stock of language. The total history and experience of a people is immanent in its language and defines its peculiar genius.

Herder's sketch "Concerning the Life Stages of Language" was his first statement of the idea of development (*Entwicklung*), which is more familiar from later works:

Just as man goes through different stages of life, so time brings about changes in everything. The entire human race, indeed even the inanimate world, every nation, and every family have the same laws of change: from the bad to the good, from the good to the excellent, from the excellent to the inferior, and then to the bad. This is the cycle of all things. So it is with every art and science: Each sprouts, bears buds, blossoms, and then withers. So it is also with language.[37]

In the childhood of their development languages were rough, monosyllabic, and high-pitched. With a mixture of gestures and cries, infantile languages expressed the two basic emotions, fear and awe, passions which subsided as political calm replaced savage violence. As man's world became more ordered, he named the objects in it, beginning with imitations of sounds made by natural creatures. Language was progressing from infancy to youth, from a language of the elementary passions to one of the sensations. Abstract concepts were introduced gradually as words for concrete things took on metaphorical connotations. Just as the early cries had been mixed with gestures, so this youthful language was supplemented by song. It was the age of minstrels and rhapsodes, the poetical stage of linguistic development. As men matured and began to search for "serious wisdom and political lawfulness," their language became more staid and its grammar more orderly. The youth of language gave way to its manhood, but something was lost in the maturing process. "The more language becomes an art, the more it distances itself from nature. The more ossified and urbane customs become, and the more passions cease to have much influence in the world, the more will language lose its natural objects. . . . Perhaps language becomes more perfect, but it also loses its true poetic character."[38] In the age of writing and of prose, language can still be beautiful, but the beauty is of an artful and self-conscious sort. It is a step on the road to the old age of language, the philosophical or scientific age, when beauty succumbs to correctness. In its youth language was rich with synonyms; in its old age philosophers either distinguish among synonyms or dismiss them from the language altogether. Grammarians rule and hold language enchained, introducing order everywhere and allowing joy nowhere. "Language loses its seductive charms, but it also becomes less of a sinner."[39]

The first edition of the *Fragments,* published anonymously, led to lively speculation about the author's identity, some literary infighting, and numerous reviews. One review, by Christian Garve, a Leipzig philosophy professor and translator of numerous English works, affected Herder so much that he undertook a revision of the *Fragments.* In his sympathetic critique Garve wrote that Herder's main problem was not literary criticism but the philosophy of language: Behind everything which Herder said about poetry there loomed the question of the reciprocal influence of language and ideas. Garve assumed that the main influence on the unidentified author was Rousseauistic primitivism and wrote: "To confess the truth, [the infancy of language], as well as the so-called *status naturalis,* seems to us to belong to the realm of philosophical romances."[40] In the state of nature, "which Rousseau describes so charmingly," feelings may well have been expressed with animalistic cries. This does not explain the origin of human language, however, since the creatures in the natural state were in fact animals and nothing more, and to jump from them to human language is an "outrageous shift." It is doubtful that Rousseau had yet made much of an impression on Herder. More likely, Garve detected the influence of Hamann, who had said that "poetry is the mother tongue of the human race."[41] Nonetheless, Herder took very seriously the charge that his sketch was a "philosophical romance."

The revision of the first section of *Fragments* was printed but never published. In the explanatory passage to the sketch Herder tried to describe early language "without romantically concocting a Rousseauistic state of nature."[42] He kept his distinction between the infancy and childhood of language, but referred to a "language" composed exclusively of gestures and cries as the utterances of "animal-men," and doubted whether this was language at all. Many passages in the second edition are taken nearly verbatim from another unfinished and unpublished work, *Attempt at a History of Lyric Poetry,* which scholars have variously dated from 1764 to 1767. Both deal more directly with the origin, as opposed to development and metamorphosis, of language than did the first edition of the *Fragments.*

Interest in origins, Herder wrote, is a favorite intellectual pastime, because man is proud of his inventions, but also because he is uncertain of his identity.

With the origin of a thing a part of its history eludes us, but a part which must explain very much about the thing, usually the most important part. As the tree from the root, so art, language, and science grow from their origin. In the grain of seed is contained the plant with all its parts, in the spermatozoon the creature with all its limbs; and in the origin of a phenomenon great treasures of explanation.[43]

But the inquirer into origins treads an unsure path, because his is a path into obscurity. Herder distinguished three basic methods of inquiring into the origins of human phenomena: historical experience, philosophical explanation, and probable conjecture.[44] Each is partially right but incomplete, and involves its own peculiar hazards. The difficulties are compounded by the common tendency to confuse origins with inventions and oversimplify the latter. Confusion is bred by speaking about the invention of language, since no invention, but least of all that of language, is "simply and suddenly there." They come about gradually with one improvement following another, so that points of commencement are hard to identify. This attack was clearly linked to Herder's critique of the understanding of language as an instrument. Herder mixed metaphors somewhat to clarify his insistence that language must be explained genetically. "All things developed little by little. . . . This great majestic flux, which rolled on sometimes as a mighty benefactor and sometimes as the tyrant of whole regions, sprang forth—from a spring, which in itself would have been unknown, if it had not borne this son."[45] Both images, of birth and of the flowing river, contrast sharply with the mechanical invention of a useful tool.

In further elaboration Herder distinguished three different meanings of *origin*. The inquirer into origins may concentrate on the causes (*Ursachen*), the source (*Quelle*), or the beginning (*Anfang*). Analysis of causes, enlightening for other purposes, is less helpful here, because causes are both external and internal, too numerous and variegated, and because causal arguments usually treat a phenomenon as though it were fully developed at its inception. Since things actually develop gradually, causal analysis does not get back to the true origins. Herder compared the beginning of something to its birth, the point at which the thing starts to exist as itself; the source he compared to the conception and gestation period, the process whereby the thing is generated and formed and develops into that which it is at birth. The person searching for the beginnings seeks the point at which the "creature" broke out into the light of day; but it was formed and nourished in obscurity long before this. "Before the first beam of light came into being, the seed of creation had already fertilized the womb of dark chaos."[46] But how can one penetrate this darkness? Will it not propel us into infinite regression? "But how in turn did the source originate? That is more difficult! It flowed forth from the hidden."[47] There is something problematic in each approach: Inquiry into sources approaches the more fundamental, but also the less certain and more obscure; the beginning may be accessible, but it is not really the original.

In the *Attempt at a History of Lyric Poetry* Herder enumerated three false approaches to the problem of origins. The first error takes subsequent reports about the birth or youth of something as though these were contemporaneous documents, themselves dating from the beginning, and as if they were the source itself. The second invents or deduces an origin according to a method developed much later. The third gives the kind of explanation which is disastrous because it puts a stop to all further inquiry into origins.[48] The first of these misguided methods Herder identified as that of "dry historians." Confronted with a complex process of development which he mistakenly interprets as discontinuous, the "dry historian" selects an arbitrary point in the process, calls it point one, and uses it as the beginning. "It starts with an approximate *beginning,* without dissecting it and without pushing back to the real origin."[49] On the second erroneous path, "one takes the science under consideration in some later state of development, observes it under far too much light, and comes up with concepts which are contradicted as much by truth as they are by history."[50] Such people see all sorts of perfection where there is none and miss the true beauties of ancient things. This is an obvious indictment of the approach to origins by arguments from design.

Out of these two there follows the third mistake, which cuts off all investigation: since we behold such brilliance from the start, we are blinded, and call out as we rub our eyes: "Divine! Divine!" This is the divine origin which is attributed to most inventions, either because one was not acquainted with any documentation and did not want to think about it himself, or because one took a later period of perfection for the beginning, without realizing that previous times were wan on account of the dimmer light. . . . What poets said figuratively was understood literally for the sake of convenience.[51]

Herder named Robert Lowth in these polemics against the idea of a divine origin of poetry. "What is the usefulness of the hypothesis that poetry is of divine origin? It does not explain anything; it requires explanation itself."[52] Most of all Herder opposed the divine hypothesis because it curtails all further discussion. Since the inscrutable acts of God are simply to be accepted, they cannot be investigated.

In the second edition of the *Fragments* Herder turned his criticism from the divine origin of poetry to that of language, and he specifically attacked Süssmilch. If Süssmilch saw a tree in full flower, he would exclaim "Divine!"; if budding, he would shout "Divine!"; if the sprout, "Divine!"; if he saw the simple seed, "Divine!" "If language had appeared on the earth adorned with all its perfection, order, and beauty, like Pallas Athena from the head of Zeus; then without hesitation I would be blinded by its brilliance, cover myself, fall down, and worship it as a divine apparition from Olympus."[53] But is this the way language appeared? There is no evidence confirming it and much that contradicts it. Süssmilch must have realized that languages can and do change, a fact which completely undercuts his argument. If this change has involved a progression in the orderliness of language, then it was not born full-blown from the deity. If it has involved deterioration, then Süssmilch cannot argue from his own language to the original.

Since language, like all human and earthly things, is in process of development, a "genetic approach" is required. Süssmilch, in contrast, tried to prove divine origin from "the nature of language." He apparently assumed that his mother tongue illustrated the nature of language par excellence—which is absurd, according to Herder. Furthermore, Süssmilch, who based so much of his proof on the correlation of language and thought, seemed unaware that his own language could have influenced his thought in a way which might have misled him to see orderliness where there was in fact none. In the *Attempt* Herder expressed his general disdain for "a priori explanations of the history of a human invention." He called them "philosophical romances" and compared them to druggists' prescriptions:" ℞ Imagination, Wit, Attention, Judgment, Gift of Expression; each in proper proportion; in this way the first poet was produced."[54] The only thing that Süssmilch demonstrated conclusively with his a priori method was that the philological spirit, the historical spirit, and the philosophical spirit all failed him. "He imagines a language the way he would like it and thus can prove anything he wants to. In details he is everywhere correct and about the whole he has said nothing."[55]

Rousseau's statement of the dilemmas concerning language origin led to the questions whether there ever could be a solution and whether the problem was worth pursuing. As the center of discussion moved over to Germany, where Rousseau was coming into such ascendancy, the more thoughtful writers focused on the nature of the question itself. Responses to Michaelis's prize essay emphasized the Berlin Academy's failure to clarify its own question about the reciprocal influence of language and opinion. Abbt and Herder refined the question of language origin and analyzed possible methods of investigation. Abbt was willing to accept the Mosaic account because it would facilitate inquiry; Herder rejected divine origin because he saw in it an end to all discussion. Their fundamental concern was the same. They judged that the question of linguistic origins was indeed fruitful and illuminating, and asked: How can the question best be approached? How can discussion best be continued?

[6]

THE CLASSIC
STATEMENT

In 1769 the Berlin Academy, on the urging of Formey, set the origin
of language as its prize essay topic for 1771. As announced (in
French, of course) it read: "Supposing that men are abandoned to
their natural faculties, are they in a position to invent language? And
by what means might they arrive at this invention by themselves? What
is required is a hypothesis which will explain the matter clearly and
satisfy all the difficulties." Herder learned of the competition and
jotted down some notes before he left Riga for several years of sojourn-
ing. In his *Travel Diary of 1769* he disparaged the academy, but spoke
of entering the contest; and in August of 1769 he wrote to his publisher, Hartknoch, about the prospect.[1]

Herder did not compose his *Treatise on the Origin of Language*
until December of 1770, a bare month before the deadline, when he
was temporarily settled in Strassburg, but then he wrote with speed
and enthusiasm. Goethe, his junior by five years and newfound friend,
read the manuscript as each folio was completed. He reacted more to
the style and wit of the essay than to the problem treated, and considered this in keeping with Herder's own attitude toward the project,
describing in some detail Herder's ironical "spirit of contradiction"
at this time.[2] Herder himself wrote later, when the work was about to
be published, and he was ready to disown it: "I am astonished and
bewildered when I read the prize essay. It was thrown together in such
haste during the last days of December, and the arguments of the opponents from whom the academy wanted to see the question rescued lay
so close to me . . . , that I don't know what demon possessed me to
write for the academy in such fashion."[3] Herder would likely have

been amused that his irreverent and ironical treatise was destined to
become the foremost classic of the literature on language origin.

The Argument

The prize essay is divided into two main parts, corresponding to the
two questions posed by the academy: Whether men could have invented language and how they might have done it. The first part is
divided into three untitled sections, which concern, respectively, the
place of language in the realm of nature, its place in the realm of
human nature, and the nature of original language. Further subdivisions are indicated by double spacing between paragraphs—unfortunately omitted from most modern editions—which signal that Herder
is about to change his sights, move on to a new polemical target, and
probably use different ammunition.

The first division of the first section contains Herder's attack on
Süssmilch and the theory of divine origin. Here it is the author's intention to show the naturalness of human language, whereas against other
theorists he would emphasize the freedom or conventionality of its
particulars.[4] Even in an animal state men expressed themselves in
audible tones and cries, as a purely physical reaction for the relief of
pain by the release of breath. No communication was intended and no
answer expected. In Herder's analysis, self-expression precedes communication as a source of language. But even this elementary form of
expression gave man's inward feelings an external form, and directed
them toward his fellow creatures, so that self-expression would necessarily become communication. Herder formulates this as a "natural
law": "Here is a sensitive being, who cannot keep to himself any of
his lively feelings, who in the first overwhelming moment, without
choice or intention, must express each of them loudly, . . . who does
not feel for himself alone."[5]

Herder locates the weakest point in Süssmilch's argument, his
theory of the alphabet and of the divinely planned economy supposedly
revealed in the reduction of all languages to twenty and some letters.
"The fact is false and the conclusion still more false."[6] The sounds of
a living language are far more numerous and variable and their reduction to an alphabet is obviously conventional. Letters are "corpses,"
which do not breathe the life of spoken language. The wealth of interjections and onomatopoeia in primitive languages makes it senseless
to speak of any alphabetic transcription which tells nothing of their
music and nuance. The omission of vowels from Hebrew script, Herder

proposes, resulted from the impossibility of writing them down at all. Primitive languages are difficult to transcribe, because "they did not originate from the letters of God's grammar, but from the wild tones of free organs."[7] The spirited tones of nature cannot be captured in script. "If we want to refer to these unmediated sounds of feeling as language, then I find its origin very natural indeed. Not only is it not supernatural, it is apparently bestial: the natural law of a sensitive machine."[8]

"But I cannot conceal my amazement that philosophers, i.e., people who seek clear ideas, could ever have come upon the idea of explaining the origin of human language out of these cries of feeling."[9] In the second division of the first section Herder shifts his aim to dispose of the naturalistic explanations of Condillac, Rousseau, Maupertuis, Diodorus, and Vitruvius. To be sure, primitive expressions of pain, fear, and pleasure allow of a physical explanation—because they are common to children and animals; whereas human language is something which the child must, and the animal cannot, learn. Herder is harshest with Condillac, quoting short passages from the *Essai* and adding, "whereof I understand nothing!" Either Condillac presupposed language, or else reflection; or if neither, then he granted his two children special dispensations and capacities which they could not have had under the stated conditions. The device of an isolated pair is artificial: "Perhaps the author knows why it was necessary to stipulate such an unnatural and self-contradictory condition in an hypothesis which supposedly traced the natural course of human knowledge."[10] Herder identifies the jumps and missing links in Condillac's argument, dissects the notions of instinct, reflection, sympathy, commerce, and custom, and to each adds: "whereof I understand nothing!" Herder curtly summarizes Condillac's theory: "In short, words originated because words existed before they existed. It seems to me that it is futile to follow the thread of this argument any further, for—it isn't tied to anything."[11]

Herder's handling of Rousseau is little kinder. "To find objections against Condillac's explanation did not exactly require a Rousseau; but to deny any possibility of a human invention of language on that account—that indeed took a Rousseauistic twist or swing or leap or whatever it's called."[12] By deducing the inadequacy of all natural explanations from the deficiencies of Condillac's, Rousseau only begged the question. And so much the worse for Rousseau that, after explaining the difficulties, he went on to endorse Condillac's theory. Maupertuis, Diodorus, and Vitruvius all failed to differentiate human language from animal noise and thoughtless signals. Since man is the only being that we know certainly to possess language, theories of its origin should begin with an inquiry into the specific difference between man and other animals. Condillac and Rousseau were doomed to failure because they did not clarify this: "The former made animals into men and the latter made men into animals."[13]

Thus Herder moves into the third subdivision of the section, where he forsakes polemics and tries to locate the difference between the "natural spheres" of animals and men. Animal psychology had been brought to the fore by Hermann Samuel Reimarus, whose *General Observations Concerning the Drives of Animals* (1760) argued that animals can learn certain things and imitate many others, but that they do not possess reason. Man, in contrast, is a creature of language and culture, who passes on his achievements through some "artistic medium." The unreflecting animals have "artistic drives" (*Kunsttriebe*), which Reimarus defined as innate abilities to make or do specific things for their own and their species' good, native talents which required little or no practice for the individual animal to develop.[14] Man lacks these "artistic impulses," so that all human arts are refined through practice and tradition. Herder rejected many of Reimarus's conclusions, while retaining his nomenclature—which introduced some terminological confusion, since art and nature, or art and instinct, were more commonly viewed as irreconcilable antinomies.

Man, according to Herder, is inferior to other animals in instinctual capacity and has no innate "artistic abilities." Each animal has its peculiar sphere of activity, but these vary greatly in breadth. The activity of the bee or spider, for example, is concentrated within a very narrow sphere. The smaller an animal's sphere of activity, the sharper will be at least one of its senses and the more likely a concentration on a single sense. If the sphere is narrow, the animal's "artistic works" may be wonderful, but the animal will likely practice only a single art, such as the spider's web-making. The narrower the sphere, the greater an animal's instinct and artistic impulse. As the sphere gains in breadth, it diminishes in concentration. "The sensitivity, abilities, and instincts of animals increase in strength and intensity in inverse proportion to the extent and multifariousness of their spheres of activity."[15] Man has no narrow and concentrated sphere of activity. His senses are directed toward everything around him and are thus individually weaker; and, having no instincts, he engages in a whole world of diverse actions. Man has no animal language of instinctive sounds because of this wide sphere, just as conversely "the smaller the sphere of animals is, the less do they have need of real language."[16] When a human child learns language—and the fact that he must learn it is proof that it is not instinctive—he transcends the stage when he expressed himself by the purely natural means of cries and whimpers, smiles and giggles. The human comes into this world as the "orphaned child of nature," naked, weak, needy, unarmed, and without instincts. It would contradict the entire "economy of nature" if that were all. "In place of instincts there must be other hidden powers dormant in him."[17]

From this open question, Herder proceeds to the second section of the *Preisschrift,* where he analyzes more precisely man's nature and its relation to language. Nature would have been a "most cruel step-mother" had she left man with nothing to compensate for his lack of instincts. "We must be overlooking some middle term which balances the different parts of this relationship,"[18] something different from instinct which is nonetheless man's peculiar "natural gift."

If we found precisely in this characteristic the cause of those lacks, and precisely in the midst of those lacks, in the abyss of that great renunciation of instincts, the seed for the compensatory substitute; then this adjustment would be a genetic proof that the true direction of humanity lies here and that the human species is different from the animals not in degrees of more or less, but in kind.

And if in this newfound character of humanity we should also discover the necessary genetic basis for the development of language in this novel sort of creature, as we found the direct basis for the animal language of each species in the instincts, then we would be directly on our goal. In that case language would be as essential to man as his humanity.[19]

In the *Fragments* Herder had opposed a genetic method to Süssmilch's a priori deduction of the origin of language from the nature of language. His remarks here indicate that his method is a deduction of the origin of language from the nature of man and that he considers this compatible with a genetic approach.

Herder defines man's *differentia specifica* as reflectiveness (*Besonnenheit*). With the loss of instinct, man won freedom. Endowed by nature to do no single work perfectly, man can still improve on all of the many works he does. In place of instinct there is a whole new disposition of human powers. Herder is even careless in naming this "total disposition," for it is not his concern to define a faculty which is man's special strength, but to look for something more fundamental than any individual faculty.[20] Herder repeatedly emphasizes that reflectiveness is not a separate power, possessed by man in addition to the various other faculties found in animals; rather it involves the whole direction and arrangement of faculties which makes man a creature sui generis. Epistemological hierarchies of both empiricists and rationalists often seemed to imply that understanding and reason were mental bonuses, the extra advantages of being human—as though man were at one moment a creature of reason, at another of sense perception, and at still others of fantasy or memory. This makes empty abstractions of man's real powers.

If a man could ever perform a single action in which he thought completely in the manner of an animal, then he would no longer be a man at all, nor capable of any human deeds. If he were without reason for a single moment, then I do not see how he could ever think with reason, or else his whole soul, the whole economy of his nature, would be changed.[21]

The different faculties are not independent and separate, but modes (*Bestimmungen*) of a single power (*Kraft*). In the same vein Herder attacks Rousseau's notion of potential reflection (*réflexion en puissance*) as a verbal deception. If potentiality has a positive tendency, then it is more than a mere possibility; and if potentiality has no particular direction, then it is in actuality very little.

The most sensuous condition of man was still human, and therefore reflectiveness was already operative, only in a less obvious degree; and the least sensuous condition of beasts was still bestial, and therefore the reflectiveness of human thoughts was never operative, even if there may have been considerable clarity of ideas.[22]

In the next division of the second section Herder moves from reflectiveness to language, and summarizes his thesis.

Man, placed in a condition of reflectiveness peculiar to him, and this reflectiveness (*Reflexion*) operating freely for the first time, invented language. For what is reflection? What is language?

This reflectiveness is characteristically his own and essential to his species. So also is language and his own invention of language.

Thus the invention of language is as natural to him as the fact that he is a man. We need only develop these two concepts: reflection and language.[23]

Man, when set out into the universe, confronts a chaotic ocean of sensations, a stream of impressions as in a dream. He shows his reflectiveness when he selects certain impressions and gives them his special attention, when he concentrates upon a single object, distinguishes certain of its characteristics, and identifies these with the object itself. Thus mere cognition (*Erkennen*) becomes recognition (*Anerkenntnis*). Recognition singles out distingishing marks (*Merkmale*) through reflection, so that objects are discerned according to their peculiar properties. These distinguishing marks become in their turn the "words of the soul," or distinguishing words (*Merkworte*), and therewith human language originates—within the psyche and without a sound having been uttered. Upon first seeing a lamb, for example, man receives a multitude of disorganized sense impressions, most of them not even peculiar to the lamb. Since man is a creature of reflectiveness, however, he does not merely perceive but perceives reflectively, distinguishing among the different impressions and selecting out the particular property which best characterizes the lamb. He may take the sheep's bleating as its distinguishing mark, saying to himself, "So! You are the bleating one!"[24] He thus identifies the lamb, locating it within the world of his experience. In effect, man has named the lamb, and this distinguishing mark becomes his distinguishing word for the lamb.

Even if he never came into the situation where he would communicate this idea to another person, and thus would never want or even be able to bleat out this distinguishing mark of reflection with his lips; nonetheless his soul has bleated inwardly, since it chose this sound as a mnemonic sign, and it bleated again, since it recognized the lamb thereby: Language has been invented! invented as naturally and necessarily for man as the fact that the man was a man.[25]

Herder concludes this section by enumerating mistaken paths along which previous theories of language origin had erred. Explanations based on the physical characteristics of the speech apparatus, on cries of passion, onomatopoeic imitation, and on convention all err because they begin with the external, spoken word, the exterior of language, instead of its deeper inward source.

The wild man, the solitary hermit in the forest would have had to invent language for himself, even if he never spoke it. It was an agreement of his soul with itself, an agreement as necessary as the fact that the man was a man. If it has been inconceivable to others how a human soul could have invented language, it is inconceivable to me how there could have been a human soul unless it had to invent language, even without a mouth and without society.[26]

The origin of language is not so much invention as discovery, man's discovery of the world about him. If natural cries and exclamations are expressions of inward feelings, an activity whereby the internal becomes external; language learning is the activity whereby the external is made internal, the appropriation of the outer world within the human soul. Parents facilitate the child's use of reason by calling things to his attention, but they do not supply rationality, for he is born "a creature of reflectiveness." "Parents never teach language without the children themselves inventing it along with them."[27]

Herder further attacks those who try to rest theories of language origin on exceptional cases, isolated children lost in some postdeluvian wilderness, wolf children, and the like. "Lay a stone on this plant: Will it not grow up to be crooked? And isn't it still an upright plant by nature?"[28] Aberrations are poor guides to the nature of a species, but even they show that man is not a creature of instinct. For all Rousseau's talk about man's natural estate, "his phantom, the natural man, this degenerate creature" is really a freakish and inconsistent monstrosity. On the one hand Rousseau endowed him with nothing more than a potentiality for reason and reflection, but on the other, with a perfectibility which enabled him to imitate whatever was his pleasure. Imitation for the perfection of the species, the sort which Rousseau imputed to the natural man, is a fully human activity, presupposing reflection and language. Apes do not imitate in this way, they simply ape. And parrots only ape sounds. If dogs could speak, they would talk back and disobey their masters. The authentic language of genuine men must include the prerogative of saying no as well as yes. And maybe. Rousseau contradicted himself by supposing a desire for perfection in the natural man and yet not granting him the freedom brought by language. *L'homme naturel* is neither man nor beast. "Let it be noted that, if one should miss the point of exact genesis, the range of error is immeasurably great on both sides: Now language is suddenly so suprahuman that God must have invented it, now so inhuman that any animal could have invented it."[29]

The synonymy in so many languages of the words for language, reason, and cause suggests the true genetic origin of language. The process of recognition and the activity of naming are parallel in character and simultaneous in time. Human nature alone must be assumed for this interpretation of language origin. It is man's nature to be reflective rather than merely reactive, to freely develop arts rather than be driven by *Kunsttriebe*. Society is no precondition, for language originates inwardly within the human soul, not for the pragmatic purpose of communication.

Yet I cannot imagine the first human thought nor the first reflective judgment without at least trying to create a dialogue within my soul. And so the first human thought by its very nature prepares the way for the possibility of a dialogue with others. The first distinguishing mark [*Merkmal*] that I apprehend is a distinguishing word [*Merkwort*] for me and a communicating word [*Mitteilungswort*] for others.[30]

Internal language, emphasizing audible characteristics, expresses itself as external, spoken language. The means of ordering the world in the individual soul become the media of communication in social intercourse.

In the third section of the first part Herder shifts from analysis of the source of language to conjectures about the primary elements of original languages, a hypothetical description of the *Ursprache*. Herder, like Hamann and the Scottish writers, emphasizes the musical quality of primitive idiom, its rhapsodic poetry and mythic fantasy. Original language was so musical because it was auditory characteristics that were singled out as distinguishing marks and audible signs that were most conveniently and expressively used as communicating words. This was because hearing has a special place among the five senses. Herder enumerates six reasons why hearing should be considered the median sense between touch and sight: its range, clarity, intensity, time, expression, and place in human development.[31] The use of the "middle sense" as the medium for articulate speech allowed greater economy than would the more complex extensions of visual or tactile sign and gesture systems. Contrary to Condillac, however, the senses cannot be understood as isolated operations. The "association of sensations" is as important as the "association of ideas." As reflectiveness underlies all mental faculties, so feeling (*Gefühl*) is the ground of all the individual senses, which are actually "modes of representation of a single positive power."[32] Herder's analysis is directed not only against the particulars, but against the whole spirit of empiricist epistemology. The senses and their data are not superadded one upon another, as per Condillac's inanimate statue or Locke's equally lifeless tabula rasa; rather the diverse senses constitute an organic and interrelated whole which cannot be isolated from the totality of human disposition. The emphasis on hearing also allows Herder to move directly into a description of original language, describing it as musical, full of the sensuous, free from grammatical rigidity, an idiom in which verbs came first because everything was lively activity, a language of sheer verbal luxury and joy—not the penurious *Ursprache* of Adam Smith or Condillac, which barely met minimal human needs.

Concluding the first part of the prize essay, Herder asserts that he has demonstrated the possibility of a human invention of language inwardly from the nature of the human soul, and outwardly from the organization of man and the analogy of all known languages. "Its genesis in the human soul is as demonstrative as any philosophical proof, and the external analogy of all ages, languages, and peoples lends it a degree of probability equal to the most certain matters of history."[33] Human origin is both a rational and a factual truth.

In the second part of the *Preisschrift* Herder formulates four "natural laws," the first of which reads: "Man is a being with freedom of thought and action, whose powers operate progressively; therefore he is a creature of language!"[34] Man is free precisely because he is not governed by instincts, but is a creature of reflectiveness and language. Freedom is more than an empty possibility, since reflectiveness is the positive tendency of human nature, already active at man's inception, when he was "perhaps not yet a reflecting creature, but nonetheless a creature of reflectiveness."[35]

The second law states: "Man is by definition a creature of the herd, of society; therefore the continuous formation of language is natural, essential, and necessary for him."[36] Man's physical weakness compels him to associate with his fellows for self-preservation, his ability to speak enables him to form such associations, and his pleasure in speaking makes him desirous of communication. Man's social character derives from both need and preference, and requires language: "The weak child, so aptly described as an *in-fant,* a nonspeaker, must appropriate language in order to enjoy its mother's milk and its father's intellect."[37] This explains the family, the tribe, and later, more complex society.

The third "natural law" says: "Since the entire human race could not possibly remain a single herd; therefore it also could not retain a single language."[38] Herder here explains the economic, practical, and geographic reasons why peoples had to diverge, and the consequent differences in their accumulated experience which would cause the diversity of languages. With the division and spreading of peoples and their cultures, "language became a Proteus on the round surface of the earth."[39] The metamorphoses of language are not discontinuous, however, since they all derive from a common source and origin.

Finally, the last "natural law": "Since in all probability the human race constitutes a progressive whole from a single origin and with one grand economy; therefore all languages are probably such also and with them the entire chain of culture."[40] There is progressive development within individual languages and in the entire history of language.

No thought of a human soul was lost; but on the other hand no skill of this race was ever there automatically and at once, as is the case with animals. As a result of the entire economy it was always in progress, always in motion: nothing invented, like the structure of a cell, but everything in the process of invention, in continuous activity, striving. How grand language becomes from this point of view! A treasury of human thoughts to which everyone contributed in his own way! A *summa* of the activity of all human souls![41]

Concluding the *Treatise,* Herder summarizes his case against divine origin. It is "refined and concealed nonsense."[42] The order of which Süssmilch speaks he imputes to language on the basis of its later developments. Two arguments for divine origin are transparent non sequiturs: the conclusion that language is divine because one cannot explain it from human nature; or that it is divine because one cannot so explain it himself, and therefore no one can so explain it. Even a rigorously deductive demonstration of the "higher hypothesis" would be false: "No one but God could invent language! However, no one but God could understand why no one but God could invent it either."[43] The theory of divine origin does not even have the testimony of Scripture in its favor. "The higher origin, as pious as it may seem, is thoroughly ungodly: At each step it belittles God with the most paltry and imperfect anthropomorphism. . . . The origin of language becomes divine in only one. appropriate regard, inasmuch as it is human."[44]

Approaching the Question

Because of the polemical spirit of the prize essay, many have seen in it a rejection of the question as asked by the academy. Some have taken it to foreshadow the attitude, so dominant later, that the problem of the origin of language is productive of neither philosophical nor philological answers. A leading authority has found in the *Treatise* an exposure of the whole inquiry as a *Scheinproblem:* "The *Treatise* not only contradicted the two extreme theses of divine and mechanistic origin of human speech; it also led to the conclusion that the question itself was without sense."[45] Herder entered three other works in competitions of the Berlin Academy and a strong case has been made that all (with the exception of the last, written when Herder was himself seeking membership) were "written with a double purpose: to make a contribution and at the same time to make fun of the Academy."[46]

There is supporting evidence for this interpretation in Herder's correspondence and in reactions to the prize essay by Herder's friends. Goethe delighted in Herder's playful work with, or for, the scholars, but he certainly did not take the question seriously: "To me the whole question seemed a somewhat idle one; for, if God created man as man, then language as well as his upright stature was created with him. . . . If man was of divine origin, then language was also; and if man, considered in the compass of nature, was a natural being, then language too was natural."[47] Herder himself concluded the prize essay with an apology for his "disobedience" in answering the academic assignment by demolishing a hypothesis rather than presenting one of his own:

And don't we usually consider things in hypothetical form little more than philosophical romances—whether Rousseau's, Condillac's, or some-one else's. Thus the author preferred to concentrate on collecting fixed data from the human soul, from the human organization, the construc-tion of all ancient and primitive languages, from the whole economy of the human race, in order to demonstrate his proposition with the sort of proof adequate to the most certain philosophical truth.[48]

And Hamann wrote that his final doubt about the *Preisschrift* was whether the "apologist for the human origin of language was ever the least bit serious about demonstrating his theme or even about treating it at all. . . ."[49] There is, then, considerable evidence that the classic statement on language origin was a classic put-on.

The put-on of questioners and the put-down of questions, how-ever, are very different things—as any serious student of Plato must know and as Hamann certainly did. Consequently, the interpretation of the prize essay as a mere dismissal of the question misses the point. That Herder was contemptuous of the academicians there is little doubt. That he would have put the question differently is probable: Just a few years earlier he had wrestled with the possible meanings of the problem. But reflection on the origin of language, even in the way the academy had fashioned the question, opened up for Herder many avenues of thought: wonder about the fundamental nature of man and whether he is a "natural" being at all, inquiry into the workings of the human spirit, concern with the dynamics of human speaking, insights into the authentic and the beautiful, new paths of investigation into human and linguistic history. It may be that Herder did not really or seriously answer the academy's question, but he can scarcely have regarded it as useless or senseless. That which cuts off free and thought-ful inquiry is useless, not a question which stimulates and inspires it.

Two contemporaneous works on language origin—both of them probably intended for or actually submitted to the same essay contest—closely followed Süssmilch's deductive method. Karl Wilhelm Jerusa-lem—the same who achieved dubious immortality in world literature when, just after his early suicide, Goethe indiscreetly used the unfortu-nate deceased as model for the title character of *The Sorrows of Young Werther*—left behind numerous manuscripts and outlines which were edited and published by Lessing. The first was a bare sketch, "That Language Was Not Miraculously Imparted to the First Man." Even the outline evinces the terse logic which Jerusalem had in mind. "To say that language came about through a miracle means that its origin cannot be explained by the soul's power of representation."[50] If language was caused by a miracle, it would have had to be either a single or a repeated miracle; but it cannot be the latter, since every miracle is a new creation. If language originated through a single miracle, either God gave man language itself, or he created man with the capacity to develop language on his own; but the latter is excluded because the soul, as a uniform substance, can possess only one fundamental capacity and that is the power of representation. If God created man in full possession of language, then he either gave man language without any knowledge of the ideas signified by words, or he gave man thought and speech simultaneously. The former is eliminated, since these would have been meaningless sounds, not language; but the latter is also excluded, for it would mean that the soul could develop ideas without experience. Ergo, man himself must have originated language. Obviously, there are presuppositions behind these premises; but the argument itself is a chain of disjunctive syllogisms.

Dietrich Tiedemann published *Attempt at a Clarification of the Origin of Language* in 1772, probably an expanded version of an essay submitted to the Berlin Academy. He attempted to deduce the origin of language from the nature of language. "Can we explain the manner of development of language, if we do not know what language is? Can we clarify the origin of anything at all, if we do not have clear concepts about it?"[51] Accordingly Tiedemann tried to describe not merely the nature of language generally, but its ideal nature, what language would be in a perfected state. From this he roughly derived the probable course of linguistic development and gradual improvement. Tiedemann reversed Süssmilch's conclusion by altering his premises. Language is perfectible, but it has not always been perfect. Primitive languages are disorderly, uneconomical, and ugly. Tiedemann's final argument for human origin runs: Language in its original state was highly disorderly; anything created by God would be perfectly ordered; ergo, God did not invent language.

Herder's mode of inquiring into language origin was deductive in a way, but distinguishable from the methods of Süssmilch, Jerusalem, and Tiedemann. He did not deduce origin from the nature of language but from the nature of man, his first important area of inquiry. He moved from his identification of reflectiveness to its relation to language generally to specific conjectures about language genesis and primitive speech. Although anachronistic, it would not stretch terminology too much to say that Herder's approach was phenomenological: He himself said that instead of hypothesizing, he was making deductions from the "fixed data of the human soul." Examining the workings of human consciousness, Herder tried to locate the critical place of language in that network of relations and interplay of forces. Although he had earlier rejected the notion of an invention of language because it suggested a machine, he now took advantage of the academicians' use of that term in their phrasing of the question: Man is indeed a language-inventor; he is creative and free when speaking— not only at a single point in the remote past, but now and always.

There is paradox in the fact that Herder started out from an inquiry into man's nature, for in a sense it was his contention that man does not have any nature, at least not natural instincts, but that everything natural to him is filtered through reflectiveness. The point was noted by Coleridge in his marginalia to Herder: "A famous word and accommodating word is that menschlich/human, or rather human/natural! It is the cousin German of Charity and employed by Herder to cover as many Follies . . . as the latter does Sins."[52] Herder himself later used a formulation which neatly captured the anomaly: "For the nature of man is art. With time everything for which there is a disposition in his being can and must become art."[53] The final question, then is this: Is this "human/natural" natural at all, or does it put man at a remove from the natural? And is it just on account of this distance that man is a being with the freedom of choice and requirement of ethical decision, and the only creature with genuine language?

[7]

MYSTIFYING RESPONSES FROM THE MAGUS OF THE NORTH

The publication of Herder's prize essay in 1772 led to a complicated series of reactions. Herder himself began to worry about the reception of the work, despite its coronation by the academy. Any jokes on the academicians seemed to have been lost on them, but the general public might be more perceptive. In 1771 Herder, who had gone from Strassburg to Bückeburg as court preacher to Count Wilhelm zur Lippe, became depressed and lonely. His parishioners were suspicious of his French-style clothes and cosmopolitan manners, and assumed that heresy must be lurking somewhere in his theology, even though he was at this point attacking deism and rationalism. But the towns-people were extremely proud of his victory in the essay contest. Herder, in contrast, wrote both to the publisher, Nicolai, and to his fiancée, Caroline Flachsland, expressing his wish that publication be suppressed.[1]

Herder's dejection deepened when Hamann wrote a very cool review of the *Preisschrift*. It came after Hamann had published a devastating review of Tiedemann's work on language origin, which he concluded by expressing his high hopes for the forthcoming prize essay, "which will give us more material and pleasure in investigations of this sort."[2] When the review appeared, however, it was curt and consisted largely of quotations to which Hamann added his own acerbic comments.

To Herder's accusation of anthropomorphism against Süssmilch and his conclusion that language is divine only in so far as it is human, Hamann remarked: "Here! Here! (by the life of Pharaoh) is God's finger! This *apotheōsis, Apokolokyntōsis,* or even *Apophtheirōsis,* probably sounds more like Galimatias than the lowest, most humble, and yet *privileged* anthropomorphism."[3] As usual in Hamann's writings, the several allusions must be explained before the point becomes clear. But Hamann could also be direct and cutting when he wanted:

We really find in Herder's style much action in the histrionic sense. But if the peculiarity and true direction of humanity consists in reflectiveness, we have found pages and passages in this prize essay where reflectiveness is operative in the author's mind to such a small degree that the *ecce homo!* would better serve as the distinguishing mark or communicating word of the unreflecting and all too human art pundit.[4]

Hamann concluded this initial review with an enigmatic passage, whose principal references (to Cervantes and Heraclitus) will be explained later:

We hope that one of our fellow-citizens, if he has not completely gone to rot in the fatherland, will yet fan some spark from the ashes of his little kitchen hearth, in order to warm up his doubts and oracles about the content and direction of the academic question and its solution. What Dulcinea is more worthy of an avenging cabalistic philologist than the individuality, authenticity, majesty, wisdom, beauty, fecundity, and boundlessness of the *higher hypothesis*—from which all systems and languages of the old and the new Babel derive their subterranean, bestial, and human origin, their fire (*kosmon tēs adikias*), and can expect their dissolution and destruction.[5]

After reading this review, Herder sank still deeper into the abysses of *Weltschmerz*. At the instigation of Hartknoch, Hamann wrote Herder a very cordial, but not apologetic letter:

As far as I have been able to pump out information . . . , you no longer understand me. This is a bad omen for our friendship, in which you can assume me to be as steadfast as is possible among us poor mortals. From the enclosed pages you will see that reviewers are finished. . . . The freedom which we take upon ourselves is granted even more generously to the friends who understand and comprehend us.[6]

Basically, Hamann conveyed to Herder that no personal animosity was intended in the review and that he would have expected Herder to understand his playfulness and freedom. As if to underscore the point, Hamann enclosed with the letter a supplement to the review, a burlesque *reductio ad absurdum* of the thesis of the prize essay. Some have taken this gesture as the oddest stroke of nastiness on Hamann's part. Taken together with the letter, however, its point seems clear: Herder should not have been bitter about the review, because such reaction mistook the freedom of friendship, the possibility of making fun of one another at the ultimate expense of the public.

The problem, Hamann wrote in the supplement, seems to revolve around the question whether original language was imparted to man in the same way as subsequent language transmission. "The scale, however, seems to tip as usual to the side of the *yes-men,* and their opponents are confronted with so many difficulties that virtually the whole analysis of the problem is thwarted."[7] The affirmative answer is far more convenient, since there would be no guide to a solution unless one assumes that original and subsequent language learning are parallel.

Even if some reader should have the cheek to take the judgment about all these difficulties by the *horns,* no sensible author would do it just to please a single *desert ram* and let his other ninety-nine *sheep* in the lurch; for in all probability the others would have already understood the prudent and secure course and, with eyes closed piously, would have nodded a clear yes to the above question.[8]

The proof is overtly specious, but, says Hamann, it remains to determine how language is imparted at the present time. There are three possibilities: instinct, invention, and instruction. Since the last of these is the "obviously correct answer," Hamann, still bluffing, wastes no words either in its defense or in refuting the first two. But how did language instruction originally take place?

Human instruction is excluded *eo ipso;* mystical instruction is ambiguous, unphilosophical, unaesthetic, and has ninety-seven more faults and defects, so that for a mere index of names and the necessary explanations of them, I would have to buy out all the supplements of the current year from the publisher of this learned and political journal, which my conscience and my good will, but most of all my pocketbook and the critical time of year forbid. There is, therefore, by reasonable necessity and good fortune, nothing left but bestial instruction.[9]

Philosophers have rightly praised the animals and considered them the first of living creatures. All man's accomplishments only imitate the animals' instinctual doings.

The borrowed fire of all the fine, free, and noble arts was a Promethean plagiarism from the *lumen naturale* of the animals. For the seed of all knowledge of good and evil, and even for the full-grown tree of the Encyclopedia, we have to thank the skepticism of some cunning beast and the refined taste of some still more cunning herd.[10]

Referring back to the previous review, Hamann surmises that its author must have been a "stranger in Israel," who did not realize that his cabalistic philologist would be turned into a beast of burden by the taskmasters. Our "countryman of sad countenance," Hamann continues with a relatively obvious allusion to Don Quixote, would probably murmur about the academic question:

What do I know about your whole topic? Why should it interest me? The dawn, midday, and sunset of all the fine arts and sciences, known (alas!) only by their fruits, have no influence on my present bliss, except that those merciless sisters interrupt the deep sleep of my contentment with allotriocosmic dreams. . . . Let your speech be yea, yea! nay, nay! All else is of the devil—and herein consists the entire spirit of laws and of the social contract, whatever names they may have.[11]

The style alone of the review and supplement indicate why Hamann was popularly known as the Magus of the North—although, when he addressed Frederick the Great, the Solomon of the North, he signed himself *Le Sauvage du Nord*. It is not only that his writings abound with cryptic allusions and puzzling formulations. It is also that Hamann maintains an ironical distance from the subjects he discusses and from the very act of writing. In another piece against the *Preisschrift*, Hamann regales:

If I had the slightest desire to make myself immortal by becoming a writer for great minds and still greater fools—with lengthy, erudite, verbose, and impertinent notes on a meagre text or with a philosophical commentary on two Latin words—then I would just use the negative part of this . . . proof as the most fruitful material for a historical-critical masterpiece. After many an edition and many a translation in our enlightened part of the world, it would perhaps occur to some Chinese emperor of the next century to canonize my masterpiece as a devotional volume, which he would therefore vigorously abridge. He would then sell this warmed-up cabbage of whims and doubts in the High German mother tongue— which is just as full of barbarism and beggar's pride as the language of the Most Reverend [Pierre] Bayle and of Mr. Henry Ophelot de la Pause—as if it were the rabbit in the moon, which inspired the holy Confucius. However, I have a heartfelt hostility against all such pig-Latin and Chinese quackeries of authorship.[12]

As to the origin of language, Hamann accuses Herder of taking the question rather flippantly. For himself, he indicates that he would defend the "higher hypothesis" of divine origin, were he to argue for any at all, but that this would be a quixotic venture, with all the elevating comedy of the pursuit of Dulcinea.

A few weeks after receiving Hamann's letter cum supplement, Herder received still another manuscript concerning language origin from Nicolai in Berlin. Hamann had submitted the manuscript to his publisher, Kanter; Kanter, not understanding it, sent it on to Nicolai for comment; Nicolai, left in total confusion by it, showed it to Mendelssohn, hoping for elucidation; since Mendelssohn could not make much of it either, he gave it back with the suggestion that it be passed on to Herder, for it apparently had something to do with the origin of language; Herder read it and returned it to Nicolai, admitting his confusion and not even sure whether it was an attack on his own prize essay. The confusion amounted to an emotional catharsis for Herder, because he realized that whatever Hamann was doing, it was undertaken in a spirit of enormous jest. He wrote to Hamann patching up the friendship from his side, and Hamann responded warmly, as though he and Herder had been engaged in a mutual conspiracy against readers:

I cannot express to you my joy that you are just the friend to fulfill my ideals. . . . My heart anticipated everything which your letter said about our misunderstanding, or rather the public's misunderstanding. . . . I still have to laugh at my Socratic grief that a disciple like Herder was so weak as to whore with the *beaux esprits* of his century and their *bon ton*.[13]

The writing in question above was *The Last Will and Testimony of the Knight of the Rose-Cross Concerning the Divine and Human Origin of Language*. Obviously the work is somewhat difficult of understanding.

The title page alone of the *Last Will and Testimony* contains ample enigmas, allusions, and cross-references. As such, it provides a good, yet finite, starting point for examining Hamann's method of writing and the philosophical attitude which this implies. The title page and verso are illustrated on page 136 with their approximate English translation on page 137. Without even advancing to the puzzles of the main text, we can already sympathize with the bewildered reactions to Hamann's piece.

The title character, the Knight of the Rose-Cross, is clearly cast in a mold with the knight-errant, Don Quixote, Dulcinea's "cabalistic

Des

Ritters von Rosencreuz

letzte

Willensmeynung

über den

göttlichen und menschlichen

Urſprung der Sprache.

———

Credidi, propter quod locutus sum.
2 Cor. IV. 13.

———

Aus einer Caricaturbilderurſchrifft
e i l f e r t i g   ü b e r ſ e ß t
vom

Handlanger des Hierophanten.
και εγω ποιησω Ιεροφαντην
Arrian Epict. III. 21.

Tempore et loco praelibatis
Motto des Rabelais.

Socrates in Platonis Philebo.

Donum profecto DEORVM ad homines,
vt mihi videtur, per Prometheum quendam
vna cum quodam lucidissimo igne descen-
dit. Etenim prisci nobis praestantiores,
DIISque propinquiores, haec nobis oracula
tradiderunt — —

THE LAST WILL AND TESTIMONY

OF THE KNIGHT OF THE ROSE-CROSS

CONCERNING

THE DIVINE AND HUMAN

ORIGIN OF LANGUAGE

———————

I believed, wherefore I spoke.
II Corinthians 4:13

———————

Hurriedly Translated
from
Caricature-Original-Hieroglyphics
by the
Acolyte of the Hierophant.

(I too shall make a hierophant.
Arrian, *Discourses of Epictetus,* III, 21.)

At the preconsecrated time and place.
Motto of Rabelais

Socrates in Plato's *Philebus*

Indeed it seems to me that a gift of the GODS to men descended through a certain Prometheus simultaneously with a certain very brilliant fire. For the ancients, being superior to us and closer to the GODS, handed down these oracles to us — —

philologist" in the original review and with "our countryman of sad countenance" in the supplement. The allusion also refers to Hamann himself, whose first published book was entitled *Crusades of the Philologist*. As such, however, the title character is Christian Rosencreuz, a fifteenth-century nobleman, crusader, and knight-errant of sorts, who traveled to "the East" (Damascus, Egypt, Fez, and Spain) in search of occult knowledge and thereafter founded the Rosicrucian Society. Like Hamann himself, Rosencreuz was known as Magus (either "magician" or "wise man"), and he established that knowledge should be communicated within his society only by means of a mysterious and cryptic language. Rosicrucianism, however, is not the only secret society referred to on the title page. The second oblique attribution of authorship refers to a hurried translation—this, no doubt a joke on Herder's hurried composition of the prize essay—by the "acolyte of the hierophant." Hierophants, literally "those who bring sacred subjects to light," were the initiating priests in the ancient Eleusinian mysteries, though in late antiquity the term designated philosophic teachers, so that the word has the same ambiguity as *magus*. For *acolyte* Hamann uses the German (*Handlanger*) rather than the Greek form. In its colloquial meaning *Handlanger* is a word used for literary hacks—and Hamann certainly would not have spared such a joke on himself. Literally a *Handlanger* is a mason's assistant, and this was the term used for initiates in German Freemasonry. Rosicrucians, Freemasons, and many others believed that the essence of some primordial wisdom was contained in the Egyptian hieroglyphs or some substitute system of ideogrammatic symbols.

To understand these references to secret societies, it is necessary to know something of the dual role played by Rosicrucians and Freemasons during the eighteenth century. On the one hand, they attracted occultists, *illuminati,* and quacks—such men as Martínez Pasqualis, Saint-Martin, or Cagliostro. But on the other hand, these societies were an important vehicle of enlightenment; in fact they were hotbeds of revolutionary ideas and activities and contributed significantly to the oncoming of the French Revolution. It was in sympathy with the latter appeal of these organizations that Herder himself joined the Freemasons in 1766. Herder was in the company of such apostles of clear and distinct rationality and common sense as Descartes, Leibniz, Lessing, Wieland, Goethe, George Washington, and Ben Franklin, all of whom were members of one or the other society. In interpreting Hamann, however, we must consider one elementary fact: He was unalterably opposed to these societies and one of the few members of the Königsberg intelligentsia who refused to join. This should deter us from simplistically interpreting Hamann as a compulsive obscurantist or pseudomystic crackpot. He sympathized with neither the occultist nor the enlightening aspects of these societies, and in *The Last Will and Testimony* he juxtaposed one against the other in ridiculous interplay: His were Caricature-Original-Hieroglyphics.[14]

The general motto on the verso is taken from Plato's late dialogue, *Philebus.* As Hamann quotes it, it reads: "Indeed it seems to me that a gift of the GODS to men descended through a certain Prometheus simultaneously with a certain very brilliant fire. For the ancients, being superior to us and closer to the GODS, handed down these oracles to us — —." The capitalization of *GODS* is, of course, Hamann's own, but there are additional distortions. The citation is an excellent example of a typical technique of Hamann's, namely to leave it to the reader to discover what is really meant; for the clue to Hamann's thought does not lie in the words he quotes, but in the two dashes. When we turn to the *Philebus* itself, we find that the passage continues: "The ancients, however, being superior to us and closer to the gods, handed down this oracle, that whatever things are said to exist are composed of both one and of many, and have both the finite and the infinite implanted in them."[15] This "oracle"—that all existing things reflect the infinite and the finite in conjunction—is, however, so crucial to Hamann's thought that it might easily serve as a one-sentence summary of his philosophy generally and of the ground for his theory of language. Nonetheless, Hamann suppresses the direct statement of his thesis and instead uses signs, the two dashes.

Once again, however, there is more to this than trivial toying with unsuspecting readers. There is a fragment of Heraclitus—and allusions to "the obscure Ephesian" will multiply as we go along—which says, "The lord to whom belongs the oracle at Delphi neither speaks out (*légei*), nor covers up (*krýptei*), but gives an indicator (*sēmaínei*)."[16] This aphorism about the ambiguity of oracles is itself ambiguous and oracular: The word *sēmaínei*, the root of *semantics,* ranges in meaning from literal physical pointing to general signification. Heraclitus's aphorism, playful with the meaning of *meaning,* is many-leveled: Literally, it refers to the practice of many ancient oracles who expressed themselves by physical gestures and signs rather than words; more generally it implies a comprehensive philosophy of language. Language does not directly reveal being, nor does it completely conceal being, but it gives man the guideposts which he must follow. (To put this somewhat differently, it is erroneous to think that we have conquered truth because we have mastered words, but it is equally misleading to think that words always divert us away from the true reality of things.) This position is near to Hamann's own and closely related to the suppressed oracle about the conjunction of the finite and the infinite in things and in language; but as a second-level irony, Hamann uses signs (dashes) to suggest it, because Plato had specifically spoken of an ancient oracle.

But Heraclitus's aphorism, and Hamann's reflected play on it, is also specifically Delphic: The consultant coming to Delphi had to meditate on the injunction "Know thyself!" Without deep self-examination and proper interpretation he risked being misled by the oracle's obscure signs and dark statements. Oedipus and Croesus are the most celebrated characters who met catastrophe because, lacking self-knowledge, they took the words of the oracle at "face value." Heraclitus's own aphorism can only be understood when we delve beneath its surface; and Hamann's seemingly innocent use of a quotation from Plato can only be understood when we go beyond its words to the dashes—signs which hardly convey deep meaning in themselves, but which alone guide us, if we are willing to follow, to Hamann's intention with this motto. Good reading, in other words, requires deep reflectiveness—Hamann's last harmless joke on Herder, in this particular instance.

We can begin to see what Hamann is up to: He uses language and writing deliberately to show things about language and writing, that is, reflectively. Still, we have barely begun with the possible inferences from the *Philebus* quotation alone, for it is indisputably related to other items on the title page. Instead of date and place of publication, Hamann uses the phrase *tempore et loco praelibatis*, which he calls the motto of Rabelais. Taken from *Gargantua and Pantagruel*, book I, chapter 42, the phrase means "at the preconsecrated time and place"; but its Rabelaisian connotations would be obvious to an ironical classicist like Hamann, since *libo* means "to drink, sip," and "pour out a libation," and only derivatively "to consecrate." Allusions and footnotes to Rabelais run throughout *The Last Will and Testimony* and Hamann's writings generally. Hamann clearly had taken notice of the "Author's Prologue" to *Gargantua and Pantagruel,* where Rabelais compares his book, as Alcibiades had compared Socrates, to a Silenus figure, ugly and obscene on the outside, beautiful and divine within. Like Heraclitus's fragments and Hamann's writings, like language generally, the exterior has to be broken through and carefully opened up (not smashed and shattered) before we can discover the true, good, and beautiful in it. For the same and self-evident reasons, although we may be prodded by circumstances or teachers, we must ultimately do the discovering ourselves, lest what we find be trite or merely "philological." Panurge, Don Quixote, and the Knight of the Rose-Cross begin to merge; as do Plato's "oracle," Heraclitus's aphorism, and Rabelais's "motto."

The interplay of citations becomes still more clear when we examine the quote from Epictetus, "I too shall make a hierophant." It is found in a chapter of Arrian's *Discourses* entitled "To Those Who Undertake the Profession of Teacher with a Light Heart," and one can easily imagine Hamann's amusement at using this in a work directed against his close friend and "disciple." In the chapter, Epictetus warns his student against precipitate publication of his thought in word or writ, and so we have the anticipation of Hamann's "hastily translated" critique of Herder's hastily composed *Preisschrift*. Rabelais's "motto" is actually a quotation from this very chapter of the *Discourses* and relates specifically to its beginning: "Those who have learned principles and nothing more are anxious to give them out immediately, just as men with weak stomachs vomit food. First digest your principles, and then you will not vomit them."[17] Vomiting and other effects of indigestion, of course, play a prominent part in Rabelais's caricature-masterpiece, and Hamann's inference from the text is rather obvious.

But the net of textual and contextual interrelations reaches further: Epictetus's admonition is essentially the same as the point of the passage from which the *Philebus* quotation is taken. The latter concerns method, specifically the proper way of relating the one and the many, infinite and finite. A little farther on in the *Philebus* passage, Socrates deplores the loose thinking of "contemporary wise men":

But wise men nowadays make out the one and the many either too quickly or too slowly. Thinking haphazardly, they go straight from the one to the infinite and have no care for the necessary intermediate steps. But this is what makes the difference between dialectical and merely sophistical argumentation. (16e–17a)

We have established specific interconnections between the title page references to Plato, Rabelais, and Arrian, and their relevance to Herder's prize essay and Hamann's criticisms of it. Lest we take all this as mere play, however, we should note that the passages concern the difference between sophistical and philosophical reasoning, that is, between that which only appears to be wise and that which is truly wise. We shall be deceived if we rely on words alone to differentiate between the reality and the appearance of wisdom; for it is only the thoughtfulness, knowledge, and experienced judgment behind words,

and that used in choosing them, which can make words wise. That is
the point of the immediate context of the words that Hamann selects
from Epictetus:

Slave, you cannot do this recklessly and in a random fashion. It demands
mature years, a certain way of life, and the guidance of God. . . . Man,
what else are you doing but vulgarizing the mysteries? In effect you are
saying, "There is a shrine at Eleusis, lo! here is a shrine also; there is a
hierophant there, *I too shall make a hierophant.* . . . The words said
are the same, so what is the difference between what is done here and
what is done there?" Most impious of men, is there no difference? The
benefit of the mysteries depends on the proper and *consecrated place and
time.* . . . But you publish and divulge the mysteries out of place and
out of season, without sacrifices or purification. You have not the dress
which the hierophant should have, nor the proper hair, nor the head-
band; you have not the right voice nor age; you have not purified your-
self in the way that he has. Instead you have merely learned the words
and recite them as though the words had some holy power in themselves.[18]

All of the passages to which Hamann alludes on the title page involve
thinking, speaking, or writing which is overhasty or premature. It
becomes eminently clear that Epictetus and Socrates are masks for
Hamann himself, who is chastising Herder for his brash prize essay.
He was dissatisfied with the way in which Herder published, that is,
made his thoughts public; the way in which he "vulgarized," that is,
made his thoughts available to the *vulgus,* an uninitiated or unen-
lightened audience. And by rude implication the *vulgus* turns out to
consist of Berlin academicians. All of this, however, is neither stated
directly, nor is it concealed entirely, but it is indicated by the hidden
interrelations of his quotations and references.

We have not nearly exhausted the allusions on the title page, and
there will be further passages from the main text which relate to the
references already explained; but this is a good point to pause and
reflect on Hamann's way of writing and his reasons for it. It is clear
that Hamann wrote obscurely and that this was his calculated intention. Yet Hamann's correspondence shows that he was entirely capable
of writing directly and clearly when he wanted to. Kant sometimes sent
Hamann books which he himself did not understand, requesting clarification, and Hamann's responses were lucid, pertinent, and direct.
Hamann could be clear, but he was not so in writings meant for publication. Letters were sent in his own name, but all of his published

writings were anonymous or pseudonymous. As the motto of the supplement to the review has it: "Ultimately the farce obliges him to mask
everything."[19] The manner of writing again hinges on the question of
what should be made public, when and how—a subject about which a
great deal can and must be said, and which goes beyond the art of
writing to basic questions of the ethics of language as such.[20] We must
remember that when Hamann refers to oracles, mysteries, hierophants,
and the like, he is alluding to the indisputably philosophical texts of
Heraclitus, Plato, and Epictetus, and not to out-of-the-way occultist
literature. Still we must ask why a writer should have chosen to speak
with so many enigmas, cryptic allusions, and obscure cross-references?

It often seems as though Hamann were writing in foreign tongues.
He himself says at the end of *The Last Will and Testimony:* "As for
all tasters who are nauseated by the French and Latin trimmings of
my dialect, I only wish that the present acolyte of the hierophant had
been a polyglot the likes of Panurge and Quintus Icilius, so that they
could not read his translation at all; for that is our good pleasure."[21]
A first reading of Hamann gives much the same impression as hearing
people converse in a foreign language: Some recurring idioms seem to
be prominent, some phrases may come through clearly, but of the
whole we understand little.

This analogy provides a convenient road on which to approach
the question of Hamann's intentions in his writings. Under what circumstances, we might ask, would people use a foreign language in the
presence of persons not in command of it? Six likely reasons come to
mind: amusement, ostentation, discourtesy, self-protection, protection
of someone else, and instruction. The first three of these—showing off,
pure play, and insult, all forms of impolitic behavior—apply to
Hamann's use of obscurity but need not detain us. Self-protection is
as obvious a reason for cryptic writing as it is for the various modes of
formal and informal cryptography. Its justification probably depends
on situation and intent; but given the various forms of violent persecution and less violent suppression to which philosophers have been subjected since antiquity, it is not surprising that much philosophical
writing is obscure. We protect others when resorting to a foreign
language if, for example, we try to conceal some horror from a child,
or the truth from someone who could not bear it.

The ethical questions here become more complex, for there are
many who would argue that concealment of the truth is never justified.
Indeed, this was stoutly maintained by many Enlightenment thinkers.[22]
Yet the maxim that one should always state the truth and state it
clearly is, among other things, only as good as the assumptions that the

truth itself is clear to us and that we can clearly state it. If, however, the truth were entirely obvious and there were no difficulty in expressing it, philosophy would be superfluous. From its beginnings philosophy has seen as its task the uncovering of the truth or of reality or of being, precisely because these are not immediately clear—because reality is covered up by appearances and because we distort the truth with prevalent opinion. But the process of discovery is a delicate one: Had the enchained prisoner in Plato's cave been dragged outside straightaway and forced to look at the sun, he simply would have been blinded and surely would not have received a philosophical education.[23] Our line of reasoning has led us directly from the fifth to the sixth reason for speaking strangely or in the manner of a stranger: The protection of others relates to the pedagogical purpose of using an alien language with those who do not fully understand it. The most obvious instance of this last, however, is when foreign language teachers speak, even with their elementary students, simply so that these can learn.

Hamann is widely known as an enemy of the Enlightenment. That he certainly was, but the basis for his opposition has often been distorted. Many have misrepresented it as enmity toward philosophy and reason (as opposed to faith, feeling, myth, inwardness, etc.), as though the cause of Enlightenment and of reason were identical. Yet there was a long-standing and ongoing tradition of philosophy which was surely not "irratonalist" and which just as surely did not share the assumptions of the Enlightenment—assumptions (or their derivative variations) which have become so generally accepted in some quarters that they constitute prevailing opinion. Philosophical thinking, however, as Hamann implied in his review of Michaelis, should not bolster prevailing opinion but undo it, even though the philosopher's speaking and writing may never be so free and open as his thinking is. By treating the truth as though it could be directly and simply stated in a journal article, a newspaper column, a panel discussion, or an encyclopedia essay, Enlightenment *philosophes* debased the truth and transformed philosophy into a more or less sophisticated form of public opinion. The very term *philosophe* virtually obliterates the distinction between philosopher and sophist. Once the enlightener would take seriously the difficulties implicit in his assumptions, he would have to dilute his maxim as follows: Everyone should state the truth as he sees it, as clearly as he can. But to rest content with "the truth as one sees it" is, in effect, to abandon the quest for truth altogether. In part at least, Hamann was an enemy of the Enlightenment because he saw the enlighteners as enemies of philosophy.

Lest this position be taken as sheer snobbery or "elitism," we should realize that Hamann thought the charge was far more appropriately leveled at those pundits and sophists who presume or pretend to hand down the truth so clearly to us. The truth—unlike opinions which happen to be true, or right, or beneficial—is something that we must necessarily discover and see for ourselves. It is akin to genuine freedom, which can never be given but only won. In a famous passage, Plato wrote that he never committed his most serious thoughts to writing.[24] One of his several reasons for saying this was that such would have been self-defeating for a philosophical instructor. If it is the dialectician's task to get his "student" to see things on his own and escape into the freedom of genuine thought, then he can hardly tell him what he must see or where his freedom must take him. This was one of the basic reasons why Socrates chose not to write and why he attacked writers as well as lecturers. Plato must have been well aware of this dilemma when he decided to write nonetheless. As a philosophical writer, he had to leave many fundamental problems to his readers and friends to disentangle and decipher, or else risk defeating his pedagogical purpose. In a different style and for a more bookish, but not necessarily more thoughtful audience, this is precisely what Hamann does: He compels his readers to track down his allusions—and thereby immerse themselves in the great philosophical classics—before they can begin to glimpse his points. This manner of writing is instructive to the careful reader in obvious and varied ways, and may even plunge him into the depths of serious, lonesome thinking.[25]

It would be interesting to know whether twentieth-century media analysts would characterize Hamann's writings—or for that matter Heraclitus's fragments or Plato's dialogues—as a cool or a hot medium. It would be curious, because it seems to be one of Hamann's points that the medium may well be the message at the level of opinion, which is so easily controlled and swayed, but that the freedom of genuine thinking always goes beyond and behind media, because they are just what their name indicates. Well-intentioned mass communication and public education, far from advancing the cause of philosophy, may turn out to be the most effective means of general manipulation. Obviously, it is impossible to know whether this was something which Hamann prophetically foresaw. Yet one cannot deny that much in our present life, including both its curses and its blessings, is the logical aftermath of Enlightenment: The mass media of today—on those occasions when they are well intentioned—are the electronic extension of the enlighteners' hope of creating the means to communicate wisdom to *le peuple*. Readers, listeners, and viewers may judge how often either the prevailing opinion promoted or the "controversial" opinions allowed approach wisdom. In any case, it is certain that philosophers are not the elite controlling public media.

This should lead us to conclude with Hamann and Epictetus that wisdom can never be identified with the language or other medium used to convey it. Wisdom always goes beyond words: Although the wise man may be our best friend, there is something strange, unfamiliar, foreign about what he says. And yet, there is a manner of speaking wisely and writing wisely, even if its wisdom may lie in hints that there is something else to say and think about. In the supplement to his review of Herder, Hamann has his Don Quixote mask say: "What do I know about your whole topic? . . . The dawn, midday, and sunset of all the fine arts and sciences . . . have no influence on my present bliss, except that those merciless sisters interrupt the deep sleep of my contentment with allotriocosmic dreams."[26] The "merciless sisters" are probably the prostitutes who disturb Don Quixote at the inn, but what of "allotriocosmic dreams"? The most likely explanation of these "otherworldly dreams" is found in the eighty-ninth fragment of Heraclitus: "For those who are awake there is one common cosmos, but every sleeper turns away to a world of his own."[27] The common cosmos—which Heraclitus generally identifies with *lógos* or "the divine law upon which all human laws are nourished"[28]—seems otherworldly to the sleeper, just as the truth seems wildly improbable to those who labor under one or another variety of prevailing opinion. Such a private world is, according to the literal translation of the Greek word, idiocy. The sleeper is "idiotic" because he does not understand the meaning of the things which he sees or of the words which he hears, because he literally has his eyes shut to the true world. The truth and the gods are not so far off when our eyes and ears and mind are open.

In the same supplement Hamann wrote: "We hope that one of our fellow-citizens . . . will yet fan some spark from his little kitchen hearth, in order to warm up his doubts and oracles about the content and direction of the academic question and its solution."[29] This apparently irrelevant metaphor can again only be explained out of a reference to Heraclitus in Aristotle. The passage reads: "Every realm of nature is cause for wonder: It is reported that, when strangers came to visit Heraclitus and found him warming himself at his little kitchen hearth, they hesitated to go in; but he bade them not be afraid to enter since, he said, 'Even here in this kitchen the gods are present also.' "[30] It is a clear inference that Heraclitus's "Lo, here are the gods also" is meant to be contrasted with Epictetus's student's "Lo, here is a shrine also." There is a difference between recognizing the presence of the gods in the world and taking the things of this world to be sacred. It is often said that every heresy is an exaggerated truth. The heresy which exaggerates the orthodox doctrine of omnipresence is pantheism. Pantheism is specifically heretical not because it views worldly things as manifestations of the divine, but because it takes the single manifestation and makes it into an object of worship, as if it had some holy power in itself. So too, the search after wisdom requires of us that we not treat words as though they had some holy power in themselves, or as though we could make them pure and holy. Both respectful and critical of the thought behind and the world beyond words, we must neither be worshipers nor iconoclasts. Silences, smiles, winks, frowns, hints must all find their way into the language of wisdom, as they so often do in Plato's dialogues.

In our catalogue of circumstances under which people would speak a foreign language in the presence of those who do not understand, we made one very obvious omission. The most natural of all cases occurs when two or more persons in a larger group actually come from a different society and naturally speak a different language. According to Plato, something quite like this is the eternal situation of the philosopher. He is a man of dual citizenship: a member of a particular society with obligations to it—including the sometimes contradictory ones of respecting that society's laws and customs and yet of refusing lawlessness when it is publicly sanctioned;[31] but also a citizen elsewhere, who is awake to the cosmos which is one for all and whose final loyalty and love is truth. In an extended sense we say that members of a specific social group, sub-, counter-, or superculture, "speak the same language," whose style and vocabulary are alien to other natives. Philosophers are neither a class nor an elite in any sociological sense—and they most assuredly are not the more-or-less accidental subset of all those who have managed to attain degrees in an academic discipline defined only with great difficulty; but this analogy is also helpful. Hamann was addressing any reader who could "speak the same language"; just as he himself felt entirely comfortable with the language of Heraclitus, Plato, Aristotle, and Epictetus. Speaking a language both foreign and common, such authors, readers, and philosophers maintain something like a transhistorical community of friendship. This is probably the main reason why Hamann wrote the way he did.[32] Hamann wished his readers pleasure, but a pleasure which only comes with time and diligence and serious thought.

We begin to see the method behind the maddening obscurity of Hamann's writings. Other authors of like sympathy abandoned the writing conventions of their time; thus Plato wrote dialogues instead of treatises and Nietzsche wrote aphorisms instead of scholarly essays or books. Hamann, in contrast, wrote mock exaggerations of the dominant scholarly-scientific-philosophic style of eighteenth-century intellectuals. Above all, he exploited the fetish of the footnote, footnotes in many languages to all sorts of obscure texts and passages: One piece, an anonymous satire-review of his own *Crusades of the Philologist,* consists almost entirely of notes, carefully arranged from Z to A.[33] (It is appropriate that the most adequate form of Hamann exegesis is the commentary, tracing down direct and indirect references with an additional array of footnotes—footnotes to Hamann's footnotes to the main texts of the ancient Greeks and Hebrews.)

What is unusual in Hamann is that the notes are meant to be systematically traced and interrelated by the reader, so that Hamann's meaning is sometimes better discovered outside of his writings than it is within them. The reader is obliged to look figuratively between the lines and literally beneath the lines. In short, a Hamann text is a grand symphony of allusions, with a counterpoint of orchestrated cross-references, in which, as with the harmonic devices of some modern music, the overtones assume as much importance as the melodic statement.

Hamann's manner of writing, which is a reflection of an underlying philosophy of language, poses special hermeneutic and exegetical difficulties for the interpreter. The commentator must follow up Hamann's allusions, often concentrating on that which Hamann has specifically omitted, but he has at hand no ready criteria to distinguish between that which was significant and insignificant for Hamann himself. All authors *do not say* an infinity of things; but with Hamann the interpreter must determine which of the things left unsaid are of importance. Although we know the contents of Hamann's library, we cannot know everything he heard, much less everything he thought.[34] Ultimately this would culminate in an elucidation of an author's silences. But can this be done? Indeed, should it be done? If a reader could genuinely understand the secret level of a philosopher's teaching, then he would also understand the reasons why the philosopher hid that level, and then he might have a moral obligation to keep the secret.[35] It would be naive to say that authors are only cryptic in times of political persecution and that since there is no hint of persecution in the twentieth century, now we can "come out" with everything. First, we can only explain that which we understand; second, persecution has not passed; third, the fear of censorship played little part in Hamann's obscurantism, for he did not even intend to publish many of his writings. Beyond this, there is the difficulty that the interpretation of an obscure writer will seem to many to be purely conjectural. Inevitably, the interpreter himself will be more convinced by his own arguments than his readers can be, for it is he who has gone through the scholarly process of elimination and found, for example, which fragments of Heraclitus are pertinent to a particular allusion and which are not. Thus even the commentator will only be persuasive to the extent that his readers undertake the pleasures and labors of reading the classic texts themselves. Could this have been Hamann's purpose?

Given all the enigmatic byplay on the title page, the opening of *The Last Will and Testimony* is surprisingly straightforward:

If one assumes that God is the origin of all effects great and small, in heaven or on earth; then every numbered hair on our heads is just as divine as the Behemoth, that beginning of God's ways. The spirit of the Mosaic laws therefore applies even to the most nauseous decomposition of the human corpse. Consequently, everything is divine and the question of the origin of evil hinges in the end on a wordplay and scholastic banter. Everything divine, however, is also human; because man can neither act nor suffer except according to the analogy of his nature, no matter how simple or complex that machine may be. This *communicatio* of the divine and human *idiomatum* is a fundamental law and the key to all our knowledge and to the whole visible economy.[36]

If we ignore the allusions for the moment, the basic argument is fairly clear: On the one hand, since all things are creations of God, language must be so; on the other hand, since the divine reveals itself in human form, language is fully human also. There is a *communicatio idiomatum,* a communication or commonness of idioms, which establishes a proportion or analogy between divine and human language; and therefore the origin of language too must be viewed as both divine and human. The basic theme is, of course, an extension of orthodox Christology, the Nicene doctrine that Christ, the Word, was fully God and fully man. Hamann continues his careful balance of these two in the second paragraph:

Since the organs of speech are in any case a gift of the *alma mater,* Nature (with which our stark men of *esprit* engage in a more absurd and blasphemous idolatry than did the vulgar masses of heathenism and of popery), and since in all philosophic probability the creator of these ingenious organs would and must have established their function, the origin of language is surely quite divine. But if a higher being, or an angel (as with Balaam's ass), should want to operate through our tongue, then all such operations, as with the talking animals in Aesop's fables, must express themselves in a manner analogous to human nature; and in this regard the origin of language, not to speak of its progress and development, can neither be nor seem to be anything but human. For this reason Protagoras already called man the *mensura omnium rerum*.[37]

For Hamann, however, man is the measure of all things not because he is their creator or judge, but because man is a vessel. In a footnote citing Tertullian and Lactantius, Hamann indicates that man is properly the discoverer, not the establisher or inventor of "the necessities of life; which existed before they were found, and the fact that they existed was not thought out by him who found them, but him who instituted them."[38] Language is like fire, Heraclitus's *lógos*: It must be discovered. One of the repeated errors of Enlightenment thinking is the confusion of these two roles. We would never say that Columbus invented America or that Newton invented gravity; yet some say that man invented language, only because they have unwittingly removed language from the realm of nature.

Some historical comments are necessary about the concept of a *communicatio idiomatum*. Hamann took the phrase from Luther, who had borrowed it from scholastic theology.[39] In his Christology, Luther used this notion to explain the coexistence of the divine and human natures of Christ. In his explanation of consubstantiation he again employed the term to emphasize that the sacramental elements are simultaneously bread and wine in their physical aspect and the body and blood of Christ in their spiritual aspect. Orthodoxy, in contrast with the more prevalent forms of intransigent or exaggerating dogmatism, involves a kind of balancing act, and here Luther was walking the line between Roman Catholicism and the new doctrines of the sacrament advanced by Calvin, Zwingli, and the Anabaptists: For the former, transubstantiation implied that the bread and wine were transformed into body and blood, but according to Luther this involved a heretical tendency inasmuch as these elements are understood as physical; in the latter, he saw the obverse heresy of derogating the physical presence altogether. Luther extended the concept still further into a general theology of the Word, according to which God created things by calling them into being or by commanding them into existence through speaking: *Opera dei sunt verba eius,* "The works of God are his words."[40] A contemporary Lutheran theologian, has coined the term *inverbation* to describe this amplified doctrine of incarnation: In Luther's exegesis of the *locus classicus* of *lógos* Christology, the first chapter of the fourth Gospel, he asserted that God revealed was not only God incarnate, but also God inverbate, God revealed in human language.[41] Luther went a step further and used the same theme to defend his exemplary but much criticized Bible translation: An adequate translation must strike a balance between the spirit and the letter of the original text.[42]

The specific doctrine of the *communicatio idiomatum* should be placed in the context of the history of theology more generally. Two related themes should be mentioned. The first was introduced over a century before the Council of Nicea by Clement of Alexandria. This was the notion of divine condescension, elaborated as *súgkatabasis, accommodatio dei,* and *Herablassung Gottes* in the respective traditions. This was the teaching that in all his revelations—nature, history, Scripture, Christ, etc.—God molded his forms of expression to the possibilities of human understanding, that is, God accommodated himself to man and man's ways. In revelation, God "comes down," humbles himself, and makes himself accessible. Often this was related to the *personae dei* in the traditional doctrine of the Trinity and to Luther's interpretation of nature and history as the *larvae dei*—in both cases, "the masks of God."[43] In taking on different forms, God "speaks" different languages. Hamann asserted that in Scripture God chose to speak in the vernacular: To the horror of contemporary rationalists and allegorists, he compared the *koiné* Greek of the New Testament to newspaper style and insisted that the Old Testament was written in a simple, commonplace, sensuous language easily grasped by the infantile mind.[44] The concept of divine condescension had its counterpart in the doctrine of analogy, and more specifically (in St. Thomas Aquinas) in the *analogia entis.* According to Thomas, there is a proportion between the divine and the human, the sacred and secular realms. The analogy between the two serves to explain, first, the order of the world—there is a proportion between God and nature, because God created the world; second, the possibility of human knowledge and science—man can understand nature because he was created in the image of God, and therefore human reason can perceive the reasonableness of the world; and, third, the possibility of human language about God. Throughout the Middle Ages there had been a strong but irksome tradition of negative theology, which asserted that the infinite nature of God could never be captured in the categories of finite human language and that therefore one could only say what God is not. This tradition was a thorn in the flesh to Christian theology because it struck at the crux of the matter, the possibility of revelation and incarnation, of God's becoming man, of God's speaking like man.[45] In Thomas's cautious phrase, human assertions about God are *non*

omnino aequivocale, not completely equivocal, so long as we are aware
that our statements are in fact analogical.[46] The hermeneutic implication of this, according to Thomas, is that we should follow an anagogical rather than an allegorical method of interpretation: Instead of
substituting a "higher" meaning for the literal, we should follow a
method which naturally leads us upward from the literal to the spiritual meaning of a text, as with a metaphor our mind should move
from the concrete image to its symbolic significance. Thus, if God's
revelation is a "coming down," man's interpretation of it should involve a "going up."

When Hamann's polemics are placed in this theological context,
we see that he is essentially accusing Herder of heresy. According to
the prize essay, "the origin of language becomes divine in only one
proper way, inasmuch as it is human."[47] To Hamann's mind this formulation was entirely misleading. To be sure, if language is fully divine
and fully human, both Süssmilch and Condillac/Maupertuis must be
rejected, but Herder was so taken with his demolition of the former
that he could not detach himself from the idea of linguistic invention
in the latter. In the end, Hamann submits, Herder's hypothesis "issues
in a divine genesis which is in fact more supernatural, more sacred,
and more poetical than the oldest Oriental story about the creation of
heaven and of earth."[48] If all phenomena are explained in strictly
immanent terms, Hamann contends, it is necessary to introduce more
ad hoc miracles than if one simply accepted the divine creation of a
reasonable natural order: It is a solution worse than Deism.

If man then, in accord with the universal testimony and example of all
peoples, times, and places, is not capable of learning to walk on his two
legs without the sociable influence of his guardians and parents, i.e., *iussus*
[on command], nor to break his daily bread without the sweat of his brow,
but least of all to attain the masterpiece of the creator's strokes; then how
could it ever occur to anyone to think of language, *cet art leger, volage,
demoniacle* (to speak with Montaigne from Plato) as an independent
invention of human art and wisdom? Our philosophers speak like al-
chemists do about the treasures of fecundity. . . . The confusion of
tongues, however, through which they deceive and are deceived, is surely
a very natural magic of automatic reason, which effortlessly transfigures
itself into a star of the first magnitude, especially for rascals of equal
blindness.[49]

What instead must be understood and emphasized is the way in which
men humanize that which is naturally given, just as the divine must be
humanized.

If the Knight of the Rose-Cross wanted to degrade the diamond stylus of his forefathers in the same way that the prevalent visionaries . . . degrade their gabbling goose quills; then . . . I would prove down their throats . . . that even eating and drinking are not innate characteristics of the human race. . . . Everything, everything militates in favor of this demonstration: the nature of the human stomach, which gulps down skin and hair, stones and lodes, as well as pills, streams of sweat and blood, whole cargoes of sighs and curses as if they were brandy; the element of hunger and thirst, whose greed, or rather attraction, makes everything, everything, everything tasty and wholesome to the princely palates of our financiers and new-dealers, Cretes and Arabians . . . ; the analogy between the cold kitchen of a Laplander, or *indiginae,* and the fire-spewing kiln of an Apicius, or *coquin pandu et parvenu;* between Fritz in a plush cradle and Fritz in a manger, both of whom would never have learned to use either a wooden or a golden spoon, had not their nurse or mother smeared pap around their open mouths and faithfully tended to the grand mystery of digestion. Indeed, won't you finally understand, you philosophers, that there is no physical link between cause and effect, between means and end, but rather a spiritual and ideal one, namely that of blind faith, as has been made known by the greatest earthly historian of his country and of the natural church.[50]

The last allusion is to Hume, whom Hamann translated and construed in a manner most un-British.[51] Hume's demolition of the physicists' concept of causality leaves open only one possibility: Apparent causation is not only a habit of mind, as Hume himself contended, but an act of faith.

The task then, according to Hamann, is to show, even more than to explain, the mystery of the natural and the naturalness of the mysterious. Thus Hamann essays a presentation of the origin of language rather than an analysis of it, "without getting himself into a fray with fad-followers."

So then, reverend brethren, imagine to yourselves, if and as well as you can, the birth of the first pair of human beings. . . . And there was the voice of a God wandering about the garden in the cool of the evening, the rational nourishment for these young children of creation, calling upon them to grow up to their political vocation, to populate the earth and master it through word of mouth. . . .

Thus Adam was God's; and God himself introduced the firstborn and eldest of our race as the feoffee and heir of a world prepared by the word of his mouth. Angels, happy to see his heavenly countenance, were the ministers and courtiers of the first monarch. All the children of God lifted their praise to the chorus of the morning stars. All tasted and saw

at first hand and on the spot the friendliness of the artisan who played
on his earth and had his fun with the human children. As yet no creature
had fallen against its will to the vanity and bondage of the transitory
system; under which it now yawns, sighs, and becomes still like the
Delphic tripod and like the antimachiavellian rhetoric of a quinsical
Demosthenes; or at most pants, gasps, and finally suffocates in the dropsi-
cal breast of a Tacitus. Every phenomenon of nature was a word—the
symbol, sense-image, and surety of a new, secret, inexpressible, but so
much the more intimate unification, communication, and communion of
divine energies and ideas. Everything which man at first heard, saw with
his eyes, gazed at, and touched with his hands, was a living word, for God
was the word. With this word in his mouth and in his heart the origin
of language was as natural, as immediate and as easy as child's play; for
human nature remains from the beginning to the end of days as much
like the kingdom of heaven as is yeast, with a small amount of which
every woman can knead three bushels of dough.

I would matagrabolize still longer, broader, and deeper, were it not
for the fact that I know much preaching exhausts the mind of auditors
these days as much as it used to tire the body of spirited speakers; and
therefore I rest content for today, after my pilgrimage in sackcloth and
ashes, in having found and named the element of language—the Alpha
and Omega—the Word.[52]

Hamann's final piece against the *Preisschrift* was *Philological
Incursions and Doubts Concerning An Academic Prize Essay,* complete with a mock Pindaric ode and an appended letter to Frederick
the Great, written in French and addressed *au Salomon de Prusse,*
recommending Herder for the presidency of the Berlin Academy.
Hamann again filled the title page with related allusions and quotations, as shown on page 156 with the corresponding translation on
page 157.

The work is the only one of Hamann's four pieces against Herder
which, according to its title, poses as an attack: The ambiguous
Einfälle means "invasions" or "sorties" as well as "random thoughts,"
"ideas," or "brainstorms"; but it is also full of mock praise. The mottos
of the title page set the satiric tone, as do the numerous footnotes to satires (mainly Horatian), references to satyrs and the
ancient festivals, comments which identify Herder as a follower of
Pan (and simultaneously Panurge), allusions to Rabelais, and the
dating in the "month of wine." It is likely that Hamann intended not
only a parody, but a sort of intellectual bacchanalia, a cathartic satyr-
play to follow the triology of tragi-ironic works—the review, supplement, and *The Last Will and Testament. Philological Incursions and*

Doubts represents the purgation of the whole Herder-Hamann controversy in pure satiric farce.

Herder is cast in the mold of a Paniscus or satyr, but as everyone knows, and as Hamann himself knew, "The great god Pan is dead." The god's demise was broadcast, and duly lamented, by Plutarch in his essay, "Why the Oracles Cease to Give Answers." It is evident that Hamann had this essay in mind while writing the set of pieces against the prize essay—and most likely also the companion piece from Plutarch's *Moralia*, "Wherefore the Pythian Priestess Now Ceases to Deliver Her Oracles in Verse."[53] The answer which Plutarch offered to these questions can be simplified in the following terms: The times are not ripe for the delivery of oracles.[54] In both *The Last Will and Testimony* and *Philological Incursions and Doubts,* Hamann draws numerous parallels between his own age and the decadent, highly superstitious phase of antiquity so clearly reflected in the works of Plutarch, the period of declining paganism and emergent Christianity. It is in this light that we must see Hamann's tirades in the latter section of *Philological Incursions and Doubts* regarding the absence or insignificance of magi in the eighteenth century—an indifference which made it unlikely that magi would even be persecuted.[55] Here lies the true significance of Hamann's quixotic assaults against the windmills of his century, its preoccupation with lengthy and pretentious books, and its failure to heed ambiguous and oracular pronouncements; for the matter of "oracles and doubts" is a continuing thread through the maze of Hamann's Herder pieces. It might be exaggerated to suggest that Hamann anticipated the Hegelian and Nietzschean proclamation of the death of God, but he certainly deplored the contemporary "silence of the oracles" and "the transitory system, under which [the creature] now yawns, signs, and then becomes still like the Delphic tripod."[56] Thus it is out of season that Hamann assumes the role of magus and casts Herder as the satyr.

Although Hamann ends *Philological Incursions and Doubts* with obscurity, parody, and excess, the initial section is clear and direct. After reiterating Aristotle's distinction between sound and language and briefly commenting on the organizational and mechanical similarities between man and the animals, Hamann asserts that the specific difference of human beings must concern their way of life.

With regard to sociability the wise Stagirite considers man to be neutral. I therefore presume that the true character of our nature consists in the judicial and magisterial dignity of a political animal, and that therefore man is related to the beast as a prince to his subjects.

Philologische
Einfälle und Zweifel
über
eine akademische Preisschrift

Ps. CXX. 4.

Sie ist wie scharfe Pfeile eines Starken, wie
Feuer in Wacholdern.

— — απομνυω,
μη τερμα προβας, ακονϑ' ωσ-
τε χαλκοπαραον, ορσαι
Θοαν γλωσσαν.
Pindar Nem. VII.

Nebst manchen Stellen mehr aus dieser O d e,
jede an seinem Ort.

Entworfen

vom

Magus in Norden.

Im Weinmonate 1772.

Gedruckt bey: Hier kommt der Drucker der allgm. Bibliothek.

— — neque ego illi detrahere ausim
Haerentem capiti multa cum laude coronam.
Horat. Satyr. I. X. 48. 49.

PHILOLOGICAL INCURSIONS AND DOUBTS

CONCERNING

AN ACADEMIC QUESTION

———

Psalm 120:4
Like sharp arrows of the mighty,
like coals of juniper.

———

— — I swear
I did not overstep the line,
when I shot forth my swift tongue,
like that bronze-tipped spear.
Pindar, Nemean Ode VII

With many other passages from this ode,
each in its place.

———

Drafted by the
Magus of the North
In the month of wine 1772.

———

Printed by: Here comes the printer of the *Allgemeine Bibliothek*
— — nor would I dare to remove
the crown fixed upon his head with great applause.
Horace, Satires I, x, 48–49.

Now, this dignity, like all honorary stations, does not presuppose any inner dignity or merit of our nature; but is, like the latter, an immediate gift of grace by the great All-Giver.

No hero or poet, whether he be the prototype of the Messiah or a prophet of the Anti-Christ, lacks periods in his life during which he has good reason to confess with David: "I am a worm and not a man."

Without the freedom to be evil there is no merit and without the freedom to be good no responsibility for one's own guilt, indeed no knowledge of good and evil. Freedom is the maximum and minimum of all our natural powers, and also the fundamental force as the purpose of their whole direction, development, and return. . . .

Without the complete law of freedom man would not be capable of any imitation, upon which all education and invention depend; for man is of all animals the greatest pantomime.

Consciousness, attentiveness, abstraction, and even moral conscience seem for the most part to be activities [*Energieen*] of our freedom.

However, it is not only undefined powers which belong to freedom, but also the republican prerogative to participate in the definition of them. These conditions were unavoidable for human nature. Thus the sphere of animals determines, as it is said, the direction of all their powers and drives through instinct in just as individual and set a way as, in contrast, the viewpoint of man reaches toward the universal and, as it were, loses itself in the infinite. . . .

Presumably the senses are related to the understanding in the same way that the stomach is to the vessels which separate the finer and higher fluids of the blood. . . . In the same way, nothing is in our understanding which was not previously in the senses, just as nothing is in our whole body which was not once in our own stomach or that of our parents. The *stamina* and *menstrua* of our reason are therefore in a precise sense revelations and traditions, which we assume as our own property, transform into our own juices and powers, and thereby grow up to our vocation of partly revealing and partly passing on the critical and archontic dignity of a political animal.

The analogy of animal economy is the only ladder to an anagogical recognition of the spiritual economy, which quite probably is the only thing capable of solving and completing the phenomena and *qualitates occultas* of that visible, abbreviated half.

Assumed then that man came into the world as an empty goatskin, this very lack makes him more capable of enjoying nature through experiences and of communing with his species through traditions. . . .

From way back philosophers have divorced themselves from the truth to the extent that they have separated what nature put together and *vice versa*, wherefore among other heresies psychology has also had its Arians, Mohammedans and Socinians, who want to explain everything from a single positive power or entelechy of the soul.

Since the secret of a marriage between such contrary natures as the outer and the inner man, or body and soul, is great, therefore, in order to come to a practical understanding of the fullness in the unity of our human nature, there is required a recognition of several differentiating earthly *Merkmale.*

Man then is not only a living field, but also the son of the field, and not only field and seed (according to the systems of materialists and idealists), but also king of the field, cultivating good seed and hostile weeds from his soil; for what is a field without seeds and a prince without land and revenues? These three then are as one in us, namely *theou geōrgion* ["God's field"; cf. 1 Cor. 3:9]: like three *larvae* on the wall are the natural shadows of a single body which has a double light behind it. — — —

Now that I have maneuvered myself into the empyreal sanctity of human nature, or to put it better, now that I have driven my peripatetic soap bubbles far enough ahead of me; they dissolve halfway into the following dew drops:

"Man learns to use and to master all his limbs and senses, thus also his ear and tongue, because he *can* learn, because he *must* learn, and because he very much *wants* to learn. Consequently the orgin of language is as natural and human as the origin of all our activities, abilities, and arts. Ignoring the fact, however, that every apprentice cooperates in his instruction relative to his inclination, capacity, and opportunity, in any case learning in the strict sense is no more invention than mere recollection."[57]

The foregoing is a fair example of Hamann's style when he is arguing directly instead of in his usual *oratio obliqua:* Although there are numerous allusions and footnotes susceptible of elaborate interpretation, the main lines of reasoning are clear. The phenomenon of meaningful human language must be related to man's dignity as a political animal, a dignity which is neither an inherent nor inevitable nobility, but a calling to sovereignty over himself and over nature. In saying that man's sociability is neutral, Hamann refers to Aristotle's reflections whether the polis is a product of nature or of art. With the alternatives formulated in this way, Aristotle answers that the polis is natural, since it arises out of the family and then the village, and because "a being without a polis, whether by nature or even by chance, is either lesser or greater than man," "either a beast or a god."[58]

For, as we say, nature does nothing in vain, and man alone possesses *lógos.* Mere sound, of course, is a sign of pain and pleasure, wherefore it is possessed by the other animals . . . , but language should make clear what is useful and what is harmful, and so too what is just and unjust;

for it is peculiar to man, in contrast with the other animals, that he alone has a perception of the good and the bad and the just and the unjust and similar things, and it is the bond of these things that makes a household and a city-state.[59]

The word *nature* in Aristotle's statements must be clearly understood, for it means that the polis is man's task and destiny; or, in one of Aristotle's most renowned formulations, "The polis came into existence for the sake of mere life, but it exists for the sake of the good life."[60] Thus the naturalness of the polis is consistent with the neutrality of human sociability; just so Socrates had emphasized that every technique is in itself neutral, for it can be used for good or bad: The best doctor is potentially the most efficient murderer, the best obstetrician is the most reliable abortionist, and the most accomplished technologist can obviously perpetrate the most bestial destruction.

For just as man when perfected is the best of animals, so he is the worst of all when separated from law and justice. And injustice is most pernicious when it is possessed of arms, but man is born possessing weapons for wisdom and virtue, which can instead be used for the very opposite purposes. Hence, when he is without virtue, man is the most impious and savage [of animals]. . . ."[61]

The endless task for man, therefore, is to define the good and the purpose of his capacities—what Hamann calls man's freedom and "republican prerogative of participating in the definition of [his powers]." The nature of this task and the difficulty of defining the good entail that the best use of man's faculties is their critical or philosophical employment, and not their use for the artificial support of modish opinions or fashionable tyrannies.

The naturalness of human language and sociability is only partly analogous to the naturalness of animal instinct, for human being is historical as well as hereditary: "The *stamina* and *menstrua* of our reason are . . . revelations and traditions." The recognition of revelations and the preservation of traditions are essential parts of man's political and linguistic task, if any good is to come of it. As in his earlier essay on Michaelis, Hamann traces these revelations and traditions back to an original *institutio* (*eine ursprüngliche Einsetzung*), which is prior to all specific or positive legislation. This original *institutio* he associated with the origin of language, in much the same way that Plato had seen the *nomothétēs* as both lawgiver and name-giver and that Aristotle had suggested that Onomacritus might have been the first true legislator. In addition, Hamann undoubtedly connected this thought in his mind with the relationship between *lógos* and *nómos* indicated by Heraclitus and elaborated in Hellenistic philosophy.[62] To paraphrase Heraclitus's fragment 114 in more modern parlance: All positive law derives from an original *institutio,* as do all specific human languages. Man must learn, cherish, and preserve revelations and traditions,. because they lead him back to the original, and this may be the only road to wisdom. As the model of the invention of language distorts some aspects of discovery, so the notion of human creativity through language should be supplemented by the more traditional idea of recollection. The way backward and the way forward are one and the same.

After this first section, Hamann summarizes Herder's arguments in the *Preisschrift* and his own criticisms.

It would be extremely laughable to present a counterproof against a truth which has not only been definitely proven but also crowned. Thus I find myself with the pleasant necessity of being able to smoke out the fashion of my century with doubts.

From the whole hovering dream of doubts which ran through my mind as I read the academic prize essay seven months ago, I collect myself now, in a moment of wakefulness, in order to concentrate fully on a single one . . . : Was this Platonic apologist for the human origin of language ever the least bit serious about demonstrating his theme or even about touching upon it?[63]

The accusation refers not only to the surface flippancy of the prize essay, but also to the superficiality of approach: Herder had not bothered to think the question through:

The whole Platonic proof consists of a vicious circle, an eternal cycle, and nonsense which is neither concealed nor fine; . . . it rests on the hidden powers of arbitrary names and socially accepted catchwords and modish ideas, and in the end issues in a divine genesis, which is in fact more supernatural, more sanctimonious, and more poetical than the oldest Oriental story of the creation of heaven and of earth. If the learned author had written in all seriousness, he would have exposed himself as wantonly and flippantly to a printed, jolting, hyperbolic-pleonastic dose of retaliation in criticism and would have opened himself to wounds and bruises! . . .[64]

The vicious circle in the argument of the prize essay is its nonsolution of the old *aporia* from Plato and Rousseau. There is also a fundamental inconsistency, which no doubt reflects the very contradictions of human being, but which Herder glides over as though he had actually demonstrated something. "The Platonic proof of the human origin of language consists of two parts, one negative, one positive. The first contains reasons why man is not an animal, and the second reasons why man is nonetheless an animal . . . , because no animal *can* invent language, and no god *may* invent language."[65] Out of his dilemma Herder concocts an apocalyptic, Neoplatonic, homuncular inventor of language which is un-animal, un-god, un-man. Herder's originator of language is no more than the *theîos anér,* the "godlike man," of the philosophical mythology of Hellenistic traditions.

In the history of our current century more than one example comes to mind how little is involved in being a creature different not in degrees but in kind from those animals which in everyday life are called subjects, in being a creature standing above them, lying above them, sitting above them, or wandering to and fro above them, which is called a tyrant or earth-god because of its freely working positive power . . . — it seems to us, I say, from the history of the present century, that nothing under the sun is easier than being such a creature, or making one, but that it is most difficult to maintain or give years to such a creature, especially when it is just baked and freshly plucked.[66]

Herder's speaking homunculus will not endure, for it is as artificial as some of the linguistic projects of those enlighteners whose fancies Herder was flattering.

After these fairly direct explanations, Hamann moves further and further into humoristic obscurantism: the mock paean, an apologia for his own crusades, a backhanded vindication of Herder, and finally the personal recommendation of Herder to Frederick the Great. One hidden theme from the last sections should be brought out, for it is a masterstroke of irony directed at both Frederick and Herder. The open letter advocating the elevation of Herder to the presidency of the Berlin Academy is filled with images taken from postexilic and Gnostic apocalyptic literature, but also with more obvious lifted phrases. Consider the language which Hamann uses in addressing the Solomon of the North:

Your Majesty is that which the Wise Men of the Century call a *Being Supreme in the Land,* and you have a Father, who will cause the superiority of *your genius* to be proclaimed above all other kings, through as many miracles as those whereby the GOD of the Jews rendered his name glorious above all the idols of the nations.

The *Magus of the North* worships you, Sire! with a devotion rivalling that which inspired of old the Wise Men of the East. . . . Because the Eternal One has loved his people, SOLOMON has been made KING of all the Prussians.

But where are the temples? the altars? the priests dedicated to the religion of the *Supreme Being of Prussia?*

Your Majesty's sublime taste, like the *Spirit of Christendom,* wishes no other cult than that of spirit and truth, no other altars than the hearts of your subjects, no other ministers than those who love and preach the truth, who love and practice virtue."[67]

However, Hamann quickly turns around this unabashed piece of emperor-worship: "Your Century, Sire, is nothing but a day of anguish, reprehensibility, and blasphemy. . . ."[68] Frederick's century, the age of Enlightenment, is an age of apostasy as filled with deification and pumpkinification as Julian's futile crusading attempt to call the pagan gods back to life.[69]

Could Herder really have been taken in by it all? Just because he desired the acclaim of his contemporaries? No, Hamann pleads in his final defense, Herder *had* to "condescend to the level of critical and archontic weakness typical of the century."[70] "As a clever administrator of an unrighteous Mammon, he could do no other than base his treatise on the revelations and traditions of his century, thus building his proof on sand, patchwork, wood, hay, and stubble."[71] "In order to make his way to the top by great victories, my friend Herder could not write in any way except as a satyr for a terrible, adulterous generation, which is neither un-animal nor un-man, but a monster with iron arm, ant-infested stomach, and the face of an Anubis—for a generation which denies God and scurries to become rich and hopes to conquer heaven and earth with various works in poetry and prose."[72] The theological language of these apologetic passages is unmistakable: Herder condescended, debased himself, humiliated himself, accommodated himself, made himself understandable—to his century. Herder revealed himself according to the analogy and measure of contemporary language. In short, Herder is made over into a comic Christ-figure, even in his dubious coronation, and the prize essay is heralded as a revelation, because it is an *accommodatio*. The best and the worst that can be said of the whole endeavor is that Herder spoke the language of his times.

We conclude with Hamann's ode to the victorious Herder:

In order that I will not be accused of having robbed the Platonic apology for the human origin of language of its poetic strength, I will improvise a fragment of the newest Genesis on the Pindaric lyre in oriental dialect, in praise and adulation of the Pythian victor.

> Courage, allons, prends ta harpe benie
> Et moque toi de son Academie — — —

He created him a nonbeast and beast from a whole grand ocean of sensations, from the whole bedazzling dream of images passing his senses, and for the act of their recognition, for the mark of his consciousness, laid out the armor before him. Raised high above beasts, not in degree but in kind of instinct, stood the Platonic hermaphrodite, a nonbeast—without instinct.

Go reign over birds of prey and creatures of sea, but be deaf and dumb! spoke the Andriantoglyph to the Protoplastes of language—for the moment you fathom the fruit of your inner and outer instinct, your mouth will be opened and you will become a beast full of instinct from inside and outside; your nonbestial traits will decay as the grass.

There stood the Platonic hermaphrodite, born dumb, in the sleep of his latent powers. But behold! in a moment it happened, in the moment he fell deeper and deeper into his element—in a whole ocean of sensations—in a whole bedazzling dream of images, in the moment that he was placed in the state of reflectiveness and enchantment, which was anyway his peculiar nature. And lo! in that very moment it happened, the first sound of the external instinct escaped from his mouth, as a sign and communicating word of his internal instinct. Thus came from the outer and inner instinct the first word, and from the nonbeast raised high above beasts through his lack of instinct came a creature driven by outward and inward instinct, *id est,* a reflective and linguistic beast. Hail the inventor of language![73]

[8]

AN ANSWER
ON THE WANE

The differences between Hamann and Herder had little immediate impact on speculations about language origin. Hamann's writings were so impenetrable that, when they were not admired as the works of a brilliant stylist, they were dismissed as the overwrought phantasms of an enigmatic eccentric. For the most part, neither Hamann's contemporary admirers nor his detractors took his philosophy seriously, and the immediate development of thought about linguistic origins proceeded as though the Herder-Hamann controversy had never occurred.[1]

The dispute did have a profound effect on Herder himself. After his initial bitterness and then bewilderment, Herder undertook to construct a theory which would be acceptable to Hamann. The main product of this attempted conciliation, *The Oldest Document of the Human Race* (1774–1776), displeased Hamann even more than the prize essay. Although his published review was qualifiedly favorable and gentle, he disparaged the work in private correspondence. Herder became confused about the entire topic, avoided mention of it in his letters to Hamann, and vacillated between the lower and higher hypothesis. Finally, within the same year, 1784, Herder published two fully contradictory theories of origin: In his preface to E. A. Schmid's translation of Monboddo, he gave qualified assent to the naturalistic theory; in part one of the *Ideas Toward a Philosophy of the History of Mankind*, he espoused divine origin. This was the end of Herder's wavering on the subject: After it he fell silent on the matter except for a brief and unoriginal essay in 1795.[2]

Despite Herder's disavowel of his response to the academic question, the prize essay and the lower hypothesis won the day. While Herder tergiversated, others accepted his work without question. The conjecture of the prize essay, daring and polemical in 1770, was a commonplace by the 1780s. Writers of the increasingly popular books on universal history, lacking time or inclination to develop their own theories of language origin, plagiarized from Herder. Johann Christoph Gatterer and August Ludwig Schlözer, both polyhistors from Göttingen, had earlier given quasidivine explanations in their works about world history: It was in keeping with the intellectual vogue of the time. Herder's *Preisschrift* revolutionized the fashion: In 1785 both of them included secular explanations in similar works. Not that the prize essay evoked no criticism aside from Hamann's; but interest in the subject waned with the growing acceptance of Herder's solution.

Critical Reactions

Some critics of the prize essay continued to defend the higher hypothesis. Matthias Claudius, the humoristic poet of pietism, took exception to the *Preisschrift* on strictly scriptural grounds. While praising much in the work, he scored Herder's failure to mention the single and incontrovertible exception to the rule of human origin, the language mentioned by Moses—"a warm translation of the Original-Language, in which a mild, inexhaustible author wrote for his friends a grandiose *Codex* of heaven and earth *en Bas Relief* and *ronde Bosse*."[3] Claudius seems to suggest that Herder explained the origin of all language except the original language.

Gottfried Ploucquet—a professor of philosophy at Tübingen, where he was Hegel's logic teacher some years later—was a member extraordinary of the Berlin Academy and thus ineligible for the essay contest; but after Herder submitted his entry, Ploucquet recorded his thoughts on the subject.[4] Concerned with the residual Cartesian problem of the guarantee of human knowledge, he saw God as the creator of both the world's external order and of the mind's capacity to understand that order. Since language is the principal vehicle of human cognition, it too must be conditioned by the divine power. Ploucquet asserted that speech is a God-given power; but since the mere faculty could not assure the truth of the contents of language, God directly instructed Adam, and thereby celestial language was accommodated to the human speech capacity. In this way, Ploucquet argued, God vouchsafed both the subjective faculty and the objective contents of language, both speech making and the speech made.

Lessing also devised an unorthodox argument for the divine origin of language. Around 1766–1769, probably aroused by publication of Süssmilch's book, Lessing contemplated an essay on the origin of language, but the project never came to fruition.[5] When he edited Jerusalem's *Nachlass* in 1776, Lessing had another opportunity to address himself to the problem. Lessing was then formulating the thoughts which would be consummated in *The Education of the Human Race* (1780), where he identified divine providence with education as the motive force behind man's progressive rationality. In his own addenda to Jerusalem's sketch, Lessing commented that Jerusalem's negative logic had indeed demonstrated that language was not imparted to man through a divine miracle, but that he had fallaciously concluded therefrom that man must have been its inventor. There is an additional alternative: That man was instructed in language through converse with higher beings and the condescension (*Herablassung*) of the creator himself. Advocates of this median position could argue: "Agreed that this converse and condescension were themselves miracles, nonetheless that which was wrought by this miracle was not miraculous: everything proceeded as naturally as it does now with the sound-making of children."[6] Even if it were possible for man to develop language entirely on his own—Lessing continues with an argument close to that of his famous work on mankind's education—the creator would not have allowed him to live for centuries, perhaps millenia, in a semihuman, prelinguistic state, but would have accelerated the process of human education by condescending to converse with man. In Lessing, the higher hypothesis becomes one aspect of the economics of divine providence.

Johann Nicolaus Tetens, professor of physics and metaphysics in Bützow and Kiel, did not mention Herder by name in his 1772 essay, "On the Origin of Languages and Writing." Nonetheless, he was clearly polemicizing against the *Preisschrift;* and in his major work, *Philosophical Essays Concerning Human Nature and Its Development* (1777), he attacked Herder directly.[7] In the earlier essay, Tetens's interest was to find some way of overcoming Rousseau's *aporiae* without resorting to gradualism. He saw no such solution in Herder: The postulate that man's reflective and linguistic nature are coeval in fact accentuates the impasse, since it does not resolve the problem of the efficient cause which impelled the development of the two. Tetens's own answer lay in the derivation of both man's language and his *Besonnenheit* from a third factor, sensibility (*Sinnlichkeit*), a mode of sensation uniquely human because of man's proclivity for associating the most heterogeneous ideas and sensory data. Although Tetens expounded this view with some care, the substitution of *Sinnlichkeit* for *Besonnenheit* hardly brings us nearer to the final ground of language. If the prize essay failed to identify the efficient cause which induced the reciprocal development of reflectiveness and language, Tetens himself only relocated the missing cause, leaving unexplained the cause of sensibility itself.

In the *Philosophical Essays,* where Tetens emphasized man's spontaneity, he attacked Herder more directly, but also Süssmilch: "[The latter] has not proved that man could not have invented language by himself, nor [the former] that he must necessarily have invented language by himself."[8] Man's capacity for language, which Herder successfully demonstrated, does not imply the necessity of human invention. In addition to aptitude and inclination, there must be favorable circumstances and some specific impetus which transforms potentiality into actuality. Tetens now located this circumstantial cause in human sociability, the *sine qua non* of linguistic development. Against Süssmilch, Tetens maintained that man surely could have devised language, but against Herder he argued that man could only have done so under propitious conditions. Yet Tetens's final solution of the difficulty is curious indeed. The "geniuses of language," he conjectured, initiated the linguistic process, once the time was ripe, and thereafter rendered special assistance as required for linguistic progress. But what created these favorable circumstances? And what brought out the latent powers of such linguistic geniuses?

Rudolf Zobel took exception both to the psychology of the prize essay and its explanation of linguistic origins. Since Herder did not observe animal activities empirically, his conclusion that reflectiveness is unique to man is arbitrary. "Good. So I want to demonstrate that dogs have language. The dog receives food from its master, and at this time the master calls it by name. This name becomes a fixed sign for the dog. He hears it: 'So! You are the feeding one!' he thinks to himself."[9] Herder could as well have demonstrated that reflection is constitutive to the nature of a dog. Like Tetens, Zobel grappled with the efficient cause that set linguistic development in motion. "It does not really follow from the fact that man is a reflective creature that he must therefore necessarily and absolutely invent language. There must have been some additional external impetus to set the power in motion and give it the necessary direction."[10]

Friedrich Heinrich Jacobi also responded to Herder's *Preisschrift.*[11] He concentrated on Herder's (and Reimarus's) notion of "artistic drives" (*Kunsttriebe*) and elaborated its application to a variety of specific animals as contrasted with man. Tetens, Zobel, and Jacobi all confused Herder's "tendency" with mere potentiality, thus misconstruing Herder's polemics against Rousseau and faculty psychology. Mere potentiality requires external agents to activate it, whereas "tendency" is self-activating unless contrary forces prevent its development. All these immediate reactions to the prize essay, whether they argued for divine or human origin, can be imagined outside the context of Hamann's more fundamental critique.

Herder Confused

If some of the respondents to the prize essay misunderstood it, Herder's own ensuing confusion is even more remarkable. Herder made his peace with Hamann, but actually he withdrew from the attack. In his letter of reconciliation in August 1772, Herder promised that he would shortly publish a work retracting the prize essay and presenting a hypothesis more to Hamann's liking. The work appeared in 1774 and 1776 as *The Oldest Document of the Human Race*. Hamann called the work a *monstrum tremendum* because of its glaring combination of primitivistic message with futuristic style: for example, Herder included whole paragraphs in which he merely amassed nouns, attempting to recreate the mood of pregrammatical language. Shifting between poetry and prose, and changing topics rapidly, Herder gave the distinct impression that rationality was not a necessary prerequisite for the invention of speech. The work purported to explain the Mosaic creation story as an elaborate allegory for the daily reappearance of the dawn: "Let there be light!" is the crucial passage. Herder fixed upon a single primordial hieroglyph, which explained all—or "The All"— and which was the "seminal germ of all human wisdom":

			A	
·		H		E
· ·	Or (Egyptian, Greek)		I	
·		O		Y
· ·			W	
·				

Herder used this "original paradigm" to explain the physical elements, physiognomic features, human anatomy, the original sounds of human speech, the first patterns of writing, and related topics. Creation, allegorized as the auroral awakening of day, is God's "visible word":

"What a pure, sublime kind of discourse! No word, no command, no advice—only the silent picture, the deed."[13] The created universe is the lasting monument whereby God instructs men through the ubiquitous primordial hieroglyph. Mixing together an odd assortment from Neoplatonic mysticism, Leibnizian monadology, and the modish fascination with things Egyptian, Herder found the macrocosmic original paradigm reflected in all microcosmic phenomena. As further support for divine origin, Herder maintained that written language preceded speech, or at least they must have developed simultaneously, like "two sisters hand in hand." The universal intelligibility of the all-important hieroglyph suggests that early linguistic development was visual rather than audible. "It was no doubt simpler to copy the thing itself . . . than to control, say, a tenth portion of exhaled breath with the haphazardly uneven, capricious sound of the mouth."[14] In direct contradiction of the prize essay, vision is taken to be the most fundamental sense and appropriate medium for language. As a pictorial copy of divine creation and of the omnipresent hieroglyph, original script was an *imitatio dei*. Since the *Oldest Document* was published anonymously, Herder directly criticized his own prize essay, stating that it was supposed to be followed by a second part containing "modifications, reservations, and applications."[15]

The new solution was no more satisfying to Hamann. In his letter of reconciliation Herder expressed surprise that the Magus should have raised such fierce objection to the prize essay:

Meanwhile it is still incomprehensible to me how . . . your version of the gift of speech differs from mine. That it is God who effects language through men—who doubts this? . . . That he did not effect it mystically, however, but through nature, animals, a pantheon of speaking tones, a compulsion of human necessities—who has assumed this more than I?[16]

Herder's disingenuous concession that a divine role could be incorporated into the framework of the *Preisschrift* left Hamann unmoved. As to Herder's new theory, although Hamann concealed his displeasure in correspondence with the author and in published remarks,[17] he was quite frank elsewhere: "You know what a rage I went into on account of the prize essay. When the *Oldest Document* appeared, that had just blown over. Fortunately, that is at rest now and I have no desire to touch off the machine again. . . . To be sure, some of my 'seminal germs' seem to have grown through Herder's diligence of pen into flowers and blossoms; but I would have preferred fruits—and ripe ones."[18]

The fourth part of the *Oldest Document,* published separately in 1776, differed in tone from the earlier ones, probably on account of the poor reviews which these received. The origin of language was treated briefly, a less mysterious version of divine origin. Attempts to explain language as "the spontaneous generation of human nature" are hypothetical at best: "Either it involves a dead linguistic capacity, which is actually recognizable only from its fruition, so that it remains eternally in question how it came to life; or else man is abandoned to the play of chance, and that is supposed to teach him language."[19] Rather than try to solve the dilemmas, Herder now satisfied himself with mere assertion: "God spoke to Adam—note the paternal education. God awakened and led him with the word of his mouth. . . . God spoke to man and man spoke. God was his word and this omnipotent word communicated itself then to all of nature. . . . Thus everything spoke after God, mimicked him, as it were, and awakened human language through overflowing compassion."[20] This is the extent of Herder's language theory as of 1776, a striking example of Abbt's apprehension that speculations about language origin might only lead to an accumulation of erasures and retractions.

The Spirit of Hebrew Poetry (1782–1783) was and is one of Herder's most popular works. Much of it is devoted to analysis of language—impassioned passages on "primitive" (i.e., Hebrew) style and expression; yet the work is further evidence that Herder had renounced all pretensions to a serious theory of the origin of language. Since he followed the lines of the Mosaic account, Herder felt compelled to speak about the problem, but evaded any specific thesis by tendering a poem, adapted from James Macpherson:

> Hail to thee! formless child of human breath,
> The sister of the angels, oh sweet speech!
> Without your faithful service, the full heart
> Would lie beneath sensation's burden crushed;
> No song of ancient times would ever touch
> A human ear; prehistory would be hushed;
> Unechoed then man's step as is the beast's;
> The wise man's soul would be his grand song's grave. . . .
>
> For you, Creator, gave to human mind
> Your second artful secret, giving sound
> A pictured form, to grasp it once again
> In weak, soft features of angelic script. . . .
>
> Come, holy shadows, come and sanctify
> My lips and speech. . . .[21]

Such poetastery hardly substitutes for a philosophical hypothesis about language origin. The desideratum is ostensibly filled in a passage of a subsequent chapter, here quoted in its entirety:

> *Euthyphron.* By the way, doesn't it strike you as a fine feature of Paradise when God leads the animals to Adam to see how he will name them? Through this firsthand recognition man formed his powers of perception, comparison, abstraction, reason, and language. The first names of his dictionary were the living sounds of animals, modified for his own speech organs and according to his own perceptions. Man gained his first intuition concerning dispositions and characters from the animals: For on the face, gait, and whole manner of life of each animal there is imprinted its individual character—peculiar, personal, constant, and immutable. Thus the deity treated man to a perpetual Aesopian fable. No poetic saga of Paradise has omitted the depiction of man in conversation with the animals: man their king, master and eldest brother; the animals all peaceful among themselves, all devoted and subject to man.[22]

The passage is of interest only for what it does not say. In light of this evasion, it is clear why Herder turned to poetry to state his views. Poetry, even inferior poetry, is at least assertive. Ten years after publication of the prize essay, Herder had almost nothing to say about the origin of language. The embryonic ideas of the prize essay had come to an abortive end.

During the very years of Herder's progressive confusion, Lord Monboddo was publishing *Of the Origin and Progress of Language* (1773–1789). Herder induced his friend E. A. Schmid to render the first two volumes into German, and he himself provided a preface, composed early in 1784. "This subject matter is almost exhausted by [Monboddo] and I believe that it is only necessary to continue along this same path in order to arrive at a precise definition and explanation of the nature of man under various circumstances."[23] Herder's minor criticisms are all expressed with great reserve: "These are all trivialities, which do not affect the heart of the work."[24] Yet there is little reason why Herder *should have* praised Monboddo, either from the standpoint of the prize essay or of his subsequent version of divine origin. Book One of Monboddo's protracted work stipulated "that language is not natural to man"; whereas the prize essay had argued the opposite. Monboddo asserted that orangutans had the "power of power" of language, that is, that the potentiality for language need not actualize itself; whereas Herder's attack on *réflexion en puissance,* his insistence that language is a human tendency which *must* express itself, directly contradicted Monboddo. Herder even singled out some of the passages which he "should have" criticized, had he been consistent, but he quickly retreated to the lame concession that the points were not so significant after all. Since Herder does not seem to have been the victim of total intellectual amnesia in other regards, the conclusion is inescapable that he had succumbed to massive confusion concerning the origin of language.

A few weeks after composing the preface to Monboddo, Herder was busily engaged in writing *Ideas for a Philosophy of the History of Mankind*. Considerations regarding language origin were included in the fourth book (Part One, 1784) and the ninth (Part Two, 1785)— after Herder had located the place of the earth within the universe, animals on the earth, and man within the animal kingdom. In the former, Herder tried to explain man's special qualities—including his rationality, artistic and linguistic capacities, freedom, religiosity, and hope of immortality—by pinpointing the physiological basis for these characteristics in man's upright gait, so that this physical factor is made the necessary condition for man's total "spiritual" being. The elevation of man's posture facilitated the development of his elevated faculties— a theorem which Herder elaborated at some length. The same faculties would have lain dormant were they not activated by human language.

Only through speech is the slumbering reason awakened! Rather, the naked potentiality, which left to itself would have remained forever dead, becomes through language a living force and actuality. . . . Therefore one can and one must view the refined organs of speech as the rudder of our reason, language as the divine spark which gradually inflamed our senses and our thoughts.[25]

Language is here taken as efficient cause, the catalyst bringing man's latent powers into play. In the same passage, Herder employed such phrases as "the language of God," "the divine gift of speech," "the divine art of ideas," and the like. He clearly implied divine origin throughout the chapter, but never elucidated his reasons. Although Herder assigned an important, even central place to language in the elaborate scheme of the *Ideas*, clearly the question of its origin was no longer crucial for him. The blatant contradictions between the position here and that taken in the preface to Monboddo indicate that Herder no longer envisioned (or cared about) the full scope of the problem.

In the ninth book of the *Ideas* Herder was more careful, partly because of Kant's caustic review of Part One. Still, the hypothesis of divine origin is left as bare assertion:

If someone should pose us with a riddle, asking how visual images and all our various sensations could be put into tones, and how these tones could be communicated with such inherent force that they express and arouse thoughts, we should no doubt consider this puzzle the brainstorm of a madman. . . . Yet the deity solved the problem *in actu*. The breath of our mouths becomes the depiction of the world, the imprint of our thoughts, the sentiment in someone else's soul.[26]

Although he once again employed the phraseology of the prize essay, Herder admitted that he had left divine origin unexplained.[27] Perhaps God's role in this theory of language was only that of the efficient cause demanded by some of the critics, a prime mover setting the linguistic apparatus in motion, the tongue wagging. Herder did not explain why he now introduced God; he explained little.

It is not surprising that Herder, when reading Rousseau's *Essay on the Origin of Languages* in 1782, wrote to Hamann blandly that the essay contained "materials already well known, but forcefully and beautifully stated."[28] It is not surprising that Herder—who in 1772 did not even want to have the prize essay published without his own reservations or rebuttal included—saw a second edition through the press in 1780 with none but stylistic revisions. It is not surprising that fourteen years later Herder—"somewhat contrary to my previous opinion,"[29] as he admitted—reversed his position once again in his *Metacritique* and supported the theory of human origin. It is apparent that these reversals, after Hamann's shattering but ambiguous critique, were not changes of mind; they were tokens of a grand renunciation.

A Solution Assumed

However much Herder himself may have become befuddled about the origin of language, or indifferent toward it, his prize essay and its hypothesis of human origin won the day in popular acceptance. During the first half of the 1780s there was a proliferation of natural and physicalistic explanations, in treatises directly related to the subject, but also in reviews, philosophies of history, and works on the culture of the ancient Greeks and Hebrews. Three things are noteworthy in this indisputable triumph of Herder's theory: the extent to which authors fell in line, even though the problem of language origin was of no immediate interest to them; the way in which human origin was simply assumed, as though it required no explanation—at least for sensible readers; and the ways in which Herder was misunderstood even by those who cited his authority.

Johann Christoph Gatterer and August Ludwig von Schlözer are egregious examples of the first phenomenon, as both shifted their positions with the prevailing intellectual winds. In a work on universal history published in 1765 Gatterer was a modified Biblicist, affirming that at least the ability to speak, if not speech itself, was innate and divinely endowed.[30] Twenty years later Gatterer's *World History in Its Total Compass* still gave credence to the scriptural account, but interpreted it as implying the human origin of language.[31] In 1772, the year that the *Preisschrift* was published, Schlözer emphasized the Tower of Babel story and the unity of mankind despite linguistic diversity.[32] In his *World History* (1785), Schlözer too admitted the human origin of language, referring to speech as a "work of nature."[33] This was à la mode; and vogues are notoriously fickle.

Johann Georg Heinrich Feder nearly parroted Herder's prize essay. Although he had shortly before declared himself incompetent to judge on technical linguistic matters,[34] in his "Summary of the Probable History of the Natural Origin of Language" (1783) Feder divided the doubters of human origin into two groups: those who exaggerated the orderliness of human speech in the belief that Greek, French, or German are typical of all language; and those who exaggerated the coarseness and childishness of the primitive mind. "But the question is this: whether, through the machinery of human nature, operating in many men who are united with one another, gradually, after hundreds of years, such a language as for instance that of the most wild savages in South America could not develop to the perfection of the Greek or the German."[35] Feder's answer is, predictably, affirmative; yet his specific reasons are of slight interest. The question had become academic, the answers repetitious.

Johann Christoph Adelung is best known as a precursor of comparative linguistics, because of his monumental *Mithridates*, an annotated compilation of the Lord's Prayer rendered in all known languages. In 1781 Adelung appended a second volume to his *German Grammar,* entitled *On the Origin of Language and the Structure of Words, Especially of German.* His main concern throughout was with etymology, and the complex of questions previously included as aspects of the problem of origin are given only brief and perfunctory treatment. In fact, Adelung disposed of them by simply stating his assumptions.

It is assumed: (1) That language was invented by men. To have it invented or immediately revealed to man by God is indeed very convenient, but it has nothing in its favor other than its convenience. The whole structure of language shows that it is very human. (2) That man did not invent language by chance, much less for pleasure or as a leisurely diversion, but that the necessity to speak is most closely connected with his nature and his destiny for social life. Thus without language he could not be man and without having invented language he could not be a reasonable creature. (3) That language was not invented by cultured men gifted with excellent insights and knowledge, but by the simple, completely coarse, and sensuous children of Nature, as they came from the hands of the Creator.[36]

Adelung was forthright: He freely admitted that he considered the solution of the problem of origin a foregone conclusion.

The next year Adelung published an *Attempt at a History of the Culture of the Human Race,* in which he showed himself an unmitigated progressist and also touched on the matter of language origin. No matter how lofty man's ultimate estate, his initial condition was lowly. It was only in his potentialities for humanity, rationality, and society that man differed from the animals. Following Herder, Adelung located the underlying capacity for all of these in man's *Besonnenheit.*[37] Adelung again simply assumed the correctness of Herder's hypothesis, and saw his own task as one of elaboration and substantiation through etymological and historical evidences.

The whole dispute [about divine and human origin] ceases to be a problem as soon as one comes to know the structure of languages; since there is nothing in evidence there which surpasses the powers of even the most coarse and sensuous human being, indeed because everything is so arranged that even the most sensuous man (one right on the borderline of the animal kingdom) not only *can* invent language, but even *must* invent it. . . . Since I cannot make use of the proof for the human origin of language here, . . . although it is so convincing that all contradiction evaporates immediately . . . , I must turn to other matters.[38]

Adelung was so confident of his readers' agreement, that he felt no need to defend the theory of human origin—no more, say, than one would belabor the arguments for the heliocentric theory.

The overwhelming acceptance of Herder's version of human origin sometimes involved ludicrous distortions, which Herder himself would no doubt have pointed out, had he not abandoned the position altogether. Adelung, copying Herder's thesis that hearing is the median sense, broke down the various tones of the "phonetic alphabet" into their original onomatopoeic meanings.[39] In his *Italian Journey,* Goethe mentioned the prize essay in the context of an incident late in 1787. His traveling companion, Karl Phillipp Moritz, had devised an etymological game, with which they wiled away the tedious interludes of their journey, and he had concocted a flippant theory of language to go with it. Maintaining that letters are not arbitrary signs but grounded in the necessities of human nature, Moritz invented an "alphabet of the understanding and of the senses," attributing to each letter-sound some inherent meaning. Originally all men spoke in these tones, but with the external influences of environment and false education, the various national languages wandered from the true path of nature, substituting conventional and inferior letter-sounds. In their game, the sojourners—much like the joking Socrates of the Cratylus— invented "true words" and "true names" derived from this "original alphabet." In mentioning the pastime, Goethe reminisced:

At that time, in the wake of Herder's prize essay and in conformity with the general intellectual tendencies, it was commonly thought: The human race did not gradually spread itself over the earth from an Oriental couple, but at a certain remarkably productive time of the world, after Nature had tried to produce the different species of animals step by step, the human race came forth then and there in many a propitious environment in a more or less fully developed state. In a most intimate relationship with the human organs and mental faculties, language was innate to man. . . .[40]

Even allowing that this occurred some seventeen years after Herder composed the prize essay and that Goethe only wrote the *Italian Journey* another thirty years later, it is still hard to see how Goethe—who was with Herder in Strassburg in 1770 and read the manuscript as it was being written—could have interpreted any of this as being in the spirit of the *Preisschrift.*

The very success of Herder's prize essay undermined interest in the question of the origin of language. Authors satisfied themselves with mere assertions or stated assumptions and to that extent ignored the substance of the question. The most fantastic and alien distortions were defended as being "in the spirit of the prize essay," as though that were a self-validating argument. And Herder himself became increasingly confused. Virtually nothing was written directly about the origin of language, particularly in Germany, between 1785 and 1795. The question's revival would require a new framework and a different focus.

THE RISE
AND FALL
OF A FINAL
SOLUTION

[9]

EXPLOSION
OF THE QUESTION

The abating curiosity about the origin of language in the aftermath of Herder's prize essay and the virtual suspension of debate
after 1785 were followed by a revival of interest a decade later. Much
of the renewed concern was inspired by the early school of German
romanticism, still embryonic in 1795 and identifiable only in retrospect,
born suddenly, growing quickly into a state of profound confusion, and
already diffuse just after the turn of the century. The romantic movement can be roughly divided into three periods: "Early romanticism"
terminates with the death of Novalis in 1801 and the abandonment of
Das Athenäum, the critical journal edited by the Schlegel brothers;
"middle romanticism" was intimately associated with the search for a
German national identity, partly in literature, but even more so in the
wars of liberation against Napoleonic conquest and occupation; "late
romanticism" dates after 1815 and the Congress of Vienna. Henrik
Steffens compared the disruption of the romantics' original harmonious
unity to a "spiritual tower of Babel," after which the individual members could no longer understand one another.[1] Nonetheless, the nineteenth-century movements which would devote attention to the origin
of language—nationalism, illuminism, idealism, comparative linguistics, even evolutionism—gestated in the womb of early romanticism.

The question of the origin of language reappeared in an "ex-
ploded" form: Sometimes the limits of the question were removed and
its scope expanded; sometimes it was so shattered that its identity is
barely recognizable, and fragments of the theme appear in wholly unexpected places; sometimes the question was nearly obliterated. The
specific problem of linguistic beginnings was often absorbed into con-

siderations of the general source, cause, and essence of language. Despite the important place that romanticism gave to historical consciousness and research, the immediate effect of its treatments of language origin was to make that question less historical in character and intent than it had been in the eighteenth century. Herder's prize essay was admired for its expansion of the problem rather than its call for intensified historical investigation. The question was significantly "dehistoricized."

The explosion of the question also brought on its fragmentation. Such fragmentation occurred in two principal ways and from opposite impulses. In the early part of the century the romanticists were so intent on an intuition or comprehension of "the All," that their written works exemplified the Anaxagorean principle *quodlibet in quolibet,* "everything [can be found] in everything."[2] In an artful attempt to recapture or recreate the original unity of form and content, of media and messages, they interlaced their themes into grandiose and intricate patterns, so that the mere recognition of the relation between parts and whole sometimes requires an intuitive leap of the romantic imagination itself. Bits and pieces of the language origin motif appear as epicycles in their mobile philosophic galaxy. The fragmentation of the question also occurred in more mundane ways as the century wore on. The rise of positivism, the successes of comparative linguistics, and the increasingly bold claims that language study had now reached a scientific level led to the demand for specialization and the division of scholarly labors. The particularization of research in the progress of "normal science" left fewer and fewer linguists willing to take on the comprehensive question of language origin. At the same time that scientists were dividing up their individual labors, the emerging phenomenon of the "two cultures" separated scientists from humanists, *Naturwissenschaftler* from *Geisteswissenschaftler,* and linguistists from poets. As individual disciplines declared their independence by seceding from philosophy, their own underlying "philosophies" became fragmentary at best.

The Question "Dehistoricized"

In 1795 Fichte published a treatise, "Concerning the Faculty of Speech and the Origin of Language." His sketch of the advancement of language—first a set of visual and vocal signs imitating natural things, transformation of these into a purely auditory system, the extension of signs in progressive levels of abstraction, concurrent refinement of grammar—is commonplace. What is striking is the confident manner in which he proposed a new method of inquiry.

In an investigation of the origin of language one cannot rely on hypotheses, on the arbitrary suggestion of special circumstances under which a language might perhaps have arisen. There are so many factors which might have guided men in the invention and elaboration of language that no inquiry could fully exhaust them; and hence with this method we would arrive at as many half-true explanations of the problem as there are investigations undertaken. One cannot content himself therefore with showing that and approximately how a language *could have been* invented; rather one must deduce the necessity of this invention from the nature of human reason: One must show that and how language *must have been* invented.[3]

A theory of language origin must be as conclusive as a deductive proof, and its premises must include demonstrable truths about language and human nature. For Fichte, language is the willful expression of thoughts and feelings through arbitrary (*willkürliche*) signs. He repeatedly emphasizes the arbitrariness of language making and of human nature. Given this, the question can be reduced to two parts:

(1) Whatever brought man upon the idea of inventing language? (2) In which natural laws does the reason lie that this idea was carried out in precisely this way? . . . Are there in human nature means which one necessarily had to employ in order to realize the idea of a language? . . . If we could find such means, then it should be possible to construct an a priori history of language.[4]

The phrase "a priori history" is the most revealing clue to the method Fichte had in mind.[5] According to common philosophical usage, where the factual is taken to be a posteriori, the phrase would seem to be self-contradictory. Nor was Fichte as clear on the point as either Vico before or Hegel after him.[6] With the phrase Fichte apparently meant the following: History is the grand pattern of human actions which follow from human nature; human nature is immediately knowable, whereas past events are at best mediately knowable; the laws of deduction are more clear and more certain than all the rules of historical evidence; therefore, the only conclusive historical explanation, of language or anything else, must be deduced from the knowable facts of human nature. The two terms of the title, the "faculty of speech" and the "origin of language," are identified, because Fichte assumed that the past origin of language must have the same explanation as the present ability to speak.

The certainty of conclusions, of course, depends on the certainty of premises. Fichte took as his own starting point the idea that the knowable fact about human nature is man's drive to subjugate nature to himself. Man, a thinking thing, an ego, is essentially rational; hence man conquers nature as he subjects it to the principles of rationality. Since language is a primary means whereby man "rationalizes" nature, language evolves necessarily: Thus Fichte constructed the groundwork for its a priori evolution. This explanation elaborates Fichte's fundamental philosophical notion of the self-positing ego. If the drive to subjugate nature is so thoroughly embedded in human character, however, why is there not an equally necessary desire of men to subjugate other men? Fichte denied that there is such a tendency, appealing to the "highest principle in man: that he should always be at one with himself."[7] This principle determines both man's need to subdue alien nature and the absence of a need to subjugate other men, for nature must be *made* rational, whereas men *are* so already and by innate character. The "natural" relationship among men, therefore, is one of equitable sociability rather than subjugation, and language is a means toward this proper human end.

For Fichte in 1795 these were the happy and inescapable facts about human nature. From these premises he confidently deduced a solution to the problem of language origin. His confidence was such that he saw no need to introduce empirical evidence in support of his thesis. He included no data from ancient or primitive languages or their historical development; nor did Fichte appeal to any philologists or linguists or any other philosophers. What, after all, could be more certain than deductive proof? Later on, Fichte became more hesitant about his premises.

Friedrich Schlegel read Fichte's essay with enthusiasm and wrote to his brother: "Anyway, the first thought is a good one. Anyone who fails to show how language *must* necessarily have developed might as well stay at home. Anybody is capable of dreaming how it *might have* originated."[8] August Wilhelm Schlegel in his turn took up the same theme when he had occasion to review Bernhardi's *Sprachlehre* in 1803:[9]

People flattered themselves that they had penetrated to the original grounds of a mode of action, when they had only arrived at the proximate cause of development. It is in this way that the question concerning the origin of language has usually been answered. Attempts to clarify this question . . . have relied partly on the observation of actual languages and partly on the reports of travelers about savage peoples. . . . Such investigations, when they are not bound to any point of certainty, are always and necessarily muddied by manifold misunderstandings and can be bandied about endlessly to no particular purpose. It is not of the essence to show that this or that *might* have contributed [to the origin of language], but that it would be necessary for it to happen this way at all times.[10]

Like Fichte, A. W. Schlegel still accepted the rationalist notion that factual or historical truths can have no more than probable and relative validity, which was directly contrary to the assumption of many later linguists that a nonhypothetical answer to the problem of origin could only be achieved through employment of a strictly historical and precisely empirical method. Schlegel desired to disentangle the "historical aspect" of the question from its "philosophical aspect, that is, the deduction of language from the nature of the human mind": "We do not view the origin of language as something that can be placed at a particular point in time; rather we consider it in the sense in which language always arises, just as the creation of the world is something which is constantly renewed."[11]

The detachment of the idea of original language from the boundaries of historical time and space seemed to imply that language lives and acts by its own independent rules and dynamics, almost as though language would exist even if there were no speakers of it. To explain the linguistic phenomena one could postulate a quasi-Kantian *noumenon,* language-in-itself or language-as-such. Thus Novalis:

From afar I heard say: Un-understandability is only a consequence of the un-understanding, which seeks that which it [already] has and thus never finds anything else. One does not understand language, because language does not understand itself, does not want to understand; pure Sanskrit would speak in order to speak, because speaking would be its pleasure and its nature.[12]

Original language is pure self-expression, but it is not so much the creativity of either philosophers, poets or legislators as that of language itself. In his "Monologue" Novalis explained poetry as "language enthusiasm": "Whoever has a fine feeling for the finger technique [of language], its measure, its musical spirit; whoever perceives in himself the gentle working of its inner nature and moves his tongue or hand accordingly, he will be a prophet."[13] He began:

Actually it is a foolish business when it comes to speaking and writing: The real conversation is a mere wordplay. One can only wonder at the ridiculous error of people in believing that they speak for the sake of things. The essential idiosyncrasy of language, that language only cares about itself—this nobody knows. That is why language is such a wonderful and fruitful mystery; for, if someone speaks simply for the sake of speaking, he expresses the most splendid and original truths. But if he wants to speak about something definite, then fickle language makes him say the most ridiculous and mixed-up rubbish. This is the cause of the hatred which so many serious people entertain against language. They notice the sportiveness of language, but they do not realize that despicable babbling is the infinitely serious side of language. If only it could be made clear to people that language is like mathematical formulae. They make up a world for themselves—they simply play with themselves, express nothing other than their own wonderful natures, and it is for exactly this reason that they are so expressive—that is why the curious interplay of relationships among things mirrors itself in them. It is because of their freedom that they are members of nature, and the world-soul expresses itself in their free motions and makes them into a delicate design and measure of things. So it is with language. . . .[14]

This personification of language, its seeming separability from the will and personality of speakers, was to reappear in postromantic disguise: Comparative linguists later claimed that they too studied language in itself, language as such—but by then the notion would be stripped of both philosophy and poetry.

Antione de Rivarol also desired to see the question of language origin removed from historical specificity. Most famous as an aphorist and author of an essay on the universality of French—which received the prize of the Berlin Academy—Rivarol was a refugee from the French Revolution and one of its most incisive critics. His comprehensive commentary on eighteenth-century philosophy, and censure of it as a source of revolutionary terror, is the lengthy but unfinished *Preliminary Discourse,* intended to serve as the preface to a new dictionary of the French language. Critical of all empiricism, *idéologie,* and analysis, Rivarol suggested that there is a mode of consciousness or sensibility in human beings which is temporally and structurally prior to any act of sensation and which is the organizing principle for all operations of the mind. He referred to this as *sentiment* and identified it with the proper concept of the self, since it is the precondition for all particular mental functions. In *sentiment* we see "the whole man"; distinctions within this totality have analytic value only and are dangerous if taken to be natural divisions. "A veritable *malheur* attaches to the dissection of the human spirit. When nature makes a man, she constructs an edifice in which all the parts are raised together; and when we explain it, we demolish it by exposing in succession the work which she performs at once."[15] The Enlighteners erred, according to Rivarol, by isolating reason from the whole self and then attempting to make it absolute as a theoretical entity and social force. The egalitarian, cosmopolitan, and philosophic aspirations of the Enlighteners were so far in excess of realistic possibilities that their fine-sounding ideals and lofty abstractions had to turn into the destructive forces of terror, fanaticism, and barbarism.[16]

For Rivarol, the historical approach to the problem of language origin misleads inquirers into elusive details, which obscure the nature of the whole self rather than clarifying it. In the initial sections of the *Preliminary Discourse,* Rivarol dealt with "the origin of speech" and "the state of the question." He doubted that there can be any explanation of primordial beginnings, because the movement of the human spirit has covered them up with "an eternal obscurity." The historical question should be replaced by the fundamental problem about language, its combination of the material and mental, sound and meaning. "It is not a question whether man could discover the variety of vowels and consonants. Inasmuch as he has in fact done so, we can conclude that he could do so. But the miracle is at work constantly, for the human race begins anew at every moment, and children cry and articulate without analyzing their articulation. . . ."[17] Rather than speak of beginnings, Rivarol used vague phrases such as "the history of language in general" or "description of the human mind in the creation of language in general." "The best history of human understanding should, in time, result in deepened knowledge of language. Speech is, in effect, the experimental physics of the soul: Each word is an event; each phrase is an analysis or development; each book is a longer or shorter revelation of sentiment and thought."[18]

When the historical dimension of the question was not subordinated, and the problem of origin not identified with source, cause, or essence, linguistic beginnings were commonly displaced into the most distant recesses of history. Curiosity was roused about such fictive topics as the language of the Golden Age, of Adam and Eve before the fall, the communication of angels and eternal spirits, and generally about the speech of the pre-Babel epoch. Although these were languages supposedly in time, they lay beyond the pale of knowable human history, immune to empirical verification or disproof. Here the "de-historicizing" of the question encouraged totally liberated and fanciful conjecture. The inherent obscurity of the problem was exploited by writers who concocted wondrous-sounding and fully irrelevant theories.

It was to this that Hegel objected in *The Philosophy of History,* when he dismissed myths of the Golden Age:

[The representation (*Vorstellung*) of a state of nature is] nothing more than an assumption of historical existence made in the twilight of hypothesizing reflection. A pretension of an entirely different sort—namely, not an assumption which proceeds from thought, but the assumption of a historical fact and simultaneously of its higher confirmation—consists in another representation which is often put forward nowadays in certain quarters. The first paradisiacal condition of man is therein taken up again—[the view which] had earlier been elaborated by the theologians after their fashion, that is, that God spoke Hebrew with Adam—but now remodeled in accordance with other requirements.[19]

Such conjectures, Hegel protested, are of little use and are more misleading than the Biblical account itself. "For the philosophical view it is fitting and worthy to take up history only at that point where rationality begins to enter into worldy existence, (not where that is still only a possibility), where there is at hand a condition in which [rationality] makes its appearance in consciousness, will, and action."[20] Here Hegel followed the lead of Kant, who acknowledged that language acquisition must have been a human event, but deliberately ignored it in his "Conjectural Beginning of Human History": "[These are skills] of which I assume that man is already possessed, in order to concentrate on the development of morality in his action and passion—which presupposses that skill."[21] Hegel, in effect, cast under philosophical suspicion all discussion of human prehistory and therewith of the primordial beginnings of language.

Friedrich Schmitthenner, a professor at Giessen, identified the very notion of an original language (*Ursprache*) with "the idea of language," "language in general as it takes on actual appearance in specific languages," "a concept which correlates with the concept of humanity in general."[22] Schmitthenner's *Ursprachlehre*, published in 1826, was in fact an essay in universal grammar based on rigid metaphysical principles and some loosely connected linguistic evidence. He specifically rejected the relevance of historical material: *"Ursprachlehre* is the science of the *Ursprache* as the idea of language. Since the idea is exempt from the changeability and fluctuation of temporal things and remains one with itself through eternal self-maintenance, *Ursprachlehre* does not really consider anything which is subject to historical development and empirical investigation."[23] An equally nonhistorical approach was attributed to Wilhelm von Humboldt by his editor and interpreter, Haymann Steinthal. Steinthal wrote—and the point is debatable—that Humboldt transformed the question of language origin out of the eighteenth-century mode: "To solve the contradictions which arise by necessity from the essence of language is to explain the origin of language. . . . [Humboldt] identified origin with essence, and changed the *wherefrom?* into a *what?*"[24] If the problem of the origin of language is not a historical question, however, does it thereby lose or gain contemporary relevance?

The Question "Politicized"

In some hands the dehistoricized version of language origin became a weapon in the arsenal of political rhetoric. In the 1790s Fichte had been a leading exponent of democratic cosmopolitanism, and he remained an apologist for the French revolutionary cause long after other German republicans had become disenchanted by the Terror and Napoleonic imperialism. In 1806, however, shortly before Napoleon's victory at Jena, Fichte confessed to the nationalistic credo in *Patriotism and its Opposite,* albeit more in resignation than in chauvinistic enthusiasm. "Cosmopolitanism is the dominant will to attain the purpose of human existence in humanity itself. Patriotism is the will to attain the same purpose first in that nation of which we are members, and then to let this success expand from that nation to the whole of humanity."[25] If the forces of international enlightenment had proved to be but another army of the night, perhaps a more modest program of national education would yield better results. In the winter of 1807–1808, in a Berlin occupied by the military forces he had once expected to be the harbingers of peace and reason, Fichte delivered his *Speeches to the German Nation.*

In the *Speeches* Fichte proposed a program of national education. He saw the current times as an age in which selfishness was in the process of destroying itself. This self-destruction was historically necessary because the self-seeking of rulers had come to dominate the advantage of individuals, because the totalitarian dictates of self-interest undermined the actual freedom of the self to determine its independent goals, and because one selfish regime would try to subjugate others and thus cause wars.[26] Patriotism, quite obviously, can induce people to transcend individual self-interest; but patriotism must be educated for it to be a power for good in the advancement of humanity. The possibilities of education are not unlimited: It cannot originate anything, but only cultivate the seeds already given. If a people is to be educated, it cannot have cut itself off from its origins or become alienated from its germinal self. Fichte concluded that the German nation met the qualifications to become, through education, the educator of and for humanity. The Germans had not severed connections with their original roots: They were what Fichte called an *Urvolk* speaking an

Ursprache. The Germans' qualifications for a program of national education did not follow from superior original endowment, but from their greater retention of it. It was not a matter of racial purity, but of spiritual continuity. The very disunity of Germany proved that this was a nation without a state: The term *German* properly referred to a cultural and linguistic entity.[27] The Germans retained their original language, neither adopting that of any conquering foreigner or conquered natives. Romance peoples, in contrast, by borrowing language and institutions from the Latins, had severed themselves from their beginnings and doomed themselves to alienation. The same was true, to a lesser degree, of Englishmen and Scandinavians. All of this did not bestow special rights so much as it gave increased responsibility to the German people. To this effect Fichte addressed his auditors in the last speech: "To you has fallen the greater fate of founding the realm of spirit and reason and destroying the domination of the world by raw physical force. . . . Of all modern peoples, it is in you that the seed of human perfectibility lies most decisively, and it is you who are entrusted with the task of caring for its progress."[28]

Fichte described the "original language" of an *Urvolk* as a living language, the derivative ones of "nonoriginal" peoples he considered dead. The German and the neo-Latin languages are as incomparable as life and death themselves. Through a living language, a speaker is indirectly related to his original forbears; in a dead language he is alienated from them. The original intuitions and sensations of the *Volk* are still expressed in a living language, and hence there is no gap between the sensuous and later abstract formulations; dead languages deal either with earthly things or floating abstractions, but these are never related to one another. A living language is immediately clear to its users; a dead language is "basically un-understandable." A living language provides a grasp upon the flow of life without conscious mediation; in a dead language the signs have no power of their own and require historical and philological clarification. The words of a living language flow necessarily from its origins; the words of a dead language are arbitrary. The roots in a living language are life and create vitality; the expressions of a dead language invite deceptive sloganeering.[29]

Such a fundamentally dead and unintelligible language easily lends itself to the misuse of beautifying human corruption, something impossible in a language which never died out. As an example I use the three notorious words, *Humanität, Popularität, Liberalität.* . . . Had we expressed to a German what those foreign words are supposed to mean (if they mean anything at all) in his own words and in the context of his own sensuous images and symbols—*Menschenfreundlichkeit, Leutseligkeit, Edelmut*—then he would have understood us.[30]

The fact that German is an *Ursprache* does not mean that it is static. On the contrary, as a living language it is always active and creative.

After millenia of change . . . it still remains the same single, living, natural power of language, which originally had to break forth just the way it did, which flowed on uninterruptedly through all modifications, and with each had to become what it did become, at the end of the process had to be what it is now, and in some time will be what it must then become.[31]

This vitality of change is Fichte's ground for asserting that a tradition of true poetic creation is only possible in a living language. And a philosophy which grasps reality and life is unthinkable in a dead language: There philosophy has as its function a sophisticated, but entirely irrelevent and trivial, explanation of the dictionary, a metacritique of language.[32] "With a people speaking a living language, spiritual education can give them a grasp upon life; for others, spiritual education and life would go each its separate way."[33]

Fichte extended the notion of originality and changed the definition of an *Ursprache*. Those things are original which flow from the first sources, and hence originality does not represent a point in time but a continuity within time. This was the step which allowed the identification of a modern language as an *Ursprache* without fanciful conjectures about Adamic speech; although Fichte did sometimes equate the original with the divine, so that the language and people who had not departed from the originals were like lingering sparks of the divine.[34] This changed conception of originality was easily wed with organistic metaphor: The original is living and growing, its life defined by the genetic laws of the organism. Whereas Fichte's earlier essay had emphasized the arbitrariness of language, the very term *Willkür* now was used as a pejorative epithet for dead languages. Living languages are not conventional: A natural force unfolds itself in them, which is their very originality.[35] In his earlier essay Fichte had identified "the orign of language" with "living languages." The question of the *Ursprache* was still detached from the specific historical past, but it was now applied to the historical present.

Fichte's *Speeches* were addressed to the entire German nation, but they were delivered to a small Berlin audience. It was several years before they achieved popularity with the general reading public and before their proposals were given serious attention by men of influence. After their success, however, the very concept of an original language was transformed. It was taken up by the more zealous nationalists and by language-purifiers, who attempted to exterminate Latin roots and French endings and replace them with homegrown alternatives. J. H. Campe produced a two-volume dictionary of Germanic substitutes for bastard foreign phrases.[36] In Campe's dictionary, *rendezvous* became *Stelldichein;* someone coached by F. L. Jahn wanted to change the *Universität* into a *Geistesturnanstalt* ("gymnasium of the spirit") ; and all German was beautified when the *Nase* ("nose") was remade into a *Gesichtsgiebel* ("gable of the face"). Until the nineteenth century, language cleansing was a marginal, mainly lower-class phenomenon. As Fichte's *Speeches* became popular, however, purification once again became the fashion, the linguistic arm of the wars of liberation. "Pure German" was pursued as a restoration of the language to its original integrity. Many writers—Joseph Görres, General von Clausewitz, and Adam von Müller among them—heralded German as an original tongue.[37] Pride of speech was a powerful motive in the drive for national status, and ultimately in the arrogance of power.

Ernst Moritz Arndt began as a disciple of Rousseau loosely tied to the romantic movement, but by 1805 he too joined the militant nationalists. In the heat of the wars of national liberation he articulated a doctrine of folk hatred. In a surreptitiously printed pamphlet, *Concerning Folk-Hatred and the Use of a Foreign Language* (1813), he advocated righteous warfare against all political, cultural, and linguistic tyranny: "The time has now come when the disgust which the upright German people has always felt for the French and Italians and their customs, can become a burning hatred . . . , when honest German will dominate instead of mendacious Romance. . . ."[38] "May this hatred glow as the religion of the German people, as a holy madness in all our hearts, and may it forever maintain us in our fidelity, honesty, and bravery."[39] In 1812 Arndt finally read Fichte's *Speeches* and thereafter referred to the originality of the German language.

Arndt viewed language as the bridge between the day and night of human life, thought projected to the level of the *Volk* soul: "The *Volk,* in its dark and secret life and action, plus individual great geniuses, create and form a language."[40] "Words are not something dead. They are the eternal archetypes [*Urbilder*] of sentiments and thoughts, fossilized and bewitched ideas, so to speak, which must be revivified in every moment by living speech and the warm, vital breath of the soul using them."[41] "Every language is the mysterious archetype, first, of a distant prehistory of which we can but dream; secondly, it is the archetype of a peculiar being and life, disclosed in large-scale association."[42] Arndt drew a curious distinction between "thinking peoples" and "speaking peoples"—soul- versus surface-oriented characters—and asserted that such peoples express themselves in different idioms.

It is precisely a speaking language which is the most dangerous. Whoever uses and practices one from his youth must necessarily see his intuitions and thoughts and feelings in an alien mirror; in the end he must see that which is innately German in a distorted way and hence all that is peculiarly his own will always remain a closed riddle for him.[43]

The catalogue of the virtues of German and the vices of French comprised a major portion of Arndt's work. French, a speaking language, lends itself to deception and linguistic malice. Like J. A. Schmeller—who, after the Congress of Vienna, argued that the Napoleonic *imperium* was not defeated so long as French was employed for negotiations and agreements[44]—Arndt felt that the use of French by educators, diplomats, and leaders was tantamount to a de facto subjugation of all Europe by the French.[45] It was for the sake of liberation that Arndt was so passionately concerned to preserve the original language and banish all vestiges of *Welschtum* and "un-Germanism." German is pure, French impure; German is decent and innocent, French sly and vain; German is true, French false.

Friedrich Baron de la Motte-Fouqué gave the conception of German as an original language a specifically patrician tone. Popular author and unabashed aristocrat, La Motte-Fouqué admired Fichte's *Speeches* and used them to argue the preeminence of Germans among Europeans and the supremacy of noblemen among Germans.

For me Germanism signifies a life which, with divine protection, has grown consistently and naturally from its own roots; Frenchdom, on the contrary, signifies a superficial experimentation with the most important matters of this world, moving from words to more words, hopping from one leap to another. . . . A historically developed language is the most unimpeachable and convincing witness for the unity and totality of all genuinely historical developments themselves.[46]

The continuum of its language gives the German people special status, and its aristocracy embodies this living tradition par excellence. The origin of the nobility is enshrouded in the same mysterious darkness as the origin of language. Unlike the English nobility, imposed through conquests on an alien population, German aristocracy is indigenous, joined in primordial solidarity with the *Volk* over which it lords. Maintenance of the purity of Germany's aristocracy and the originality of its language will assure its bright future and continued vitality.

Friedrich Ludwig Jahn became famous in his own land and infamous elsewhere through publication in 1810 of the nationalist manifesto, *Deutsches Volkstum*. In it he attacked the two alternatives to nationalism: individualism and cosmopolitanism. It is a "sweet illusion" that individuals can be self-determining ends in themselves, for everyone is born into a community which speaks a particular language and exemplifies a unique mode of thinking and feeling. It is also an illusion that anyone can transcend his community and identify with universal humanity. Humanity per se makes no appearance on the world-historical stage; rather the universal realizes itself by playing the roles of different peoples. The *Volk,* therefore, is the synthetic medium between individual man and universal humanity. *Volkstum* is the power of creativity which imbues the true and vital *Volk,* "its immanent nature, its motion and life; its power of propagation and ability to reproduce."[47] An equally influential work was the *Deutsche Turnkunst* (1816), the definitive exposition of the true German "athletic culture." Jahn was an active organizer of public athletic clubs and university fraternities, the *Burschenschaften,* which supplied many volunteers for the liberation armies. In *Deutsche Turnkunst* Jahn, like a Hobbesian sovereign, established definitions, devising an entire new gymnastic vocabulary which was *echt deutsch.*

By the time Jahn published the *Deutsche Turnkunst* he had appropriated the reinterpretation of *Urvolk* and *Ursprache* as extensible in time through organic development. The extended notion of originality led to a peculiar mixture of archaisms with neologisms in Jahn's vocabulary proposals and in his inimitable style. "The German language combines pure originality with far-ranging possibilities for further development, considerable age with youthful vigor. . . . In the flexibility for development lives the rejuvenation of language, the fountain of its immortality. In German the word-sources can be plumbed to their depths, but they will never be dried up."[48] To maintain the original purity of the mother tongue and its vital generative force, all coinages must be made from the indigenous primitive roots.

No word is to be considered extinct so long as the language is not dead; no word obsolete so long as the language still retains its youthful power. There is blessing and prosperity in buried roots which, though they are still green, can upon full growth bear trunks, branches, and twigs. The shoots and sprouts of the age-old basic roots announce a new spring after the long winter's numbness. . . . Unless the radicles are cultivated, language will be overladen like a packhorse and beast of burden, and it will finally succumb under the weight of the heavy mixture [of foreign elements]. Every original word which is brought back into usage is a copious spring, which nourishes the central stream, waters the valley path, and provides a flood tide for all who live in high places.[49]

To be sure, the metaphors are mixed, but no matter: "As an original language [German] has a clarity for its dowry which is lacking in all after-languages."[50]

Aftersprachen was the term of Jahn's invention to denote secondary or nonoriginal languages. The semiarchaic prefix *after-*, which can imply both posteriority and falsity, gives a clue to the xenophobia which animated Jahn's thought about language. Nonoriginal languages, like French, distort and confuse; they are really only pseudo-languages. Jahn suggested that people blush less at obscenities in foreign languages, that lies sound prettier in foreign languages, that a father who has his daughter learn French is no better than one who offers her up for prostitution, and that the use of French had made German men impotent and German wives dishonored. "Every man has just one mother; one mother tongue is enough for him also."[51] It is only "After-Germans" and perverted "linguistic weaklings" who think that German need go a-begging at foreign doors. Use of foreign words and phrases is the result of ignorance, laziness, pretension: "Multilingualism is the den of iniquity from which all the fogginess of books steams up."[52]

Foreign words, even when they are declared naturalized citizens one hundred thousand times, never get into the true blood. A foreign word always remains a mongrel, without any power of reproduction. . . . To Frenchify is to falsify—it is an emasculation of the original potency, a poisoning of the language spring, an obstruction of the developmental possibilities, and total linguistic nonsense.[53]

One can only guess how Father Jahn's obsessive concern with linguistic virility may have impressed his athlete devotees. But the *Ursprache* had a more spiritual aspect too: "The mother tongue is the original wisdom [*Urwissenschaftslehre*], which mediates sensuousness and spirituality, which marries sense and intellect. The mother tongue is the renewal of all revelation. . . ."[54] With the expanded concept of an *Ursprache* Jahn could fully identify original language with the Germanic mother tongue.

The French theocrats—Joseph de Maistre, Louis de Bonald, and Félicité de Lamennais—also put a specifically political slant on their theories of the divine origin of language. Bonald was the systematist of neo-Catholic conservatism, its scholastic apologist.[55] Although Bonald affirmed both the adequacy and necessity of divine revelation, he was not content with the mere assertion of it, but worked out arguments in demonstration of its rationality. Unlike Descartes, he insisted that philosophical reasoning must begin with an act of faith rather than with doubt; like him, he sought an indubitable first principle.[56] The primitive gift of speech was the fact which Bonald took as his starting point, his substitute for the *cogito, ergo sum*. Since there is no thought prior to language, the question of the origin of ideas is secondary to that of the origin of speech. Since man's sociability and his power of speech are coeval, neither language nor political society can have been deliberative inventions. The contract theory of either society or language shatters on its assumption that man could have lived without language and outside of society.

In sum, language is necessary in the sense that human society could not have existed without language any more than man could have lived outside of society: a new proof that man is not the inventor of language. Man discovers that which is useful or pleasurable, he even invents that which is evil; but he does not invent that which is necessary for him to be what he is, which exists before him and outside of him.[57]

If there can be no precedence between language and society, man must be both a speaking and social being by nature and necessity.

Against Rousseau's contract theory Bonald used Rousseau's analysis of the *aporiae* regarding language origin. Characterizing the various explanations of language origin as theistic, deistic, and atheistic—depending on whether they made God the actual donor of language, the giver only of the potentiality, or assigned God no role at all—Bonald asserted that the *aporiae* made nonsense of all theories but the first. Only "theophobia," the dogmatic refusal to allow any supernatural solutions, would lead anyone to admit the impasses and yet deny divine origin. It is not "theomania" but plain reason which supports the higher hypothesis. Going beyond negative proof, Bonald saw in the gift of speech the substance of original revelation and quintessence of primitive legislation.

[Natural religion] has been revealed through speech, and it is natural to men in the society of the primitive family, isolated from all other society; whereas [revealed religion] has been revealed through Scripture, and it is natural to men united in a national body. Undoubtedly, natural religion is a ray which God makes to light in our souls; but speech is the distinct light of the sun, without which it would make no impression on us. Speech is the light which illuminates every human being coming into this world.[58]

As the *lumen naturale,* original language constitutes true and authoritative law surpassing conventional human regulations.[59]

The original *institutio,* of which Hamann had spoken cryptically, was explicitly identified by Bonald with the corresponding traditions of nation and church, of secular and sacred history. Pierre Maine de Biran criticized this whole approach. By making original language into a *corpus,* Maine de Biran argued, Bonald was guilty of the same error as "atheistic" mechanists: He treated language as a wholly exterior phenomenon, as though no thoughtfulness went into the generation of it, as though it required no conscious appropriation by men. "The perpetual sophism of M. de Bonald consists in the fact that he takes as his model a language completely formed. . . ."[60] By positing a divine perfection at the commencement of linguistic history, Bonald ignored the "internal language of consciousness," without which language is little more than noise, at best unthinking verbal repetition. In the lofty terms of the higher hypothesis, Maine de Biran concluded, Bonald actually demeaned both speech and men—all for a politically convenient explanation of language origin.

In the competitive nationalism which developed during the eighteenth and nineteenth centuries, no country had a monopoly on chauvinistic excess and its curious rationalizations. Authors found shreds of linguistic, Biblical, ethnographic, or climatic evidence to identify the original language of Paradise with their own mother tongue. The presence of amber deposits convinced J. G. Hasse that the Garden of Eden was located in Eastern Prussia in the warmer days of prehistory.[61] Rowland Jones and James Parsons, Irishmen, had no doubt that the modern European language most nearly approximating the original was Gaelic.[62] Vincenzo Gioberti appealed to Vico's *ricorsi* to explain the primacy of Italian: He hazarded the guess that modern Italian was no corruption of decadent Latin, but a restoration of the pristine purity of its primary stage.[63] P. F. J. Müller, a student of Fichte who took his teacher literally, proved to his satisfaction that Adam conversed with Eve in original German.[64] Count Gobineau used the origin and history of language as a piece in his fabric of "scientific" analysis of racial inequalities: "Languages, unequal among themselves, are in perfect accord with the relative value of the races."[65] The fault of philologists, Gobineau found, was their assignment of a single origin to language: Languages are as polygenetic as the races that speak them.[66] J. Kempe had it down to the detail that God first spoke to Adam in Swedish, but Adam responded in Danish.[67]

No less self-serving were those theories which zealously proclaimed the universality and clarity, rather than the originality, of French or English. Rivarol wrote the classic paean to *la grandeur du Français:* "Ce qui n'est pas clair n'est pas français; ce qui n'est clair est encore anglais, italien, grec ou latin"[68]—and clarity demands that the slogan go untranslated. Bertrand Barère, on behalf of the Committee of Public Safety, called for *instituteurs de la langue française* to eliminate all "inequalities of language" by prohibiting the use of foreign languages and dialects in the French provinces:

The so-called Breton language, the Basque language, the German and Italian languages, have perpetuated the reign of fanaticism and superstition; have assured the domination of priests, noblemen, and patricians; have prevented the Revolution from penetrating into new and important departments; and have been able to favor the enemies of France.[69]

Federalism and superstitution speak Breton; emigration and hatred of the Republic speak German; counterrevolution speaks Italian; and fanaticism speaks Basque. Let us smash these instruments of harm and error.[70]

Jeremy Bentham demonstrated with a series of grammatical considerations—but never with his own style—that no language in the world matched modern English in economy and clarity.[71] And Noah Webster dreamed that America had "the fairest opportunity of establishing a national language . . . that ever presented itself to mankind."[72]

Within a century and a half, North America will be peopled with a hundred millions of men, *all speaking the same language.* Place this idea in comparison with the present and possible future bounds of the language in Europe—consider the Eastern Continent as inhabited by nations, whose knowledge and intercourse are embarrassed by differences of language; then anticipate the period when the people of one quarter of the world, will be able to associate and converse together like children of the same family. Compare this prospect, which is not visionary, with the state of the English language in Europe, almost confined to an Island and to a few millions of people; then let reason and reputation decide, how far America should be dependent on a transatlantic nation, for her standard and improvements in language.[73]

Webster's linguistic Americanism was unconcealed and unabashed.

In politically inspired language theory, truth, beauty, and virtue were regularly identified with original (or universal) language itself, rather than with the utterances that speakers might make within language. For Jahn and Arndt, French and Italian were intrinsically mendacious quâ languages, German was by nature pure and true. For Bonald original language was the very content of primitive revelation and legislation. For Rivarol French was clear per se. For Webster linguistic history had a manifest destiny: the conquest of Babel through the triumph of American English. If there is so much intrinsic virtue in so many languages, however, then why is human error and corruption so pervasive?

The Question "Demythologized"

During the same decades when international events turned the political theory of romanticists from cosmopolitanism to nationalism, there was a growing and changing concern with myth. Here too the problem of language and its origin occupied an important place. And once again, the grand hopes for the revelation of a new mythology turned sour in a grand disillusionment about the possibility of any theophany whatsoever. Henri Saint-Simon and Auguste Comte, the founders of positivism, called for a new religion, the demythologized religion of humanity and secular devotion to "the Great Being." By the dialectical twists of history, philosophy, and language itself, however, positivism has come to be identified with that stance which is most stridently antimetaphysical and antireligious. Positivism moved from the visionary myth of a new gospel to the nullifidian demolition of all myths.

The evocation of a new mythology was one of the programmatic ideas of early romanticism, enunciated in Friedrich Schlegel's "Discourse on Mythology" in 1800.[74] In his early *Fragments* Herder had already stated his conviction that a new myth was needed if poesy was to be revitalized. Friedrich Schlegel wrote to Novalis about the coming dawn of a new religion: In a letter of 1798 he conceded immodestly that the aim of his literary endeavors was to write a new Bible.[75] Ludwig Tieck, August Ludwig Hülsen, Heinrich Steffens, and Schelling all ruminated on the topic.[76] Since the epoch of human naiveté was past, Schlegel argued, the new mythology would have to be a self-conscious product of art.

For [the new mythology] will come to us in a manner just the opposite of the way the ancient former one came. . . . The new mythology . . . must be the most artistic of all artistic works, for it should encompass all others, it should provide a new bed and vessel for the olden, eternal wellspring of poetry, and it should itself be an infinite poem which veils the seeds of all other poems.[77]

Such an artful and historically conscious mythology would be the foundation for a new intellectual unity—philosophy, science, and poetry all rendered in a single medium.

Asserting the need for a new mythology did not create any new myths. It was the romantics themselves who insisted that myths are not invented, that their origination is as spontaneous and mysterious as that of language itself. If it is beyond human power to breathe life into new gods, historically conscious poets and philosophers could but lament the death of the old ones. In 1802, Hegel wrote of "the feeling whereon rests the religion of modern times—the feeling: God himself is dead."[78] A year earlier, Friedrich Hölderlin, the tortured poet, wrote with bitter poignancy:

> But, my friend, we have come too late. True, the gods are living,
> But over our heads, above in a different world.
> Endlessly there they act and—see how the heavenly spare us!—
> Care very little, it seems, whether or not we exist.
> For not always, indeed, a feeble vessel can hold them,
> Only at times can mankind bear the full weight of the gods.
> Only a dream about them is life henceforth. . . .[79]

The old gods were dead or dying, the new powerless to be born. Instead of a new myth, there was a new mythography. Friedrich Creuzer, Adam von Müller, Johann Arnold Kanne, Joseph Görres, the Grimm brothers, and many others turned to writing about the old myths—Greek and Hebrew, Indian and Persian, Norse and Germanic—without conceiving any new ones. Mythophilia ran high in the first decades of the nineteenth century, as expectations of the new advent ran low.

Schelling's *Philosophy of Mythology* and *Philosophy of Revelation,* both published posthumously, were based on lectures delivered during his later years in Munich and Berlin. Rejecting allegorist and naturalist, poetical and philosophical interpretations of myth, Schelling instead advanced the notion of a "theogonic process." Myth is the progressive self-revelation of the Absolute in human consciousness and, simultaneously, the self-creation of the Absolute as such. As with language, it is only misleading to speak of the "invention" of myth, whether by poets or philosophers, sovereign rulers or social groups: Myth and language develop according to dynamic laws and rationales of their own. In a passage later quoted by Steinthal and Nietzsche, Schelling wrote: "Since without language . . . one could imagine no consciousness whatsoever, the ground of language cannot be laid in consciousness, and yet, the more deeply we penetrate into it, the more decisively is it revealed that its depth far surpasses that of the most conscious accomplishments."[80] Myth and language are not so much the products of consciousness, as consciousness is the product of myth and language.

According to Schelling, the history of man's religions is the record of God's self-becoming. The process falls into three or four principal stages. First there was original or relative monotheism, which Schelling called *Eingötterei,* with its connotation of idolatry. Such monotheism is only relative because the "absolutely-One God excludes the very *possibility* of other gods, whereas the relatively-one god only in fact [happens to] have no others before, with, or after him."[81] Duotheism develops when different peoples worship different single gods, or the same people different ones in the various stages of its history. The great religious revolution, polytheism as such, Schelling related to the Tower of Babel story, which he took to represent "a crisis of religious consciousness," "the time at which new gods entered into consciousness."[82] Polytheism, the full flower of mythology, was finally replaced by the absolute monotheism of revelation, which Schelling identified generally with "the essential truth of mythology" and specifically with Christian revelation.

The stages of mythic consciousness corresponded neatly with linguistic types. First language was monosyllabic—Schelling proposed Chinese as the original language; then it became disyllabic; finally polysyllabism emerged triumphant.[83] As to content, the history of language moved from a poetical expression of the mythic to the philosophical presentation of the mythological.

In a very different context and with a different intent, French positivist schemes of world history were parallel to romanticist projections in detail and configuration. Comte's "law of the three stages" had humanity progressing from a theological to a metaphysical to the positive or scientific level. Whereas most romantics spoke of the fall away from mythic consciousness, however, Comte spoke of its conquest and the rise above it. Comte's treatment of language—not a critical concern, although it did receive a full chapter in the *System of Positive Polity* (1851)—fit his purposes as needed. Language originated during the theological stage, human childhood, when men thought in images and myths and the suitable language was metaphorical and poetic. In the adolescence of humanity, metaphysical mentality required a language of abstract concepts—albeit these are, on Comte's analysis, really mythical images abstracted and absolutized. The positive stage will require a new linguistic type, though Comte was imprecise about its features and felt that such a universal language could only develop after mankind was united in *humanité*.

More specifically, Comte located the origination of language between the family and the emergence of the "social organism." It was the power of language that led from the self-sufficient family to the larger social unity of mutual dependency. He vacillated between a strictly social and a biological interpretation.

Without the convincing light thrown on the study of the human mind by the study of animals, we should never have got rid of the empty specula- tions of metaphysicians on human language. . . . All these insoluble questions take a new form or disappear altogether, as soon as we cease to study man apart from the other races of which he is the master. . . . The comparisons furnished to us by the study of animals are of immense importance in guiding us to the Positive theory of human language; as this is the only means of tracing it to its proper biological origin.[84]

Just a few pages later in the same chapter, however, Comte argued to the contrary that language, though instinctively begun, is a creation of the social community: "Mankind collectively, therefore, is the true author of Language, and its true guardian."[85] A running theme in Comte's chapter is his comparison of language with religion. "It is with Religion that Language must be directly compared; since both spontaneously relate to human life in its totality. They both alike arise out of the very functions which it is their object to regulate. . . . Lan- guage, like Religion, is inspired by the Heart, and created by the Intel- ligence."[86] And the language of the future, like the religion of human- ity, should harmoniously unite all mankind.

Ernest Renan published *On the Origin of Language* in 1848. He had abandoned his studies for the priesthood three years earlier, largely because he could not reconcile his philological findings—he was an acknowledged expert in Semitics—with the teachings of the Church. His work on language origin was written while he was drafting *The Future of Intelligence,* whose publication he delayed until 1890, two years before his death. Renan thought that the origin and history of language could provide the surest clues to "the embryogeny of the human spirit."

Such a science would no doubt be more difficult than one which proposes to ascertain the present state of human consciousness. Nonetheless, there are sure means which could conduct us from the present age to the primitive. Direct experimental knowledge of the latter is impossible for us; but induction, exercised upon the present, could let us reascend to the spontaneous age, of which the reflective epochs are but the blossom.[87]

Renan used the organistic analogy, embryogeny, repeatedly. He too believed in the progress of science, but he challenged the view that advancement had been a cumulative process. So, too, language was not formed step by step or by "successive juxtapositions," but like "Minerva from the head of Zeus."[88] Language was complete at the beginning, the spontaneous creation of individuals and group together, of all faculties operating simultaneously, of the *génie du race*. "Languages should be compared, not to a crystal which is formed by agglomeration around a nucleus, but to a germ which develops by its own internal force. . . . Only artificial unities result from superimposed marriages and successive extensions."[89] Renan saw the same sense-oriented, myth-minded spontaneity in primitive language as did the romantics.

Renan referred to himself as "a born priest," but was roundly condemned by all ordained ones. His religious quest continued throughout his life, but he pathetically remarked that no student of comparative religion could retain the old faith.[90] And so he turned to the "religion of science." He replaced Comte's three stages with a sequence borrowed from Victor Cousin: The first age was religious but unscientific, the second scientific but irreligious, whereas the future will be scientific *and* religious. He also replaced Comte's positive science of sociology and put in its stead philology. He saw philology as the comprehensive science which philosophy had once been: Only in times of decadence—late antiquity, the late Middle Ages, and late modernity—is philosophy practiced as a specialized discipline. The new science of philology would be "the science of humanity," encompassing all religious and intellectual history, *"l'expérimentation universelle de la vie humaine."*[91] Metaphysics must be banned from philosophy and the supernatural from religion, but they would live on in the afterglow of historical and philological research. The early romantics had envisioned that science and natural philosophy might once again become poetical, integral, accessible to the generality of men. Renan reversed this: Instead of science becoming poetical, poetry and myth would be subsumed under science. And then, Renan dreamed, science pursued in the proper spirit—not for curiosity or utility, but with pious devotion—would in fact be religious. "Thus science is a religion; science alone will henceforth create the symbols; science alone is able to resolve for man the eternal problems of which his nature imperiously demands a solution."[92] Renan's search ended with the *amor dei intel-*

lectualis. So this philosophic-minded philologist saw his calling, but would the practitioners of scientific linguistics agree?

The Question "Spiritualized"

In the later, diffused phases of romanticism, many authors became absorbed in the movements of mystical illumination and esoteric wisdom, still popular from the eighteenth century. François Hemsterhuis, Louis Claude de Saint-Martin, Joseph de Maistre, Franz von Baader, and Friedrich Schlegel during his last years—these are only the best known of the *illuminati*. Illuminism was the obscurantist side of the secular enlightenment and then of romanticism, a kind of intellectual underground with diverse political and religious ties, which nearly gained general respect and influence but was overshadowed by other developments. The themes in illuminist writings recur so insistently and merge so confusingly one with another, that it is difficult to detect any pattern of development in their thought (and sometimes even any outlines of that thought), but the topic of the origin of language was a repeated motif in their grand schemes of universal significancy. *Illuminati* regularly cited Hamann with a *Magus dixit*—though Hamann himself found some of their effusions laughable[93]—and almost without exception they held to the theory of divine origin.

The freedom of illuminist fantasies was safeguarded by the obscurity of prehistory. They used the *aporiae* concerning language origin, taken directly from Rousseau, in support of the higher hypothesis, but also as a device to forestall any critical or scientific examination of their conjectures. Ultimately, after all, language origin was totally inexplicable—especially for opponents of divine genesis. This convenient self-protection was made all the more secure by the illuminists' penchant for speculation about the very most primordial circumstances—reaching even into the chaotic darkness of the prehuman era with imaginings about the communication among spirits and angels, and beyond that about the divine language itself. Certainly, they had ready-made insulation against all historical testing of their hypotheses when they claimed to describe the original word spoken by God in the act of creation, the speech of God with man before the *lapsus,* the *Ursprache* before the Babylonian confusion, or the language of the Golden Age. Following Saint-Martin and Jakob Böhme, Baader employed the concept of the *deus sermo.* God was interpreted as a being whose existence is his speaking, whose creative power is a kind of language through which he calls things out of nothing and into being.[94] "If God did not speak, then everything would be silent," said Baader.[95] The divine *fiat* represents the ultimate creativity of original language, and human creativity is an echo of the original. God's omnipotence lay in the primordial identity of speech and action, of thought, language, and being. Saint-Martin saw the same simultaenity of word and deed as characteristic of Adamic language in the perfect order of Eden.[96] "Before man sank into that fatal sleep whereby the world of sense fell to his lot," wrote Schlegel, man was master of nature by a linguistic dominion which made all human wishes into natural commands.[97] Man named and controlled the animals through the God-given gift of speech, the true meaning of the cipher of the breath of life inhaled by Adam.

The *illuminati* located the great breaking point of linguistic history either at the Fall or at the Tower of Babel. They generally agreed that the confusion of tongues was the child of human depravity. Saint-Martin contrasted the original *langue* with the historical *langages*.[98] Friedrich Schlegel made the otherwise unsupported suggestion that the curse of Cain was his inability to speak the same language as his brethren.[99] After Babel or its functional equivalent, it was widely held, the one natural language was replaced by the many conventional tongues with their arbitrary modes of signification. Hebrew, Sanskrit, and all other "primitive" languages accessible to historical research are at best the fossilized remains of the pure *Ursprache*.

Johann Arnold Kanne envisioned that the divine language itself could be reconstructed from the ruins. In his manuscripts for a *Panglossium* Kanne anticipated Grimm's "law of sound shift"—indeed some have credited him with its discovery.[100] In the changing intensity of labials, dentals, and gutturals he saw ultimate proof that all languages derive from one original, of which Hebrew was the first but already corrupted offshoot. By following the thread of shifting sounds Kanne hoped to find his way back to the absolute original and thereby gain a glimpse into the "depths of divinity." If mystical union was to have a linguistic dimension, the gap beyond Babel had to be bridged.

In illuminist schemes of linguo-redemptive history, Babel was overcome by Pentecost.[101] This was roughly equivalent to the victory of Christ over the first Adam in more orthodox plans of salvation. If the divinely inspired original language could not be reconstructed from its remnants in postlapsarian history, perhaps it could yet be regained in enthusiastic transport. Saint-Martin surmised that the assembled apostles spoke the *Ursprache* itself, the direct gift of the Holy Spirit. Justinus Kerner—physician, poet, theosophist—darkly identified the fiery gift of tongues, sleep-talking, the psycholinguistic effects of animal magnetism, and "inner language"—of which "one word . . . frequently expressed more than whole lines of ordinary language, [so] that, after death, in one single symbol or character of it, man would read his whole life."[102] The Apocalypse, in turn, would bring a restoration of original language with its complete unity of the inner and the outer word, its identity of speech and action. Saint-Martin foresaw a verbal purgation on the Day of Judgment, when the idle words of sinful men would be read and expunged from the divine record. Since man's original sin was against the Word, and since the Word existed in anguish during human history, at the end of history, "the substance of men's words will rise up in judgment against them. . . ."[103] Thereafter, God and man would once again converse in the fully spiritual *Ursprache*—though it is not clear whether this would be the music of the spheres or complete silence. Baader explained that the final unveiling, the great revelation, would have to remove and annihilate all the enshrouding signs.[104] And, according to Saint-Martin, on the Last Day "the tongue will be silent, it will not be able to say anything else, and it will not be necessary for it to speak any more, since Being itself will act through us and in us.[105] The *eschaton* of the history of language is that there should be no more language.

Some illuminists and transcendentalists so generalized the concept of language itself that the question of its origin became but an aspect of their pantheistic vision. Nature could be viewed, not merely as the art of God, but as the very "speech of God." Saint-Martin thought the universe dumb, needing the flicker of human speech for animation; but other writers found nature veritably loquacious: They found ciphers in the stars, hieroglyphs in the animals, symbols in the plants. Fascination with ubiquitous hieroglyphs relegated man's verbal and spoken language to secondary status. Many an author took up the old occasional theme that writing had been invented before speech. Johann Jakob Bachofen contrasted the power of symbols with the weakness of words.

Symbols awaken presentiment [*Ahnung*]; language can only explain. Symbols strike all the strings of the human spirit simultaneously; language necessarily confines itself to a single thought. The symbol plants its roots in the most hidden depths of the soul; language, like a soft breeze, barely touches the surface of the understanding. The former are directed inward, the latter outward. Only symbols are capable of combining the most diverse things in a single, unified total impression. Language strings individual things together and always brings things to consciousness piecemeal—things which would have to be presented to the soul in a single flash to have their full force. Language makes the infinite finite; but symbols abduct the mind beyond the boundaries of the finite and becoming into the kingdom of the infinite and world of being. They awaken presentiments, they are signs of the unspeakable. . . .[106]

Appropriately, these comments on the superiority of mute, nonverbal images came in a work on sepulchral symbolism. The exegetes of universal symbolistics extended the concept of language in the direction of a romantically conceived infinity, and therewith it became infinitely imprecise. All was potential language in a world full of hieroglyphs.

Ralph Waldo Emerson was one of the American transcendentalists who took up this theme from the Germans. In a chapter on language in his first book, *Nature,* he enumerated the rudiments: "(1) Words are signs of natural facts. (2) Particular natural facts are symbols of particular spiritual facts. (3) Nature is the symbol of spirit."[107] Emerson repeatedly emphasized that things as well as words are emblematic, that nature is metaphorical, that "words and deeds are quite indifferent modes of the divine energy."[108]

Man is a monad receptive to the significancy of the universe, but the poets exhibit the fullest measure of sensitivity to the "picture-language" of nature. "The poets made all the words. . . . For though the origin of most of our words is forgotten, each word was at first a stroke of genius, and obtained currency because for the moment it symbolized the world to the first speaker and to the hearer. . . . Language is fossil poetry."[109] The nomothetic powers of the poet do not depend on his active creativity, but his passive receptivity: "The condition of true naming, on the poet's part, is his resigning himself to the divine *aura* which breathes through forms, and accompanying that."[110] The poet makes the world transparent by reformulating the natural symbol as a verbal one. "The poet, by an ulterior intellectual perception, gives [the natural symbols] a power which makes their old use forgotten, and puts eyes and a tongue into every dumb and inanimate object. . . . The poet turns the world to glass, and shows us all things in their right series and procession."[111] Although Emerson described poets as "liberating gods," who "are free and . . . make free," the poet's powers are ultimately passive and mimetic, for the possibilities of genuine creativity were exhausted by the maker of the original poetry of nature itself: "For poetry was all written before time was. . . ."[112] Man's historical retreat from nature and the life of virtuous simplicity had a corrupting influence on his language as well as his morals, but primitive language was pure poetry, the original natural symbols themselves.[113]

An influential extension of the concept of language was Gotthilf Heinrich von Schubert's analysis of the symbolism of dreams. Schubert did not consider the flow of somnial images the absolute *Ursprache*, but something close to it. Prophecy, poetry, and dreams all derive from the single original language of God in nature, "a dream world in the flesh, a prophetic language in living hieroglyphic forms."[114] "Nature [is] an apocalypse in forms and vital natural images. . . . It is the same language which was spoken from the beginning and is still spoken by the higher regions of the spiritual world."[115] Schubert found the figures of somnolent fantasy better suited to human nature than the words of rational language: They are immediately and universally understood without a conscious learning process. Governed by different laws of association than the grammar and syntax of articulate language, dreams capture the chaotic interplay and covert connexity of things and give archetypal expression to the hidden, the unconscious, the divine.

That language of images and hieroglyphs, which higher wisdom has employed for all its revelations to men, is in the highest and most perfect degree that which the language of poetry is at a lesser level and the picture-language of dreams at the lowest and most imperfect level— . . . an original and natural language of the human soul. [Might it not be] . . . the real wakeful speech of a higher region! Whereas we, although we consider ourselves awake, have actually sunk into a multimillenial sleep, or in any case we have fallen for the echo of its dreams; and, like sleepers with regard to the fully audible talk of people standing around, so we can grasp only a few dark words from that language of God.[116]

Dreaming may be an escape from the conscious and rational world, but it is an escape into a higher reality, the *plērōma*, the fullness of pure spirituality and divinity, original being.

The explosion of the concept of language consummated in "hiero-astronomy."[117] It was guessed that the final secrets of the universe might revolve with the celestial bodies and that the most original idiom could be the language of the stars. Baader and Johann Wilhelm Ritter—the physicist who found romantic wisdom confirmed in his discovery of ultraviolet rays—discussed the foundation of a new journal, *Der Siderismus*. Görres spoke of the "grammar of the planets" as a prototype of human history.[118] Friedrich Schlegel confided in a letter (which his brother found most disconcerting) that he contemplated writing a treatise on the "sidereal language" and its two dialects as a basis for the earliest language of revelation and mythology.[119] In the spirit of hiero-astronomy Schubert produced what is surely one of the most curious oddities among theories of language origin. In a chapter of his *Views from the Nightside of Natural Science,* Schubert glowingly described the original harmony between man and nature in the epoch before the oldest human documents, an age when "the mind of man did not control nature, but rather nature controlled the mind of man. . . ."[120] But thereafter, "the cool winds of the last night watch are followed by the dawn of day, and in a few moments, abandoned by the maternal wings, the delicate race becomes numb. . . . Then the voice of bold enthusiasm is silenced, and man no longer understands nature."[121] These rhapsodic descriptions supported the common explanation of man's earliest language as the product of inspiration, poetic and prophetic. But Schubert also suggested an alternative solution to the riddle of language origin. Perhaps in a previous age the revolutions of the heavenly bodies may have caused atmospheric vibrations which created a virtual symphony of natural sounds and which literally produced the original harmony of the universe and music of the spheres. Man's language could have originated spontaneously when he sang along with the melody of the stars and planets according to to the "harmonic law of the whole." "In this way the most ancient natural wisdom and language itself may have arisen as an immediate revelation of Nature to man."[122] Schubert added, of course, that there was no direct verification or scientific proof for his theory; but he failed to mention that therefore, conveniently, it was also not subject to disproof. In all these "spiritualizers" of language origin, one must wonder whether there is any clear definition of language at all. Or has that too disappeared in the boundless infinite?

Conclusion: Humboldt on the Origin of Language?

It is an open question whether Wilhelm von Humboldt was seriously concerned with the specific problem of the origin of language. Steinthal maintained that for Humboldt the matter of origin was one with the definition of language as such.[123] Whereas some thinkers so stretched the concept of language that their speculations have become mere curiosities, Humboldt took pains to clarify both the idea of language and the question of origins in general, even if he put forward no particular thesis regarding the origin of language in particular.

The classical distinction which Humboldt employed to elucidate the nature of language was that between *érgon* and *enérgeia.* "One must not consider language as if it were a dead product, but far more as a producing."[124]

Language, conceived in its true essence, is something which passes away constantly and in every moment. Even its preservation in writing is only an incomplete, mummylike preservation, for which it is first necessary that we try to resensualize the live delivery. Language itself is not a work (*érgon*), but an activity (*enérgeia*).[125]

As Herder had said of language—and Hegel of logic—it cannot be understood either as a tool or as a *factum*.[126] Like Hegel's "here and now," the immediate "facts" of language vanish before us, as our speech changes literally under our noses and our written words pass away behind us. If language is a product at all, it is an always unfinished product, and therefore a true account of it must be a genetic one.

In the first instance Humboldt emphasizes spontaneity: not simply the creativity of individuals, but the activity of nations and of spirit itself. "[Language] possesses spontaneity or self-activity, which reveals itself visibly to us even though its essence is inexplicable; and from this perspective it is not a production of activity but an involuntary emanation of spirit, not a work of nations but a gift bestowed upon them by their inner fate. They make use of it without knowing how they have formed it."[127] This spontaneity is not indeterminate, however, for activity has purpose and direction. Humboldt explicitly builds on Aristotle's use of the term *enérgeia*, which did not mean mere capacity, but actuality, the antonym of potentiality (*dýnamis*). Since all things move from potentiality to actuality by becoming what they are intended to be—that is, by self-realization—Aristotle often used *enérgeia* as a synonym for *entelechy*, the inherent goal or *télos* which things have in themselves because there is purpose in the cosmos. Humboldt calls this principle *Geisteskraft*, the power of spirit or mind. Language and the human direction of nations are "thoroughly and inseparably activities of the same intellectual capacity. Inasmuch as a people, in the development of its language as the instrument of that human activity in it, creates freedom from within, it simultaneously seeks and achieves the object itself, thus something other and higher; and insofar as it achieves this by means of poetic creation and meditative presentiment [*Ahndung*], this simultaneously reflects back into language."[128] Ultimately the *enérgeia* of language is the transformation of matter into idea and of articulated sound into thought. "As little as the nature of these creative powers admits of complete penetration, this much is clear: that in them there always rules a capacity to master the given material from the inside out and to transform or subordinate it to ideas."[129] "For insofar as [language] reveals itself to us in creative independence, it loses itself beyond the realm of appearances in ideal being."[130]

Humboldt's view of language as *enérgeia* does not cancel out language as *érgon,* but rather illuminates the objective aspects of language. Language is not only the organ of inner existence but of national character as well. "As inward as language is throughout, it has nonetheless simultaneously an independent, external existence, which exercises power [over] against man."[131] In the first instance the objective independence of language derives from the fact that we speak languages handed down to us: "Since every [language] has received material from previous generations out of an earlier time unknown to us, the spiritual activity which elicits the expression of thought is, therefore, always also directed toward something already given; it is not purely generative [*erzeugend*], but transformational [*umgestaltend*]."[132] Every speaker has a "historical investment" and the "relationship of the past to the present interlinks with the deepest element in the formation" of language. All individual activity must be understood as an aspect of the whole, a totality which strengthens individual creativity, gives it its context, and is the ultimate aim of thought through language. The objective spirit of language further shows itself in the need for a recognition of other persons. "The articulated sound tears itself from the breast in order to arouse an echo in the ear of another individual. Thereby man discovers that there are around him beings with the same inner needs, who are thus able to encounter the manifold longing latent in his feelings."[133] In this discovery, the search for objectivity reestablishes subjectivity, the subjectivity of another human being as well as oneself. "Subjectivity is robbed of nothing, since man always feels himself one with man; indeed it is strengthened, since the representation transformed into language does not now belong exclusively to one object."[134]

Mediation is the fundamental principle of language, whether it be mediation between man and man or between man and nature. "As the individual sound mediates between the object and man, so language as a whole intervenes between him and nature, which affects him inwardly and outwardly. He surrounds himself with a world of sounds, in order to take up the world of objects into himself and to fashion it."[135] "Just as no concept is possible without [language], so there can be no object for the soul [without it], for every external thing only attains its complete essentiality through the mediation of the concept."[136] Subjectivity and objectivity are mediated through one another. "All speaking, from the simplest on, ties that which is individually perceived to the common nature of humanity."[137] "One could say with equal truth that the entire human race speaks one language or that every individual possesses his own individual language."[138] Through mediation the principles of subjectivity and objectivity are fulfilled. They overcome and are overcome in the realization of the whole.[139] The whole of language lies within each individual and each people, for language is not developed in isolated parts, as it is not learned in isolated words.[140] Language learning is not a cumulative process of acquisition in the separate areas of vocabulary, grammar, and phonetics; it is a progress of understanding which moves in spurts and bounds as new horizons of the whole suddenly appear. Language is "the eternally self-repeating work of the spirit in making articulated sound capable of expressing thought."[141] This working of the spirit is the task of the listener as well as the speaker, since understanding and language are operations of the same capacity.[142] Language is even the decisive element in silence.[143] Constant renewal in speech, for which spirit provides ever new and old materials, is the true link between past and future, for "language has this beginningless and endless infinity for us."[144]

This infinity without beginning and without end is the most important clue to Humboldt's considerations of linguistic beginnings and linguistic ends. One must consider in their necessary relations the beginnings of language and the ends of mankind. As with the Aristotelian cosmos, the motion of thought leads in infinite circularity; just as language itself is for us a finite circle: "Through the same act, by means of which [man] spins language out of himself, he threads himself into language, and each language draws a circle around the people to which it belongs. . . ."[145] Although there are hidden and mysterious aspects to both, the beginnings of language are as fathomable, and only as fathomable, as the ends of humanity.

Aspiration is the true nature of man, and elevation or ennoblement his proper end. All extraneous limitations upon human aspiration—that is, those which are not rightly self-imposed because of general human finitude or because of the more specific limits of individual capacity—are contrary to nature to the extent that they restrict self-fulfillment, prevent (like a stone cast upon a seedling) examples of nobility from growing and the flowers of excellence from blooming, and therefore allow and even encourage the predominance of the base and the power of the corrupt. *Geisteskraft,* the cultivation of man's inner being, is the end toward which human activity can and should tend, and it is simultaneously the means of achieving the goal of humanity. *Geisteskraft* is the exercise of those powers which "actually make man human and therefore are the plain definition of his being."[146] Nations and peoples attain their dignity and have their explanation in "the production of human *Geisteskraft* in ever new and often intensified form."[147]

[It is] the highest goal of all spiritual motion, the final idea of which world history must strive to deliver itself clearly. For this elevating or widening of inward being is the only thing which the individual, to the extent that he participates in it, can take as an indestructible possession; and in a nation it is out of it that great individuals unfailingly and repeatedly develop.[148]

Language is both midwife and child of this aspiration. "The heterogeneity [of language] can be viewed as the striving with which the power of speech, universally bestowed upon man, breaks forth in more or less favorable fashion, aided or hindered by the *Geisteskraft* inherent in the peoples."[149]

The producing of language is an inner need of humanity: not merely an external one for the maintenance of mutual intercourse, but one latent in our very nature, indispensable for the development of our spiritual powers and for the acquisition of a world-view, which man can only attain insofar as he brings his thought to clarity and definiteness in common thinking with others. . . . Language is one of the sides from which universal human *Geisteskraft* emerges in constantly active efficacy. In other words, one glimpses in it the striving to gain existence in reality for the idea of language perfection. The tracing and presentation of this striving is the task of the linguist in its final, but simplest, analysis.[150]

Through language man uncovers and realizes his humanity within and without himself. Language begins in the elementary need for existence, and it ends in the most elevated need for human self-realization: "In the merely vegetative existence of man on this earth, the individual's need for help leads to association with others and requires understanding through language for the possibility of communal undertakings. Just so, however, spiritual cultivation, even in the loneliest isolation of the soul, is only possible through [language]. . . ."[151]

When inquiring into beginnings we must keep our eye steady upon ends. But in searching for ultimate beginnings and ends, we must go beyond sensible evidence. "We must abstract more from the ways in which [language] serves for the designation of objects and communication of understanding, and instead go back to its origin, so closely intertwined with inner spiritual activity. . . ."[152] The further we go, the more difficulties we encounter.[153] The deeper one descends into prehistory, the more the mass seems to melt together and individuals to disappear. "There is, finally, an epoch in which we glimpse only [language], where it does not merely accompany spiritual development, but completely takes its place."[154]

For language must first be introduced into the circles over which it will pour its light through a still dark and undeveloped feeling. How is this breaking-off of the existence of individuals unified with the progressive development of the race? Perhaps in a region unknown to us? That remains an impenetrable secret. *But the effect of this feeling of impenetrability is an outstanding and important moment in the formation of inner individuality, inasmuch as it awakens a respectful reserve in the face of the unknown, which is surely left over after the disappearance of everything knowable.* It is comparable to the impression of night, in which, too, it is only the individually scattered sparks of bodies unknown to us that take up the place of all the customary visible things.[155]

In this sense, a knowledge of original language is a knowledge of our ignorance.

For Humboldt, the question of the origin of language—whether understood historically, essentially, or in some other sense—belongs to that realm of problems which are unsusceptible of any direct and final explanation. The obstacles or knots are there from beginning to end, resisting final solution, because "spiritual power cannot be penetrated to its very essence and its effects cannot be calculated beforehand."[156] The model of mechanical cause and effect cannot satisfactorily explain it, because "all spiritual advancement can only proceed from inner expression of power and insomuch it always has a hidden and unexplainable ground, because it is self-moving."[157] In his emphasis on the self-moving, Humboldt discloses the precise basis for the organicism which dominated German philosophy from Herder on: From the human vantage point, it is life which is the immediate mystery, and the purpose of life the ultimate mystery. This hidden aspect of the object is better illuminated by biological metaphors than by the model of mechanistic physics which dominated French philosophy from Descartes on. "All becoming in nature, but above all organic and living becoming, eludes our observation. No matter how exactly we research the prior conditions, there is always a gap between the last of these and the appearance, the cleft which separates something from nothing."[158]

What are science and philosophy to say or do in the face of this unknown? "It may seem that one had better leave this point untouched. But this is impossible, if one wants to trace the course of development of the human spirit, even in its rawest outlines. . . ."[159] One cannot undertake science in the spirit that one is forbidden to explain precisely that which needs to be explained. In delineating the tasks of linguistic science Humboldt suggests a more precise answer. The goals of linguistic research should be defined by the purposes of language itself, as these relate to the ends of humanity. Since these ends are aspiration and elevation, "it is especially important for practical application, that we should not rest content with any lower principles of explanation, but that we should really ascend to the highest and ultimate. . . ."[160] In its specific inquiries, linguistics may concentrate on particular phases of language, but these will clarify little unless they are understood as aspects of the whole. More than that, since language points beyond itself, the inquiry into language should point beyond the linguistic phenomena as such—to that human good which language indicates, that good which is both the source of language and its aim.

Finally, if that good is not always clear, if beginnings and ends are intertwined, and if the beginnings are shrouded in dark mystery, what is the linguist or philosopher to do with that knotty problem, the origin of language? "While acknowledging that we are standing at a boundary, over which neither historical research nor free thought is able to lead us, we must faithfully record the fact and its immediate consequences."[161]

However much one may fix and objectify in [language], separate and dissect, there is always something unrecognized left over in it; and precisely this, which eludes research, is its very unity and breath of life. Since languages are so constituted, the presentation of the form of any particular one can never be entirely complete in the sense here stated, but can only ever succeed to a certain degree—but one which is satisfactory for the surveying of the whole. Therefore, however, by virtue of this concept, the way is no less [clearly] prescribed on which the linguist must track down the secrets of language and try to unveil its essence.[162]

The linguist must not only note, but recognize the importance of the impasse of the origin of language, for it derives from the very nature of the object of his inquiry. Would it not then remain the principal task of linguist and philosopher alike to find as much clarity as mortals can about the nature of the human good?

[10]

RECONSTRUCTION
OF THE *URSPRACHE*

From the diverse and fragmented movements during the first half of the nineteenth century, retrospective histories of linguistics have singled out some writers, scholars, and books as belonging to the prehistory, emergence and establishment of scientific language study—comparative grammar or Indogermanistics, as it came to be called. In fact, the immediate affiliations and philosophic commitments of these figures were diverse, and the nature of "the method," "the profession," and "the science" were still very much in dispute and in process of articulation. Since it was the comparative method which proved to be decisive for the successes of historical linguistics, reconstructions of the history of linguistics in the later nineteenth and twentieth centuries have included those students of language who anticipated or employed that method and generally excluded those who followed a less historical approach.

The term *comparative grammar,* first used by Friedrich Schlegel in his book on Indian language and philosophy, was specifically used in analogy to *comparative anatomy.* During the eighteenth century, classificatory biology advanced rapidly from systems such as those of Buffon and Linnaeus to the deeper—that is, less superficially taxonomic—insights of Cuvier in zoology and Candolle in botany. Candolle's *History of Succulent Plants* appeared from 1799 through 1803, and Cuvier, the more articulate theorist and methodologist and student of Kantian philosophy, published his *Lessons on Comparative Anatomy* from 1800 to 1805—just the years when Schlegel was studying Sanskrit and preparing his book. Earlier biologists had classified plants and animals by comparing individual parts, as in Linnaeus's system based on the variations of stamens and pistils, but Cuvier argued that groupings of this sort were superficial and artificial.[1] Organisms, he insisted, are characterized by the indivisibility of the parts from the whole in which they function; an adequate taxonomy must, therefore, clarify this functioning of parts within the whole. Thus comparative anatomy must go beyond merely descriptive classification and penetrate into the internal dynamics of the organism. Cuvier claimed that biology must be deductive as well as inductive. If the biologist understands the organic relation between parts and whole, then, given some of the parts, he should be able to deduce the whole. Cuvier himself was not especially interested in the problem of evolution, and he deliberately eschewed all questions relating to the origins of life or of the genera and species. Clearly, however, the comparative method, with its use of deduction, could add an historical dimension to biology, because it provided a means for "reconstructing" past forms of life.

The development of comparative grammar was closely related to the interpretation of language as an organism. Thus it was quite understandable that linguists would claim that their pursuits should be numbered among the natural sciences. Comparative linguists also rejected as superficial earlier classifiactory schemes and stipulated that comparison should discern the inner structure of language and determine how its elements functioned in terms of the whole. Reconstruction was also a principal device of historical linguists, who deduced individual roots and whole protolanguages by analogy. For linguistic reconstruction, as much attention had to be given to spoken language as earlier humanists had given to written documents. In the transition from philology to linguistics, languages were studied, not for the literary traditions which they embodied, but for their place in the historical continuum; and thus it was argued that linguistics studied language for its own sake, language as such, regardless of its spoken or written contents.

The new science of language, at first, offered great hopes of solving the problem of language origin, of providing a solution with certitude instead of a creation of unmethodical conjecture. The comparative method of reconstruction seemed to provide a road back to the origins, at least relatively, and that was admittedly one reason why scholars started out upon it. At the same time that this road was being traveled, however, and the method applied with greater and greater exactitude, the origins were being displaced into a more and more remote past. Friedrich Schlegel, at the beginning of the nineteenth century, could still look upon Sanskrit and Hebrew as languages which were at or near the beginning in an absolute sense; but by the time of Schleicher and Darwin, shortly past the middle of the century, such "ancient traditions" could no longer be maintained except by wishful thinkers. Within half a century the scope of human history had expanded at a rate beyond expectations and even comprehension. Method had improved, and there was considerable success in reconstructing the roots of extant language families, but the ultimate object had become inaccessible. Despite the advancement of science, the question of the origin of language remained elusive.

Prehistory of the New Science of Language

Friedrich Schlegel was by no means the first to propose the Indo-European hypothesis. A long line of earlier scholars, going back to J. J. Scaliger and Leibniz, had suggested correspondences between European languages and those of India and Persia.[2] In 1786 Sir William Jones, a colonial judge in Calcutta and devoted Orientalist, asserted that Sanskrit, Greek, and Latin, and probably Gothic, Celtic, and Old Persian "have sprung from some common source, which, perhaps, no longer exists."[3] Although linguists later in the century were contemptuous of Schlegel's dilettantism and viewed his researches as prescientific, they nonetheless grudgingly conceded him the honor of being the first to envision the proper basis of comparative method for linguistics.

In 1802 Schlegel left Jena for Paris, where he founded a new journal, *Europa,* marking a new phase of romanticism. There he also studied Persian with Antoine Léon de Chézy and Sanskrit with Alexander Hamilton, both distinguished Orientalists. He continued to amass materials, until in 1808 he published *On the Language and Wisdom of the Indians*—a watershed work, not because it was the first, best, or most accessible introduction to Sanskrit, but because in it Schlegel envisioned a whole new way of studying language. It was Schlegel's visionary hope that his book would have an even more general influence than the substantial one it did have. At its beginning and conclusion Schlegel revealed his fondest wish, that the book might initiate a new renaissance, a rebirth of the classical culture and philosophy of the Indians which would be as broad in its reprecussions as was the rediscovery of Greek and Roman antiquity in the late Middle Ages. The new mythology of which Schlegel was a prophet in earlier writings was now replaced by an altered vision, the revival of an old but unfamiliar mythology. Schlegel even hesitatingly suggested that Indian wisdom was something close to the original revelation.[4] Schlegel's book was filled with enthusiasm for the discovery of a relatively unknown chapter of ancient history and filled with hope for a future social and artistic renewal.

The lasting effect of *On the Language and Wisdom of the Indians* lay not in any renascence which it inspired, but its suggestion of a method for the historical study of language. "There is, however, one single point, the investigation of which ought to decide every doubt, and elucidate every difficulty: The structure or comparative grammar of the [languages] furnishes as certain a key to their general analogy, as the study of comparative anatomy has done to the loftiest branch of natural science."[5] The kind of comparison Schlegel had in mind concerned the "internal structure" and "living organism" of the language. Previous linguistic classifications, some of them more comprehensive and elaborate than Schlegel's own, had limited their comparisons to the words of different languages. Words can, of course, be borrowed from one language to another; but such loan words only prove that there has been contact between the peoples involved, not that there is any essential relationship between their languages. The very notion of essential relationships, as opposed to accidental ones, only arises when the philologist considers it necessary to go beyond the words of a language to its grammatical structure and internal form. "We must not judge of these varieties from the first impressions communicated by sound or form, but rather by their inner and essential character, which can be appreciated only by researches penetrating far beneath the mere external veil."[6]

Earlier grammarians also erred in using a Latin model, which they then imposed on other languages. Others saw in grammar the mirror of the systematics of universal reason: They took the grammatical homogeneity of all languages as confirmation of the universality and consistency of logical laws and schemata. On reflection, the *petitio principii* is glaring: Languages were forced into a Latinate mold, and the twisted image was then used to prove the grammatical similarity of all the languages so twisted. Schlegel called for a new grammar without the old presuppositions. The new grammar, however, would prove to have some presuppositions of its own.

Schlegel distinguished two basic types of language: organic and mechanical. "Modifications of meaning, or different degrees of signification, may be produced either by inflection or internal variations of the primitive word, or by annexing to it certain peculiar particles, which in themselves indicate the past, the future, or any other circumstance."[7] As with so many passages from this work, this was a rather loose suggestion, not entirely accurate, but very influential for the further development of linguistics. It anticipated the threefold typology advanced by August Wilhelm Schlegel ten years later, which was dominant for some time. August Wilhelm divided languages into an analytic group, which has no inflection whatsoever and thus alters meaning by the use of additional isolated words; a synthetic group, in which meaning is varied by inflection; and an agglutinating group, in which new words are formed by the composition of different root words.[8] With less precision, Friedrich Schlegel simply contrasted inflecting and noninflecting languages. Flexional languages are organic, according to Schlegel, because their changes of form are similar to animate metamorphosis, whereas root-isolating and agglutinating languages are mechanical, because they are based on the inanimate principles of accumulation and agglomeration. The roots in inflected languages have powers like those of living seeds.

In the Indian and Greek languages each *root* is actually that which bears the signification, and thus seems like a living and productive germ, every modification of circumstance or degree being produced by internal changes. . . . Those languages, on the contrary, in which the declensions are formed by supplementary particles . . . have no such bond of union; their roots present us with no living productive germ, but seem like an agglomeration of atoms, easily dispersed and scattered by every casual breath. They have no internal connexion beyond the purely mechanical adaptation of particles and affixes.[9]

Schlegel's understanding of linguistic roots is clearly parallel to Fichte's explanation of the original elements of an *Ursprache* and Jahn's effusions about its "life-giving seeds."

Schlegel devoted an entire chapter of *On the Language and Wisdom of the Indians* to the specific question of the origin of language. "Hypotheses concerning the first origin of language would either have been discarded altogether, or would have assumed an entirely different form, had they been founded on historical investigation, instead of being wrested into forced compliance with arbitrary theories."[10] Earlier, for Schlegel and for Fichte, it was historical evidence which was shabby and uncertain, susceptible of interpretation; certainty required logical deduction. Now, according to Schlegel, history provided the only valid method. This new pointer toward a different road meant more than the obvious requirement that we adduce historical evidence for those phenomena that we would consider original in language. It meant that language can only be understood in its historical development, because language *is* its history. The origin of language itself has a history: "I shall be content if I have proved satisfactorily, in general terms, the fixed principles on which a comparative grammar and genuine historical foundation—an authentic history, in short, of the origin of language— . . . may be constructed."[11] Schlegel's chapter on the origin of language amounted to little more than a temporary suspension of the question: The final word on language origin must await further and more precise comparative studies, and we would know how language originated only when we understood the whole history of language thoroughly. Advancement in the study of linguistic history would surely bring with it an answer clear and certain, beyond doubt.

Despite Schlegel's cautious postponement of any definitive answer, he still speculated about origin. In keeping with his division between organic and mechanical languages, he postulated a polygenetic theory of origin: The mother languages for each of the different language groups must have arisen at different times and places. Mechanical languages developed by simultaneous processes of accretion and refinement. Rude and barbaric in their beginnings, they arose out of spontaneous expressions akin to animal cries. Grammar and euphony came only as latter-day correctives. Since these beginnings were so coarse, it is of little moment to know about the origin of mechanical languages. In contrast, since flexional languages are organic, knowledge of their origin can help preserve their life-giving roots. Either at their birth or shortly thereafter organic languages were fully refined, their grammars complete, their clarity superior. Organic language was founded on "the clear perception of the natural signification of things. . . . The primitive roots . . . and the grammatical construction . . . both spring from the same original source—a deep feeling, and a clear discriminating intelligence."[12] The changes that organic languages undergo are those of life and growth. The different idioms in a language group are but the varied metamorphoses of a single original. Related organic languages are fundamentally one, all deriving from the same prototype. Schlegel's term *organic,* then, does not only refer to the grammatical structure of a given language, but also to its historical relations.

Schlegel's book on the Indians and Fichte's *Speeches to the German Nation* were published in the same year and, without any direct influence of one on the other, they both involved a significant extension of the notion of an *Ursprache.* They both saw primordial language as the ideal and inexhaustible source for later language.

The Indian grammar offers the best example of perfect simplicity, combined with the richest artistic construction. It is necessary, however, to presuppose one property of the mind, in order to explain . . . the origin of that language: a peculiarly fine feeling of the separate value and

appropriate meaning . . . of the radical words or syllables; a perception
of the whole activity and influence of which we can hardly be fully sensible, the ear now being dulled and confused by a multiplicity of various
impressions, and the original stamp of each word being obliterated by
long use.[13]

Like Fichte, Schlegel was concerned with origins as a means of preserv-
ing the roots, as a fount of life and power, as a way of imbibing primordial wisdom. From the middle of the eighteenth century on, German thinkers had rejected the French bias that the linguistic process
was one of gradual but constant improvement, the progression of
systems of increasingly clarified relations. With the importance now
attached to Sanskrit, there seemed to be proof for their contention,
for Sanskrit grammar was every bit as "complex" as that of modern
European languages. To the contrary, many argued, the "perfection"
and "completeness" of Sanskrit grammar—its superior clarification of
relations through more extensive inflection—signified that the history
of language was a continuous fall away from original clarity. Was
original language then a model of perfection? or even of wisdom? Was
it something like a Platonic form with a self-activating principle of
motion? And could modern science recapture its essence or details?

The Genetic Laws of a Mysterious Organism

Rasmus Rask was the first to formulate the laws of sound change which
would lead to the fulfillment of Schlegel's high expectations for the
systematic development of historical linguistics. Although his importance was recognized by few contemporaries, because he wrote in
Danish, Rask made the breakthrough toward methodical comparison
in a prize essay on the origin and history of Icelandic, written in 1814
and publisher in 1818.[14] The first rule Rask laid down was that similarities of vocabulary are insufficient confirmation of linguistic kinship:
There must be similarity of grammatical structure, or, where that is
not evident, logical intermediate steps which would explain grammatical dissimilarities. By a second principle, he established that identical
or nearly identical formations are not so important as is a consistent
pattern of similarities and dissimilarities. Rask himself worked out elaborate tables of comparison of nominal and verbal inflection, and also
of the most common phonetic shifts, which showed the relation of
Icelandic to Gothic and other Germanic languages. At the same time,
he proved that the Baltic and Slavic languages do have a common

source; whereas Finnish and Lappish, despite many cognates, are unrelated to Scandinavian and Germanic languages, because there is no grammatical correspondence, and hence the cognates must be loan words. Thus Rask gained an imperfect but comprehensive view of the Indo-European family and formulated a rationale for the dynamics of change within it.

Jacob Grimm, in the first volume of his *Germanic Grammar* (1819), acknowledged his debt to Rask, but placed little emphasis on phonology, instead beginning with an exposition of morphology. Directly upon its publication, Grimm became dissatisfied and began to revise. The second edition of the first volume appeared in 1822 and commenced with a section "Of Letters," a systematic analysis of historical phonology. As later refined, Grimm stated the law of sound shift as follows: "The *mediae* [voiced stops] of the sounds produced with each of the three organs [labials, dentals, and palatals] become *tenues* [voiceless stops], the *tenues* become *aspiratae* [fricatives] and the *aspiratae* become *mediae*. Therewith the cycle is completed and would have to commence once again in a similar manner."[15] Grimm's point is illustrated in the diagrams he constructed:

	Labials		*Dentals*			*Palatals*		
Greek	B (med)	P F	D (med)	T	TH	G (med)	K	CH
Gothic	P (ten)	F B	T (ten)	TH	D	K (ten)	CH	G
O.H.G.	F (asp)	B P	TH (asp)	D	T	CH (asp)	G	K

Thus a Greek *b* (voiced labial) would become *p* (voiceless labial) in Gothic and *f* (labial fricative) in Old High German; whereas Greek *p* changed to Gothic *f* and Old High German *b*; and so on.

Grimm's theory, although seminal, left many matters unexplained. The scheme only explained the sound shift of some consonants and of no vowels, and it could not show why some sounds, even within the same word, went through the prescribed cycle, whereas others did not. Application of Grimm's "law" seemed to be a hit-and-miss affair, leaving a multitude of exceptions—which led later linguists to charge that it was no law at all. In was only later in the century, after Verner's and Grassmann's laws had been formulated, and the notion developed of a "phonetic environment" affecting sound change, that the neogrammarians would postulate that all phonetic laws must be exceptionless. Finally, Grimm had no way of explaining how change was initiated or why the cycle always came to an end at the third stage, regardless of the starting point. For explanation of the reasons for change Grimm relied on a half-romantic, half-Hegelian *Sprachgeist*. Why does the pattern of sound shift not repeat itself after reaching the third stage? "Precisely because the spirit of language has completed its course, it does not seem to want to begin anew."[16]

Franz Bopp began a concentrated study of Sanskrit in 1814 and finally published in six volumes the first definitive or paradigmatic work in comparative linguistics, *Comparative Grammar of Sanskrit, Zend, Greek, Latin, Lithuanian, Gothic, and German* (1833–1852). Bopp complained that earlier students of language had treated it as a vehicle for cultural content and repository of historical information.[17] Rather than examine what was done with language, Bopp proposed to explain what happened in and to language itself, for only then would linguistics attain to that "higher and more scientific" level at which it would be a "history and natural description of language, . . . [which could] trace the natural-historical laws according to which occurred its development or destruction or rebirth from previous ruination."[18]

It was Bopp's intention to approach language without philosophical or cultural presuppositions. He harbored the same desire preciously expressed by Friedrich Schmitthenner: "[The grammarian] must be neither a Kantian, nor a Fichtean, nor a Schellingean, but must be precisely and only a Language-ian [*Sprachianer*]."[19] The objectivity of the new approach would yield more reliable results, but it would also impose restrictions on the investigator. The method could successfully establish the original roots from which Indo-European languages were derived, but it could not show why any of those roots came into being or why they came to mean what they did. The price of accuracy was the renunciation, at least temporarily, of certain levels of meaning and cause. "In this book I intend to give a comparative description of the organism of the languages mentioned in the title, bringing together all of their related aspects, and exploring their physical and mechanical laws as well as the origin of the forms which signify grammatical relations. *The only thing which we will leave untouched is the secret of the roots, that is, the basis for the naming of the original concepts.*"[20]

The word *organism* in the above quotation betrays the fact that Bopp's new scientific approach was not wholly without presuppositions. It had already become commonplace to refer either to language in general or to languages of a particular kind as "organic." In the second half of the eighteenth century and especially in Germany, organistic metaphors were used in deliberate contrast with the mechanism dominant in French philosophy. At the time, physics, and especially mechanics, was still the prevailing model for scientific thought, and philosophy as well. Authors favoring organistic analogies—Vico, Herder, Goethe, most romantics, for example—also tended to doubt

the adequacy of modern science. For some this involved a general distrust of science as such; but the more thoughtful specifically criticized
the mechanists for claiming to explain more than they possibly could
explain. Even Descartes needed God to set things in motion—to bring
them to life. Life is the phenomenon which mechanics cannot explain,
the great mystery and symbol for everything mysterious. Despite that,
it is clear that the organism could also serve as a new model of scientific
explanation, and so it became with the rapid rise of the biological
sciences. In a sense, then, those who intended to take the study of language out of the hands of natural scientists used a metaphor which was
destined to put it back in those same hands. Bopp himself reflects this
tension between mystery and scientific law. In his use of organistic analogies Bopp was pulled backward to a romanticist understanding of language and forward toward the later conception of linguistics as a natural science.

The grammatical forms and collective organism of the languages [studied
by comparative linguistics] are the production of their earliest period of
life, when they blossomed forth with the whole strength of youth, like
blossoms and fruits from a young stalk. Languages should be considered
organic natural bodies, which are formed according to fixed laws, develop
because they possess an inner principle of life, and gradually die off
because they do not understand themselves any longer. Thus they cast
off or mutilate or misuse (i.e., use for different purposes than those intended at their origin) their members and forms, which were at first significant, but gradually became more of an extrinsic mass.[21]

This mix of metaphors shows how tentative the biological model still
was.

Karl Ferdinand Becker tried to carry out a consistent and systematic analysis of language as an organism. In an organism, each part
functions in the context of the whole, and so it is with language. An
organism is not a collection of organs brought together by some external form, but develops according to its internal design and powers, and
so it is with language. Ultimately, an organism is its own purpose,
that is, life itself is the end of a living being, and so it is with language.
In language everything is dynamic. Although the absolute origin of
language is hidden in darkness and the first words are unknowable,
Becker felt certain that man's original conception was that of motion
and his first words, whatever their sounds and syllables, must have
expressed this.[22] If language supplies its own self-moving purpose,
however, can linguists or philosophers of language come to terms with
that purpose?

According to Becker, it is as natural for man to speak as it is for him to move and learn to walk, as it is for his body to grow. As thinking beings, men inevitably speak; it is not a matter of choice. "Man speaks because he thinks, whereas he is only silent because he wants to be; actually man does not learn to speak at all, but he does have to learn to be silent."[23] This curious point deserves some reflection. It is strange that Becker considered silence the opposite of language. The rests and pauses in a sonata or symphony are surely not nonmusic: The musical sound and the silence are both parts of the more meaningful whole which we call music in a broader and deeper sense. (So too with the dancer's stillness, stops, and poses, and even his touching of the dance floor.[24]) The clear lesson of this analogy is that a comprehensive analysis of music must consider more than the production of sounds. Becker, although he read his Hegel as well as his Humboldt, did not look for the totality in this instance. Becker wrote that we speak because we think; but it is often the case that we are silent because we think. We are consciously silent when there is some discrepancy between what we are thinking and what we desire or are able to express. In a most general sense thought is the realm of silence which lies behind our speaking. Therefore, the silence of thought is part of the totality of language which must be explained. No matter how language-bound thought may be or vice versa—if, for example, all languages reveal the universal laws of thought or the a priori forms of judgment, as Becker himself maintained—nonetheless, when someone speaks, we can never be certain that he is saying what he thinks.[25] Discrepancies between thought and speech may be accidental or intentional; in either case, and clearly in the latter, they lead to ethical questions. Silence is sometimes a despicable crime; but compulsive talking is not the norm, and phatic speech is not the exemplar. Despite Becker's emphasis on the internal laws which govern organisms, he did not especially look toward this most inward aspect of language. Rather, his organistic model led him to assert that grammar (*Sprachlehre*) should ultimately become a physiology of language. Of course, his would not be a mechanistic physiology, but one cannot help noticing its similarity to the goals of Gassendi and La Mettrie.

Jacob Grimm's lecture-essay, *On the Origin of Language,* is a good example, and very nearly the last, of the fusion of *mysterium* and *scientia* in the organistic conception of language. Grimm delivered his lecture to the Berlin Academy of Sciences in 1851—after Schelling had delivered a tribute to Herder's prize essay and Hamann's responses, and had called for a reopening of the question of language origin[26]— and then revised it into a popular essay. Grimm spoke of the rise of linguistics to the level of a genuine science during the preceding half century, but he also spoke of language as a form of revelation. He still raised seriously the possibility of a divine origin of language, but finally rejected it, not so much on linguistic as on theological grounds. Romantic metaphor, mythical references, and remnants of an older nomenclature are intermixed with scientifically established data in the essay. Herder's explication, Grimm conceded, was unsatisfactory, but he attributed this less to Herder himself than to factors beyond his control—the state of linguistic research when Herder wrote. Grimm concluded his essay, much as he had begun it, with homage to "the genius of the man who made up for that which he lacked in depth of research and rigor of learnedness by a sensitive tact and a lively feeling for the truth. . . . [Herder's answer] still hits the mark, even though, on other grounds than those available to him, the difficult question concerning the origin of language must still be posed and the answer ratified."[27] Even in such an assessment Grimm showed himself a man between two ages.

Despite advances of research, Grimm saw the origin of language as an enduring puzzle. One can affirm, with Friedrich Schlegel, that the answer to origin lies in the total history of language; one can study and reconstruct that history; one can examine Sanskrit and hypothesize beyond it to some parent language. And still the question persists: "How can the beginning of language be measured across such an abyss? Does not the entire question fall into the realm of impossibilities?"[28] Analogies between linguistics and the natural sciences bring us little closer to "the shores of its origin." The view of language history as a process of natural evolution does not as such favor either divine creation or human invention, but leaves the question open. Physicalistic explanations are disproved by the fact that children learn the language not of their race but of their country, not of their biological ancestors but of their immediate environment. On the other hand, "if language is uncreated, that is, not produced immediately by divine power, but formed through the freedom of man himself, . . . the linguist . . . can go even further than the natural scientist, because he is dealing with something human and grounded in our history and freedom . . . ; whereas in contrast all created things have no history at all. . . ."[29] In such statements Grimm seems to affirm and deny natural and linguistic evolution at one and the same time. Grimm sees language in terms of a mixed metaphor, with different elements predominating at different times: a freely spiritual organism.

For Grimm, the fundamental question about language has been and shall remain whether language was created *for* man or *by* man.

History shows that earlier stages of language had greater grammatical clarity and poetic beauty than later ones—which might support the notion that man was created with an initial perfection matched by a perfection of language. Yet, such an argument is contradicted by the Biblical account itself, the story of Adam's naming of the animals and of the Tower of Babel. In addition, the notion that God himself gave man language implies that early men had a distinct advantage over others, which would be contrary to divine justice and mercy. Finally, Grimm once again revived the old *aporia* concerning language origin and used it against the divine explanation. "If the first men were able to take in God's words, that is, to understand them, then it would seem unnecessary to reveal a language to them, which they would already have had to possess as the condition for such understanding."[30] Grimm concluded that language must be a human creation of some sort, since the assumption that it is a divine gift presumes that man is equal to the gods, whereas the assumption that it is an innate physical capacity makes man into a beast.[31]

The mix of elements in Grimm's essay reveals the basic tension in the organistic understanding of language. Grimm used details of linguistic history as established by the comparative method, but he also used ancient myths and fables as evidence for some of his conclusions. He viewed language as a fundamental enigma: "Truly, the origin of language is mysterious and miraculous, and yet it is surrounded by other miracles and mysteries."[32] Yet, two pages later, Grimm called for confirmation of his thesis by further research. Grimm was one of the last linguists who had come to maturity in direct contact with the early romantic movement. His essay is an unsynthesized combination of remnants of romanticism with prospects of the new linguistic science. The next steps in language study would see the tension of the organistic framework divided into two contrary ways of interpreting language. A century earlier a fundamental question was whether language itself was poetical or mechanical. The same basic concern will now reappear in a new form: What is the proper model for linguistic science?

Idealist Linguistics or Materialist Linguistics?

The most prominent philosophical idealists among practicing linguists were Karl Wilhelm Heyse and Haymann Steinthal, both professors at Berlin. Heyse was a student of Hegel himself, and Steinthal of Heyse. Heyse's *System of the Science of Language,* published posthumously by Steinthal from the author's notes, is a highly structured edifice of

Hegel-like divisions and progressions. On the one hand, it moves from the universal idea of language to its particular manifestations; on the other, it moves from language as subjective spirit (the act of speaking) to language as objective spirit (the history of national languages) to language as absolute spirit. The study of language, according to Heyse, underwent parallel developments: *Grammaire raisonnée* derives principles from the "subjectively reflective understanding"; whereas comparative linguistics studies the objective spirit of language, virtually disregarding the mental processes of speakers. "Philosophical *Sprachlehre* begins with the plurality of languages, but with the unity of the language-idea."[33]

Heyse explained the origin of language out of the dynamic interplay between the idea of language and its necessity. "Speaking, language considered subjectively, is externalization of the inward, presentation and expression of that which goes on inside of men. Language, considered objectively, is the means for the externalization of the inward."[34] More precisely, language is the most adequate means of expressing the free and therefore self-conscious spirit. Reason, man's difference from the beasts, is the freedom of consciousness, and as such its development is simultaneous with language. Heyse attacked Becker and others carried away with the organistic analogy: "Every organism lives through and for itself, is its own purpose. Language, however, does not speak itself; it does not lead an independent existence, but is an *organon* which serves the spirit."[35] There is a "need of the thinking spirit to express itself," and this need finds satisfaction in language, where there is a "reconciliation of spirit and matter," a reconciliation in which the material *organon* becomes the willing servant of the mind, and spirit thus gains its freedom. "The revelation of the spirit through language necessarily becomes communication; the one-sided externalization of thought becomes an exchange of thoughts; and language [*Sprache*] becomes dialogue [*Gespräch*]."[36]

Heyse offered little in the way of an empirical explanation of language origin. The initial stages of linguistic development belong to an unknowable prehistory impossible to reconstruct. Analogies with the language learning of children are misleading, since speech acquisition involves both the individual, spontaneous development of the capacities for thought and articulation as well as the transmission of an objectively given language as the material used to develop those capacities. "Without the subjective capacity and need for language, the objective language would be dead matter; and without this latter, the capacity would not develop."[37] The obstacle in the way of a solution is fundamental: From the perspective of form, speaking is a natural activity of the *merely* conscious mind, but with regard to content, thought and language are both acts of the *freely* self-conscious mind. Heyse resolved the dilemma in grand Hegelian fashion:

Language is produced by the conscious, free spirit by way of the natural development of its innermost essence itself. With this development of the spirit, freedom and necessity coincide completely. When freedom is not simultaneously necessity—that is, when it does not operate according to universal and eternal laws based in the essence of the free spirit—then it is individual whim, incidental caprice, or the mere opinion of the subject.[38]

Strictly natural acts represent necessity with no freedom; strictly individual acts, freedom without necessity; hence neither can explain language origin. Heyse's reflections lead him directly to a metaphysics of history. Language is reconciliation of matter and spirit, and the orgin of language is the wedding of freedom and necessity.

Steinthal was seldom so precisely orthodox. He was one of the most variously interpreted linguists of the century, belittled by some as an unreconstructed idealist, and either praised or censured by others as a pioneer in materialist linguistics. In the four very different editions of his work on language origin he attended more to the history of theories of origin than he did to the history of language itself.[39] He was convinced that the forces which evoke utterances in modern men are the same which first brought language to birth. "Our inquiry into the origin of language does not concern a singular, more or less accidentally coalesced occurrence of primordial times, but the timeless and unchanging origin of a power and activity in the consciousness of man generally, or the laws of the life of the soul, according to which language comes into being—today, just as in primordial times and at all times."[40]

The priority of psychological over historical verification fit Steinthal's view of speaking as creative action. Although modern men speak a transmitted language, Steinthal insisted, their situation is not fundamentally different from that of the first makers of articulate speech. Every human being says things which are new and entirely his own, even while using an already established linguistic medium—the argument long since advanced by Descartes against mechanism. Steinthal contrasted the native speaker at a loss for words with the foreigner searching for verbal equivalents. "The latter searches mechanically in his memory or his pocket dictionary; but when we are wanting for words in our mother tongue, actually that is not a toilsome search but an aggravated birth."[41] Language is perpetual birth, emanation, creation, genesis—not the one-time invention of a static product. All of the basic aspects of language origin—man's disposition toward language, his breaking forth in speech, his linguistic development—can be studied outside of any historical context. The task of the linguist, therefore, is closest to that of the psychologist:

Language is not a thing like gunpowder, but an event, like an explosion; it is not an organ, like the eye or ear, but an ability and activity, like seeing and hearing. . . . As the physiologist has the task of identifying the conditions under which men of all races saw and heard; so, it is the linguist's task to understand that state of the soul which, because of the elements working in it, is forced to express itself in sound, to break out in sounds. As human nature remains eternally the same, so too does this task. It is essentially the same for the primitive man, for the child, and for us all with reference to every act of speech.[42]

Despite Steinthal's strict demarcation of the provinces of physiologist and linguist, however, the first half of the nineteenth century had seen important advances in the physiology of speech, phonetics, and historical phonology.[43] Karl Moritz Rapp devised a system of phonetic transcription and published a four-volume physiology of speech between 1836 and 1841. The accomplishment suggested to Rapp the opposite of Steinthal's conclusion: "Language . . . is a natural product, for it was not brought about by the will of any individual nor by human reflection; rather the human spirit organized the linguistic substance unconsciously. As such, the regularity of language is as external and as material as the regularity of external nature."[44]

The successes in phonetics and the conception of language as an organism conspired to foster the notion that linguistics is properly a natural science, similar to the other *Naturwissenschaften* in goal and method. The question whether linguistics was a *Geisteswissenschaft* or a *Naturwissenschaft* dominated theoretical discussion during the 1860s and 1870s, especially in Germany and France. Abel Hovelacque and Michel Bréal, influential members of the newly founded *Société de linguistique* in Paris, adopted the viewpoint of the later Schleicher. Hovelacque wrote: "For in point of fact languages are born, grow, decay, and perish like all other living things. . . . It is precisely this conception of the *life* of language, that . . . distinguishes the modern science of language from the unmethodical speculations of the past."[45] By the time of the neogrammarians, in the late 1870s and after, interest in the dispute waned. In the late century the majority of linguists considered the argument settled in favor of the naturalists. Although they generally shunned broad theoretical questions in favor of more specific problems and field work, the concensus was that the method of the naturalists had produced more concrete and verifiable results than the philosophical perorations of idealists.

Many of the linguistic naturalists thought of themselves as fighters for the secular truth against received dogma. Thus, for example, Hovelacque: "If it cannot be admitted, without falling into metaphysical and childish conceptions, that the lingual faculty was acquired all of a sudden, without cause, without origin—in fact, *ex nihilo*—it must be allowed to be the result of a progressive development of the organs of speech."[46] Although a shabby non sequitur as argument, Hovelacque's comment discloses the quixotic strain in the stance of the naturalists. To a great extent they were fighting against straw men, for the remaining defenders of divine origin were authors of little reputation and less influence.[47]

An exchange between one linguist and one Biblicist shows the animus which inspired the two embattled camps. Franz Kaulen, a pastor from Bonn, attacked all the new linguists as heretical and godless, and it fell to the lot of August Friedrich Pott to be singled out as candidate designate for the role of anti-Christ. For all the vaunted results of the new science, Kaulen argued, it shed no light on the fundamental question, the origin and diversity of language. Despite the futility of all their etymological researches, linguists have contemptuously turned their backs on the Biblical account. "Ever since linguistics, which grew up in the innermost bosom of the church, has come to stand in more or less conscious opposition to revealed truth, the edifice of linguistic scholarship has become a Tower of Babel, whose completion will be made impossible by the fundamental differences of outlook among its builders."[48]

Pott, the linguist most directly accused, rose to the challenge with a book which was not only a counterattack against Kaulen, but which attempted to expose under the light of empirical science all mythical and theological explanations of language origin. It was with some misgivings that Pott undertook this task: "Nothing is more difficult than the total and permanent obliteration of errors, if those errors are wholly or partially grounded in religious prejudice."[49] Some myths about language are so unfounded that the effort of scholarly disproof seems wasted. Nonetheless, the forces of benightedness being so strong, Pott took upon himself one of the burdensome chores of scientific progress, the exact modern refutation of those vague ancient tales. With painstaking detail Pott showed why each particular in the old myths, whether of Moses or of Ovid, was contradicted by scientific truth. It is as though the ancient myths and Pott's modern refutations were written in two different languages.

The discrepancy between the idealist and materialist approaches to language derived in the end from the dual aspects of language itself—language as sound with meaning, as thought expressed in a physical medium. It was, in effect, the nature of language which made feasible both the idealist's and the materialist's method; just as the nature of man allows for him to be variously studied. Yet, neither the nature of man nor of language is a simple or obvious given, not even a clearly separable duality. The approach chosen also serves as a way of discovering, or obscuring, that nature. Baron C. C. J. von Bunsen— Prussian diplomat, friend of Humboldt and Max Müller, and a conscientious amateur in the world of learning—charged that idealist and materialist linguistics were both defective:

The materialists have never been able to show the possibility of the first step. They attempt to veil their inability by the easy, but fruitless assumption of an infinite space of time, destined to explain the gradual development of animals into men. . . . But neither has its counterpart, the spiritualist system of philosophy, been able to give a totally satisfactory explanation of the phenomena, and in particular of the origin of language, and therefore has not been able to drive the other theory from the field; for as the one cannot take the step from matter to thought, so the other cannot take that from thought to matter.[50]

Theoretically, idealists like Heyse and Steinthal were as deeply interested in the physical as the mental side of language; indeed their specific concern was with the reconciliation of linguistic form and matter. As Feuerbach and Marx said of Hegel, however, the reconciliation was often more in idea than in actuality. Steinthal's classification of languages, for instance, betrayed an unexamined "formalistic" bias. All languages join form and matter, but in the inflected languages form dominates matter. Thus, Steinthal inferred, inflected languages represent a more perfect linguistic type.[51] This was no less circular than the argument of some materialists that, inasmuch as the physical aspects of language lend themselves more easily to clear description and precise analysis, therefore linguistics will be more scientific if it concentrates on these alone. When the contrary rationales for method come into open conflict, the danger is that one side of language itself may be ignored. Then comes, by one group of disputants, a pursuit of the fruits of empirical study regardless of their partiality and, by the other, a "philosophic" withdrawal away from the particulars of concrete evidence. At that point both groups effectively renounce any attempt to understand the whole as anything more than an empty abstraction. And when that happens it is doubtful whether the two sides to a dispute can even address one another meaningfully any longer: Although they are ostensibly "talking about the same things," it is questionable whether they are even "seeing the same things."

A Fable in the *Ursprache*

August Schleicher reflected in his own career the metamorphoses undergone by comparative philology as a whole after its scientific revolution. Schleicher began as a Hegelian, but in the end he totally rejected idealism and turned to Darwinism. He began his career as a philologist, but ultimately he divided the concerns of philology sharply from those of linguistics. In his earliest works he viewed language as a phenomenon in the realm of spirit; in the latest ones he saw it as a product of nature, to be studied with the methods of *Naturwissenschaft*. When Schleicher published his first book in 1848, the revolution in linguistics had not yet been completed: Both the method and content of the discipline were still in dispute. By the time of his death in 1868, the revolutionary phase was past, the paradigms for linguistic research were established in the works of Bopp and Schleicher himself, and "normal science" ensued.[52] When Bopp died, Schleicher and Adalbert Kuhn wrote obituary remarks lamenting the death of the founder of linguistics as a science.[53] When Schleicher himself died, the memorial was written by his student and collaborator, Johannes Schmidt. Continuing the theme of the earlier eulogy, Schmidt repeated that Bopp was indeed the founder, but that Schleicher had secured the foundations.[54]

Born in 1821, Schleicher pursued higher studies in Leipzig, Tübingen, and Bonn and in the course of these peregrinations moved from theology to philosophy to philology. In Tübingen he was a student of Ferdinand Christian Baur, who introduced him to the historical treatment of philosophy; and it was there that Schleicher became a convinced Hegelian and decided that the historical study of language should have first priority. In Bonn, Schleicher was especially influenced by Friedrich Wilhelm Ritschl, eminent expert in textual criticism and reconstruction. Ritschl's method of constructing a *stemma* or "genealogical tree" to represent manuscript variants bore its stamp in Schleicher's later nontextual reconstruction.[55] Schleicher also developed an intense avocational interest in botany—another area which, he thought, provided clear linguistic analogs.

Schleicher's first book, *On the Comparative History of Language*

(1848), included a substantial section of introductory material in which he expounded his broad view of linguistic development. He adopted Hegel's notion that ultimate origins belong to an era of prehistory permanently obscure, and argued that the total development of language falls into two parts, first its prehistorical evolution and then the documented changes which occur after man has gained historical consciousness. The first of these was a time of "language formation" (*Sprachbildung*), the actual forming of languages from primitive elements into the highly regulated idioms known to us from the dawn of history. No matter whether a language was isolating, agglutinating, or inflecting, it reached its zenith somewhere around the point when man became a consciously historical being. The prehistory of language was the true period of linguistic progress, for it was the formation of language itself which was then the principal task and activity of spirit. Not so in the historical age: *Sprachbildung* and history are mutually exclusive. With man's entrance into history, languages are already completed, and thus language became a means rather than an end for spirit. Language continued to change, but now by the diversification of established parent languages. Far from being advances, these historical changes have been linguistically regressive:

The powerful nature of earlier periods of the world, forcefully active and swelling with creative potency, has come down to mere reproduction in our own time; it no longer begets anything new, once the world spirit in man has come out of its otherness; ever since the human spirit . . . came to itself in history, there has been no more productivity in the unconscious creation of man's concrete image, language.[56]

Languages are simplified during the historical era, their structures undermined, as syntactical distinctions and circumlocution replace inflection. But language in decline is spirit victorious, part of the process whereby spirit gains its freedom. In prehuman times, spirit was in the bondage of nature; in the prehistorical era, it was captured in the sounds of language; but the human self-consciousness which emerged in history was a release of spirit from all captivity: Instead, language came to be enslaved by spirit.

Schleicher's division between linguistic prehistory and history was the line separating conjecture from scientific knowledge. There can be no scientific verification of speculations about prehistory. Schleicher's gingerly treatment of the accepted linguistic typology illustrates his caution. He essayed a strictly Hegelian analysis of the relationship among isolating, agglutinat'ng, and inflecting languages. In isolating languages, matter predominates, since relations are not explicitly expressed but implicitly indicated by word order and sentence structure. In agglutinating languages, meaning and relation still do not form an organic unity: As the word *agglutination* implies, the different elements are merely "glued together." Union is achieved in the inflecting languages, where there is a "return to the phonetic unity of meaning and relation [*Beziehung*]. . . ."[57] This makes a neat Hegelian triad; but, although Schleicher found it suggestive, he refused to make any inferences from it about the prehistorical formation of language. The science of language can establish the changes which occurred from the fully formed parent languages to daughter languages during the historical age, but it cannot explain the origin of the parent languages.

Since the creation of language is prior to history, it follows, in Schleicher's Hegelian terms, that it cannot be the work of self-consciousness. In that case, some other force must have operated. In one passage from his first book Schleicher nearly exposed the bridge which would lead him from Hegelianism to his later conception of linguistics as a natural science:

The systematic part of language research, in contrast with the historical part, has . . . an undeniable similarity with the natural sciences. This is particularly obvious in the division of languages into classes. . . . This similarity of the science of language with the natural sciences is on account of that prehistorical epoch, since language is for the human spirit what nature is for the world spirit, the condition of otherness. . . .[58]

In his second book, *The Languages of Europe in Systematic Perspective* (1850), Schleicher made this point more emphatically and removed it from its Hegelian context. The first section of that work was entitled "Linguistics and Philology." Although these two disciplines supply one another with supporting materials, Schleicher said, they are entirely different in method and in object. "Linguistics stands in contrast with philology and has language as such for its object; thus it has no direct concern with the historical life of the peoples who speak the languages studied, but rather it constitutes a part of man's natural history."[59]

The philologist is concerned with history, which commences at the point where the free human will comes into existence; whereas the object of linguistics is languages, whose constitution lies entirely outside of the willful determination of any individual, as little so, for example, as it would be possible for a nightingale to exchange its song for that of a lark.[60]

Themes from the first volume are carried over into the second, though with changes and without the regular references to some *ipse dixit* out of Hegel. But Schleicher openly retracted his earlier assertion that language belongs to the spiritual side of man, because language has a history.[61] Rather, language merely shows a becoming (*Werden*), like all natural phenomena, and not history in any accurate sense; hence language belongs to the "unfree and natural side of man."

Schleicher spent the next ten years without publishing a major book. He devoted his time to collecting data, working out individual problems, and perfecting the comparative method of reconstruction. During this period Schleicher refined his notion of the "family tree" of Indo-European languages with a protolanguage (*Ursprache*) and parent languages (*Grundsprachen*). The metaphor of the tree was intended quite literally. The trunk was proto-Indo-Germanic, from which branched out, on the one side, the Slavo-Germanic *Grundsprache*, and on the other side, the Ario-Graeco-Italo-Celtic *Grundsprache*, each subdivided approximately as the names suggest. Thence the "tree" ramified into the various known Indo-European languages and ended with a final column, the twigs, the various dialects of known languages. The roots of the tree remained hidden in the ground of prehistory. With the comparative method Schleicher was able to reconstruct word forms of the parent languages and of the Indo-European *Ursprache* itself. The systematic extension of the tree metaphor led Schleicher to some highly debatable hypotheses. The tree implied a process of increasing bifurcation and diversification, ending with the different dialects as "twigs." From this Schleicher concluded that the *Ursprache* and *Grundsprachen* were dialect-free and that the number of different languages spoken by Indo-Europeans increased at a geometrical rate during the historical epoch. The reconstructed protolanguage loomed as an uncorrupted linguistic ideal. Occasionally Schleicher argued that the reconstructed forms were really more certain than words from languages preserved in documents, since texts are subject to the vicissitudes of history, climate, and human ignorance, whereas deduction is certain. Wilhelm Streitberg made the point:

The Indo-Germanic *Ursprache*, as Schleicher conceives it, is thus necessarily a perfect *Idealsprache*, which is not subject to the "sound laws" and cannot be subject to them. For in the same moment when the first sound law would begin to take effect, that is, the first signs of decline would be recognizable, it would cease to be an *Ursprache* at all, namely the final goal in the backward and upward direction of Indogermanistics: There would still be one spot to be wiped out, one law of sound change still to be worked back to its conclusion.[62]

For Schleicher, the beginning of linguistic history was a state of suspended historical animation. What, then, gave to this *Ursprache* its "principle of motion"?[63]

With these ten years of specialized labors behind him, Schleicher was again ready to make a comprehensive statement about the nature of language and the proper method for its study. This came in *The German Language* (1860) and the *Compendium of the Comparative Grammar of Indogermanic Languages* (1861—1862). In a long introductory section to the former, Schleicher retained many themes from his earlier works, but changed their emphasis. For example, he continued to differentiate between the prehistorical development and the historical decline of language; but now he stressed the unconscious forces which molded language before history. He implied that the free use of language by historically conscious men is not the concern of linguistics—or *Glottik,* as he now preferred to call it—since there the linguist is perpetually distracted by the contents of written or spoken evidence rather than giving exclusive attention to the linguistic matter itself. This suspension of the intentions of speakers was slowly leading Schleicher to the point where he would imply that language per se— which, by circular definition, came to mean language as the linguist studies it—could be explained out of the set of unconscious forces and unfree laws determining its verbal and syntactic elements. The final step in this reasoning was to infer that, since language is defined as its observable elements, then linguistics is an observational science.

Schleicher now felt that reconstruction and the more sophisticated classification of languages provided sufficient clues for the formulation of hypotheses about the origin of language.[64] He maintained that there was probably an original polygenesis of language and that it would therefore be misguided to attempt to reconstruct proto-protolanguages connecting the major language families.[65] He thought it probable that all languages at the dawn of human life were isolating ones, that some remained so, whereas others advanced to an agglutinating stage, and a few became inflectional. Moving closer to the postulate that a single law governed all linguistic development in both the prehistorical and historical eras, Schleicher suggested that the main difference was that prehistorical change went from the simple to the complex, whereas there was a process of simplification during the historical age. On the general question of linguistic beginnings, Schleicher emphasized the unconscious element. Resorting to the time-honored *aporia,* he argued that language cannot have been a human invention, because inventions are made by conscious and thinking beings, which men cannot have been before the acquisition of language. "Man can no more invent a language than he can a rose or a nightingale."[66]

Schleicher became still more emphatic in his assertion that linguistics is an observational science, which yields objective results. In a monograph on the differentiation between noun and verb, Schleicher argued that the distinction, far from being universal, is consistently carried out only in the Indo-European languages. His principal support for this contention was the argument that there can be no grammatical differentiations unless there is a discernible and regular phonetic difference attached to them. "In other words, do function and sound, content and form coincide in language, or are there functions without any audible expression, contents which take no appearance in form? Do there exist in the language-feeling [*Sprachgefühl*] of the speaker any grammatical categories which he does not signify in any phonetic way?" Schleicher answered his own question in the negative, because "even in language the spirit (function) never moves separately from its body (sound)."[67] Beyond the correspondence of phonetic and semantic elements, Schleicher averred that the internal form of language is inseparable from its external form: "It can be demonstrated by observation that the functional formation [*Gestaltung*] of language, its inner form, is different in different languages, indeed that this difference is in complete correspondence with the difference expressed in sounds and forms."[68] "Thus we steadfastly hold to the conviction that there is nothing which goes on in the [mind of the] speaker which is not expressed in sound, and that the sound is the unexceptionable and in fact the only witness for the function, and that therefore a language possesses only those functions which are audibly expressed."[69] From the disputable proposition that there are no phonetic elements in language of which man is not conscious, Schleicher inferred the even more debatable conclusion that there is nothing in human consciousness which is not audibly expressed. This fallacious conversion was then used to justify a strengthened version of his earlier argument: Since there can be nothing unobservable in language, linguistics can only be an observational science.

Schleicher was now ready for the final step, the proposition that linguistics is a natural science which deals with physical evolution. Schleicher took this step in two works, *Darwinian Theory and the Science of Language* (1863) and *The Meaning of Language for the Natural History of Man* (1865). The former was an open letter to Ernst Haeckel, Schleicher's junior colleague at Jena. Because of Schleicher's interest in botany, Haeckel had prodded him to read *The*

Origin of Species. Schleicher was immediately taken with the idea that Darwinism could be applied to the evolution of language and that Darwin's theories about the origin of species ran parallel to his own on the life of language. The proper study of language must also adopt an evolutionary standpoint. In language too there is a struggle for existence and survival of the fittest, which causes the intermediate forms (*Mittelformen*) to become extinct. The relationships among genera, species, and subspecies are the same.

To a certain extent there will also be a correspondence with the actual origin of plant and animal organisms: The simple cell is probably the common original form of them, as the simple root is of languages. . . . The cells must probably be presumed to have developed *en masse* at a certain period of the life of our globe, and so too with the simple meaning-carrying sounds [*Bedeutungslaute*] in the world of languages. These initial forms of organic life, which cannot even be classified with either the plant or animal kingdom, later developed in different directions. Exactly so with the roots of language.[70]

Schleicher went beyond analogy: "Languages are natural organisms, which, unregulated by the will of man, arise according to certain laws, grow and develop, and then become old and die out. . . . Glottics, the science of language, is therefore a natural science; its method is in particular and in general the same as that of the rest of the natural sciences."[71]

Schleicher's last book was a defense against critics of the pamphlet on Darwinism. In it Schleicher went still further: "Language is the audibly perceptible symptom of the action of a complex of material relations in the formation of the brain and the speech organs. . . ."[72] Schleicher now hypothesized that the various original languages developed differently because of varying climatic and environmental conditions. He called for more intense research in the comparative anatomy of the speech organs, insisting that this should explain the difference between speaking and nonspeaking animals as well as variations in the tongues that men employ. Minimal differences in the speech apparatus, Schleicher hinted, may have maximum effect upon the sounds produced. Study of the speech organs should provide a more reliable basis for racial and genetic classification than cephalic index or skeletal formation, for "the natural system of languages is in my opinion simultaneously the natural system of humanity."[73] Schleicher now identified the "rise of linguistic forms" with "the development of the organs which form language."[74]

To the end Schleicher retained his distinction between the history of language and its prehistory, adding a still earlier stage for the anatomical development of the organs themselves. But Schleicher now asserted something quite different: "The same laws of life, which we are actually able to observe [in known languages], we assume to apply in all essentials to those periods of time which are inaccessible to direct observation, and thus also to the first origin of language. . . ."[75] He compared the linguist to a chemist studying the sun: He cannot go and directly observe the ultimate object of his investigation, but he knows enough about the effects and consequences to have a good idea of its nature. Herewith Schleicher opened the door for the scientific reconstruction of linguistic prehistory. For that Schleicher himself did not yet claim to have either the method or the data. But Schleicher had clearly gone beyond the limits previously set for linguistic reconstruction: the proto-languages of the historically documented language families.

In 1868, the year of his death, Schleicher produced what was, in a symbolic sense at least, the capstone of his linguistic researches. He published a fable of his own making in reconstructed proto-Indo-Germanic. Prior to this he had only deduced individual words and forms, but the composition of these into sentences and paragraphs was an obvious possibility. Although Schleicher has often been ridiculed for the fable, it was the logical outcome of the method he pursued. The following is the story which Schleicher wrote in *Urindogermanisch*:

Avis akvāsas ka

Avis, jasmin varna na ā ast, dadarka akvams, tam, vāgham garum vaghantam, tam, bhāram magham, tam, manum āku bharantam. Avis akvabhjams ā vavakat: kard aghnutai mai vidanti manum akvams agantam.

Akvāsas ā vavakant: krudhi avai, kard aghnutai vividvantsvas: manus patis varnām avisāms karnanti svabhjam gharmam vastram avibhjams ka varnā na asti.

Tat kukruvants avis agram ā bhugat.[76]

Critics could argue whether this fable was an invention in an invented language or a deduction in a deduced language. But, at the end of his life, Schleicher evidently judged that the question of the origin of all language could be scientifically resolved, and that the question of the origin of Indo-European had been solved.

[11]

THE LAST
PHASE

Significant discussion of the origin of language waned during the last three or four decades of the nineteenth century, and by the 1890s it was nearly dead. Darwinism gave final impetus to interest in the topic: Darwin himself offered an explanation, and it evoked controversy among supporters and opponents of the new doctrine. There was also some indirect interest among a few philosophers and poets, but their concerns were far removed from those of the now established linguists. Increasingly, self-respecting professionals in the science of language retreated from the question and, in the end, became openly contemptuous of it. As a rule, the only aspect of the question considered admissible by linguists was the origin of language in children, the psychology of language learning. Wilhelm Wundt, who devoted a volume of his ten-volume *Folk Psychology* to the development of language, was given a good hearing in the linguists' scholarly journals, largely because he specifically restricted the scope of the question. Other authors were abruptly dismissed as dilettantes. It was not simply a split between professionals and amateurs, however, but of linguistic scientists from all others who concerned themselves with language. The two sides of language, its mental and physical aspects, were now conveniently separated in the "two cultures" of its respective students. The task of envisioning the whole was abandoned, or at least postponed, in favor of the more precise examination of the parts.

The charge of dilettantism was not always misdirected. There was, for example, the case of Christoph Gottlieb Voigtmann, a teacher at the Gymnasium in Coburg. Voigtmann tried to draw the line against Max Müller, particularly, and generally against all the new-fangled students of language. Voigtmann complained that contemporary linguists, although "very learned," went against nature, because they "sought the roots not in, but . . . behind the natural sounds."[1] For his part, Voigtmann went directly to nature and derived all the utterances of human speech onomatopoeically from the sounds of roosters and cuckoos—representing respectively (and consistently with the metaphysical implications of it all) the principles of permanence (the domesticated chickens) and change (the migratory and undomestic cuckoos). All the beauties and subleties of later human idiom began in the throats of singing fowl. The most natural of human arts sprang from the same source: The very words *cano* and *canto* (Latin "to sing") derived by internal consonant shift from the primordial *cuckoo*. Perhaps the most ingenious of Voigtmann's inventive etymologies was his derivation of *weil* (German "because") : It was generated by the addition of initial and terminal consonants to the root *Ei* (German "egg")—which not only returns to the natural motifs, but gives a capsule explanation of all dilemmas of causation, the chicken-and-the-egg problem. In a hilarious review Johannes Schmidt dubbed Voigtmann the "chief cuckoo."[2]

During this same period the principal explanations of language origin received names which would prove popular enough to hold for a century. One of the most widely read works on the subject, especially in the English-speaking world, was Max Müller's *Lectures on the Science of Language*. Müller denominated the onomatopoeic or imitative explanation, which he associated with Herder, the "bow-wow theory"; the expressive, emotive, or interjectional account, which he associated with Condillac, Müller called the "pooh-pooh theory."[3] There were minor eddies of disagreement whether Müller himself subscribed to the "ding-dong theory," which he attributed to Lorenz Oken and Heyse, the thesis that linguistic beginnings derived from the fact that all natural things have vibrating resonance.[4] It was inevitable that new nicknames would be tried out. A. H. Sayce devised an explanation whereby "just as the Darwinian hypothesis . . . evolves the animal creation out of a primeval mass of gelatinous matter of infinite potentialities, so too [this] theory of language evolves the manifold creations of speech out of the unformed and undeveloped primitive sentence."[5] Gloating, Sayce called his hypothesis "the jelly-fish theory of language."

Although serious concern with language origin was ebbing among linguists and philosophers, there was, from a sheerly quantitative standpoint, probably no period when more was written about it.[6] The list of essays or books, written between 1860 and 1890, announcing some theory of language origin in their titles, is lengthy indeed. Except for a few responses to the challenge of Darwinism, however, they were all written by nonlinguists. Frederick W. Farrar was a clergyman, Horatio Hale a lawyer and amateur ethnologist, Lazarus Geiger and Ludwig Noiré professors of philosophy. Nor were the conclusions of these works impressively new or, for the most part, important. Farrar and T. Hewitt Key still defended the mimetic "bow-wow theory"; Hensleigh Wedgwood opted for the interjectional "pooh-pooh theory."[7] Geiger, as a Kantian, emphasized the mind's active role in the genesis of language and reason.[8] Noiré arrived at the idea that language originated in the sounds of communal labor, thereby inventing the novel "heave-ho theory."[9]

Another striking feature of the more serious works about language origin composed during the last phase is the new consciousness of the history of language theory. Beginning with Steinthal, it became accepted practice to commence with a historical review of the important opinions on the subject. These usually started either with the Greeks or the controversies of the mid-eighteenth century. This was the format followed by Geiger and Noiré, Max Müller and A. H. Sayce. It was also during the 1860s that there appeared the first flurry of works dealing specifically with the history of linguistics as a science.[10] Such monographs, as well as the frequent historical and biographical notices in the professional journals, began to appear only when it was clearly accepted what the parameters of the discipline in fact were. Only by the 1860s was linguistic science cohesive enough, distinct and stable enough, for histories of *Sprachwissenschaft*. Only then were things quiet enough for this type of historical reflection, which created an almost establishmentarian version of the history of linguistics, with each step leading in a rational line to the advent of the neogrammarians.[11] Linguistics had reached something like a plateau, from which some of the journeymen themselves could look back in comfort and even with a measure of self-congratulation, for their success had exceeded all expectations.

The Missing Link in Linguistic Evolution

Charles Darwin published his epoch-making *The Origin of Species by Means of Natural Selection* in 1859. In it he did not discuss the evolution of human speech, and made but one brief reference to language as a model for classificatory schemes.[12] In fact, the *Origin* was a very cautious work, which only implied that the human species developed according to the same evolutionary laws as did the others. It was,

nonetheless, an implication seized upon immediately, the most controversial item in the public dispute which raged over the Darwinian
theory. There were many writers in the next decade who applied the
doctrine to the origin and history of language—Schleicher, T. H.
Huxley, Canon Farrar, Hensleigh Wedgwood, Ernst Haeckel, W. H. J.
Bleek. Darwin himself first treated the subject in *The Descent of Man*
(1871). Even there he was cautious and deferred to the judgment of
those he considered more expert in this field—Farrar, Wedgwood, and
above all Schleicher.

Darwin's most extensive discussion of language was in a chapter
of *The Descent of Man* comparing the mental powers of man with
the lower animals, dealing with reason, the use of tools, self-consciousness, the sense of beauty, the belief in God, and the moral sense, along
with language. It was his purpose, here as elsewhere, to show the
genealogical links among species without obliterating specific differences. Darwin concurred in the view that "the habitual use of articulate language" is a human peculiarity, but he then added several quali-
fiers. Although articulate language is peculiarly human, human
language is not exclusively articulate: like other animals, men utter
"cries of pain, fear, surprise, anger" and some of these are "more
expressive than any words."[13] Furthermore, it is not the understanding
of articulate words which is distinctively human, since dogs, for instance, can respond to them. Nor is it the act of articulation, for parrots
are capable of that. Rather, Darwin concluded, "the lower animals
differ from man solely in his almost infinitely larger power of associating together the most diversified sounds and ideas."[14] As a *differentia
specifica,* language is a difference of degree and not of kind.

According to Darwin, the nearest analogue to human language
is the singing of birds. He took the evidence to indicate that the varied
species of birds learn their distinctive sounds by association with their
kind rather than uttering them by instinct. There is an instinctual
tendency among birds to vocalize and make sounds of some sort, but
the specific sound patterns are learned. There is a similar combination
of heredity and learning in human language, which is an art, to be
sure, but an art which men have a native predisposition to acquire.
Its essential characteristics, articulation and conventionality, are not
part of its natural foundation and impulse. Thus Darwin saw language
as distinctive and then again not so distinctive. Darwin ventured that
"some unusually wise ape-like animal" may have imitated the growl
of some other beast and thus taken the "first step in the formation of a
language."[15] He went on to say that even dogs clearly show that they
can form general ideas, albeit not such extensive ones as men do. Once

again Darwin saw a clear difference between human speech and other forms of expression and communication, but no distinct break between them. As with all such gradualistic schemes, Darwin's final problem was to locate the prior cause. The use of the speech organs could have led by inheritance to their improvement, but did a more efficient brain lead to more articulate speech or vice versa? Darwin decided that there was reciprocal influence. Such gradualism covers up the implicit or modified teleology of "natural selection" and "the preservation of favored races." As the more sophisticated defenders of divine agency said of God, so did Darwin imply of the evolutionary process, that it endowed man with the capacity and inclination for language in general, whereas the particulars were left to human convention.

Darwin also thought that the basis for human language might be the use of the voice for purposes of sexual selection and mating. It is a point further elaborated in *The Expression of the Emotions in Man and Animals,* first planned as a chapter of *The Descent of Man,* then published a year later as a separate book. The voice was first used as a means to entice, and to ward off competition. George Darwin attributed to his father the view that "man is indebted for language not entirely to the vast utility of so perfect a means, but partly to the philoprogenitive nature of his ancestors."[16] From this additional link between human language and animal expression, Darwin inferred that articulate language was preceded by music.[17] He drew heavily on material worked out by Herbert Spencer, for whom all nuances of the voice—loudness, quality, timbre, pitch, interval, rate of variation— were "the physiological results of variations of feeling."[18] Thus, for example, the volume or pitch of an utterance is in direct proportion to the intensity of pleasure or pain which evoked it. Spencer argued, somewhat differently from Darwin, that all music was originally vocal and that it arose as an exaggeration or idealization of that part of human speech which constituted the "natural language of the passions." He summed up his thesis:

Thus we find all the leading vocal phenomena to have a physiological basis. They are so many manifestations of the general law that feeling is a stimulus to muscular action. . . . The expressiveness of these various modifications of voice is therefore innate. . . . When the like sound is made by another, we ascribe the like feeling to him; and by a further consequence . . . have a certain degree of it aroused in ourselves.[19]

The expressive theory of language origin, once favored by poets and critics against mechanical scientists, was now appropriated by biological scientists. The tendencies of earlier organicists now disappear, however, since it is clear that both Spencer and Darwin understood the "expression of the emotions" in a stimulus-response framework—the very framework that previous expressive theories were intended to overcome.

Applications of the main outlines of Darwinian theory to the later history of language were soon forthcoming. As the social Darwinists saw the emergence of a rule of the strong in political and economic institutions, so linguistic Darwinists could look for a survival of the fittest in grammatical and lexical evolution. Darwin himself, after pointing out the frequency with which useless vestigial elements are retained in languages, drew the analogy.

Languages, like organic beings, can be classed in groups under groups. . . . Dominant languages and dialects spread widely, and lead to the gradual extinction of other tongues. . . . Distinct languages may be crossed or blended together. . . . The survival or preservation of certain favoured words in the struggle for existence is natural selection.[20]

Sir Charles Lyell devoted an entire chapter of *The Antiquity of Man* to a demonstration of the law of gradual transmutation in the history of languages, and Ernst Haeckel reiterated these ideas.[21] When the work of Haeckel's cousin from South Africa, W. H. J. Bleek, *On the Origin of Language,* was published in Germany and England, Haeckel wrote the preface. Language, Haeckel wrote, along with other physical and moral characteristics, was unshakable proof that the South African tribes stood "at the lowest stage of human development, and made the smallest advance beyond the ape."[22] Haeckel praised the contributions of Bleek, who had "manifold opportunities for becoming more closely acquainted with those lower races of men, who in every respect remind us of our animal ancestors, and who, to the unprejudiced comparative student of nature, seem to manifest a closer connection with the gorilla and chimpanzee of that region than with a Kant or a Göthe."[23] Bleek emigrated to South Africa as colonial librarian, and he there studied exotic languages, but he traveled with the commonplace intellectual baggage of positivism and white supremacy. Linguistic Darwinism provided a most convenient rationalization for empire.

The attack against Darwinism in linguistics was led by Max Müller. Born and educated in Germany, Müller took British citizenship after his engagement by the East India Company as editor of the *Rigveda.* As the first professor of comparative philology at Oxford, Müller exerted great influence on a generation of English students, many of whom knew comparative linguistics only through the filter of Müller's popular lectures. Müller was a prolific and enthusiastic writer, and the difficulty of summarizing his position was already observed by W. D. Whitney: "It is never entirely easy to reduce to a skeleton of logical statement a discussion as carried on by Müller, because he is careless of logical sequence and connection, preferring to pour himself out, as it were, over his subject, in a gush of genial assertion and interesting illustration."[24] The crucial assertions were "No Reason Without Language: No Language Without Reason"—motto for both *The Science of Language* (1861–1864) and *The Science of Thought* (1887)—and "Language the Barrier between Man and Beast" or "Language the Rubicon, and no brute will dare to cross it." Carefully expounded, such slogans might serve as a shorthand for a serious refutation of certain aspects of Darwinism. Unfortunately, however, Müller favored the appeal to authority as a debating device: No true philosophers would deny the arguments of Kant; thus the evolutionists are clearly not true philosophers.

On balance, Müller's basic objections against evolutionary theory combine a dubious assertion with a distortion of Darwin's actual position. "If it can be proved," said Müller, "that man derives his origin genealogically, and, in the widest sense of the word, historically, from some lower animal, it is useless to say another word on the mind of man being different from the mind of animals."[25] This facile dismissal does not hold true, even for those who maintain that the difference between animal and human intelligence, as well as language, involves more than the degree of mental powers, but a breakthrough into distinctly new possibilities. Studies of animal behavior may be unsuited to illuminate the nature of those new possibilities, but that does not entail that there are no links between animals and men. The classical distinction between causes and conditions was not meant to lead to the dismissal of inquiry into the conditions of phenomena or their evolution. On the contrary, the isolation of cause should clarify the preconditions for a phenomenon and identify the causes required beyond the physical conditions. In like manner, Müller first distorted, and only then refuted, the evolutionist's notion of insensible gradation, as though it implied that there are no specific differences whatsoever. Müller used the affirmation that human language is unique to dismiss all inquires into transitions. "Why allege a transition, if we do not know anything about it? It is in alleging such a transition that we raise our ignorance to the rank of knowledge."[26]

Friedrich Engels allowed the evolutionary link between man and animals, and yet insisted on the distinctiveness of human existence.

Engels dealt with language origin in "The Part Played by Labour in the Transition from Ape to Man," a chapter of *Dialectics of Nature*. According to Engels, man exists in a completely different relationship to nature than do the animals.

In short, the animal merely *uses* external nature, and brings about change in it simply by his presence; man by his changes makes it serve his ends, *masters* it. This is the final, essential distinction between man and other animals, and once again it is labour that brings about this distinction.[27]

The essential factor in man's evolution, therefore, is not the mutation of physical organs, but man's changing relation to nature. Erect stature and the opposable thumb were physical changes, but their importance lay in enabling men to work, bringing men closer together in joint activity and mutual support.

In short, men in the making arrived at the point where *they had something to say* to one another. The need led to the creation of its organ; the undeveloped larynx of the ape was slowly but surely transformed by means of gradually increased modulation, and the organs of the mouth gradually learned to pronounce one articulate letter after another.[28]

The advancement of speech and labor, in their turn, led to further development of the brain, and the full evolution of *homo sapiens* as a speaking, working being who could make the world his own.

Among linguists themselves, William Dwight Whitney, the foremost American philologist, led the attack on Max Müller. In a prolonged debate which eventuated in malicious personal recriminations, Whitney moved from respectful but critical reviews to openly hostile critiques and finally to a book-length exposé of inconsistencies culled from the pages of Müller.[29] Müller, Whitney charged, "is so penetrated with a sense of the supreme importance of language to man, that he cannot bear to admit anything which seems to him to derogate from it."[30] Müller, he objected, goes from the proposition that language is immensely important to thought, which is absolutely true, to the stipulation that no thought is possible without language, which is the exaggeration of a truth, to the concluding absurdity that thought and language are identical.[31] The alleged correlation is unenlightening so long as the terms go undefined.

Although Whitney raised these objections, he did not commit himself to Darwinism, or, for that matter, to any theory of language origin. He stoutly maintained that linguistic meaning is conventionally established, but how the conventions themselves were established he did not answer.[32] Whitney would not allow himself to be pushed into unsubstantiated and unverifiable speculations. In the end, he felt, the evolutionist can make no contribution to linguistic theory and "linguistic science has no more to say about the evolution of animal life than of vegetable life, or of geologic structure."[33] The biologist deals with natural structures, and the linguist with conventional meanings. Whitney excluded both gradual transition and abrupt breakthrough in linguistic evolution.

No steps between the wholly instinctive expression of the animals and the wholly . . . conventional expression of man will ever be discovered. . . . There is neither *saltus* [leap] nor gradual transition in the case: no transition, because the two are essentially different; no *saltus,* because human speech is an historical development out of infinitesimal beginnings. . . .[34]

Whitney, of course, rejected all theological explanations as well. With all of these alternatives excluded, however, one is forced to wonder not only how but whether language ever originated.

The Dark Depths of the Unconscious

Numerous authors during the nineteenth century thought that the wellsprings of language lay beneath the surface of consciousness. It was a dominant theme in the early works of Ernst Moritz Arndt.[35] Schopenhauer suggested, with little elaboration, that language originated instinctually rather than rationally.[36] Eduard von Hartmann devoted a chapter of his *Philosophy of the Unconscious* (1869) to "The Unconscious in the Origin of Language."[37] As with so many of his chapters, however, instead of coming to specifics, Hartmann combined repeated assertions of his thesis with ponderous intimations of the grand seriousness of it all. Théodule Ribot, a French experimental psychologist, wrote occasional essays dealing with the origin of speech and evolution of abstraction. He concluded: "The completely developed languages . . . bear throughout the print of the unconscious labor that has fashioned them for centuries: They are petrified psychology."[38] Freud also commented briefly on the origin of language:

The original sounds of speech served for communication, and summoned the speaker's sexual partner; the further development of linguistic roots accompanied the working activities of primal man. These activities . . . were performed in common and were accompanied by rhythmically repeated utterances. In this way a sexual interest became attached to work. Primal man made work acceptable, as it were, by treating it as an equivalent and substitute for sexual activity. The words enunciated during work in common thus had two meanings; they denoted sexual acts as well as the working activity equated with them. As time went on, the words became detached from the sexual meaning and fixed to the work. . . . In this way a number of verbal roots would have been formed, all of which were of sexual origin and had subsequently lost their sexual meaning.[39]

The theories of libido, sublimation, and dream symbolism are all suggested in this interpretation of the origin of language from the combined impulses of sexuality and labor.

Nietzsche gave more careful consideration to the role of the unconscious in language. In an early fragment of 1869 or 1870, "Of the Origin of Language," he argued that language was not the conscious work either of individuals or of any collective. He supported his thesis on three main grounds: Conscious thought is only possible with the help of (therefore, after) language; conscious thinking is actually detrimental to the vitality of language; and language is too complex to be an individual invention, too uniform to be the outcome of mass agreement.[40] Language, therefore, is a product of instinct, which Nietzsche was at pains to define: It is not conscious, but it is also not mechanical or external stimulation, but "the most individual accomplishment of the individual or a mass, springing from its character, . . . the innermost kernel of one's essential being."[41] In another fragment, about a year later, "On Music and Words," Nietzsche refined this notion of instinct and introduced the contrast between the Dionysian and Apollonian, the vital unconscious impulse and conscious artistic control. According to this fragment, original language is musical, and original music vocal: There is in language an original "tonal substratum," upon which both verbal and gesture symbolism are overlaid.[42] Unlike the multiplicity of articulate languages, this "tonal substratum" is common to all, since it is the direct expression of the will and of "all degrees of pleasure and pain." A similar theme is incorporated in Nietzsche's first major book, *The Birth of Tragedy from the Spirit of Music* (1872):

The world-symbolism of music can never be exhaustively attained in language, because [music] symbolically relates to the original contradiction and original pain in the heart of the primordial One, and thus symbolizes a sphere which is beyond and before all appearance. In comparison with it, every appearance is only an image; hence language, as the organ and symbol of appearances, can never at all make outwardly evident the innermost depths of music. . . .[43]

On the surface of language there is conscious rationality; beneath language and penetrating it there is unconscious impulse. Nietzsche does not deny language any more than he does the Apollonian—so long as they do not inhibit the forces of life, and men do not succumb to "the seduction of language and the fundamental errors of rationality petrified in it."[44]

Nietzsche was still a young professor of classics at Basel when he published *The Birth of Tragedy*. The work was ill received by the scholarly community and Nietzsche became increasingly embittered against the "professional establishment" in philology and linguistics. He delivered blistering polemics in *The Future of our Educational Institutions* (1872), *Wisdom and Science in Combat* (1873), and *We Philologists* (1874).

Consciously or unconsciously, a host of [philologists] have come to the conviction that direct contact with classical antiquity is useless and hopeless for them. . . . With all the more enthusiasm this troop has plunged into the science of language: Here, in this endless field of newly plowed soil, where presently even the most mediocre gifts can be usefully employed . . . ; here where the novelty and uncertainty of methods brings constant danger of fantastic errors . . . ; here everyone is welcomed with open arms, including him in whom Sophocles and Aristophanes never evoked an unusual impression or a noteworthy thought, but who can be successfully employed at some etymological loom or in the collection of scattered remains of defunct dialects—and he spends his day knotting and untying, collecting and dispersing, running to and fro consulting books. . . . And suddenly it all becomes clear: Why is he an expert in language at all? Why did those authors write Greek and Latin? And with a light heart he begins to etymologize, right off from Homer, bringing in Lithuanian and Church Slavonic, and above all the sacred Sanskrit, as though Greek lessons were only a pretext for a general introduction to linguistics and as though Homer only suffered from one principal failure—namely that he did not write in proto-Indo-Germanic.[45]

In their search for ever more original word forms, the linguists completely miss the critical question regarding origins, the impulses which lie beneath all such surface appearances.[46] Nietzsche was skeptical of contemporary philology, the new linguistics, and historicism generally. He doubted, for example, that the study of language could corroborate ethnic relationships: "A victorious language is nothing more than a massive . . . sign of a successful conquest."[47] Nietzsche elaborated this thought later, when he saw expressions of the unconscious less in terms of music than the will to power. In *Beyond Good and Evil* and

The Genealogy of Morals Nietzsche suggested that the denominators of "good and bad" or "good and evil" were the legislators of morality. He generalized: "The right of the masters to give names goes so far that one should allow the origin of language itself to be conceived as an expression of the power of the rulers. They say, 'That is that and that,' they seal with a sound every thing and each event and thereby, as it were, take possession of it."[48]

The importance of the unconscious is also treated in Nietzsche's crucial essay, *Concerning Truth and Deception in an Extra-Moral Sense* (1873). In was here that Nietzsche began to develop his theory of truth, along with the notion of man as both deceiver and deceived.

In man this art of dissimulation comes to its pinnacle: Here deception, flattery, lying and fraud, talking behind the back, making false representations, living in a false light, going disguised, cloaking convention, theater-playing for others and for oneself, in short, the continual fluttering to and fro around the single flame of vanity, is so much the rule and law that there is virtually nothing less comprehensible than the way in which an honest and pure impulse toward truth could have arisen among men.[49]

Man is deceived not only in his relations with other men, but also in his perspective on nature. He thinks that he sees nature as it is, but it turns out that "the legislation of language also establishes the first laws of truth" and the thing-in-itself is for the language-maker "totally beyond reach and not at all worth striving for."[50]

What then is truth? A mobile army of metaphors, metonymies, anthropomorphisms, in short a sum of human relations which became poetically and rhetorically intensified, extended and adorned, and which, after long usage, seemed to a people to be fixed, canonical and binding. Truths are illusions of which one has forgotten that they are illusions, metaphors which have been used up and become sensuously powerless, coins which have lost their face and now only serve as metal, no longer as coin.[51]

Truth, in the final analysis, is unconscious lying: "Naturally, man forgets that this is the way things stand with him; and thus he lies in this fashion unconsciously and according to the habit of centuries—and precisely *through this unconsciousness,* this forgetfulness, he comes to a feeling for the truth."[52] If language is absolutely man-made, the elaborate "cover-story" for the will to power, then truth too is a strictly human construction, a horizon about which we deceive ourselves that it constitutes the end of the world and the limits of our knowledge.

The French symbolist poets also made occasional reference to the view that language wells up from the unconscious. They neither saw the poet as drawing upon the common language, nor the common people as the universal poet of all language, as did so many earlier romantics. Rather, the poet defied common usage and reached back into the deepest darkness of his psyche and the "primitive resources in language."[53] For Mallarmé, "Language, in the hands of the mob, leads to the same facility and directness as does money. But in the Poet's hands, it is turned, above all, to dream and song."[54] The poet is prophet and seer, misunderstood and feared, but also respected by other members of society. In their ability to transform language, poets are "magicians": Mallarmé spoke of the "magic charm of art"; Rimbaud included a section on the "alchemy of the word" in *A Season in Hell;* and Baudelaire wrote: "To know how to use a language is to practice a kind of evocative magic."[55] The symbolists spoke of the divine origins of poetic language, if not of the language of the common man. Baudelaire appealed to the gods, "the sick muse," and *"la muse vénale"* in quick succession. The poet's divinely inspired play may just be the play of language itself.

If the poet is to be pure, the poet's voice must be stilled and the initiative taken by the words themselves, which will be set in motion as they meet unequally in collision. And in an exchange of gleams they will flame out like some glittering swath of fire sweeping over precious stones, and thus replace the audible breathing in lyric poetry of old—replace the poet's own personal and passionate control of verse.[56]

The symbolist poets claimed that their inspiration derived from "language itself"; the comparative linguists claimed that they studied "language itself." The former excluded the commonly accepted surface of language; the latter, everything but the commonly accepted surface, whether that be the subconscious impulse or conscious thought behind language. The two groups spoke to their own mutual exclusion. What should the poets and linguists, the artists of language and the scientists of language, now have to say to one another? Can one imagine conversations between Mallarmé and Hovelacque, Rimbaud and Bréal, Nietzsche and Leskien? These would surely be among the strangest of the "dialogues of the dead." They were contempories in the same lands, but they seem to be speaking different languages.[57] Could there be a more egregious example of the "two cultures"?

[12]

ANNIHILATION
OF THE QUESTION

The *Société de linguistique de Paris* was founded in 1865, and its constitution approved by ministerial decision the next year. Among its dozen bylaws the first two specifically limited the scope of acceptable inquiries:

Article I: The Society of Linguistics has as its object the study of languages, and of legends, traditions, customs, and documents which could clarify ethnographic science. All other objects of study are rigorously forbidden.

Article II: The Society will accept no communication dealing with either the origin of language or the creation of a universal language.[1]

The Philological Society of London did not make its ban official, but it avoided involvement in the linguistic aspects of the Darwinism controversy, and its highest officer expressed his personal disapproval of speculations as to language origin. In 1873, the second year of his presidency, Alexander J. Ellis reviewed before the Society Müller's lectures on Darwinism and finally dismissed the entire matter.

I conceive such questions to be out of the field of philology proper. We have to investigate what *is*, we have to discover, if possible, the invariable unconditional relations under which language *as we observe it*, forms, develops, changes, or at least to construct an empirical statement of definite linguistic relations, and ascertain how far that statement obtains in individual cases. Real language, the go-between of man and man, is a totally different organism from philosophical language, the misty ill-understood exponent of sharp metaphysical distinctions. Our work is with the former. We shall do more by tracing the historical growth of one single work-a-day tongue, than by filling wastepaper baskets with reams of paper covered with speculations on the origin of all tongues.[2]

The luxury of speculative generalizations must be replaced by "real work," the empirical and detailed study of "real language," a task requiring that scholars be willing to work for carefully defined and limited objectives. Some, such as Ellis himself, merely wanted to postpone general questions, "to relegate these philosophical questions on origins to a period when more is known of actualities and development, and to work, with 'a long pull, a strong pull, and a pull altogether,' to make the real living organism intelligible, and to track its growth day by day."[3] Others suspected that the asking of such questions would be speculative and futile under any circumstances and that the proper goal of science should be the collection of empirical data for its own sake. Thus Honoré Chavée, writing in a journal founded shortly after the Parisian Society, identified "positive linguistics" with "comparative philology": "For many centuries, people have philosophized about languages and language, but here, as in the other natural sciences, they always wanted to proceed from a priori concepts, never from the comparative observation of facts."[4] "I do not want to invent anything or create anything of whole cloth; I have no fetishism of the a priori. I only want to contribute to the examination of the internal life of words the care which one ordinarily gives to the study of changes, even to the accidents undergone by their exterior figure, corporeal or syllabic."[5]

One must not underestimate the immediate validity and ultimate value of many of the specialized studies undertaken. To some extent it was the very success of applications of the comparative method which dampened interest in the origin of language: To the degree that linguists were successful in reconstructing protolanguages, they found that the deduced structures were not fundamentally different from later language. Therefore, such reconstructions did not seem to solve the basic problems which earlier framers of the question had hoped that they might. Thus it seemed reasonable to abandon general theory in favor of detailed analysis. Increasingly, in the 1870s and 1880s, the leading professional journals came to be dominated by articles like: "Lithuanian *aug* = German *ang*," "Gr. ἱππεῦ = skr. *áçvayo*," "*ana–*," "On the Letter *L* and its Diverse Modifications," "The Letter *O* in Provençal Dialects," "The Root *Vert* in the Brittanic Dialects."[6] Minutes of the sessions of the *Société* included a section of "Communications" with entries like the following:

M. Bréal is dealing with the effects of analogy on the form of Latin adverbs. After *hâc* (*viâ*), *quâ* (*viâ*), there was formed *citrâ, ultrâ* and a quantity of other adverbs; after *quô* (cf. *it clamor caelô*) there was *retrô, ultrô,* etc. Then M. Bréal, taking up the text of a remark by M. Renan in the *Prêtre de Nemi,* developed the idea that *mûnia,* "institutions," and *moenia,* "walls," are etymologically identical.

M. Halévy brought to the attention of the Society certain Hungarian words which were evidently borrowed from an Iranian language. The name for gold *arany* (with the article *az arany,* which is a confusion for *a zarany*) corresponds to Zend *zaranyem.* The name for silver *erzüst,* for *erüst,* is Zend *erezatem.*

Work of precision and detail is both important and fascinating and it should not be belittled. Nevertheless, there is always a dual question about such labors: What whole is the detail meant to illuminate? And what is the whole which provides the details with context and meaning? The minute researches so prevalent in journals of the later nineteenth century give the impression of linguists who humbly esteemed themselves mere journeymen in the scientific enterprise, but who had the proud confidence of having placed one brick in a structure which would one day be complete and even grand—that, after many still more detailed studies, the whole would finally be mastered and a total picture would emerge. But, one is compelled to ask, would there be a picture at all, or merely a collection of possibly related parts? It may well be true, as the enticing maxim has it, that "the good Lord lives in details." Normally, however, our observation is only as keen as our awareness of the distinctions we are searching for and the criteria we are ready to apply, so that we will surely find "the gods" here only if it is "the good Lord" we are looking for.

Critical reviews are also a telling measure of what was considered acceptable by the emerging establishment in linguistics. Fairly typical was a review by Johannes Schmidt, respected professor in Bonn, of a book by August Boltz, a nonprofessional popularizer.[8] In 1868 Boltz published a series of "popular letters" to convey to the public at large the principal discoveries and hypotheses of the new linguistics. Throughout, Schmidt's review displayed a deep-seated disdain for the author's lay status. Boltz had done his homework, Schmidt conceded, but he could not attain the thoroughness and depth possessed exclusively by the professional linguist, and only that would justify popularizations. General introductions written by acknowledged members of the guild, such as Müller, Sayce, and Whitney, were greeted with less open hostility, but also with aloofness. Such works, it was often said, were too *geistreich*—and there may be no better omen of the changing times than the semantic shift whereby a word which literally means "rich in spirit" came to denote an empty cleverness. The order of the new day, the standard of last appeal for the reviewers, was *Gründlichkeit,* thoroughness, which for all its virtues is necessarily earthbound.

The validity of *Ursprachen* in the narrow sense, the reconstructed protolanguages of Schleicher, was also cast in doubt. Schleicher did not particularly trouble himself whether there was any proto-Indo-European people corresponding to the proto-Indo-European language: His idea of a language hardly required that it have any speakers, since it was virtually self-speaking. When ethnologists found no evidence, indeed negative evidence, for the existence of a single *Urvolk,* however, Schleicher's heirs were faced with a massive dilemma: If they denied that the *Ursprache* was dialect-free, they were left either with a laughable self-contradiction or with no *Ursphache* at all, as Wilhelm Streitberg pointed out;[9] if, however, they denied that there ever was an *Ursprache,* they had on their hands a thriving, growing tree without any roots. Johannes Schmidt, himself a student of Schleicher, found that the evidence did not support his mentor's favored metaphor of a linguistic family tree. If analogy is necessary, Schmidt argued, a "wave theory" would be more appropriate: Linguistic change occurred, as it were, with an undulating momentum flowing from dialect to dialect. In that case—in any case, on the evidence as Schmidt read it—the language spoken by the so-called "original Indo-Europeans" was not dialect-free, there was no initial unity, there never was a proto-Indo-European language in any precise sense. "Thus the *Ursprache* remains for now, if we consider it as a whole, a scientific fiction. To be sure, research is significantly facilitated by this fiction, but that which we today can call *Ursprache* is no historical individual."[10]

As had been the case a century earlier, interpreters of world history adopted the prevailing attitude toward language origin. Eduard Meyer—himself a professional historian, but knowledgeable in linguistics as an ancillary discipline—published the first installment of his exhaustive *History of Antiquity* in 1884. He succinctly summarized the new position:

The notion, so influential in the beginnings of modern linguistics, that the investigation of the historical development of a language family could provide a historical look at the origin and beginning stages of language, has long since proved to be an illusion. . . . Language as such, that is, the insoluble connection of a group of sounds with a specific meaning, is an absolute given for linguistic science, whose origination cannot be explained with the means at hand.[11]

Schleicher, then, did not merely err in thinking too confidently that his reconstructed forms were indisputable deductions from perfectly inducted empirical evidence; Schleicher had in fact reconstructed a "scientific fiction."

Even if proto-Indo-European were a real language susceptible of accurate reconstruction, what would it tell us about the absolute beginnings of human speech? It would itself be a developed language, learned by its speakers, not invented by them. *Its* genesis would be the new question, ad infinitum, in perpetual regress into that darkness where no evidence is visible. In less than a century the presumed extent of human and terrestrial life expanded like a dizzying receding horizon.[12] Herder and Hamann, even Sir William Jones and Friedrich Schlegel, still spoke of Hebrew and Sanskrit as idioms from the dawn of human life and history. These were languages spoken only a few millenia ago. Sir Charles Lyell reckoned the history of higher forms of life in thousands of centuries rather than the thousands of years of Judaeo-Christian chronologies. T. H. Huxley estimated that man evolved a million or more years ago. In 1856 fossils were found in a valley near Düsseldorf: The age of Neanderthal man—who was presumed to be a speaking creature, since primitive implements were also discovered—was reckoned at a minimum of 25,000 years. Such sudden displacement of points of origin could easily have a vertiginous effect. Perhaps it was only possible to maintain balance by holding close to familiar shores, while admitting that the best-known beginnings were not the true beginnings at all. Friedrich Schlegel had proposed that rigorous historical research alone would solve the problem of origin. An important factor in the refinement of the comparative method of reconstruction was the desire for the long-awaited answer. But even as the method was perfected, the goal receded.

For some of the newly emerging disciplines, those which branched off from philosophy through increased specialization, linguistics was an important auxiliary science. E. B. Tylor in anthropology and Wilhelm Wundt in psychology both borrowed corroborative evidence from studies of language and addressed themselves to the question of its origin. Both were given respectful consideration in the journals of linguistics, and both were extremely cautious in their approaches. In his *Researches into the Early History of Mankind* (1865) and then in *Primitive Culture* (1871), Tylor dedicated whole chapters to early language. He discussed extensively the use of sign language among the deaf and dumb, with copious references to the innovators in this field during the eighteenth and nineteenth centuries. He analyzed the manual and pictorial signs used by American Indians and the gestures employed by contemplative monks who had taken vows of silence. The implication was that there are parallels among the means of communication used by deaf-mutes, savages, children, and the first human beings; but Tylor was careful to reiterate that the implication was strictly probable. "The idea that gesture language represents a distinct separate stage of human utterance, through which man passed before he came to speak, has no support from facts. But it may be plausibly maintained. . . ."[13] Mere plausibility is the best that can be hoped, because "we know so little about the Origin of Language, that even the greatest philologists are forced either to avoid the subject altogether, or to turn themselves into metaphysicians in order to discuss it."[14] Despite Tylor's various suggestions, he despaired of any final solution:

Steinthal's masterly summary of these speculations in his 'Origin of Language' is quite melancholy reading. It may indeed be brought forward as evidence to prove something that matters far more to us than the early history of language, that it is of as little use to be a good reasoner when there are no facts to reason upon, as it is to be a good bricklayer when there are no bricks to build with.[15]

Wilhelm Wundt found potential "building bricks" in the data of experimental psychology. Wundt elaborated his final views on language in 1900 in the first volume of his ten-volume *Folk Psychology: An Examination of the Developmental Laws of Language, Myth, and Custom.* Rejecting the theories of invention, imitation, natural sounds, and miracle, Wundt referred to his own explanation of language origin as the *Entwicklungstheorie,* theory of development. His focus was on language as an aspect of developmental psychology. "The problem of the origin of language, therefore, can only be pursued to the extent that one restricts it to the question how the expressive movements peculiar to man and adequate to his level of consciousness became linguistic sounds and thence gradually the symbols of mental contents. . . ."[16] Inferences from psychological analysis to historical fact are possible but not necessary, indirect rather than direct.

The blackout on discussion of language origin was not total, but those rare linguists who continued to concern themselves after the 1890s proceeded with great circumspection. Otto Jespersen is among the isolated examples. Jespersen almost apologized for his undertaking, quoting Whitney:

No theme in linguistic science is more often and more voluminously treated than this, and by scholars of every grade and tendency; nor any, it may be added, with less profitable result in proportion to the labour expended; the greater part of what is said and written upon it is mere windy talk, the assertion of subjective views which commend themselves to no mind save the one that produces them, and which are apt to be offered with a confidence, and defended with a tenacity, that are in inverse ratio to their acceptableness. This has given the whole question a bad repute among sober-minded philologists.[17]

Nevertheless, Jespersen continued, "linguistic science cannot refrain for ever from asking about the whence (and about the whither) of linguistic evolution."[18] But it must reject the bulk of previous theorizing and adhere to a strictly critical evaluation of evidence.

While the propounders of [earlier] theories of the origin of speech . . . made straight for the front of the lion's den, we are like the fox in the fable, who noticed that all the traces led into the den and not a single one came out; we will therefore try and steal into the den from behind. They thought it logically correct, nay necessary, to begin at the beginning; let us . . . begin with languages accessible at the present day, and let us attempt from that starting-point step by step to trace the backward path. . . .[19]

When Jespersen's *Progress in Language* (1894) was reviewed by Michel Bréal, he was sympathetic to the work, since it at least disposed of the cranky mourners of linguistic regression. Nonetheless, Bréal remarked that theories of language origin reveal more about their authors than they do about the subject.[20]

The neogrammarian movement in Germany, less than a revolution, more than a changing of the guard, also helped to make official the proscription of the question of language origin. The *Junggrammatiker* are best known for their principle that the laws of sound change are without exception.[21] Linguistic flux is governed by mechanico-organic laws, subject to neither human will nor divine reason, but regular and explicable nonetheless. As the Slavologist, August Leskien, stated: "If one admitted optional [*beliebige*], accidental variations which cannot be brought into any orderly relation, then one would in effect show up the fact that the object of his investigations, language, is not susceptible of scientific explanation."[22] Thus, according to Leskien, the linguist's view of science should determine his view of the object of his science. The scientific linguist can look neither beneath the phenomena, behind the data, nor beyond historical evidence; and therefore he must abandon the pursuit of origins. As Hermann Osthoff and Karl Brugmann wrote in their definitive work:

Only the comparative linguist who abandons the hypothesis-laden atmos-
phere of the workshop in which the Indo-Germanic root-forms are forged,
and who steps out into the clear light of graspable reality and presence,
in order to gain some instruction about things which gray theory never
teaches . . . —only he can come to a right understanding of the manner
of life and change of linguistic forms and attain the methodical principles,
without which it is impossible to achieve any believable results in studies
of language history and without which especially any attempt to penetrate
those spaces of time which lie beyond the historical transmission of language would be like a voyage without a compass.[23]

There is in this metaphor-laden admonition both half-truth and
double jeopardy. Do not go into the darkness, because it is dark; and
besides, how could you see in the darkness if your vision is inaccurate in
daylight clarity? Or to reverse the image: Do not go into the sunlight,
it will blind you; stay in the twilight, it is the only preparation for such
frightening brilliance. For practical purposes the question of the origin
of language had been effectively abolished. Alexander J. Ellis put it
in simpler and more sparing words: We philologists have to investigate
what *is*. But the question remained, then and now: What *is* language?
Indeed, what *is?*

NOTES

Prolegomena

1. Cf. Arno Borst, *Der Turmbau von Babel: Geschichte der Meinungen über Ursprung und Vielfalt der Sprachen und Völker,* 3 vols. in 5 (Stuttgart, A. Hiersemann, 1957–1961).
2. Cf. Arthur O. Lovejoy, *The Great Chain of Being: A Study of the History of an Idea* (Cambridge, Mass., Harvard University Press, 1936), chap. IX.
3. Equivocation is a logical fallacy; equivocity, of course, is not.

Chapter 1

1. Cf. Giambattista Vico, *On the Study Methods of Our Time* [*De nostri temporis studiorum ratione*], trans. and intro. Elio Gianturco (Indianapolis, Bobbs-Merrill, 1965).
2. Vico, *The New Science,* bk. II, par. 384, trans. T. G. Bergin and M. H. Fisch (Ithaca, N.Y., Cornell University Press, 1948), p. 108. Reprinted from *The New Science of Giambattista Vico,* translated from the 3rd ed. (1744), by Thomas Goddard Bergin and Max Harold Fisch. Copyright 1948 by Cornell University. Used by permission of Cornell University Press.
3. Thomas Hobbes, *De cive; or, The Citizen,* chap. XVIII, par. 4, in *Works,* ed. W. Molesworth (London 1839–1845), vol. VII, p. 183. Cf. Arthur H. Child, "Making and Knowing in Hobbes, Vico and Dewey," University of California Publications in Philosophy, XVI, no. 13 (Berkeley, University of California Press, 1953), pp. 271–310.
4. Cf. Joseph Cropsey, "Hobbes and the Transition to Modernity," *Ancients and Moderns: Essays on the Tradition of Political Philosophy in Honor of Leo Strauss,* ed. Joseph Cropsey (New York-London, Basic Books, 1964), pp. 213–237.
5. I.e., *Psóphos émpsychos.* Aristotle, *De anima,* bk. II, chap. viii, p. 420b28–34. Cf. *Politics,* bk. I, chap. i, 10–11, p. 1253a11–18: "Mere sound, of course, is a sign of pain and pleasure, wherefore it is possessed by other animals . . . , but speech (*lógos*) should make clear what is useful and what is harmful, and so too what is just and unjust; for it is peculiar to man, in contrast with the other animals, that he alone has a perception of the good and the bad and the just and the unjust and similar things, and it is the bond of these things that makes a household and a city-state."
6. Ideas about the recurrent order of world history developed gradually in Vico's mind: From 1710 until his death he constantly revised the writings which

expounded his fundamental new idea. We will not concern ourselves with Vico's intellectual development, however, but simply take as most authoritative the last edition of *The New Science,* published just after his death in 1744.

7. Vico, *The New Science,* bk. II, par. 401, pp. 114–115.

8. Vico offers confusing and contradictory comments about the story of the Tower of Babel, which immediately follows the Biblical account of the flood: cf. ibid. bk. I, pars. 62–63, pp. 34–35 with bk. II, pars. 369–371, pp. 100–102.

9. Ibid., bk. IV, par. 929, p. 306; bk. II, par. 431–432, pp. 125–126; bk. II, par. 437, p. 129.

10. Ibid. bk. II, par. 438, p. 129.

11. Cf. ibid., bk. II, par. 427, pp. 123–124.

12. Like Augustine, Vico rejected Varro's distinction of three types of theology, poetic, natural, and civil. In its place he established his own trichotomy: the poetic or civil theology of theological poets, the natural theology of metaphysicians, and Christian or revealed theology. Cf. ibid. bk. II, par. 366, p. 99. Cf. St. Augustine, *The City of God,* bk. VI, chaps. ii–x. The works in question by Varro, *Antiquitates rerum humanarum* and *Antiquitates rerum divinarum,* have been lost.

13. Vico, *The New Science,* bk. I, pars. 238–239, 241–242, p. 70.

14. Ibid. bk. II, par. 446, p. 134.

15. Ibid.

16. Cf. ibid. bk. I, par. 91, p. 43; bk. II, pars. 424–427, pp. 122–123; bk. II, par. 499, p. 150.

17. Ibid., bk. II, pars. 391 and 393, pp. 110–111. These are the third and fifth of the seven "principal aspects" of the new science which Vico enumerated: (1) a rational civil theology of divine providence; (2) a philosophy of authority; (3) a history of human ideas; (4) a philosophical criticism, which will "render true judgment upon the founders of the nations," a "natural theogony which will give us a rational chronology of poetic history"; (5) an ideal eternal history traversed in time by the histories of all nations; (6) a system of the natural law of nations; (7) principles of universal history, which has "hitherto lacked its beginning, and . . . its continuity as well." Ibid., bk. II, pars. 385–399, pp. 108–113). This set of principles is clearly symmetrical in arrangement, with the marriage of philology and philosophy—the method of Vico's science—standing as the fourth and middle aspect.

18. Cf. Vico, "Dell'ingegno umano dei detti acuti e arguti e del riso," *Opere,* ed. Fausto Nicolini (Milan-Naples, R. Ricciardi, 1953), pp. 926–932.

19. Cf. Vico, "Della mente eroica" (1732), *Opere,* pp. 909–926.

20. Vico, *The New Science,* bk. II, par. 412, p. 119.

21. Cf. ibid., bk. II, par. 437, p. 129; bk. II, par. 379, p. 106. The passages from Homer are *Iliad,* bk. I, ll. 403–404; bk. XIX, l. 291; bk. XX, l. 74; *Odyssey,* bk. XII, l. 61; bk. X, l. 303f.

22. Cf. Ibid., bk. I, par. 227, p. 69; bk. II, par. 431, p. 126. Cf. Plato, *Cratylus* 400e–401a; cf. Plato, *Critias* 121c.

23. Ibid., bk. I, par. 346, p. 92; bk. II, par. 399, p. 113.

24. In Italian, *scienza del bene e del male.* Ibid., bk. II, par. 365, p. 98. The passage from Homer is *Odyssey,* bk. VIII, ll. 63–64, and should be translated "The Muse greatly loved him and gave to him both good and ill; she deprived him of his eyes, but gave him pleasurable song."

25. Ibid., bk. V, par. 1096, p. 373. This is also a mistranslation or misquotation of Seneca, *Naturales quaestiones,* bk. VII, par. 31.

26. For general treatments of this transformation, see the following works: Leonora Cohen Rosenfield, *From Beast-Machine to Man-Machine: Animal Soul in French Letters from Descartes to La Mettrie,* (New York, Oxford University

Press, 1941); Hester Hastings, *Man and Beast in French Thought of the Eighteenth Century,* The Johns Hopkins Studies in Romance Literatures and Languages, vol. XXVII (Baltimore-London-Paris, Johns Hopkins University Press, 1936); Albert G. A. Balz, "Cartesian Doctrine and the Animal Soul: An Incident in the Formation of the Modern Philosophical Tradition," *Cartesian Studies* (New York, Columbia University Press, 1951), pp. 106–157; Keith Gunderson, "Descartes, La Mettrie, Language and Machines," *Philosophy: The Journal of the Royal Institute of Philosophy* XXXIX (1964), pp. 193–222.

27. Descartes, *Discourse on Method,* pt. V, in *The Philosophical Works of Descartes,* trans. Elizabeth S. Haldane and G. R. T. Ross (Cambridge, Cambridge University Press, 1931), vol. I, p. 116.

28. Ibid.

29. Ibid., pp. 116–117.

30. Descartes, *Meditations on First Philosophy,* Med. II, in *The Philosophical Works,* vol. I, p. 153.

31. Cf. Noam Chomsky, *Cartesian Linguistics: A Chapter in the History of Rationalist Thought* (New York-London, Harper & Row, 1966), pp. 3–31; see also Chomsky, "Language and the Mind: II," *Columbia Forum* (Fall 1968), pp. 23–25; and Chomsky, *Language and Mind* (New York, Harcourt Brace Jovanovich, 1968), pp. 1–20.

32. Géraud de Cordemoy, *A Philosophicall Discourse Concerning Speech, Conformable to the Cartesian Principles* [*Discours physique de la parole*] (Savoy 1668), "Preface," end of par. 4 (no pagination). Reprint: intro. Karl Uitti, in *Language, Man and Society* (New York, AMS Press, 1974).

33. Ibid., p. 13.

34. Ibid., p. 9.

35. Ibid., p. 16.

36. Descartes, "Fifth Set of Objections: Relative to Meditation II, 7," *Objections and Replies,* in *Philosophical Works,* vol. II, p. 146.

37. Cf. Diodorus Siculus, *Historical Library,* bk. I, chap. 8; Vitruvius, *On Architecture,* bk. II, chap. 1.

38. Epicurus, "Letter to Herodotus," in Diogenes Laertius, *Lives of Eminent Philosophers,* bk. X, 75–76, trans. R. D. Hicks (London-Cambridge, Mass., The Loeb Library, 1950), vol. II, pp. 605–607. (Translation revised.)

39. The Stoics generally accepted Aristotle's differentiation between sound-making and speech, and were mainly concerned with form and grammar rather than the sounds or composition of individual words. They also experimented with etymology in an attempt to recover the "true *lógos.*" Chrysippus (frag. 152) went so far as to claim that every word is naturally ambiguous. Cf. Paul Barth, *Die Stoa,* 3rd ed. (Stuttgart, Frommann, 1922), pp. 85–90; cf. Haymann Steinthal, *Geschichte der Sprachwissenschaft bei den Griechen und Römern,* 2nd ed. (Berlin 1890), vol. I, pp. 331ff.

40. Lucretius, *De rerum natura,* bk. V, ll. 1087–1090. The main passage on language origin is bk. V, ll. 1028–1090.

41. Julien Offray de la Mettrie, *Man a Machine,* ed. and trans. Gertrude Carman Bussey (La Salle, Ill., Open Court, 1912 [1961]), p. 104. For the development of La Mettrie's thought cf. Aram Vartanian, *La Mettrie's "L'Homme machine": A Study in the Origins of an Idea;* Critical Edition with an Introductory Monograph and Notes (Princeton, Princeton University Press, 1960).

42. La Mettrie, ibid., p. 105.

43. Ibid., p. 141.

44. Cf. Wolfgang von Kempelen, *Mechanismus der menschlichen Sprache, nebst der Beschreibung einer sprechenden Maschine* (Vienna 1791).

45. Cf. P. Camper, *De l'orang-outang et de quelques autres espèces des singes* (n.p., 1779); cf. also Camper, "Account of the Organs of Speech of the Orang Outang . . . in a Letter to Sir John Pringle, F.R.S.," *Philosophical Transactions of the Royal Society of London* LXIX (1779), pp. 139–159; cf. Hester Hastings, op. cit., pp. 125–132.

46. Cf. Gottfried Wenzel, *Neue, auf Vernunft und Erfahrung gegründete Entdeckungen über die Sprache der Tiere* (Vienna 1800); cf. Wenzel, *Neue Entdeckungen über die Sprache der Tiere: Mit einem Wörterbuch der Tiersprache und Übersetzungen aus der Tiersprache* (Leipzig, n.d.).

47. Cf. Abbé [Guillaume Hyacinthe] Bougeant, *Amusement philosophique sur le langage des bêtes* (1739), ed. Hester Hastings (Geneva-Lille, Droz, 1954); cf. Cyrano de Bergerac, *Les Estats et empires de la lune* (1657).

48. La Mettrie, *Man a Machine*, p. 104.

49. Ibid., p. 105.

50. Quoted in F. Max Müller, *The Science of Language* (London 1870), vol. II, p. 254.

51. Cf. Antoine Court de Gébelin, *Monde primitif, analysé et comparé avec le monde moderne, consideré dans l'histoire naturelle de la parole: Origine du langage et de l'écriture*, bk. I, chap. XIV, "Principes sur lesquels repose l'art étymologique" (Paris 1775), vol. III, pp. 38–49.

52. Charles de Brosses, *Traité de la formation mécanique des langues et des principes physiques de l'étymologie*, "Discours préliminaire" (Paris 1765), vol. I (no pagination).

53. "Differences of language are immediately dependent upon the organs of speech; so that, in cold countries, the nerves of the tongue must be more rigid and less active than in those that are warmer. . . . Hence it happens that all northern languages have more monosyllables, and are more burdened with consonants." (Johann Joachim Winckelmann, *Geschichte der Kunst des Altertums*, bk. I, chap. iii, §4 (1764), in *Werke*, ed. Heinrich Meyer and Johann Schulze (Dresden 1809), vol. III, p. 47.) Cf. Thomas Abbt, "Von der Verschiedenheit der Sprachen" (1765/1766), *Vermischte Werke*, ed. Friedrich Nicolai (Frankfort-Leipzig 1783), vol. VI, pp. 99–110.

54. Cf. Nicolas-Sylvestre Bergier, *Les élémens primitifs des langues découverts par la comparaison des racines de l'Hébreu avec celles du Grec, du Latin et du Français* (Paris 1764); cf. Abbé Copineau, *Essai synthétique sur l'origine et la formation des langues* (Paris 1774).

55. Court de Gébelin, *Monde primitif . . . : Grammaire universelle et comparative* (Paris 1774), vol. II, pp. ix–x.

56. Cf. Hans Aarsleff, *The Study of Language in England, 1780–1860* (Princeton, N.J., Princeton University Press, 1967), pp. 73–114.

57. John Horne Tooke, ΕΠΕΑ ΠΤΕΡΟΕΝΤΑ, or *The Diversions of Purley*, 2nd ed. (London 1798), vol. I, pp. 531–532.

58. William Hazlitt, "The Late Mr. Horne Tooke," *The Spirit of the Age* (1825), in *Complete Works*, ed. P. P. Howe et al. (London, J. M. Dent, 1932), vol. XI, pp. 55–56.

59. Cf. Franz Wüllner, *Über die Verwandschaft der Indogermanischen, Semitischen und Tibetanischen, nebst einer Einleitung über den Ursprung der Sprachen* (Münster 1838), pp. 44–68.

60. Alexander Murray, *History of the European Languages: Researches into the Affinities of the Teutonic, Greek, Celtic, Slavonic, and Indian Nations* (Edinburgh 1823), vol. I, p. 28.

61. Ibid., pp. 31–32.

62. In the Soviet Union a similar theory held dictatorial sway for a time. Nikolai Jakoblevitch Marr was a linguist-charlatan, whose domination of Russian

linguistics served to retard it as much as did Horne Tooke's over English philology. All languages, according to Marr, derive from four original elements; *Sal, Ber, Yon,* and *Rosh,* the irreducible substructure from which all linguistic variation dialectically proceeded. As part of the ideological superstructure, language is a function of class consciousness, whose historical relations derive from the links of conflict or alliance in the master-slave relationships among peoples. Marr also held that language is one of the tools of production. Marr himself died in 1934, but Marrism was dogma in Soviet linguistics until 1950, when a conference of memorial tribute proved fatal to Marr's teachings. The issue was finally settled by the ukase of Stalin. If language were a tool of production, Stalin jibed, "chatterboxes would be the richest people in the world." [J. Stalin, "On Several Problems in Linguistics," (*Pravda,* July 4, 1950, p. 3), *The Soviet Linguistic Controversy,* trans. John V. Murra, Robert M. Hankin, and Fred Holling; Columbia University Slavic Studies (New York, King's Crown Press, 1951), p. 86.] However, language is not part of the superstructure either: "Language is generated not by one base or another . . . , but by the entire historic development of society. . . . This is the reason why language can serve equally both the old, dying order and the new, emerging one, both the old base and the new, both exploiters and exploited." [J. Stalin, "On Marxism in Linguistics," (*Pravda,* June 20, 1950, p. 3), ibid., p. 70.]

63. Cf. Rowland Jones, *The Origin of Language and Nations, Hieroglyfically, Etymologically, and Topografically Defined and Fixed, After the Method of an English, Celtic, Greek and Latin English Lexicon* . . . (London 1764); cf. Jones, *Hieroglyfic Language* . . . (London 1768); cf. Jones, *The Philosophy of Words* . . . (London 1769); cf. Jones, *The Circles of Gomer* . . . (London 1771); cf. Jones, *The Io-Triads* . . . (London 1773).

64. James Gilchrist, *Philosophic Etymology, or Rational Grammar* (London 1816), pp. xx–xxi.

65. Cf. W. Hornay, *Ursprung und Entwicklung der Sprache. Ersther Theil: Enthüllung des Ursprungs der Sprache* (Berlin 1858), pp. 132ff.

66. F.-G. Bergmann, *Origine et formation des langues* (Paris 1842), pp. 3–4. Cf. Bergmann, *Résumé d'étude d'ontologie générale et de linguistique générale; ou, Essai sur la nature et l'origine des êtres, la pluralité des langues primitives, et la formation de la matière première des mots,* 2nd ed. (Paris 1869).

67. Cf. Paul Friedländer, *Plato,* (New York, Pantheon, 1958–1969), vol. I, pp. 118–123; cf. Johan Huizinga, *Homo Ludens: A Study of the Play-Element in Culture* (Boston, Beacon Press, 1955), pp. 150ff.

68. Cf. Plato, *Cratylus* 407e–408.

Chapter 2

1. Thomas Hobbes, *Leviathan,* pt. I, chap. 4, in *Works,* ed. W. Molesworth (London 1839–1845), vol. III, p. 25.

2. George Berkeley, introduction to *A Treatise Concerning the Principles of Human Knowledge,* par. 22, in *The Works,* ed. A. A. Luce and T. E. Jessop (London 1948–1957), vol. II, p. 39; cf. *An Essay Towards a New Theory of Vision,* par. 147, ibid., vol. I, p. 231.

3. Cf. Donald F. Henze, "The Linguistic Aspect of Hume's Method," *Journal of the History of Ideas* XXX (1969), pp. 116–126.

4. Cf. Thomas Reid, *Essays on the Intellectual Powers of Man,* Essay V, in *Works,* ed. Sir William Hamilton (Edinburgh 1863), vol. I, pp. 389ff.

5. Cf. John Locke, *An Essay Concerning Human Understanding,* bk. I, chap. i, par. 8, ed. A. C. Fraser (Oxford 1894), vol. I, pp. 32–33.

6. Ibid., bk. II, chap xxiii, par. 1, vol. I, p. 390.

7. Ibid., bk. III, chap. iii, par. 6, vol. II, pp. 16–17.

8. Cf. ibid., bk. II, chap. xi, pars. 6–11, vol. I, pp. 205–208; bk. III, chap. vi, pars. 22, 25–27, vol. II, pp. 73–74, 75–78.

9. Cf. ibid., bk. III, chap. vi, par. 25. vol. II, p. 75; bk. III, chap. xi, par. 5, vol. II, pp. 149–150. Cf. David A. Givner, "Scientific Preconceptions in Locke's Philosophy of Language," *Journal of the History of Ideas* XXIII (1962), pp. 340–354.

10. Locke, ibid., bk. III, chap. i, par. 5, vol. II, p. 5.

11. Cf. David Hartley, *Observations on Man, His Frame, His Duty, and His Expectations* (London 1749), vol. I, p. 272: "When the visible Objects impress other vivid Sensations . . . with sufficient Frequency, . . . these Sensations must leave Traces, or Ideas, which will be associated with the Names of the Objects, so as to depend upon them. Thus an Idea, or nascent Perception, of the Sweetness of the Nurse's Milk will rise up in that Part of the Child's Brain which corresponds to the Nerves of Taste, upon his hearing her Name. . . ."

12. Cf. Hartley, "To Apply the Foregoing Account of Words and Characters to the Languages and Method of Writing of the First Ages of the World," ibid., pp. 297–315.

13. The original section was in verse and published as *The Grumbling Hive; or, Knaves Turn'd Honest* (1704). Additional sections, including six dialogues, were published in 1714 and 1723.

14. Bernard de Mandeville, *The Fable of the Bees; or, Private Vices, Publick Benefits,* ed. F. B. Kaye (Oxford, Oxford University Press, 1924), vol. I, pp. 36–37.

15. Cf. Jonathan Swift, ["Essay upon the Art of Political Lying"], *The Examiner,* Nov. 9, 1710, in *The Examiner and Other Pieces Written in 1710–1711,* in [*The Prose Works*], ed. Herbert Davis (Oxford, Basil Blackwell, 1957–1968), vol. III, pp. 8–9; Cf. Oliver Goldsmith, "On the Use of Language," *Essays* (Boston, The Bibliophile Society, 1928), vol. II, p. 21; cf. Goldsmith, "On Deceit and Falsehood," ibid., pp. 141–148.

16. Mandeville, *Fable of the Bees,* vol. II, pp. 289–290; cf. pp. 284–312.

17. Adam Smith, "Considerations Concerning the First Formation of Languages, and the Different Genius of Original and Compounded Languages," *The Early Writings of Adam Smith,* ed. J. Ralph Lindgren (New York, A. M. Kelley, 1967), pp. 243–244.

18. The most pertinent fragments are "Essay on Language" and "Fragments on Universal Grammar," *The Works,* ed. John Bowring (Edinburgh 1843), vol. VIII, pp. 295–338 and pp. 339–357. Less directly related are the "Essay on Logic" and "A Fragment on Ontology," *The Works,* pp. 213–293 and pp. 193–211; and some sections and appendices of the *Chrestomathia, The Works,* vol. VIII, pp. 1–191, especially pp. 185–191. They were composed in 1813 and after. Sections from these manuscripts and other works, together with a long introductory essay, are contained in C. K. Ogden, *Bentham's Theory of Fictions,* 2nd ed., International Library of Psychology, Philosophy and Scientific Method (London, Routledge and Kegan Paul, 1951).

19. Bentham, "Conjectural History of Language," an unpublished fragment (1826), contained in the London University College Collection, Box 102, pp. 275–279; here quoted from Mary P. Mack, *Jeremy Bentham: An Odyssey of Ideas* (New York-London, Columbia University Press, 1963), p. 158.

20. Bentham, "Essay on Language," p. 323.

21. Bentham, *Chrestomathia,* Appendix IV, Sec. xviii, p. 119.

22. Bentham, "A Fragment on Ontology," p. 198.

23. Ibid., p. 199. Cf. "Essay on Language," p. 331.

24. Bentham, "Essay on Logic," p. 242. Cf. p. 249.

25. Bentham's detection of Blackstone's misleading use of terms was one of the early factors leading him to political theory. "Grammar and legislation must work in concert. A good grammarian is a powerful friend of ignorance, and a powerful enemy to corruption: the same flaws in language which serve as pitfalls to ignorance are lurking holes to corruption." ["Prefat to Bern Prize Code" (1779), a fragment contained in London University College Collection, Box 27, p. 157; here quoted from Mack, op. cit., p. 153]. He was suspicious of the slogans of active politicians and the terminologies of political philosophers. He exposed and disambiguated Jacobin rhetoric in the *Anarchical Fallacies* (c. 1791).

26. There is some indication that Bentham thought of his work in this area as an extension of the "art of measurement" with regard to pleasures and pains first examined in Plato's *Protagoras* 356cff. Perhaps so, but it should be remembered that the unphilosophical and unliberated inhabitants of Plato's cave were also very precise measurers and namers of the shadows on the wall. Cf. Plato, *Republic*, bk. VII, 515b, 516c–d, 516e–517a.

27. Cf. Nietzsche, *Jenseits von Gut und Böse*, pt. IX, §268, *Werke*, ed. Alfred Baeumler (Leipzig, Kröner, 1930), vol. IV/ii, p. 214; *Werke*, ed. Karl Schlechta (Munich, Carl Hanser, 1966), vol. II, pp. 740–741: "The history of language is the history of a process of abbreviation—; people bind themselves to this quick understanding more and more narrowly." Cf. George Orwell, "Politics and the English Language," *A Collection of Essays* (Garden City, N.Y., Doubleday/Anchor, 1954), pp. 162–177. Cf. Orwell, *1984*, appendix.

28. Bentham, *Nomography: or the Art of Inditing Laws*, in *The Works*, vol. III, p. 267.

29. Bentham, *Memoirs*, chap. XXII, in *The Works*, vol. X, p. 569.

30. Bentham, *The Rationale of Reward*, bk. III, chap. i, in *The Works*, vol. III, pp. 253–254.

31. In Bentham's early writings, the good will of governors was taken for granted. After public rejection of his proposals for prison reform embodied in the Panopticon, his confidence was somewhat undermined; but even then he had implicit faith that competition and enlightened self-interest would transmute private vices into public benefits. He saw in liberal democracy the political machinery which could channel the self-seeking of rulers into the greatest happiness for the greatest number. Together with businessmen and industrialists, Bentham helped found the Liberal party, but his political theory did not end with individualism. He considered himself a nationalist; or, more precisely, he advocated internationalism—the very term *international* is a Bentham neologism—an internationalism which was in fact universal competition based on national self-interest, and which should in the end eliminate the causes of war. Bentham concluded his *Principles of International Law* with a 14-point "Plan for an Universal and Perpetual Peace."

32. Cf. Arthur O. Lovejoy, *The Great Chain of Being: A Study of the History of an Idea* (Cambridge, Mass., Harvard University Press, 1936), chap. IX.

33. Étienne Bonnot de Condillac, *An Essay on the Origin of Human Knowledge: Being a Supplement to Mr. Locke's Essay on the Human Understanding*, trans. Nugent (London 1756), pp. 7–8. Reprint: intro. James H. Stam (New York, AMS Press, 1974).

34. According to Condillac's scheme, the progressive operations of the mind are perception (the mind's reception of sense data), consciousness (the mere awareness of perceptions), attention (concentration on certain perceptions over others), and reminiscence (recognition that some perceptions have occurred before). Beyond these, but still prior to reflection, come imagination (the

ability to revive perceptions as recollected images), contemplation (the power to preserve "the perception, the name or the circumstances of an object which is vanished out of sight"), and memory (retaining only the name or circumstances of perceptions, when it is impossible to revive the image itself). The more advanced faculties are based on reflection and language: abstraction (the formation of general ideas by association and comparison, compounding and decompounding), judgment (affirmative or negative conclusions drawn about abstract ideas), understanding, and reason. In combination with these the awareness of pleasure and pain yields desire and passion, love, hatred, hope, fear, and volition.

35. Although this point was anticipated by Berkeley, his works were still untranslated; Condillac read no English, and seems to have relied on comments by Voltaire. Cf. Pasquale Salvucci, *Linguaggio e mondo umano in Condillac,* Pubblicazionni dell'università di Urbino, Serie di Lettere e Filosofia, vol. V (Urbino 1957), pp. 117–119; cf. Isabel F. Knight, *The Geometric Spirit: The Abbé de Condillac and the French Enlightenment,* Yale Historical Publications, Miscellany 89 (New Haven-London, Yale University Press, 1968), p. 95.

36. Condillac, *An Essay,* pt. II, sec. i, p. 169.

37. On the use of the period after the flood as a device, cf. Andrew Dickson White, *A History of the Warfare of Science with Theology in Christendom* (New York, Dover, 1960), vol. I, pp. 225–248.

38. Cf. William Warburton, *The Divine Legation of Moses,* bk. IV, chap. 4 (London 1738–1741), vol. II, p. 81.

39. Condillac, *An Essay,* pt. II, sec. i, chap. i, §2, pp. 172–173.

40. Cf. Jules Paul Seigel, "The Enlightenment and the Evolution of a Language of Signs in France and England," *Journal of the History of Ideas* XXX (1969), pp. 96–115; cf. Seigel's introduction to *Diderot's Early Philosophical Works,* ed. and trans. Margaret Jourdain (New York, AMS Press, 1973); cf. Herbert Josephs, *Diderot's Dialogue of Gesture and Language: "Le Neveu de Rameau"* (Columbus, Ohio State University Press, 1970).

41. Condillac, *Langue des Calculs,* bk. II, chap. iv, in *Œuvres complètes* (Paris 1803), vol. XXXI, p. 268.

42. Cicero, *Tusculan Disputations,* bk. I, par. 9.

43. Anne Robert Jacques Turgot, "Premier discours. Sur les avantages que l'établissement du Christianisme a procurés au genre-humain," *Œuvres,* ed. Pierre Dupont de Nemours (Paris 1808–1811), vol. II, p. 44.

44. Frank E. Manuel, *The Prophets of Paris: Turgot, Condorcet, Saint-Simon, Fourier, and Comte* (Cambridge, Mass., Harvard University Press, 1962), p. 19.

45. Denis Diderot, *Lettre sur les aveugles à l'usage de ceux qui voient* (Paris, Bibliothèque de la Pléiade, 1951), p. 866: "The author of the *Essai sur l'origine des connaissances humaines,* [i.e., Condillac], judiciously remarks that, whether we elevate ourselves up to the heavens or descend down into the abysses, we still never get out of our own selves, and it is never anything other than our own thought that we perceive; but this is the conclusion of the first of Berkeley's dialogues and the foundation of his whole system."

46. Turgot, "Réflexions sur les langues: Annexe de l'article 'Étymologie'," *Œuvres,* vol. III, pp. 86–87.

47. Alexander Pope, *An Essay on Man,* ep. I, ll. 289–296.

48. Cf. Manuel, *The Prophets of Paris,* pp. 45–51; cf. Charles Frankel, *The Faith of Reason: The Idea of Progress in the French Enlightenment* (New York, King's Crown Press, 1948), pp. 120–127; cf. Karl Löwith, *Meaning in History: The Theological Implications of the Philosophy of History* (Chicago, University of Chicago Press, 1949), pp. 91–103.

49. Condorcet, *Sketch for a Historical Picture of the Progress of the Human Mind,* trans. June Barraclough (London, Weidenfeld and Nicolson, 1955), p. 173.

50. Cf. Condorcet, *Essai sur l'application de l'analyse à la probabilité des décisions rendues à la pluralité des voix* (Paris 1785). Reprint: (New York, Chelsea, 1972). Cf. Condorcet, "Tableau général de la science, qui a pour objet l'application du calcul aux sciences politiques et morales" [published posthumously in 1795 in the *Journal d'instruction sociale*], *Œuvres,* vol. I, pp. 539–574.

51. Cf. Gilles-Gaston Granger, "Langue universelle et formalisation des sciences: Un fragment inédit de Condorcet," *Revue d'histoire des sciences et de leurs applications* VII (1954), pp. 197–219. The fragmentary manuscript reproduced by Granger, MS 885 of the Institut de France, was most likely composed in connection with the *Sketch.*

52. Condorcet, *Sketch,* p. 199.

Chapter 3

1. Cf. Allan Bloom, "An Outline of *Gulliver's Travels,*" *Ancients and Moderns: Essays on the Tradition of Political Philosophy in Honor of Leo Strauss,* ed. Joseph Cropsey (New York-London, Basic Books, 1964), pp. 238–257. I am indebted to Bloom's essay for several points made in this section.

2. Ibid., p. 249.

3. Jonathan Swift, *Gulliver's Travels,* pt. III, chap. ii, in [*The Prose Works*], ed. Herbert Davis, (Oxford, Basil Blackwell, 1957–1968), vol. XI, p. 159.

4. Ibid., pt. III, chap. iv, p. 176.

5. Cf. Marjorie Nicolson and Nora M. Mohler, "The Scientific Background of Swift's *Voyage to Laputa,*" in Nicolson, *Science and Imagination* (Ithaca, N.Y., Cornell University Press, 1956), pp. 110–154.

6. Swift, *Gulliver's Travels,* pt. III, chap. v, p. 185.

7. Ibid., pt. IV, chap. iv, p. 240. Cf. Plato, *Cratylus* 429d. Consider also the fragments of Parmenides.

8. Swift, ibid., pt. IV, chap. v, p. 248. (Emphases added.)

9. Ibid.

10. Ibid., p. 250.

11. Ibid., pt. IV, chap. viii, pp. 267–268.

12. Ibid., pt. IV, chap. iii, p. 237.

13. Cf. Aristotle, *Politics,* bk. I, chap. ii, 9–16; bk. VII, chap. xiii, 11–12.

14. Cf. Swift, *Gulliver's Travels,* pt. IV, chap. iii.

15. Cf. Thomas S. Kuhn, *The Structure of Scientific Revolutions,* 2nd ed., International Encyclopedia of Unified Science, vol. II, no. 2 (Chicago, University of Chicago Press, 1970).

16. Cf. Richard Foster Jones, *Ancients and Moderns: A Study of the Rise of the Scientific Movement in Seventeenth-Century England* (St. Louis, Washington University Press, 1961).

17. Monboddo does not cite Aristotle, so that it is uncertain which terms he is translating. "Energy" is surely a translation of *enérgeia* and "habit" is from *habitus,* the usual Latin for Aristotle's *héxis.* The second and final categories, however, might both be *dýnamis,* since Aristotle used that term to refer to specific faculties or powers, as well as potentiality in general, or "mere power." On the other hand, since Aristotle's use of *entelécheia* is often loose, Monboddo might have had this in mind, but logically it should be the first rather than the second category.

18. James Burnet, Lord Monboddo, *On the Origin and Progress of Language,* 2nd ed. (Edinburgh 1774), vol. I, pp. 13–14. (Monboddo issued second edi-

tions of the first two volumes before completing the work; there was only one edition of all other volumes.) Reprint: intro. Regna Darnell (New York, AMS Press, 1974).

19. Ibid., pp. 338–340.

20. Cf. ibid., pp. 201–206, 415–421.

21. James Boswell, *Journal of a Tour of the Hebrides with Samuel Johnson, LL.D.,* [August 26, 1773], ed. Frederick A. Pottle and Charles H. Bennet (New York, Viking Press, 1936), p. 80.

22. Ibid., [August 16, 1773], p. 27.

23. Boswell, *The Life of Samuel Johnson, LL.D.,* [Sept. 30, 1769], ed. Herbert Askwith (New York, The Modern Library, 1931), p. 348.

24. Ibid., [May 8, 1773], p. 468.

25. Adam Ferguson, *Essay on the History of Civil Society,* 4th ed. (London 1773), pp. 12–13. The first edition of Ferguson's *Essay* appeared in 1767, but Monboddo's ideas were known in intellectual circles some time before the publication of his books.

26. Ibid., p. 10.

27. Ferguson, *Principles of Moral and Political Science; Being Chiefly a Retrospect of Lectures Delivered in the College of Edinburgh* (Edinburgh 1792), vol. I, p. 24. Reprint: intro. L. Castiglione (New York, AMS Press, 1973).

28. Ibid., p. 42.

29. Cf. Arthur O. Lovejoy, "Monboddo and Rousseau," in *Essays in the History of Ideas* (New York, Capricorn Books, 1960 [1948]), pp. 48–61; cf. also Lovejoy, "The Supposed Primitivism of Rousseau's *Discourse on Inequality,"* in *Essays,* pp. 14–47.

30. Alexander Pope, *An Essay on Criticism,* pt. I, ll. 132–135, 139–140.

31. Vico, *The New Science,* bk. III, pars. 875–876, 879, p. 290. Reprinted from *The New Science of Giambattista Vico,* translated from the 3rd ed. (1744), by Thomas Goddard Bergin and Max Harold Fisch. Copyright 1948 by Cornell University. Used by permission of Cornell University Press.

32. Cf. ibid., bk. III, par. 788, p. 272; par. 806, p. 276; par. 875, p. 290.

33. Ibid., par. 821, p. 281.

34. Ibid., par. 787, p. 272.

35. Vico, *Il Diritto universale,* ed. Fausto Nicolini (Bari, G. Laterza, 1936), vol. III, p. 698. The Horatian reference is to *Ars poetica,* l. 359.

36. Thomas Blackwell, *An Enquiry into the Life and Writings of Homer* (London 1735), p. 40.

37. Ibid., pp. 58–59.

38. Ibid., p. 46.

39. Robert Wood, *An Essay on the Original Genius and Writings of Homer* (London 1824 [1769]), p. 79.

40. Ibid., pp. 150–151.

41. Ibid., p. 172.

42. The first edition of Wood's *Essay* in 1769, shortly before his death, was limited and distributed mostly among friends; an accessible version first appeared in 1824. Already in 1763, however, Wood sent a copy of the draft to Michaelis, who showed it to Heyne. Heyne spread the news with a review of Wood in the *Göttinger Gelehrte Anzeigen.* Bodmer and Breitinger then incorporated Wood's Homer in their new literary criticism.

43. Cf. Friedrich August Wolf, *Prolegomena ad Homerum sive de operum Homericum prisca et genuina forma variisque mutationibus et probabili ratione emendandi* (Halle 1795). Wolf only became acquainted with Vico by way of Melchiorre Cesarotti, an Italian poet, classicist, and translator of the *Iliad.* Wolf obtained a copy of *The New Science* in 1802 and published an apprecia-

tion five years later. Cf. Wolf, "Giambattista Vico über den Homer," *Museum der Alterthumswissenschaften* I (1807), pp. 555–570.

44. Cf. Jean Astruc, *Conjectures sur les mémoires originaux dont il paraît que Moïse s'est servi pour composer le livre de la Genèse* (Brussels 1753). Important forerunners of Biblical criticism were Richard Simon—*Histoire critique du Vieux Testament* (1678) and *Histoire critique du texte du Nouveau Testament* (1689)—and Spinoza. Cf. Spinoza, *Tractatus politicus,* chaps. III–IV; cf. *Tractatus theologico-politicus,* chaps. VII, XII, XV–XVII, XX; cf. Leo Strauss, "How to Study Spinoza's *Theologico-Political Treatise,"* in *Persecution and the Art of Writing* (New York, Free Press, 1952), pp. 142–201.

45. Cf. Johann Gottfried Eichhorn, *Urgeschichte,* ed. Johann Philipp Gabler, 3 vols. (Altdorf-Nürnberg 1790–1793). Cf. Christian Hartlich and Walter Sachs, *Der Ursprung des Mythosbegriffs in der modernen Bibelwissenschaft* (Tübingen, J. C. B. Mohr, 1952), pp. 20–47.

46. Christian Gottlob Heyne, "Sermonis mythici interpretatio ad causas ac regulas suas revocata," *Göttingische Gelehrte Anzeigen* (1811), p. 2009.

47. Cf. Carl Ullman, *Historisch oder Mythisch: Beiträge zur Beantwortung der gegenwärtigen Lebensfrage der Theologie* (Hamburg 1838).

48. Cf. M. H. Abrams, *The Mirror and the Lamp: Romantic Theory and the Critical Tradition* (New York, Oxford University Press, 1953).

49. Cf. Walter Jackson Bate, *From Classic to Romantic: Premises of Taste in Eighteenth-Century England* (Cambridge, Mass., Harvard University Press, 1946); cf. René Wellek, *History of Modern Criticism* (New Haven, Conn., Yale University Press, 1955), vols. I and II.

50. Figures as diverse as Charles Avison, Count Algarotti, James Beattie, Hugh Blair, John Brown, the marquis de Chastellux, and Johann Nikolaus Forkel, all wrote works asserting the original unity of music and poetry or calling for their reunification.

51. In all his operas beginning with *Orfeo ed Euridice* (1762), Christoph Willibald Gluck combined choreography, dramatics, instruments, and voice in one grand effect.

52. Cf. John Brown, *A Dissertation on the Rise, Union, and Power, the Progressions, Separations, and Corruptions, of Poetry and Music* (London 1763), pp. 45–46: "For the *Chief* would now no longer pride himself on the Character of *Poet* or Performer; nor the *Man* of *Genius* and *Worth* descend to the Profession of *Lyrist, Singer* or *Actor:* Because these Professions, which had formerly been the Means of inculcating everything laudable and great, would now (when perverted to the contrary Purposes) be disdained by the Wise and Virtuous. Hence the Power, the Utility, and Dignity of *Music* would sink into a general Corruption and Contempt."

53. William Wordsworth, preface to the second edition of the *Lyrical Ballads, The Poetical Works of William Wordsworth,* ed. Thomas Hutchinson (London, Oxford University Press, 1916), p. 940.

54. Cf. James Harris, "A Discourse on Music, Painting and Poetry," in *Three Treatises* (London 1744), pp. 47–103.

55. Cf. Adam Smith, "On the Nature of That Imitation Which Takes Place in What Are Called the Imitative Arts," in *Works,* ed. Dugald Stewart (London 1811), vol. V, pp. 241–318.

56. Cf. James Beattie, *Essays: On Poetry and Music, as They Affect the Mind; on Laughter and Ludicrous Compositions; on the Usefulness of Classical Learning* (London 1762); cf. Beattie, *The Theory of Language* (London 1788), pp. 95–107; Reprint: intro. Kenneth Morris (New York, AMS Press, 1974).

57. William Jones, "Essay on the Arts Commonly Called Imitative," *Works,* ed. Lord Teignmouth (London 1807), vol. X, p. 378.

58. Cf. Daniel Webb, *Observations on the Correspondence Between Poetry and Music* (London 1769).

59. Cf. Webb, *Some Reasons for Thinking That the Greek Language Was Borrowed from the Chinese: Notes on the Grammatica Sinica of Mons. Fourmount* (London 1787). On this point Webb was following the lead of a namesake: cf. John Webb, *An Historical Essay Endeavoring a Probability That the Language of the Empire of China is the Primitive Language* (London 1669).

60. Cf. Northrop Frye, "Towards Defining an Age of Sensibility," *ELH, a Journal of English Literary History* (1956), pp. 144–152. Reprinted in *Eighteenth-Century English Literature,* ed. James L. Clifford (New York, Oxford University Press, 1959), pp. 311–318.

61. Two articles which summarize changes in the conception of genius are Herbert Dieckmann, "Diderot's Conception of Genius," *Journal of the History of Ideas* II (1941), pp. 151–182; and Herman Wolf, "Die Genielehre des jungen Herder," *Deutsche Vierteljahrschrift für Literaturwissenschaft und Geistesgeschichte* III (1925), pp. 401–430. Cf. also Walter Kaufmann, "Heralds of Original Genius," in *Essays in Memory of Barrett Wendell* (Cambridge, Mass., Harvard University Press, 1926); cf. Milton C. Nahm, *Genius and Creativity: An Essay in the History of Ideas* (Baltimore, Johns Hopkins Press, 1956); cf. Donald M. Foerster, *Homer in English Criticism: The Historical Approach in the Eighteenth Century* (New Haven, Yale University Press, 1947).

62. Wood, *An Essay on the Original Genius,* p. 177.

63. William Duff, *An Essay on Original Genius and its Various Modes of Exertion in Philosophy and the Fine Arts, Particularly in Poetry* (London 1767), pp. xx–xxiii.

64. Ibid., pp. 89–90.

65. Cf. Ernest Lee Tuveson, *The Imagination As a Means of Grace: Locke and the Aesthetics of Romanticism* (Berkeley-Los Angeles, University of California Press, 1960).

66. Hobbes, *Leviathan,* pt. I, chap. 2, p. 6.

67. Cf. Immanuel Kant, *Critique of Judgement,* pt. I, bk. ii, §§46–50.

68. A good summary of the provenance of the term *imagination* as used by Coleridge is R. L. Brett, "Coleridge's Theory of the Imagination," *English Studies,* n.s. II (1949), pp. 75–90.

69. Friedrich Schiller, "Sprache," *Votivtafeln,* no. 47, *Sämtliche Werke,* Horenausgabe (Munich-Leipzig 1910–1922), vol. XII, p. 193:

> Warum kann der lebendige Geist dem Geist nicht erscheinen?
> *Spricht die Seele,* so spricht, ach! schon die *Seele* nicht mehr.

70. The Germans distinguish between *originell* and *original* to separate the two senses of *originality.*

71. Edward Young, *Conjectures on Original Composition* (1759), *Works* (London 1773), vol. V, p. 95. (Emphasis added.)

72. Ibid., p. 105.

73. Ibid., pp. 89, 104, 118.

74. Ibid., pp. 120–121.

75. Cf. J. S. Smart, *James Macpherson: An Episode in Literature* (London, D. Nutt, 1905), especially pp. 200ff.

76. Cf. Edward B. Hungerford, *Shores of Darkness* (Cleveland-New York, World Publishing Co., 1963), pp. 29–33.

Chapter 4

1. It has been well remarked, and paradoxically, that "with Rousseau there begins what we may call the second wave of modernity, [even though] this great and

complex counter-movement consisted in the first place in a return from the world of modernity to pre-modern ways of thinking." Cf. Leo Strauss, "What is Political Philosophy?" *What is Political Philosophy? and Other Studies* (New York, The Free Press, 1959), p. 50.

2. Cf. Roger D. Masters, introduction to Jean-Jacques Rousseau, *The First and Second Discourses,* trans. Roger D. and Judith R. Masters, ed. Roger D. Masters (New York, St. Martin's Press, 1964), pp. 1–26. Consider especially the last three quotations in the introduction (pp. 25–26): "The subjecting of man to law is a problem in politics which I liken to that of the squaring of the circle in geometry" (from *Considerations on the Government of Poland*). "Common readers, pardon my paradoxes: they must be made when one thinks seriously; and, whatever you may say, I would rather be a man of paradoxes than a man of prejudices" (from *Émile*). "I would wager that at this point a thousand people will again find a contradiction with the *Social Contract.* That proves that there are even more readers who ought to learn to read than authors who ought to learn to be consistent" (from *Jugement sur la polysynodie*).

3. Jean-Jacques Rousseau, *Discours sur l'origine et les fondements de l'inégalité parmi les hommes,* in *Œuvres complètes,* ed. V. D. Musset-Pathay (Paris 1823–1826), vol. I, p. 246.

4. Ibid.

5. Ibid., p. 247.

6. Ibid., pp. 247–248.

7. Ibid., p. 248.

8. Cf., for example, *Cratylus* 436b5.

9. On Socrates' use of deliberate ambiguities, puns, and traps, cf. Maurice H. Cohen, "The Aporias in Plato's Early Dialogues," *Journal of the History of Ideas* XXIII (1962), pp. 163–174; cf. also Rosamund K. Sprague, *Plato's Use of Fallacy* (New York, Barnes & Noble, 1962).

10. In many dialogues this structure is quite obvious, in others not so. In the *Apology,* for example, Socrates' dialogue with the Athenian people, he begins with an astonishing confession of self-ignorance: "How you, o men of Athens, have been affected by my accusers, I do not know; but for my own part I nearly forgot who I was, so persuasively did they speak." And after the final verdict, Socrates concludes: "But now it is the hour to go on our ways, me to die and you to live; and which of the two is the better deed—that is unclear to everyone except God." The conclusions of the *Meno* and the *Ion,* in which virtue and rhapsody respectively are interpreted as divine gifts, should also be considered indirect statements of an *aporia.* There are many more Platonic dialogues in which this basic structure is concealed.

11. The role of listeners to Socratic conversations has been neglected in Plato scholarship. Martin Heidegger comments on Glaucon's role listening to the middle sections of the *Republic* as the one who "manifests awakening wonder": cf. *Platons Lehre von der Wahrheit: Mit einem Brief über den Humanismus* (Bern, Francke Verlag, 1954 [1947]), p. 5. The entire *Republic* might be interpreted in terms of its several listeners.

12. Cf. Aristotle, *Metaphysics,* bk. IV, chap. v, 18; cf. also *Metaphysics,* bk. I, chap. vi, 2.

13. Cf. Plato, *Laches* 186c; cf. *Symposium* 175d–e, where Socrates uses a similar tactic to show up Agathon's failure to understand wisdom.

14. The *Essay* had a complicated history. Some of its materials were first intended as an article on melody and on the moral implications of music and art; these sections were begun in 1749 and were to be submitted to the *Encyclopedia,* for which Rousseau was then the main contributor on music. After composing the Second Discourse, Rousseau expanded those sections, made them center on the problem of language, and changed the title from "Principles of Melody" to the

present one. This Rousseau wanted to use together with the Second Discourse, but he finally decided against it. At another time he considered publishing it along with a new edition of his *Dissertation on Modern Music* (1743), but he also abandoned that plan. In 1761 he considered including it in a collection of essays, *Political Institutions,* but this plan did not come to fruition either. The *Essay* was first published posthumously in 1781.

15. Rousseau, *Discours sur l'origine,* p. 253.

16. Cf. the first and last sentences of the preface: "The most useful and the least advanced of all forms of human knowledge is, it seems to me, that concerning man; and I dare say that the inscription of the temple of Delphi alone contained a precept more important and difficult than all the thick tomes of the moralists." (Ibid., p. 215.) Rousseau closed the preface with a quote from Persius:

> Quem te Deus esse
> Jussit, et humana qua parte locatus es in re,
> Disce. (*Satire* III, 71–73)

"Learn who it is that God has ordered you to be and in what human place you are in fact located" (p. 220)—which is one way of rephrasing the Delphic maxim.

17. Ibid., p. 216.

18. Ibid., p. 215.

19. Cf. Ibid., pp. 239–240: "The beast, which has acquired nothing and which therefore has nothing to lose, always stays with its instinct, [but is it not the case that] man, losing again by old age or other accidents all that which his *perfectibility* had made him acquire, thus falls back even lower than the beasts themselves? It would be sad for us to be forced to admit that this distinctive and almost unlimited faculty is the source of all the sorrows of mankind, that it is this which, by virtue of time, tears him from that original condition in which he passed tranquil and innocent days; that it is this which, bringing to birth over the centuries his enlightenment and his errors, his vices and his virtues, over the long run renders him the tyrant both of himself and of nature."

20. Ibid., p. 215. Cf. Plato, *Republic,* bk. X, 611.

21. Rousseau, ibid., p. 218.

22. Cf. Rousseau, *Essai sur l'origine des langues, où il est parlé de la mélodie et de l'imitation musicale,* in *Œuvres complétes,* vol. II, p. 423, where Rousseau defends the thesis that language must have arisen from passions rather than needs. The natural effect of the first needs, Rousseau says, was to separate men rather than bring them together. "It would be absurd that the cause which separated men [i.e., needs] should become the means which would unite them [i.e., language]."

23. Ibid., p. 435.

24. Cf. Plato, *Phaedrus* 274–278; *Epistle* II 314c; *Epistle* VII 344c–d; et al.

25. Rousseau, *Essai sur l'origine des langues,* pp. 428–429.

26. Ibid., p. 415.

27. Cf. Rousseau, *Discours sur l'origine de l'inégalité,* p. 238, and note (k), pp. 336–344. The Montaigne reference is to the beginning of the forty-second essay of the first book of *Essais,* "Of the Inequality That Is Among Us."

28. Rousseau, *Essai sur l'origine des langues,* p. 421.

29. Consider Rousseau's comments about translation: "I have reflected a hundred times while writing that it is impossible, in a long work, always to give the same sense to the same words. There is no language rich enough to furnish enough terms, turns, and phrases as there are modifications of ideas. . . . Definitions would be very nice if only one did not have to employ words to make them. Despite that, I am convinced that one can be clear, even with the

poverty of our language, not by always giving the same meaning to the same words, but by working things out so that, each time a word is used, the meaning which one gives it is sufficiently determined by the ideas which relate to it, and so that each sentence in which the word appears serves, so to speak, as its definition." *Émile; ou, De l'éducation,* bk. II, in *Œuvres complètes,* vol. III, pp. 160–161.

30. Cf. Rousseau, *Essai sur l'origine des langues,* p. 495: "Thus our popular languages have become as perfectly useless as eloquence. Societies have assumed their last form: one does not change anything any more except with cannons or with coins; and since the only thing left to say to people is 'Give your money!' it is said with placards on street corners or with soldiers stationed on the premises. For that it is unnecessary to assemble a single person; on the contrary, it is necessary to keep one's subjects apart—that is the first maxim of modern politics."

31. Cf. C. E. Vaughan, *The Political Writings of Jean Jacques Rousseau* (Cambridge, Cambridge University Press, 1915), vol. I, pp. 434ff.

Chapter 5

1. Cf. Adolf Harnack, *Geschichte der Königlich Preussischen Akademie der Wissenschaften zu Berlin* (Berlin, Reichsdruckerei, 1900), vol. II, p. 71 and vol. I, p. 94. The academy was originally founded as the Brandenburg Society of Sciences, but was redesignated when the elector of Brandenburg became hereditary king of Prussia.

2. Consider these comments by Süssmilch lamenting the nonpayment of an allowance which had long been assured him: "I am despondent and dubious about the desired outcome, partly because my book is written in German, partly because the academy is to be subjected to the revisions of d'Alembert, from which nothing but injury can be expected for the Germans. The decline of the academy will surely ensue, because the few Frenchmen are insufficient and there is not a single genuine scholar among them anyway. The hour of fate has struck for the academy." (Ibid., vol. I, p. 357.) On the "Frenchification" of the academy, cf. ibid., pp. 269–316.

3. Cf. Turgot, *Remarques critiques sur les Réflexions philosophiques de M. de Maupertuis,* in *Œuvres,* ed. Pierre Dupont de Nemours (Paris 1808–1811), vol. II, pp. 102–164.

4. Pierre Louis Moreau de Maupertuis, "Dissertation sur les différents moyens dont les hommes se sont servis pour exprimer leurs idées," *Œuvres* (Lyon 1756), vol. III, p. 438.

5. Ibid., p. 449.

6. Cf. ibid., pp. 450, 466.

7. Maupertuis, "Des devoirs de l'académicien: Discours prononcé dans l'Académie royale des sciences et belles-lettres" (1753), ibid., p. 301.

8. For the impact of *Die göttliche Ordnung,* particularly on Thomas Malthus, see F. S. Crum and W. F. Wilcox, "A Trial Bibliography of the Writings of Johann Peter Süssmilch, 1707–1767," *Publications of the American Statistical Association,* vol. V: 39 (1896–1897), pp. 310–314.

9. Cf. Johann Peter Süssmilch, *Versuch eines Beweises, dass die erste Sprache ihren Ursprung nicht vom Menschen, sondern allein vom Schöpfer erhalten habe* (Berlin 1766), p. iv(b); pp. 13–14.

10. Cf. Jakob Carpov, *Tractatus de lingua ejusque perfectione* (n.p. 1740).

11. Süssmilch, *Versuch eines Beweises,* pp. 23–24.

12. In the introductory material to *Versuch eines Beweises,* Süssmilch says that Rousseau's work came into his hands only after his draft was completed, though he does take Rousseau to confirm his own position.

13. Christian Wolff, *Philosophia prima, sive ontologia,* pt. I, sect. iii, chap. iii, §279 (Frankfort-Leipzig 1736), p. 227. Cf. §294, p. 236. Reprint: ed. Joannes Ecole (Hildesheim, Georg Olms, 1962).

14. Moses Mendelssohn, *Sendschreiben an den Herrn Magister Lessing in Leipzig* (1756), *Gesammelte Schriften,* ed. Julius Guttman et al. (Berlin, Akademie-Verlag, 1931), vol. II, p. 106.

15. Johann David Michaelis, *De l'influence des opinions sur le langage et du langage sur les opinions: Dissertation qui a remporté le prix de l'Académie royale des sciences et belles lettres de Prusse en 1759,* trans. Prémontval (Bremen 1762), p. 8. Reprint: *A Dissertation on the Influence of Opinions on Language and of Language on Opinions* (1769), intro. James H. Stam (New York, AMS Press, 1973), p. 2.

16. Moses Mendelssohn, letter 72, *Briefe, die neueste Literatur betreffend* IV (Berlin-Stettin 1759), p. 365.

17. Ibid., pp. 365–366.

18. Ibid., p. 370.

19. Johann Georg Hamann, "Versuch über eine akademische Frage," *Kreuzzüge des Philologen,* in *Sämtliche Werke,* ed. Josef Nadler (Vienna, Herder, 1949–1957), vol. II, p. 121.

20. Ibid., p. 122.

21. Ibid., pp. 125–126.

22. Aristotle, *Politics,* bk. II, chap. ix, 5, p. 1274a25–30.

23. Cf. Plato, *Phaedrus* 275b, *Philebus* 49a–d, and *Republic,* bk. VI, 490e–496e.

24. Plato, *Sophist* 233c.

25. Hamann, "Versuch über eine akademische Frage," p. 121.

26. Cf. Plato, *Republic,* bk. V, 476ff.

27. Hamann, "Versuch über eine akademische Frage," p. 125.

28. Jean Henri Samuel Formey, "Réunion des principaux moyens employés pour découvrir l'origine du langage, des idées, et des connoissances des hommes," *Anti-Émile* (Berlin 1763), pp. 211–253.

29. Cf. Herodotus, *The Persian Wars,* bk. II, chap. ii.

30. Thomas Abtt, "Allerhand Muthmassungen über den ältesten Zustand der Menschen," *Vermischte Werke,* ed. Friedrich Nicolai (Frankfort-Leipzig 1783), vol. VI, p. 147.

31. Ibid., p. 152.

32. Ibid., p. 164.

33. Cf. Kant's similar use of the Mosaic account in "Muthmasslicher Anfang der Menschengeschichte" (1786), in *Werke,* ed. Wilhelm Weischedel (Frankfort on the Main, Insel, 1960–1964), vol. VI, pp. 85–102.

34. Abtt, "Allerhand Muthmassungen," p. 151.

35. Cf. Herder, *Über Thomas Abbts Schriften: Der Torso von einem Denkmaal, an seinem Grabe errichtet* (1768), in *Sämmtliche Werke,* ed. Bernhard Suphan et al. (Berlin 1877–1913), vol. II, pp. 249–294.

36. Herder, *Über die neuere deutsche Literatur: 1.–3. Sammlung von Fragmenten, als Beilagen zu den "Briefen, die neueste Literatur betreffend"* (1767–1768), in *Sämmtliche Werke,* vol. I, p. 147.

37. Ibid., pp. 151–152.

38. Ibid., p. 154.

39. Ibid., p. 155.

40. Christian Garve, "Über die deutsche neue Literatur," *Neue Bibliothek der schönen Wissenschaften und der freyen Künste* IV: 1 (1767), p. 74.

41. Hamann, *Aesthetica in Nuce: Eine Rhapsodie in kabbalistischer Prose* (1762), in *Sämtliche Werke,* vol. II, p. 197.
42. Herder, *Über die neuere deutsche Litteratur: Fragmente,* 2nd ed. (1768), in *Sämmtliche Werke,* vol. II, p. 69.
43. Ibid., p. 62; cf. Herder, *Versuch einer Geschichte der lyrischen Dichtkunst* (1767?), in *Sämmtliche Werke,* vol. XXXII, pp. 86–87.
44. In the revision of the *Fragmente* the last phrase was changed to *poetical conjecture,* apparently because of Garve's criticism. Cf. *Über die neuere deutsche Litteratur: Fragmente,* 2nd ed., p. 61; cf. *Versuch,* p. 85.
45. Herder, *Versuch,* pp. 89–90; cf. *Über die neuere deutsche Litteratur: Fragmente,* 2nd ed., p. 64.
46. Ibid., p. 90.
47. Herder, *Über die neuere deutsche Litteratur: Fragmente,* 2nd ed., p. 64.
48. Cf. Herder, *Versuch,* p. 91.
49. Ibid.
50. Ibid.
51. Ibid., p. 92.
52. Ibid., p. 99.
53. Herder, *Über die neuere deutsche Litteratur: Fragmente,* 2nd ed., p. 66.
54. Herder, *Versuch,* p. 103.
55. Herder, *Über die neuere deutsche Litteratur: Fragmente,* 2nd ed., pp. 67–68.

Chapter 6

1. Cf. Herder, *Journal meiner Reise im Jahr 1769,* in *Sämmtliche Werke,* ed. Bernhard Suphan et al., vol. IV, pp. 405–406; cf. Herder, to Johann Friedrich Hartknoch, Aug. 1769, *Johann Gottfried Herders Lebensbild,* ed. Emil Gottfried von Herder (Erlangen 1846), vol. II, p. 248.
2. Johann Wolfgang von Goethe, *Dichtung und Wahrheit,* pt. II, bk. 10, *Gedenkausgabe der Werke, Briefe und Gespräche,* ed. Ernst Beutler (Zurich, Artemis, 1948–1954), vol. X, p. 442.
3. Herder, to Friedrich Nicolai, February 1772, *Herders Briefwechsel mit Nicolai,* ed. Otto Hoffman (Berlin 1887), p. 70.
4. Cf. Herder, *Abhandlung über den Ursprung der Sprache,* in *Sämmtliche Werke,* vol. V, p. 5: "Already as an animal man has language." This opening sentence to the *Treatise* must be understood in the polemical context, not as an unqualified assertion.
5. Ibid., p. 6.
6. Ibid., p. 13.
7. Ibid., p. 14.
8. Ibid., p. 17.
9. Ibid.
10. Ibid., p. 18.
11. Ibid., p. 20.
12. Ibid.
13. Ibid., pp. 21–22.
14. Cf. Hermann Samuel Reimarus, *Allgemeine Betrachtungen über die Triebe der Thiere, hauptsächlich über ihre Kunsttriebe,* chap. IV, §§56–57, 2nd ed. (Hamburg 1762), pp. 94ff.
15. Herder, *Abhandlung,* p. 24.
16. Ibid.
17. Ibid., p. 26.
18. Ibid., p. 27.

19. Ibid.

20. Herder mostly uses the word *Besonnenheit,* but he varies his terms freely, some-times using *Besinnung* ("consciousness"), or *Vernunft* ("reason"), or simply *Reflexion* ("reflection").

21. Herder, *Abhandlung,* p. 30.

22. Ibid., pp. 33–34.

23. Ibid., p. 34.

24. Ibid., p. 36.

25. Ibid., p. 37.

26. Ibid., p. 38.

27. Ibid., p. 41.

28. Ibid., p. 42.

29. Ibid., p. 46.

30. Ibid., p. 47.

31. According to Herder, sight has the widest range of sensitivity, touch the nar-rowest, and hearing is midway between them. Hearing is median with regard to clarity and exactness: "All the obscure characteristics of touch which flow into one another are ignored by hearing, so also the overly precise and fine distinctions made by sight" (ibid., pp. 65–66). Touch is too forceful, sight too indifferent, but hearing stands in the middle as to intensity. As to the time in which they are operative: In touch, everything comes upon us at once, but in forceful, sporadic moments; in sight, everything comes upon us at once, but as a confused multitude of things placed next to one another; in hearing, impres-sions are more easily distinguishable because they are extended temporally in linear arrangement. Hearing is the middle sense with regard to its expression: Tactile sensations are so instantaneous and dark that they cannot be expressed; objects of sight are clear and often constant—generally one can continue to stare at them—so that it is often more instructive to point than to talk about them. In contrast, auditory sensations come and go: Their duration is enough to make them distinguishable; yet, since they are transitory, they must be imi-tated if they are not to be lost. Finally, the sense of touch is the earliest devel-oped in the newborn; whereas the sense of sight grows with age and may even become more discriminating as the physical faculty falters. Vision is the sense most susceptible and needing of education; whereas touch requires little. Again, hearing is the median sense: The musical ear can be trained to hear the finest distinctions; but everyone who has a functioning ear, even the tone-deaf, can detect an infinity of differences among auditory stimuli.

32. Herder, *Abhandlung,* p. 64. Cf. Martin Schuetze, "The Fundamental Ideas in Herder's Thought: Part V: Herder's Psychology," *Modern Philology* XXI: 1 (August 1923), pp. 29–48; cf. Robert T. Clark, "Herder's Conception of 'Kraft,'" *PMLA* LVII: 3 (Sept. 1942), pp. 737–752.

33. Herder, ibid., pp. 89–90.

34. Ibid., p. 93.

35. Ibid., p. 95: ". . . zwar noch kein Geschöpf von Besinnung, aber schon von Besonnenheit . . ."

36. Ibid., p. 112.

37. Ibid., p. 118.

38. Ibid., pp. 123–124.

39. Ibid., p. 127.

40. Ibid., p. 134.

41. Ibid., p. 136.

42. Ibid., p. 144.

43. Ibid., p. 145.

44. Ibid., p. 146.

45. Robert T. Clark, *Herder: His Life and Thought* (Berkeley-Los Angeles, University of California Press, 1955), p. 132.

46. Clark, "Hamann's Opinion of Herder's *Ursachen des gesunden Geschmacks*," *Modern Language Notes* LXI (1946), p. 99.

47. Goethe, *Dichtung und Wahrheit,* pt. II, bk. 10, pp. 445-446.

48. .Herder, *Abhandlung,* p. 147.

49. Hamann, *Philologische Einfälle und Zweifel über eine akademische Preisschrift,* in *Sämtliche Werke,* vol. III, p. 41.

50. Karl Wilhelm Jerusalem, "Dass die Sprache dem ersten Menschen durch Wunder nicht mitgetheilt seyn kann," *Philosophische Aufsätze von Karl Wilhelm Jerusalem, mit G. E. Lessings Vorrede und Zusätzen,* ed. Paul Beer (Berlin 1900), p. 11.

51. Dietrich Tiedemann, "Vorrede,"· *Versuch einer Erklärung des Ursprungs der Sprache* (Riga 1772), unpaginated.

52. G. A. Wells, "Man and Nature: An Elucidation of Coleridge's Rejection of Herder's Thought," *Journal of English and Germanic Philology* LI (1952) pp. 321-322. Coleridge's marginalia are reprinted in this article from his copies of Herder and Kant held by the British Museum. This comment was in the flyleaf of Herder's *Briefe, das Studium der Theologie betreffend.* On the general problem of art, nature, and human nature, cf. Henry V. S. Ogden, "The Rejection of the Antithesis of Nature and Art in Germany, 1780–1800," *Journal of English and Germanic Philology* XXXVIII (1939), pp. 597–616.

53. Herder, *Briefe zur Beförderung der Humanität,* coll. II, let. 25, §11, in *Sämmtliche Werke,* vol. XVII, p. 117. Whether or not Herder knew it, this was an almost exact quotation of Adam Ferguson, *Essay on the History of Civil Society,* 4th ed. (London 1773), p. 10.

Chapter 7

1. Cf. Herder to Friedrich Nicolai, February 1772, *Herders Briefwechsel mit Nicolai,* ed. Otto Hoffman (Berlin 1887), p. 70; cf. Herder to Caroline Flachsland, February 1772, *Aus Herders Nachlass,* ed. Heinrich Düntzer and Ferdinand Gottfried von Herder (Frankfort on the Main 1857), vol. III, p. 178.

2. Johann Georg Hamann, *Zwo Recensionen nebst einer Beylage, betreffend den Ursprung der Sprache,* in *Sämtliche Werke,* ed. Josef Nadler (Vienna, Herder, 1949–1957), vol. III, p. 16.

3. *Ibid.,* p. 18. *Apokolkyntōsis,* literally meaning "pumpkinification," refers to a Roman work usually attributed to Seneca, sometimes to Petronius, *Ludus de morte Claudii.* On the death of a Roman emperor it was customary for some poet to laud his apotheosis. After the death of Claudius, however, instead of a "deification," an anonymous satire described his "pumpkinification." *Apophtheirōsis* in this form is apparently a term of Hamann's coinage, meaning "abortion" or "destruction." *Galimatias* is a term of unknown etymology used to describe a confused tongue or, generally, gibberish.

4. *Ibid.,* p. 17.

5. *Ibid.,* p. 19. For the reference to the kitchen hearth at the beginning of the paragraph, cf. Aristotle, *On the Parts of Animals,* bk. I, chap. v, p. 645a17–21.

6. Hamann to Herder, June 14, 1772, *Briefwechsel,* ed. Walther Ziesemer and Arthur Henkel (Wiesbaden, Insel, 1955–   ), vol. III, pp. 7–8.

7. Hamann, *Zwo Recensionenen,* p. 20.

8. *Ibid.*

9. *Ibid.,* pp. 21–22.

10. *Ibid.,* p. 22.

11. Ibid., pp. 23–24. "Merciless sisters" refers to the prostitutes who disturb Don Quixote at the inn. *Allotriocosmic* means "otherworldly" and evidently alludes to the eighty-ninth fragment of Heraclitus. The scriptural quotation is from Matt. 5:37. The "spirit of laws" and "social contract" obviously refer to Montesquieu and Rousseau respectively.

12. Hamann, *Philologische Einfälle und Zweifel über eine akademische Preisschrift,* in *Sämtliche Werke,* vol. III, pp. 43–44.

13. Hamann to Herder, Oct. 6, 1772, *Briefwechsel,* vol. III, pp. 16–17.

14. The possible wordplays which Hamann had in mind with the term *Caricatur-bilderurschrift* are many. *Caricatur* in the eighteenth century could mean "caricature," but it also could mean (and certainly could have been intended by Hamann as a pun on) "characteristics," as in Shaftesbury or in Leibniz's universal characteristics. This in turn could involve a translinguistic pun, since Herder's *Merkmal,* which we have translated as "distinguishing mark," would customarily be translated as "characteristic." An unusual division of the elements of the word would yield *Caricat-Urbilder-Urschrift,* with the latter two elements meaning "original images" and "original writing," and both giving a hint of original language. The usual translation of *Bilderurschrift* is "hieroglyphics," which might indicate another translinguistic pun with Epictetus's "hierophant." By the nature of the case it is impossible to determine with certainty how many of these puns (or perhaps more) were consciously intended by Hamann; but it is fairly certain that some were.

15. Plato, *Philebus* 16c. Hamann cites this passage in Latin, probably because the word *oracula* is less ambiguous than Plato's *phémē,* which can mean "oracle," "legend," "tradition," or "saying." This rendering fits with Hamann's plea in the review for a cabalistic philologist who would express his "oracles and doubts" about the academy's question and Herder's answer.

16. Heraclitus, fragment 93 (Diels-Kranz numeration).

17. Arrian, *Discourses of Epictetus,* bk. III, chap. 21.

18. Ibid. (Emphasis added.)

19. Hamann, *Zwo Recensionen,* p. 20.

20. Cf. Leo Strauss, *Persecution and the Art of Writing* (New York, Free Press, 1952); cf. Leo Strauss, "On a Forgotten Kind of Writing," *What Is Political Philosophy? and Other Studies* (New York, Free Press, 1959), pp. 221–232.

21. Hamann, *Des Ritters von Rosencreuz letzte Willensmeynung über den göttlichen und menschlichen Ursprung der Sprache,* in *Sämtliche Werke,* vol. III, p. 33. Cf. Rabelais, *Gargantua and Pantagruel,* bk. II, chap. 9. Quintus Icilius was the name that Frederick the Great gave to Karl Gottlieb Guichard, a general, but also a polyglot and knowledgeable classicist.

22. For a statement of the main positions taken, cf. Lester Gilbert Crocker, "The Problem of Truth and Falsehood in the Age of Enlightenment," *Journal of the History of Ideas* XIV (1955), pp. 575–603.

23. Cf. Plato, *Republic,* bk. VII, 514aff.

24. Cf. Plato, *Epistle* VII 341c. I here ignore the philological debate about the genuineness of this text, because Hamann himself evidently accepted it.

25. "Socrates [referring to Heraclitus] spoke of readers who could swim. A confluence of ideas and impressions in that lively elegy of the philosopher perhaps made these same sentences into a multitude of small islands, with no methodological bridges or ferries to connect them." (Hamann, *Sokratische Denkwürdigkeiten* [1759], in *Sämtliche Werke,* vol. II, p. 61.) For the Socratic reference to Heraclitus, cf. Diogenes Laertius, *Lives of Eminent Philosophers,* bk. II, chap. v, 22.

26. Hamann, *Zwo Recensionen* pp. 23–24.

27. Heraclitus, fragment 89.

28. Heraclitus, fragment 114.
29. Hamann, *Zwo Recensionen*, p. 19.
30. Aristotle, *De partibus animalium*, bk. I, chap. v, p. 645a 17–21.
31. Cf. *inter alia* George Anastaplo, "Human Being and Citizen: A Beginning to the Study of Plato's *Apology of Socrates*," *Ancients and Moderns: Essays on the Tradition of Political Philosophy in Honor of Leo Strauss*, ed. Joseph Cropsey (New York-London, Basic Books, 1964), pp. 16–49; Martin A. Bertman, "Socrates' Defence of Civil Disobedience," *Studium Generale* XXIV (1971), pp. 576–582; Ronald F. Hathaway, "Law and the Moral Paradox in Plato's *Apology*," *Journal of the History of Philosophy* VIII (1970), pp. 127–142; Gregory Vlastos, "Socrates on Obedience and Disobedience," *The Yale Review* (Summer 1974), pp. 517–534.
32. Compare this comment on authorship by Hamann: "To ask Him who is no longer asked in our enlightened century and no longer heard, the Muse went and said: 'Since it is so with me, why have I become an author?'" (*Hamburgische Nachricht*, in *Sämtliche Werke*, vol. II, p. 244.) The allusion is to Genesis 25:22, when Rebecca approaches God and says: "If it is so with me, why have I become pregnant?" (Translated from the Luther translation.) Parallels between authorship and pregnancy are obvious, as in Plato's *Symposium*.
33. Cf. Hamann, "Beurtheilung der *Kreuzzüge des Philologen*," in *Sämtliche Werke*, vol. II, pp. 257–274.
34. There is a list of the books owned by Hamann which serves as an effective control against purely speculative interpretation. Cf. Nora Imendörfer, *Johann Georg Hamann und seine Bücherei* (Königsberg, Ost-Europa Verlag, 1938). A list is also contained in the fifth volume of Nadler's edition.
35. Cf. Leo Strauss, "A Moral Dilemma," *Persecution and the Art of Writing*, pp. 55–60.
36. Hamann, *Des Ritters von Rosencreuz letzte Willensmeynung*, p. 27.
37. Ibid.
38. Ibid.; cf. Tertullian, *Apologeticus adversus gentes*, chap. XI.
39. Cf. Gustaf Wingren, *The Living Word: A Theological Study of Preaching and the Church*, trans. Victor C. Pogue (Philadelphia, Fortress Press, 1960), pp. 204–215; cf. Gerhard Ebeling, *Evangelische Evangelienauslegung: Eine Untersuchung zu Luthers Hermeneutik* (Darmstadt, Wissenschaftliche Buchgesellschaft, 1962), pp. 246ff, pp. 338–340.
40. Luther, *Psalmen-Vorlesung* (1513–1514), in *Werke*, Kritische Gesamtausgabe (Weimar 1883–), vol. III, p. 152. Cf. Wolfgang M. Zucker, "Linguistic Philosophy and Luther's Understanding of the Word," *The Lutheran Quarterly* XV (1963), pp. 195–211.
41. Cf. Ebeling, *Evangelische Evangelienauslegung*, pp. 362–365.
42. Cf. Luther, "Sendbrief vom Dolmetschen" (1530), *Werke*, vol. XXX/2, pp. 627–646.
43. Cf. Fritz Blanke, *Der verborgene Gott bei Luther* (Berlin, Furche Verlag, 1928); cf. Blanke, "Hamann und Luther," *Hamann-Studien* (Zürich, Zwingli Verlag, 1956), pp. 54ff; cf. Blanke, "Gottessprache und Menschensprache bei J. G. Hamann," *Hamann-Studien*, pp. 83–97. Note Hamann's references to the Lutheran doctrine on pp. 40 and 47 of *Philologische Einfälle und Zweifel*.
44. Cf. Erik Peterson, "Das Problem der Bibelauslegung im Pietismus des 18. Jahrhunderts," *Zeitschrift für systematische Theologie* I (1923), pp. 468–481. Hamann's part of this dispute is contained in the *Kleeblatt hellenistischer Briefe* (1759–1760), in *Sämtliche Werke*, vol. II, pp. 167–184.
45. It was especially irksome that the principal authority for negative theology was Pseudo-Dionysius the Areopagite. Cf. Ronald F. Hathaway, *Hierarchy and the*

Definition of Order in the Letters of Pseudo-Dionysius: A Study in the Form and Meaning of the Pseudo-Dionysian Writings (The Hague, Nijhoff, 1969), pp. xxiii–xxiv.

46. Cf. St. Thomas Aquinas, *Summa theologica,* pt. IA, quest. xiii, art. 5.

47. Herder, *Abhandlung über den Ursprung der Sprache,* p. 146.

48. Hamann, *Philologische Einfälle und Zweifel über eine akademische Frage,* in *Sämtliche Werke,* vol. III, p. 42.

49. Hamann, *Des Ritters von Rosencreuz letzte Willensmeynung,* pp. 30–31. The word *iussus* in the passage is taken from Ovid, *Metamorphoses,* bk. I, fable X, l. 399. The Montaigne reference is to "Of Vanity" (*Essays,* bk. III, no. 9); the Plato to *Ion* 534b.

50. Ibid., pp. 28–29.

51. Cf. Hamann, *Dialogen die natürliche Religion betreffend,* in *Sämtliche Werke,* vol. III, pp. 245–274.

52. Hamann, *Des Ritters von Rosencreuz letzte Willensmeynung,* pp. 31–33. Hamann explains in a note that *matagrabolize* is taken from Rabelais (*Gargantua and Pantagruel,* bk. III, chap. 22) based on *mataiographobolizein,* literally, "to take soundings by acting foolishly with nugatory writings." Cf. the next footnote for the reference to the stilled "Delphic tripod." "Anti-machiavellian rhetoric" is no doubt a sarcastic allusion to Frederick the Great's *Anti-Macchiavel* (1740), which Frederick composed while he simultaneously pursued machiavellian policies toward Silesia in the War of the Austrian Succession.

53. Clear references are contained in both the *Letzte Willensmeynung* and *Philologische Einfälle und Zweifel.* Demetrius, mentioned on p. 30 of the *Letzte Willensmeynung,* is a character in Plutarch's essay. The references to the navel on the same page may be related to the beginning of that essay. Still more clear are the passages on p. 32 of the *Letzte Willensmeynung* and p. 50 of *Philologische Einfälle.* Hamann's cryptic comments about a "political arithmetic" and a "divine arithmetic" probably refer to Plutarch's mathematical computations of the possible length of a daemon's life in "Why the Oracles Cease to Give Answers," pars. xi–xiii, *Opera moralia.*

54. Plutarch, "Why the Oracles Cease to Give Answers," pars. xlix–lii; cf. Plutarch, "Wherefore the Pythian Priestess Now Ceases to Deliver Her Oracles in Verse," pars. xxiii–xxx.

55. Cf. Hamann, *Philologische Einfälle und Zweifel,* pp. 45, 49, 50.

56. Hamann, *Des Ritters von Rosencreuz letzte Willensmeynung,* p. 32.

57. Hamann, *Philologische Einfälle und Zweifel,* pp. 37–41.

58. Aristotle, *Politics,* bk. I, chap. i, 9, p. 1253a4–5; bk. I, chap. i, 12, p. 1253a29.

59. Ibid., bk. I, chap. i, 10–11, p. 1253a9–18.

60. Ibid., bk. I, chap. i, 8, p. 1252b30–31.

61. Ibid., bk. I, chap. i, 12, p. 1253a36–37.

62. Cf. Carl Andresen, *Logos und Nomos: Die Polemik des Kelsos wider das Christentum* (Berlin, W. de Gruyter, 1955).

63. Hamann, *Philologische Einfälle und Zweifel,* p. 41.

64. Ibid., p. 42.

65. Ibid., p. 43.

66. Ibid., pp. 44–45.

67. Ibid., p. 57.

68. Ibid.

69. Cf. Hamann, *Des Ritters von Rosencreuz letzte Willensmeynung,* p. 33; cf. Hamann, *Vetii Epagathi Regiomonticolae hierophantische Briefe,* in *Sämtliche Werke,* vol. III, p. 144.

70. Hamann, *Philologische Einfälle und Zweifel,* p. 50.

71. Ibid.

72. Ibid., p. 51.
73. Ibid., pp. 45–46.

Chapter 8

1. The same was not the case in the nineteenth century, when both Hegel and Kierkegaard studied Hamann seriously. Cf. Hegel, "Über Hamann's *Schriften*" (1828), in *Sämtliche Werke,* ed. Hermann Glockner, vol. XX, pp. 203–275. Kierkegaard's references to Hamann are scattered throughout his works.
2. Cf. Herder, "Von der Gabe der Sprachen am ersten christlichen Pfingstfest," *Christliche Schriften: Erste Sammlung,* in *Sämmtliche Werke,* vol. XIX, pp. 3–59.
3. Matthias Claudius, [Review of Herder's *Abhandlung über den Ursprung der Sprache*] (1772), *Werke: Asmus omnia sua secum portans, oder Sämmtliche Werke des Wandsbecker Boten,* ed. Urban Roedl (Stuttgart, Cotta, 1954), p. 93.
4. Cf. Gottfried Ploucquet, *De origine sermonis* (1771).
5. Cf. Gotthold Ephraim Lessing, "Von dem Ursprung der verschiedenen Sprachen" [Essay projected but never written, notes arranged by Franz Muncker], in *Sämtliche Schriften,* ed. Karl Lachmann, 3rd ed., [rev. Franz Muncker] (Stuttgart 1886–1907), vol. XV, p. 119; cf. Lessing, *Collectanea,* §27, *Sämtliche Schriften,* vol. XV, p. 152, and *Entwurf zum Laokoon,* §25, ibid., vol. XIV, pp. 427–428.
6. Lessing, "Zusätze des Herausgebers" [Lessing's appendix to his edition of Karl Wilhelm Jerusalem's *Philosophische Aufsätze*] (1776), in *Sämtliche Schriften,* vol. XII, pp. 296–297.
7. Cf. Wilhelm Uebele, "Herder und Tetens," *Archiv für Geschichte der Philosophie* XVIII (1905), pp. 216–249; cf. idem, *Johann Nicolaus Tetens nach seiner Gesamtentwicklung betrachtet, mit besonderer Berücksichtigung des Verhältnisses zu Kant,* Kant-Studien, Ergänzungsheft no. 24 (Berlin 1911).
8. Johann Nicolaus Tetens, "Einige Anmerkungen über die natürliche Sprachfähigkeit des Menschen," *Philosophische Versuche über die menschliche Natur und ihre Entwicklung* XI (Leipzig 1777), vol. I, p. 772.
9. Rudolf Zobel, *Gedanken über die verschiedenen Meinungen der Gelehrten vom Ursprunge der Sprachen* (Magdeburg 1773), p. 114.
10. Ibid., p. 113.
11. Cf. Friedrich Heinrich Jacobi, "Betrachtung über die von Herrn Herder in seiner Abhandlung vom Ursprung der Sprache vorgelegte genetische Erklärung der thierischen Kunstfertigkeiten und Kunsttriebe," *Werke,* ed. Friedrich Roth and Friedrich Köppen (Leipzig 1825), vol. VI, pp. 243–264. Elsewhere, Jacobi used the thesis of the prize essay in an aphorism: "All philosophizing is only a further fathoming of the invention of language" (*Fliegende Blätter,* pt. I, in *Werke,* vol. VI, p. 165).
12. Herder to Johann Heinrich Merck, October 1770, *Briefe aus dem Freundekreis von Goethe, Herder, Höpfner und Merck,* ed. Karl Wagner (Leipzig 1847), pp. 10–11; cf. Herder, *Älteste Urkunde des Menschengeschlechts,* in *Sämmtliche Werke,* vol. VI, pp. 288–303, 336–345.
13. Herder, *Älteste Urkunde,* p. 286.
14. Ibid., p. 297.
15. Ibid., p. 299.
16. Herder to Hamann, August 1, 1772, *Hamanns Briefwechsel,* ed. Walther Ziesemer and Arthur Henkel, vol. III, p. 10.
17. Cf. Hamann, "Christiani Zacchaei Telonarchae Prolegomena über die neueste

Auslegung der ältesten Urkunde des menschlichen Geschlechts: In zweyen Antwortschreiben an Apollonium Philosophum" (1774), *Sämmtliche Werke,* vol. III, pp. 123–133.

18. Hamann to Johann Friedrich Hartknoch, October 25, 1774, *Briefwechsel,* vol. III, p. 116.

19. Herder, *Älteste Urkunde,* pt. IV (1776), vol. VII, p. 30.

20. Ibid., pp. 30–31.

21. Herder, *Geist der ebräischen Poesie* (1782), in *Sämmtliche Werke,* vol. XI, pp. 242–244. By his own admission, though much to his chagrin, Herder was an inferior poet, so that it is only necessary to make perfunctory apology for the translation.

22. Ibid., pp. 326–327.

23. Herder, Preface to *Des Lord Monboddo Werk von dem Ursprunge und Fortgange der Sprache,* übersetzt von E. A. Schmid (Riga 1784), *Sämmtliche Werke,* vol. XV, p. 183.

24. Ibid., p. 187.

25. Herder, *Ideen zur Philosophie der Geschichte der Menschheit,* bk. I, chap. iv (1784), in *Sämmtliche Werke,* vol. XIII, pp. 138–139.

26. Herder, *Ideen,* bk. II, chap. ix (1785), ibid., p. 355.

27. Cf. ibid., p. 367.

28. Herder to Hamann, July 11, 1782, *Hamanns Briefwechsel,* vol. IV, p. 404.

29. Herder, *Verstand und Erfahrung: Eine Metakritik zur Kritik der reinen Vernunft* (1799), in *Sämmtliche Werke,* vol. XXI, p. 209.

30. Cf. Johann Christoph Gatterer, *Handbuch der Universalhistorie nach ihrem gesammten Umfang von Erschaffung der Welt bis zum Ursprung der meisten heutigen Reiche und Staaten* (Göttingen 1765).

31. Cf. Gatterer, *Weltgeschichte in ihrem ganzen Umfange* (Göttingen 1785–1787), vol. I, pp. 5–6.

32. Cf. August Ludwig von Schlözer, *Vorstellung einer Universalhistorie* (Göttingen-Gotha 1772).

33. Cf. Schlözer, *Weltgeschichte nach ihren Haupttheilen im Auszug und Zusammenhange* (Göttingen 1785).

34. Cf. Johann Georg Heinrich Feder, "Über Adelungs *Deutsche Sprachlehre,*" *Berlinische Monatschrift* I:4 (April 1783), pp. 392–403.

35. Feder, "Abriss der wahrscheinlichen Geschichte des natürlichen Ursprungs der Sprache," *Berlinische Monatschrift* II:5 (November 1783), p. 393.

36. Johann Christoph Adelung, *Über den Ursprung der Sprache und den Bau der Wörter, besonders der Deutschen: Ein Versuch* (Leipzig 1781), p. 7.

37. Cf. Adelung, *Versuch einer Geschichte der Cultur des menschlichen Geschlechts* (Leipzig 1782), p. 10.

38. Ibid., pp. 12–13.

39. Cf. Adelung, *Über den Ursprung,* pp. 19–20.

40. Johann Wolfgang von Goethe, *Italienische Reise,* pt. III (1817), in *Gedenkausgabe der Werke, Briefe und Gespräche,* ed. Ernst Beutler (Zurich, Artemis, 1948–1954), vol. XI, p. 507.

Chapter 9

1. Henrik Steffens, letter of Sept. 11, 1814, *Briefe an Ludwig Tieck,* ed. Karl von Holtei (Breslau 1864), vol. IV, p. 65.

2. Cf. Anaxagoras, fragment 6. Cf. Hegel, "Vorrede," *Phänomenologie des Geistes,* in *Sämtliche Werke,* ed. Hermann Glockner (Stuttgart, Friedrich Frommann, 1949–1959), vol. II, p. 22.

3. Johann Gottlieb Fichte, "Von der Sprachfähigkeit und dem Ursprunge der Sprache," *Sämmtliche Werke,* ed. I. H. Fichte (Berlin 1846), vol. VIII, p. 301.

4. Ibid., pp. 303–304.

5. A few years earlier Fichte contrasted the "a priori origin" with the "empirical origin" of the concept of revelation. Cf. Fichte, *Versuch einer Kritik aller Offenbarung* (1792), §§4–6, in *Sämmtliche Werke,* vol. V, pp. 75–106.

6. For Vico providence and "ideal eternal history" give content to "empirical" history; for Hegel it is precisely rationality which reveals itself in history. As he puts it in the famous formulation of the *Philosophy of Right* (1821): "Whatever is rational (*vernünftig*), that is actual (*wirklich*); and whatever is actual, that is rational." (Hegel, "Vorrede," *Grundlinien der Philosophie des Rechts,* in *Sämtliche Werke,* vol. VII, p. 33). In Hegel's early writings, however, prior to the *Phenomenology* (1807), there is much the same ambivalence toward history as can be found in Fichte.

7. Fichte, "Von der Sprachfähigkeit," p. 305.

8. Friedrich Schlegel, letter of Dec. 23, 1795, *Friedrich Schlegels Briefe an seinen Bruder August Wilhelm,* ed. Oskar Walzel (Berlin 1890), p. 262.

9. August Ferdinand Bernhardi also identified linguistic psychogenesis and ontogenesis. Cf. Bernhardi, *Allgemeine Sprachlehre* (Berlin 1803), 2 vols., and *Anfangsgründe der Sprachwissenschaft* (Berlin 1805).

10. August Wilhelm Schlegel, "Miscellen," *Europa: Eine Zeitschrift,* ed. Friedrich Schlegel (Frankfort on the Main 1803), vol. II/i, pp. 193–194.

11. August Wilhelm Schlegel, *Die Kunstlehre: Vorlesungen über schöne Literatur und Kunst* (1801), in *Kritische Schriften und Briefe,* ed. Edgar Lohner (Stuttgart, Kohlhammer, 1962–1967), vol. II, p. 235, Cf. Schlegel's proposal of a "natural history of art," "an explanation of its necessary origin," which would be at once an hypothesis as to the origin of language, the development of poetry, and the progression of human consciousness: ibid., p. 230.

12. Novalis (Friedrich von Hardenberg), *Die Lehrlinge zu Sais* (1798), in *Shriften,* ed. Paul Kluckhohn and Richard Samuel (Stuttgart, Kohlhammer, 1960–), vol. I, p. 79. The terms *un-understandability* (*Unverständlichkeit*) and *un-understanding* (*Unverstand*) are used with specific reference to Kant. According to Kant's distinction between understanding (*Verstand*) and reason (*Vernunft*), the understanding, as the faculty of discursive language and logic, resists going beyond its own rules and categories.

13. Novalis, "Monolog" (1798), ibid., vol. II, p. 672. The title is deliberate and ironic: One can hardly explain soliloquy in terms of useful communications where words act as social coins or coinages. In monologue language comes into its own, it is language for the sake of language.

14. Ibid.

15. Antoine de Rivarol, *Discours préliminaire du nouveau dictionnaire de la langue française* (Paris, An V [1797]), p. 20.

16. "The eternal nature of things is fundamentally opposed to such vast pretensions. . . . Thus when science rises too high, people ultimately treat it like magic; admired in exact proportion to their ignorance. . . . Thus it is certain that to the degree that it rises, science slips down to a vulgar level. It is progress in concentration and not the expansion of enlightenment which should be the goal of the best minds; despite all the efforts of a philosophic century, the most civilized empires will always be just as close to barbarism as the most polished iron is to rust: With nations as with metals it is only the surfaces which are brilliant." (Ibid., pp. 194–195.) "The most eloquent of these [Enlightenment] philosophers has said that children are necessarily small

philosophers; then it must be that philosophers are necessarily big children."
(Ibid., p. 194.)

17. Ibid., p. 2.

18. Ibid., p. 133

19. Hegel, *Vorlesungen über die Philosophie der Geschichte,* in *Sämtliche Werke,*
vol. XI, p. 93.

20. Ibid., p. 95.

21. Kant, "Mutmasslicher Anfang der Menschengeschichte," in *Werke,* ed. Wilhelm Weischedel (Frankfort on the Main, Insel, 1960–1964), vol. VI, p. 87.

22. Friedrich Schmitthenner, *Ursprachlehre: Entwurf zu einem System der Grammatik mit besonderer Rücksicht auf die Sprachen des indisch-teutschen Stammes: das Sanskrit, das Persische, die pelasgischen, slavischen und teutschen Sprachen* (Frankfort on the Main 1826), pp. 18–19.

23. Ibid., p. 29.

24. Haymann Steinthal, *Der Ursprung der Sprache, im Zusammenhange mit den letzten Fragen alles Wissens: Eine Darstellung der Ansicht Wilhelm v. Humboldts, verglichen mit denen Herders und Hamanns* (Berlin 1851), p. 10.

25. Fichte, *Der Patriotismus und sein Gegentheil: Patriotische Dialoge vom Jahre 1807,* in *Sämmtliche Werke,* vol. XI, pp. 228–229. [Vol. XI is vol. III of *Nachgelassene Werke,* ed. I. H. Fichte (Bonn 1834–1835).]

26. Cf. Fichte, *Reden an die deutsche Nation,* in *Sämmtliche Werke,* vol. VII, pp. 270–273, 265.

27. Cf. Fichte, *Politische Fragmente* (1814), in *Sämmtliche Werke,* vol. VII, p. 565.

28. Fichte, *Reden,* pp. 496–498.

29. Cf. ibid., Speeches IV and V passim, pp. 311–344.

30. Ibid., pp. 321, 324.

31. Ibid., p. 315.

32. Ibid., pp. 332–333.

33. Ibid., p. 329.

34. Cf. ibid., Speech VIII, pp. 488–497; cf. also Fichte, *Grundzüge des gegenwärtigen Zeitalters,* lect. I, in *Sämmtliche Werke,* vol. VII, pp. 11–13.

35. Ibid., p. 314.

36. Cf. Joachim Heinrich Campe, *Wörterbuch zur Erklärung und Verdeutschung der unserer Sprache aufgedrungenen fremden Ausdrücke* (Braunschweig 1801), 2 vols.

37. Cf. Arno Borst, *Der Turmbau von Babel,* vol. III/ii, pp. 1555–1558, 1562–1565.

38. Ernst Moritz Arndt, *Über Volkshass und über den Gebrauch einer fremden Sprache* (n.p. 1813), p. 15.

39. Ibid., p. 19.

40. Arndt, "Unsere Sprache und ihr Studium," *Geist der Zeit,* pt. IV (1818), in *Werke,* ed. August Leffson and Wilhelm Steffens (Berlin-Leipzig-Vienna-Stuttgart, n.d.), vol. IX, p. 185.

41. Arndt, "Über deutsche Art und über das Welschtum bei uns," *Geist der Zeit,* pt. IV, in *Werke,* vol. IX, p. 145.

42. Arndt, "Unsere Sprache," p. 169.

43. Arndt, "Über deutsche Art," pp. 150–151.

44. Cf. Johann Andreas Schmeller, *Soll es Eine allgemeine europäische Verhandlungs-Sprache geben?* (Kempten 1815).

45. Cf. Arndt, *Über Volkshass,* pp. 48–49.

46. Friedrich de la Motte-Fouqué, *Etwas über den deutschen Adel, über Ritter-Sinn und Militair-Ehre in Briefen von Friedrich Baron de la Motte Fouqué und Friedrich Perthes in Hamburg* (Hamburg 1819), pp. 15–16.

47. Friedrich Ludwig Jahn, *Deutsches Volkstum* (Lübeck 1810), p. 6.
48. Jahn, *Die Deutsche Turnkunst zur Einrichtung der Turnplätze* (Berlin 1816), pp. xxii–xxiii.
49. Ibid., pp. xxv–xxvi.
50. Ibid., pp. xxiii–xxiv.
51. Jahn, *Deutsches Volkstum,* p. 185.
52. Jahn, *Die Deutsche Turnkunst,* p. xxi.
53. Ibid., p. xxii.
54. Jahn, *Werke,* ed. Karl Euler (Hof 1884–1887), vol. II/2, p. 598.
55. De Maistre's discussions are less systematic than Bonald's and more eclectic. The most important passages are in *Essai sur le principe générateur des constitutions politiques et des autres institutions humaines,* §§XLVII–LIX (written 1809, publ. 1815), *Œuvres complètes* (Lyon 1884–1893), vol. I, pp. 286–301. Lamennais repeats in exact outline the theory of Bonald in *Essai sur l'indifférence en matière de religion* (1817–1820) (Paris, Garnier, [1869]), vol. II, pp. 141ff, 191. Lamennais changed over the years from a theocratic royalist to a theistic democrat to a secular democrat. The *Essai* falls within the first period.
56. Cf. Louis de Bonald, *Recherches philosophiques sur les premiers objets des connaissances morales* (1818), chap. I, in *Œuvres complètes,* ed. Abbé Jacques Paul Migne (Paris 1859), vol. III, col. 44; cf. Bonald, *Démonstration philosophique du principe constitutif de la société* (1830), Intro., in *Œuvres complètes,* vol. I, col. 17.
57. Bonald, *Recherches philosophiques,* col. 88.
58. Bonald, *Législation primitive, considérée dans les derniers temps par les seules lumières de la raison* (1802), in *Œuvres complètes,* vol. I, col. 1071.
59. "The knowledge of the true relations among beings, revealed or transmitted by this authority, is called LAW, from *legere* (to read), because that transmission, given to the first domestic society with speech in the very beginning, was later set in writing for the first public society." (Ibid., col. 1212.)
60. Pierre Maine de Biran, "Origine du langage," *Examen critique des opinions de M. de Bonald* (1818), *Œuvres inédites,* ed. Ernest Naville (Paris 1859), vol. III, p. 247.
61. Cf. Johann Gottfried Hasse, *Preussens Ansprüche als Bernsteinland das Paradies der Alten und Urland der Menscheit gewesen zu seyn* (Königsberg 1799).
62. Cf. Rowland Jones, *The Origin of Language and Nations, Hieroglyphically, Etymologically, and Topographically Defined and Fixed* (London 1764); cf. James Parsons, *Remains of Japhet, Being Historical Enquiries into the Affinity and Origin of the European Languages* (London 1767).
63. Cf. Vincenzo Gioberti, *Del Primato Morale e Civile degli Italiani* (1843), Collezione di Classici Italiani, vols. 24–26 (Turin 1920), vol. III, p. 51.
64. Cf. Peter Franz Josef Müller, *Die Ursprache* (Düsseldorf 1815).
65. Joseph Arthur de Gobineau, *Essai sur l'inégalité des races humaines* (1854) bk. I, chap. xv, 4th ed. (Paris, n.d.), vol. I, pp. 187–214.
66. Cf. ibid., p. 189.
67. Cf. Léon de Rosny, *De l'origine du langage* (Paris 1869), p. 20.
68. Rivarol, *De l'universalité de la langue française: Sujet proposé par l'Académie de Berlin en 1783* (Paris, An V [1797]), p. 32.
69. Barère's speech is contained in *Réimpression de l'ancien Moniteur, seule histoire autentique et inaltérée de la Révolution française depuis la réunion des états-généraux jusqu'a consulat (Mai 1789–Novembre 1799)* (Paris 1847), vol. XIX, p. 318.
70. Ibid., p. 319.

71. Cf. Jeremy Bentham, "Fragments on Universal Grammar," *The Works,* ed. John Bowring (Edinburgh 1843), vol. VIII, p. 341.
72. Noah Webster, *Dissertations on the English Language* (Boston 1789), p. 36. Reprint: ed. Harry R. Warfel (Gainesville, Fla., Scholars' Facsimiles & Reprints, 1951).
73. Ibid., pp. 21–22.
74. Cf. Friedrich Schlegel, "Rede über die Mythologie," *Gespräch über die Poesie* (1800), in *Kritische Ausgabe,* ed. Ernst Behler, Jean-Jacques Anstett and Hans Eichner (Munich-Paderborn-Vienna-Zurich, Ferdinand Schöning, 1958–   ), vol. II, pp. 311–328.
75. Friedrich Schlegel to Friedrich von Hardenberg (Novalis), Oct. 20, 1798, *Friedrich Schlegel und Novalis: Biographie einer Romantikerfreundschaft in ihren Briefen,* ed. Max Preitz (Darmstadt, Hermann Gentner, 1957), p. 130.
76. For material on the "new mythology," cf. Fritz Strich, *Die Mythologie in der deutschen Literatur von Klopstock bis Wagner* (Halle on the Saale 1910), 2 vols; cf. Oskar Walzel, *German Romanticism,* trans. Alma Elise Lussky (New York, Capricorn Books, 1966 [1932]), pp. 68ff et al.
77. Friedrich Schlegel, "Rede über die Mythologie," p. 312.
78. G. W. F. Hegel, *Glauben und Wissen,* in *Sämtliche Werke,* vol. I, p. 433.
79. Friedrich Hölderlin, "Brod und Wein," stanza VII, *Hölderlin: His Poems,* trans. Michael Hamburger, with a critical study, 2nd ed. (London, Harvill Press, 1952), p. 151. Used by permission of Michael Hamburger.
80. F. W. J. von Schelling, *Einleitung in die Philosophie der Mythologie,* in *Sämmtliche Werke,* ed. K. F. A. Schelling (Stuttgart-Augsburg 1856–1861), vol. II/I, p. 52.
81. Ibid., p. 127.
82. Ibid., pp. 132–133.
83. Cf. ibid., pp. 133–136.
84. Auguste Comte, *System of Positive Polity* (1851–1854), trans. Frederic Harrison (London 1875–1877), vol. II, p. 189. Reprint: Research and Source Works Series #125 (New York, Burt Franklin, 1966).
85. Ibid., p. 217.
86. Ibid., p. 183.
87. Ernest Renan, *De l'origine du langage,* 2nd ed. (1858), in *Œuvres complètes,* ed. Henriette Psichari (Paris, Calmann-Lévy, 1947–1962), vol. VIII, p. 37.
88. Ibid., p. 53.
89. Ibid., p. 54.
90. Cf. Lucien Lévy-Bruhl, *History of Modern Philosophy in France* (Chicago-London, Open Court, 1924), pp. 404–405; cf. D. G. Carlton, *Positivist Thought in France During the Second Empire 1852–1870* (Oxford, Oxford University Press, 1959), pp. 104–125; cf. Richard M. Chadbourne, *Ernest Renan* (New York, Twayne, 1968), pp. 44–53.
91. Renan, *L'Avenir de la science* (written 1848, publ. 1890), in *Œuvres complètes,* vol. III, p. 939.
92. Ibid., p. 814.
93. "I read the book [Saint-Martin's *Des erreurs et de la vérité*] certainly, with enormous appetite, but with little nourishment. Many of the brothers found it more appetizing than I. . . ." [Hamann to J. G. Herder, Sept. 15, 1781, *Briefwechsel,* ed. Walther Ziesemer and Arthur Henkel (Wiesbaden, Insel, 1959), vol. IV, p. 335.]
94. Cf. St. Paul in Rom. 4:17.
95. Franz von Baader, *Erläuterungen zu sämtlichen Schriften von Louis Claude de Saint-Martin,* in *Sämtliche Werke,* ed. Franz Hoffman, Julius Hamberger, et al. (Leipzig 1860), vol. XII, p. 354.

96. Cf. Louis Claude de Saint-Martin, *Des erreurs et de la vérité; ou, Les hommes rappelés au principe universel de la science* (Edinburgh 1775), pp. 456–457; cf. Saint-Martin, *Pensées mythologiques; Cahier des langues*, ed. Robert Amadou, in *Les Cahiers de la tour Saint-Jacques*, vol. VII (n.p., 1961), pp. 182–184.

97. Friedrich Schlegel, "Recension von Rohde (1820)," *Sämmtliche Werke*, Zweite Original-Ausgabe (Vienna 1846), vol. VIII, p. 247.

98. Cf. Saint-Martin, *Des erreurs et de la vérité*, pp. 466–467.

99. Cf. Friedrich Schlegel, *Philosophische Vorlesungen, insbesondere über Philosophie der Sprache und des Wortes*, lect. III, (1828–1829), in *Kritische Ausgabe*, vol. X, p. 369. Reprint of English translation by A. J. W. Morrison, intro. J. B. Robertson, *The Philosophy of Life, and Philosophy of Language, in a Course of Lectures*, (New York, AMS Press, 1974), p. 402.

100. Kanne destroyed his first *Panglossium* manuscript after his conversion to "positive Christianity." The second, composed shortly before his death in 1824, is in the library of the University of Erlangen (nr. 500a). Sections of the second are printed in Erich Neumann, *Johann Arnold Kanne: Ein vergessener Romantiker: Ein Beitrag zur Geschichte der mystischen Sprachphilosophie*, Diss. (Erlangen 1927), pp. 77–82.

101. This theme was anticipated by Clement of Alexandria, Origen, and Luther, among others.

102. Justinus Kerner, *The Seeress of Prevorst, Being Revelations Concerning the Inner-Life of Man and the Inter-Diffusion of a World of Spirits in the One We Inhabit* (New York 1845), p. 47. Cf. Franz von Baader, *Fermenta Cognitionis*, bk. I, in *Sämtliche Werke*, vol. II, pp. 181–182.

103. Saint-Martin, *Man: His True Nature and Ministry*, trans. Edward Burton Penny (London 1864), p. 368; cf. pp. 478–481.

104. Cf. Baader, "Über den Einfluss der Zeichen der Gedanken auf deren Erzeugung und Gestaltung" (1820–1821), *Sämtliche Werke*, vol. II, pp. 125–136.

105. Saint-Martin, *Man: His True Nature and Ministry*, pp. 347–348.

106. Johann Jakob Bachofen, *Versuch über die Gräbersymbolik der Alten*, in *Gesammelte Werke*, ed. Karl Meuli et al. (Basel, B. Schwabe, 1943–1958), vol. IV, pp. 62–63.

107. Ralph Waldo Emerson, *Nature* (1836), in *The Complete Essays and Other Writings*, ed. Brooks Atkinson (New York, Modern Library, 1940), p. 14.

108. Emerson, "The Poet," *Essays: Second Series*, in *The Complete Essays*, p. 322.

109. Ibid., p. 329.

110. Ibid., p. 332.

111. Ibid., pp. 328–329.

112. Ibid., p. 322; cf. pp. 334–335.

113. Cf. Emerson, *Nature*, pp. 16–17.

114. Gotthilf Heinrich von Schubert, *Die Symbolik des Traumes*, 3rd ed. (Leipzig 1840), p. 33.

115. Ibid., p. 70.

116. Ibid., pp. 23–24.

117. The term was used with bemused contempt by Jean Paul Richter in his preface to Kanne's *Erste Urkunden der Geschichte oder allgemeine Mythologie*. Cf. Jean Paul Richter, *Sämtliche Werke*, ed. Eduard Berend (Weimar, H. Böhlaus, 1927–1944), vol. I/XVI, pp. 281–285.

118. Cf. Joseph Görres, *Über die Grundlage, Gliederung und Zeitenfolge der Weltgeschichte* [Lectures delivered in Munich in 1830], in *Gesammelte Schriften*, ed. Wilhelm Schellberg et al. (Cologne, Gilde Verlag, 1926–1958), vol. XV, p. 262.

119. Friedrich Schlegel, letter of April 26, 1823, *Friedrich Schlegels Briefe an seinen Bruder August Wilhelm*, ed. Oskar Walzel (Berlin 1890), p. 639.

120. Gotthilf Heinrich von Schubert, *Ansichten von der Nachtseite der Natur-wissenschaft,* 4th ed. (Dresden-Leipzig 1840), p. 3.
121. Ibid., pp. 5–6.
122. Ibid., p. 38; cf. pp. 37–40.
123. Cf. Haymann Steinthal, *Der Ursprung der Sprache, im Zusammenhange mit den letzten Fragen alles Wissens: Eine Darstellung der Ansicht Wilhelm v. Humboldts, verglichen mit denen Herders und Hamanns* (Berlin 1851), p. 10.
124. Wilhelm von Humboldt, *Über die Verschiedenheit des menschlichen Sprach-baues und ihren Einfluss auf die geistige Entwicklung des Menschenge-schlechts,* in *Gesammelte Schriften* (Berlin, Königlich Preussische Akademie der Wissenschaften, 1903), vol. VII, p. 44. In the more recent *Werke in fünf Bänden,* ed. Andreas Flitner and Klaus Giel (Stuttgart, Cotta, 1964) this work is in vol. III, pp. 368–756: The pagination of the *Akademie-Ausgabe* is provided at the top of the pages. Although Humboldt's publica-tions in linguistics go back to 1817—when he edited the last volume of corrections and additions to Adelung's *Mithridates*—and despite the im-portance of some of the earlier work, this analysis is confined to the post-humously published *On the Heterogeneity of Human Language Structure and Its Influence on the Spiritual Development of the Human Race*—the introductory volume to the work Humboldt projected on the Kawi language of Java, which he had been working on for five years at his death in 1835.
125. Ibid., pp. 45–46.
126. Cf. Herder, *Über die neuere deutsche Literatur,* in *Sämmtliche Werke,* vol. I, p. 147; cf. Hegel, *Phänomenologie des Geistes,* "Einleitung," in *Sämtliche Werke,* vol. II, p. 67, and the two prefaces and introduction to the *Wissen-schaft der Logik.*
127. Humboldt, *Über die Verschiedenheit,* p. 17.
128. Ibid., p. 42.
129. Ibid., p. 24.
130. Ibid., p. 42.
131. Ibid., pp. 21–22.
132. Ibid., p. 47.
133. Ibid., pp. 36–37. In an earlier essay on the classical dual form Humboldt put special emphasis on the second personal pronoun: "Thus the word must gain substantiality and language must further itself in someone who hears and repeats. This primordial form of all languages is expressed pronominally through the distinction of the second person from the third. *I* and *he* are actually different objects [*Gegenstände*], and with them everything is actually complete, for in other terms they mean *I* and *non-I.* But *you* is *he* placed in relation to *I.* As *I* and *he* depend on inner and outer perception, in *you* there is spontaneity of choice. It too is a *non-I,* but not, as with *he,* in the sphere of all beings, but in another, that of action through mutual influence. In *he* itself there is thereby, besides a *non-I,* a *non-you.* . . ." ("Über den Dualis" (1827), *Gesammelte Schriften,* vol. VI, p. 27.) "Man longs for . . . a *you* corresponding to the *I* [and thereby], through the return reflec-tion from an alien mental power, the concept first seems to attain its de-terminateness and certainty. . . . Between mental power and mental power, however, there is no other mediator than language." (Ibid.) Humboldt's analysis stands in sharp contrast with the treatment by Adam Smith.
134. Humboldt, *Über die Verschiedenheit,* p. 56.
135. Ibid., p. 60.
136. Ibid.
137. Ibid., p. 56.

138. Ibid., p. 51.
139. Cf. ibid., p. 63, pp. 47–48.
140. Cf. ibid., pp. 57–58.
141. Ibid., p. 46.
142. Cf. ibid., p. 58.
143. Cf. ibid., p. 55.
144. Ibid., p. 62.
145. Ibid., p. 60.
146. Ibid., p. 25.
147. Ibid., p. 13.
148. Ibid., p. 14.
149. Ibid., p. 19.
150. Ibid., p. 20.
151. Ibid., p. 36.
152. Ibid., p. 44.
153. Cf. ibid., p. 38.
154. Ibid., p. 16.
155. Ibid., pp. 33–34. (Emphasis added.)
156. Ibid., p. 15.
157. Ibid., p. 26.
158. Ibid., p. 39.
159. Ibid.
160. Ibid., p. 43.
161. Ibid., p. 39.
162. Ibid., pp. 48–49.

Chapter 10

1. For fuller discussion of Cuvier's methodology, cf. Ernst Cassirer, *The Problem of Knowledge: Philosophy, Science, and History Since Hegel*, trans. William H. Woglom and Charles W. Hendel (New Haven, Yale University Press, 1950), pp. 118–136. Cf. also Henry M. Hoenigswald, "On the History of the Comparative Method," *Anthropological Linguistics* V (1963), pp. 1–11; cf. W. S. Allen, "Relationship in Comparative Linguistics," *Transactions of the Philological Society* (Oxford 1953), pp. 52–108.
2. Cf. Giuliano Bonfante, "Ideas on the Kinship of the European Languages from 1200 to 1800," *Cahiers d'histoire mondiale* I (1953–1954), pp. 679–699. Cf. George J. Metcalf, "The Indo-European Hypothesis in the 16th and 17th Centuries," *Studies in the History of Linguistics: Traditions and Paradigms,* ed. Dell Hymes (Bloomington, Ind., Indiana University Press, 1974).
3. Sir William Jones, "On the Hindus," *Works,* ed. Lord Teignmouth (London 1807), vol. III, pp. 34–35.
4. At one point Schlegel suggested that the pantheistic philosophy of the Vedas may have been "the first growth of error and superstition." Friedrich Schlegel, *On the Language and Wisdom of the Indians,* in *Aesthetic and Miscellaneous Works,* trans. E. J. Millington (London 1900), p. 516.
5. Ibid., p. 439.
6. Ibid., p. 458.
7. Ibid., p. 446.
8. Cf. August Wilhelm Schlegel, *Observations sur la langue et la littérature provençales* (Paris 1818).
9. Friedrich Schlegel, *On the Language,* p. 449.
10. Ibid., p. 453.

11. Ibid., p. 464.

12. Ibid., p. 455.

13. Ibid., pp. 445–446.

14. Cf. Rasmus Rask, *Undersøgelse om det Gamle Nordiske eller Islandske Sprogs Oprindelse* (Copenhagen 1818).

15. Jacob Grimm, *Geschichte der deutschen Sprache* (Leipzig 1848), vol. I, p. 393.

16. Ibid., pp. 292–293.

17. Cf. Franz Bopp, *Vergleichende Grammatik des Sanskrit, Zend, Griechischen, Lateinischen, Litthauischen, Gothischen und Deutschen* (Berlin 1833), vol. I, pp. xiii–xiv.

18. Bopp, *Vocalismus, oder sprachvergleichende Kritiken über J. Grimms Deutsche Grammatik und Graff's Althochdeutschen Sprachschatz, mit Begründung einer neuen Theorie des Ablauts* (Berlin 1836), p. 3.

19. Friedrich Schmitthenner, *Ursprachlehre* (Frankfort on the Main 1826), p. v.

20. Bopp, *Vergleichende Grammatik,* vol. I, p. iii. (Emphasis added.)

21. Bopp, *Vocalismus,* p. 1.

22. Cf. Karl Ferdinand Becker, *Organism der Sprache,* 2nd ed. (Frankfort on the Main 1841), p. 4 and pp. 71ff.

23. Ibid., p. 6.

24. Cf. Heinrich von Kleist, "Über das Marionettentheater" (1810), *Werke,* ed. Wilhelm Waetzoldt (Berlin-Leipzig-Vienna-Stuttgart, Bong, n.d.), vol. V, pp. 73–79. Cf. Humboldt, *Über die Verschiedenheit,* p. 55.

25. Cf. Plato, *Symposium* 174d–175e. What did Socrates think while he was caught up in meditation before entering Agathon's house? Agathon desperately wanted to know and even thought that he would "get wisdom" if Socrates told him. But we do not know, because Socrates would not say.

26. Cf. Friedrich Wilhelm Joseph von Schelling, "Vorbemerkungen zu der Frage über den Ursprung der Sprache" (November 25, 1850), *Sämmtliche Werke,* ed. F. K. A. Schelling (Stuttgart-Augsburg 1861), vol. I/X, pp. 419–426. The brief lecture summarizes the positions of Herder and Hamann—the author sides with Hamann despite his praise of the prize essay—and concludes with a Latin poem which Schelling had composed some twenty-five years earlier.

27. Jacob Grimm, *Über den Ursprung der Sprache,* in *Kleinere Schriften* (Berlin 1864), vol. I, p. 298.

28. Ibid., p. 259.

29. Ibid., pp. 260–261.

30. Ibid., p. 273.

31. Cf. ibid., p. 275.

32. Ibid., p. 296.

33. Karl Wilhelm Ludwig Heyse, *System der Sprachwissenschaft,* ed. H. Steinthal (Berlin 1856), p. 16.

34. Ibid., p. 23.

35. Ibid., p. 60.

36. Ibid., p. 43.

37. Ibid., p. 47.

38. Ibid., p. 64.

39. Haymann Steinthal, *Der Ursprung der Sprache im Zusammenhange mit den letzten Fragen alles Wissens* (Berlin 1851); 2nd ed. (Berlin 1858); 3rd ed. (Berlin 1877); 4th ed. (Berlin 1888).

40. Steinthal, *Einleitung in die Psychologie und Sprachwissenschaft* (Berlin 1871), pp. 88–89. Cf. Steinthal, *Grammatik, Logik und Psychologie: Ihre Principien und ihr Verhältnis zu einander* (Berlin 1855), pp. 225ff.

41. Ibid., p. 88.

42. Ibid., pp. 85–86.

43. Cf. Ludwig O Livier, *Über die Urstoffe der menschlichen Sprache und die allgemeinen Gesetze ihrer Verbindungen* (Vienna 1821); cf. Johann Karl Friedrich Rinne, *Die natürliche Entstehung der Sprache aus dem Gesichtspuncte der historischen oder vergleichenden Sprachwissenschaft* (Erfurt 1834); cf. August Friedrich Pott, *Etymologische Forschungen auf dem Gebiete der Indo-Germanischen Sprachen* (Lemgo 1833–1836), 2 vols.

44. Karl Mortiz Rapp, *Versuch einer Physiologie der Sprache nebst historischer Entwicklung der abendländischen Idiome nach physiologischen Grundsätzen* (Stuttgart-Tübingen 1836–1841), vol. I, p. 2.

45. Abel Hovelacque, *The Science of Language: Linguistics, Philology, Etymology,* trans. A. H. Keane (London-Philadelphia 1877), p. 8.

46. Ibid., p. 30.

47. The German defenders of divine origin in the postromantic period included Peter Franz Josef Müller, *Die Ursprache,* 2nd ed. (Cologne 1826); Friedrich Karl Hermann Kruse, *Freimüthige Bemerkungen über den Ursprung der Sprache, oder Beweis, dass die Sprache nicht menschlichen Ursprungs sey* (Altona 1827); Philip Christian Kayser, *Über die Ursprache, oder über eine Behauptung Mosis, dass alle Sprachen der Welt von einer einzigen, der noachidischen, abstammen* (Erlangen 1840); Ignaz Gaugengigl, *Der Ursprung der Sprache* (Passau 1854); and Franz Kaulen below. Cf. also George Smith, *The Origin and Progress of Language* (Philadelphia, American Sunday School Union; London, Religious Tract Society, [1848]).

48. Franz Kaulen, *Die Sprachverwirrung zu Babel: Linguistisch-theologische Untersuchungen über Gen. XI, 1–9* (Mainz 1861), p. v.

49. August Friedrich Pott, *Anti-Kaulen, oder Mythische Vorstellungen vom Ursprung der Völker und Sprachen* (Lemgo-Detmold 1863), p. v.

50. Christian Charles Josias von Bunsen, "On the Results of the Recent Egyptian Researches in Reference to Asiatic and African Ethnology, and the Classification of Languages," *Three Linguistic Dissertations Read at the Meeting of the British Association in Oxford by Chevalier Bunsen, Dr. Charles Meyer, and Dr. Max Müller* (London 1848), pp. 285–286.

51. Cf. Steinthal, *Die Classification der Sprachen dargestellt als die Entwicklung der Sprachidee* (Berlin 1850); and Steinthal, *Charakteristik der hauptsächlichsten Typen des Sprachbaues* (Berlin 1860). Cf. Brigit Beneš, *Wilhelm von Humboldt, Jacob Grimm, August Schleicher: Ein Vergleich ihrer Sprachauffassung* (Winterthur, P. G. Keller, 1958), pp. 103ff.

52. Cf. Thomas S. Kuhn, *The Structure of Scientific Revolutions* (Chicago-London, University of Chicago Press, 1962), pp. 10–12, pp. 35–51.

53. Cf. Adalbert Kuhn and August Schleicher, "Nachruf: Franz Bopp, geboren den 14. sept. 1791 zu Mainz, gestorben den 23. oct. 1867," *Zeitschrift für vergleichende Sprachforschung* XVII (1868), pp. 156–160.

54. Cf. Johannes Schmidt, "Nachruf: August Schleicher, geboren den 19. feb. 1821 zu Meiningen, gestorben den 6. dec. 1868 zu Jena," *Zeitschrift für vergleichende Sprachforschung* XVIII (1869), pp. 315–320.

55. Cf. Henry M. Hoenigswald, "On the History of the Comparative Method," *Anthropological Linguistics* V (1963), p. 8.

56. August Schleicher, *Zur vergleichenden Sprachengeschichte: Sprachvergleichende Untersuchungen,* vol. I (Bonn 1848), p. 17.

57. Ibid., p. 10.

58. Ibid., pp. 27–28.

59. Schleicher, *Die Sprachen Europas in systematischer Übersicht: Linguistische Untersuchungen,* vol. II (Bonn 1850), p. 1.

60. Ibid., p. 2.

61. Cf. ibid., pp. 10–11 fn.

62. Wilhelm Streitberg, "Schleichers Auffassung von der Stellung der Sprachwissenschaft," *Indogermanische Forschungen* VII (1897), pp. 371–372; cf. Johannes Schmidt, "Schleichers auffassung der lautgesetze," *Zeitschrift für vergleichende Sprachforschung* XXVIII (1887), pp. 303–312.

63. Aristotle's fundamental criticism of the Platonic theory of forms was that the ideas contained no principle of motion: Thus comprehensive explanation required the addition of efficient and final causes to the formal and material causation implied in Plato's theory. Cf. Aristotle, *Metaphysics*, bk. I, chap. ix, 9–27.

64. Cf. Schleicher, *Die deutsche Sprache* (Stuttgart 1860), pp. 37–47.

65. On this point Schleicher had a running dispute with Rudolf von Raumer, who thought that Indo-European and Semitic languages were genetically related and that elements of an Aryo-Semitic protolanguage could be deduced. Cf. Raumer, *Gesammelte sprachwissenschaftliche Schriften* (Frankfort on the Main-Erlangen 1863) and Schleicher's review in *Beiträge zur vergleichenden Sprachforschung* IV (1864–1865), pp. 242–247; cf. Raumer, *Herr Professor Schleicher in Jena und die Urverwandschaft der semitischen und indoeuropäischen Sprachen: Ein kritisches Bedenken* (Frankfort on the Main 1864) and Schleicher's rebuttal in the same. volume of the *Beiträge*, pp. 365–368; cf. Raumer, *Fortsetzung der Untersuchungen über die Urverwandschaft der semitischen und indoeuropäischen Sprachen* (Frankfort on the Main 1867).

66. Schleicher, *Die deutsche Sprache*, p. 40.

67. Schleicher, "Die Unterscheidung von Nomen und Verbum in der lautlichen Form," *Abhandlungen der philologisch-historischen Classe der Königlichen Sächsischen Gesellschaft der Wissenschaften* IV: 5 (Leipzig 1865), pp. 501–502.

68. Ibid., p. 503.

69. Ibid., p. 505.

70. Schleicher, *Die Darwinische Theorie und die Sprachwissenschaft: Offenes Sendschreiben an Herrn Dr. Ernst Häckel,* 2nd ed. (Weimar 1873), p. 27.

71. Ibid., p. 7.

72. Schleicher, *Über die Bedeutung der Sprache für die Naturgeschichte des Menschen* (Weimar 1865), p. 8.

73. Ibid., pp. 17–18.

74. Ibid., p. 26.

75. Ibid., p. 24.

76. Schleicher, "Eine fabel in indogermanischer ursprache," *Beiträge zur vergleichenden Sprachforschung* V (1868), pp. 207–208. Schleicher included a German translation with his fable. The English translation follows:

[The] sheep and [the] horses

[A] sheep, [on] which [there] was not wool (a shorn sheep), saw horses, that [one] carrying [a] heavy wagon, that [one] [a] big load, that [one] carrying [a] man quickly. [The] sheep spoke [to the] horses: [The] heart becomes cramped [in] me (I am very sorry), seeing [the] man driving [the] horses.

[The] horses said: Hear, sheep, [the] heart becomes cramped [in those] having seen (we are very sorry, since we know): [the] man, [the] master makes [the] wool [of the] sheep [into a] warm garment [for] himself and [there] is not wool [on the] sheep (but the sheep have no more wool, they are shorn; they are even worse off than the horses).

Having heard this [the] sheep turned (disappeared) [on the] field (it made a quick escape).

Chapter 11

1. Christoph Gottlieb Voigtmann, *Dr. Max Müllers Bau-Wau-Theorie und der Ursprung der Sprache* (Leipzig 1865), pp. 10–11.
2. Cf. Johannes Schmidt's review in *Zeitschrift für vergleichende Sprachforschung* XV (1860), pp. 235–237.
3. Cf. F. Max Müller, *The Science of Language: Founded on Lectures Delivered at the Royal Institution in 1861 and 1863,* 7th ed. (New York 1891), vol. I, pp. 494–512.
4. Cf. Müller, *The Science of Thought* (New York 1887), vol. I, pp. 207–208.
5. Archibald Henry Sayce, "The Jelly-Fish Theory of Language," *Contemporary Review* XXVII (1876), p. 718.
6. The following writers published essays, pamphlets, or books between 1860 and 1890 which referred to the problem of language origin in their titles: In Germany: C. Abel, F. Bergmann, O. Caspari, T. Curti, L. Geiger, G. Jaeger, W. Krause, M. Schleis von Löwenfeld, A. Marty, L. Noiré, L. Reinisch, C. F. Riecke, E. von Schmidt, F. Schulz, C. Schumann, P. Schwartzkopff, O. S. Seemann, L. Stein, A. Stengel, P. Tesch, C. G. Voigtmann, W. Wackernagl, H. Waeschke, W. J. A. Werber, C. Wirth, R. Zimmermann; in France and Italy: L. Alotte, A. d'Assier, L. de Backer, R. de la Grasserie, F. de Moor, L. de Rosny, V. de Vit, E. Drival, P. Heger, R. Kleinpaul, H. Mazzoleni, J. P. Rambosson, P. Regnaud, L. Richard, C. Schoebel, S. Zabarowski; in England and America: F. W. Farrar, H. Hale, M. Kavanagh, T. H. Key, Count G. A. de Goddesand Liancourt, F. Pincott, M. S. Terry, H. Wedgwood. Although it is no objective criterion, it is worthy of mention that virtually none of these names—Leo Reinisch and Anton Marty are the exceptions—appear in the standard histories of linguistics, and very few turn up in their respective national biographical dictionaries, and then usually for reasons other than their work on language origin.
7. Cf. Frederick W. Farrar, *Origin of Language* (London 1860) and *Chapters on Language* (London 1865); cf. T. Hewitt Key, *Language: Its Origin and Development* (London 1874); cf. Hensleigh Wedgwood, *On the Origin of Language* (London 1866).
8. Cf. Lazarus Geiger, *Ursprung und Entwicklung der menschlichen Sprache und Vernunft,* vol. I (Frankfort on the Main 1868); vol. II, ed. Alfred Geiger (Stuttgart 1872).
9. Cf. Ludwig Noiré, *Der Ursprung der Sprache* (Mainz 1877), pp. 323ff; and *Max Müller und die Sprach-Philosophie* (Mainz 1879).
10. Cf. Georg Curtius, *Zur Chronologie der indogermanischen Sprachforschung,* Abhandlungen der Königlich Sächsischen Gesellschaft der Wissenschaften, Philosophisch-historisch Klasse V: 3 (Leipzig 1867); cf. Theodor Benfey, *Geschichte der Sprachwissenschaft und orientalischen Philologie in Deutschland* (Munich 1869); cf. Rudolf von Raumer, *Geschichte der germanischen Philologie* (Munich 1870); cf. Haymann Steinthal, *Geschichte der Sprachwissenschaft bei den Griechen und Römern* (Berlin 1863).
11. Cf. Henry M. Hoenigswald, "Fallacies in the History of Linguistics," *Studies in the History of Linguistics: Traditions and Paradigms,* ed. Dell Hymes (Bloomington, Ind., Indiana University Press, 1974), pp. 346–358.
12. Cf. Charles Darwin, *The Origin of Species by Means of Natural Selection,* chap. XVI, 6th ed. (New York 1899), pp. 214–215.
13. Darwin, *The Descent of Man and Selection in Relation to Sex,* 2nd ed. (New York 1899), p. 86.
14. Ibid., p. 87.

15. Ibid., p. 89.

16. George Darwin, "Professor Whitney on the Origin of Language," *Contemporary Review* XXIV (1874), p. 901.

17. Cf. Charles Darwin, *The Descent of Man,* chap. XIX, especially pp. 584–586.

18. Herbert Spencer, "On the Origin and Function of Music" (1857), *Essays on Education and Kindred Subjects,* ed. Charles W. Eliot (London-New York, Everyman, [1910]), p. 316.

19. Ibid., pp. 320–321.

20. Darwin, *The Descent of Man,* p. 92.

21. Cf. Charles Lyell, *The Geological Evidences of the Antiquity of Man, with Remarks on Theories of the Origin of Species by Variation,* chap. XXIII (London, 1863); cf. Ernst Haeckel, *The History of Creation or the Development of the Earth and Its Inhabitants by the Action of Natural Causes* (1868), trans. E. Ray Lankester, 6th ed. (New York 1914), vol. II, pp. 405ff.

22. Ernst Haeckel, editor's preface to W. H. J. Bleek, *On the Origin of Language,* trans. Thomas Davidson (New York-London 1869), p. iv.

23. Ibid., p. v.

24. William Dwight Whitney, "Darwinism and Language," *North American Review* CXIX (1874), p. 63.

25. F. Max Müller, "Lectures on Mr. Darwin's Philosophy of Language II," *Fraser's Magazine* (March 29, 1873), p. 661.

26. Ibid., p. 663.

27. Frederick Engels, "The Part Played by Labour in the Transition from Ape to Man," *Dialectics of Nature,* trans. Clemens Dutt (New York, International Publishers, 1940), p. 291. This work was composed between 1872 and 1882 and published posthumously.

28. Ibid., p. 283.

29. The main works involved in the quarrel between Müller and Whitney were: Whitney, "Darwinism and Language," op. cit., pp. 61–88—actually an attack on Müller and Schleicher; George Darwin, "Professor Whitney on the Origin of Language," op. cit., pp. 894–904—mainly a summary of Whitney's arguments against Müller; Müller, "My Reply to Mr. Darwin," *Contemporary Review* XXV (1875), pp. 305–306—a personal attack on Whitney centering on the strife between Whitney and Steinthal; Whitney, "Are Languages Institutions?" *Contemporary Review* XXV (1875), pp. 713–732—a personal defense and an attack on Müller. Whitney summarized his case for anathematization in *Max Müller and the Science of Language* (New York 1892).

30. Whitney, "Darwinism and Language," p. 81.

31. Whitney, *Max Müller and the Science of Language,* p. 30.

32. In addition to Whitney's polemics against Müller, cf. his "Strictures on the Views of August Schleicher Respecting the Nature of Language and Kindred Subjects," *Transactions of the American Philological Association* (1871), pp. 35–64, especially pp. 38ff, pp. 50ff; cf. Whitney, "φύσει or θέσει—Natural or Conventional?" ibid. (1874), pp. 95–116.

33. Whitney, "Darwinism and Language," p. 88.

34. Ibid., p. 87.

35. Cf. Ernst Moritz Arndt, *Fragmente über Menschenbildung* (1805), ed. Wilhelm Münch and Heinrich Meisner, Manns Bibliothek pädagogischer Klassiker, vol. 42 (Langensalza 1904).

36. Cf. Arthur Schopenhauer, *Parerga und Paralipomena,* vol. II, chap. xxv, §307, in *Sämmtliche Werke,* ed. Julius Frauenstädt (Leipzig, F. A. Brockhaus, 1922), vol. VI, p. 600.

37. Cf. Eduard von Hartmann, *The Philosophy of the Unconscious,* trans. William Chatterton Coupland (London 1893), vol. I, pp. 293–300.

38. Théodule Ribot, "The Evolution of Speech," *The Open Court* XIII (1899), p. 272.
39. Sigmund Freud, *Introductory Lectures on Psycho-Analysis,* lect. X, in *The Standard Edition of the Complete Psychological Works,* ed. and trans. James Strachey et al. (London, Hogarth Press, 1963), vol. XV, p. 167.
40. Friedrich Nietzsche, "Vom Ursprung der Sprache," *Gesammelte Werke,* Musarionausgabe (Munich, Musarion Verlag, 1922), vol. V, pp. 467–468.
41. Ibid., p. 468.
42. Nietzsche, "Über Musik und Wort," ibid., vol. III, pp. 340–341.
43. Nietzsche, *Die Geburt der Tragödie,* sec. 6, *Werke,* ed. Alfred Baeumler (Leipzig, Kröner, 1930), vol. I/i, p. 76; *Werke,* ed. Karl Schlechta (Munich, Carl Hanser Verlag, 1966), vol. I, pp. 43–44.
44. Nietzsche, *Zur Genealogie der Moral,* First Essay, sec. 13, Baeumler, vol. V/i, p. 36; Schlechta, vol. II, p. 789.
45. Nietzsche, *Ueber die Zukunft unserer Bildungsanstalten,* pt. II, lect. 3, Baeumler, vol. I/ii, pp. 456–457; Schlechta, vol. III, pp. 222–223.
46. Cf. Nietzsche, *Morgenröte,* bk. I, §44, Baeumler, vol. III/i, p. 44; Schlechta, vol. I, p. 1044.
47. Nietzsche, *Wir Philologen,* "Plan und Gedanken zur buchmässigen Ausführung, §128," Baeumler, vol. I/ii, p. 576.
48. Nietzsche, *Zur Genealogie der Moral,* First Essay, sec. 2, Baeumler, vol. V/i, p. 16; Schlechta, vol. II, p. 773.
49. Nietzsche, "Über Wahrheit und Lüge im aussermoralischen Sinn," Baeumler, vol. I/ii, p. 606; Schlechta, vol. III, p. 310.
50. Ibid., Baeumler, pp. 607–608; Schlechta, p. 311.
51. Ibid., Baeumler, p. 611; Schlechta, p. 314.
52. Ibid., Baeumler, pp. 611–612; Schlechta, p. 314.
53. Stéphane Mallarmé, "Crisis in Poetry," *Selected Prose Poems, Essays, & Letters,* trans. Bradford Cook (Baltimore, Johns Hopkins Press, 1956), p. 35.
54. Ibid., pp. 42–43.
55. Ibid., p. 40; Arthur Rimbaud, "Alchimie du verbe," *Une Saison en enfer, Délires II, Œuvres complètes,* ed. Rolland de Renéville and Jules Mouquet (Paris, Gallimard, 1963), pp. 232–238; Charles Pierre Baudelaire, "Théophile Gautier," *Baudelaire as a Literary Critic: Selected Essays,* intro. and trans. Lois Boe Hyslop and Francis E. Hyslop, Jr. (University Park, Pa., Pennsylvania State University Press, 1964), pp. 167–168.
56. Ibid., pp. 40–41.
57. Consider this comment by Samuel Butler: "English will be the universal language, but each profession will, by and by, come to have a subordinate dialect of its own which will be hardly understood by those of another profession. The longer we can delay this the better." *Further Extracts from the Note-Books of Samuel Butler,* ed. A. T. Bartholemew (London, J. Cape, 1934), p. 177.

Chapter 12

1. "Statuts," *Bulletin de la Société de linguistique de Paris* I (1871), p. iii.
2. Alexander J. Ellis, "Second Annual Address of the President of the Philological Society, Delivered at the Anniversary Meeting, Friday 16th May, 1873," *Transactions of the Philological Society* (1873), pp. 251–252.
3. Ibid., p. 252.
4. Honoré Chavée, "La Science positive des langues indo-européennes: son présent, son avenir," *Revue de linguistique et de philologie comparée* I (1867), p. 1.
5. Chavée, "Idéologie positive I: Familles naturelles des idées verbales dans la parole indo-européenne," ibid., p. 138.

6. Cf. in the order mentioned, H. Weber in *Zeitschrift für vergleichende Sprachforschung* XXII (1874), pp. 88–89; Jacob Wackernagel, ibid. (1879), pp. 295–303; Siegfried Goldschmidt, ibid., p. 426; A. Dufriche-Desegnettes in *Bulletin de la Société de linguistique de Paris* III (1875–1878), pp. lxxi–lxxiv; Paul Meyer in *Mémoires de la Société de Linguistique de Paris* I (1868), pp. 145–161; J. Loth in the *Bulletin* V (1881–1884), p. cii.

7. "Séance du 21 novembre 1885," Bulletin VI (1885–1888), p. lv.

8. Cf. August Boltz, *Die Sprache und ihr Leben: Populäre Briefe über Sprachwissenschaft* (Leipzig 1868). Schmidt's review is in *Zeitschrift für vergleichende Sprachforschung* XVII (1868), pp. 449–451.

9. Cf. Wilhelm Streitberg, "Schleichers Auffassung von der Stellung der Sprachwissenschaft," *Indogermanische Forschungen* VII (1897), pp. 360–372.

10. Johannes Schmidt, *Die Verwandschaftsverhältnisse der indogermanischen Sprachen* (Weimar 1872), p. 31.

11. Eduard Meyer, *Geschichte des Altertums*, 3rd ed. (Stuttgart-Berlin 1910), vol. I/i, p. 4.

12. Cf. Francis C. Haber, *The Age of the World: Moses to Darwin* (Baltimore, Johns Hopkins Press, 1959); cf. John C. Greene, *The Death of Adam: Evolution and Its Impact on Western Thought* (Ames, Ia., Iowa State, 1959).

13. Edward B. Tylor, *Researches into the Early History of Mankind and the Development of Civilization* (New York 1878), p. 15.

14. Ibid.

15. Ibid., p. 56.

16. Wilhelm Wundt, *Die Sprache, Völkerpsychologie: Eine Untersuchung der Entwicklungsgesetze von Sprache, Mythus und Sitte*, pt. I (Leipzig 1900), vol. I, p. 606.

17. William Dwight Whitney, *Oriental and Linguistic Studies* (New York 1873–1874), vol. I, p. 279; quoted in Otto Jespersen, *Language: Its Nature, Development and Origin* (London, G. Allen & Unwin, 1922), p. 412.

18. Jespersen, op. cit.

19. Ibid., pp. 417–418. Jespersen's thesis, briefly, is that language was at first musical, with single "words" expressing whole ideas and feelings and used, in effect, as unanalyzed sentences. From such raw beginnings language progressed with increasing differentiation of its parts and clarity of its meaning.

20. Cf. Michel Bréal's review in *Journal des Savants*, Année 1896, pp. 381–389, 459–470.

21. Cf. Hermann Paul, *Prinzipien der Sprachgeschichte*, 5th ed. (Halle, Max Niemeyer, 1920), pp. 67–73. Paul's *Prinzipien* was adapted in English by Herbert A. Strong, Willem S. Logeman, and Benjamin Ide Wheeler, *Introduction to the Study of the History of Language* (London 1891). Reprint: intro. Keith Percival (New York, AMS Press, 1973). Cf. Strong, p. 40: "If we say that a law of sound-change admits of no exceptions, we can only mean that, within the limits of some definite language or dialect, all cases which fulfill the same phonetic conditions have had the same fate. . . . It must be clear . . . that laws of sound-change, in the correct meaning of this term, must be consistent and absolutely regular." Like Jespersen, Paul still made passing reference to the problem of the origin of language: cf. *Prinzipien*, pp. 35–36; Strong, pp. 11–12. Cf. also Paul, "Der Ursprung der Sprache: Vortrag gehalten im Zweige München des Allgemeinen Deutschen Sprachvereins den 12. Jan. 1907," *Allgemeine Zeitung*, Beilage 1907, Heft 13 and 14.

22. August Leskien, *Declination im Slawisch-Litauischen und Germanischen* (Leipzig 1876), p. xxviii.

23. Hermann Osthoff and Karl Brugmann, *Morphologische Untersuchungen* (Leipzig 1878), vol. I, pp. ix–x.

INDEX

Italicized entries refer to the main expository passages concerning an author or subject.

76 77 78 79 9 8 7 6 5 4 3 2 1